YALE UNIVERSITY PUBLICATIONS
IN ANTHROPOLOGY

NUMBER EIGHTY-THREE

THE EXCAVATIONS AT COROZAL, VENEZUELA: STRATIGRAPHY AND CERAMIC SERIATION

Anna Curtenius Roosevelt

NEW HAVEN
PUBLISHED BY

DEPARTMENT OF ANTHROPOLOGY
AND THE PEABODY MUSEUM
YALE UNIVERSITY
1997

LEOPOLD J. POSPISIL
Editor
ANNE F. WILDE
Associate Editor

Copyright © 1997 by Anna Curtenius Roosevelt
All rights reserved. This book may not be reproduced, in whole or in part, in any form (except by reviewers for the public press), without written permission from the publishers.
International Standard Book number: 0-913516-17-1
Composition: PEGASUS
Printing: BOOKCRAFTERS

Contents

1. INTRODUCTION 1
   A. Background of the Research 1
   B. Tropical Lowland Archaeology in South America 3
   C. Parmana Archaeological Project 10
   D. Research on the Ceramic Sequence 16
2. THE EXCAVATIONS AT COROZAL 23
   A. The Site and Its Region 23
   B. The 1975 Excavations 28
   C. Mapping and Excavation Methods 30
   D. Introduction to the Stratigraphy 38
   E. Description of the Strata 41
   F. Interpretation of the Stratigraphy 69
   G. The Dating Problem 73
      1. Relative Dating 74
      2. Absolute Dating 75
      3. Accelerator and Thermoluminescence Dating Program ... 80
3. THE CERAMIC SERIATION 87
   A. The Parmana Ceramic Sequence 87
   B. Method of Ceramic Analysis 95
      1. Procedures 96
      2. Defining Modes 97
      3. Statistical Tests of Significance 102
      4. Cross-Regional Ceramic Comparisons 105
   C. Description of the Ceramic Modes 107
      1. Corozal Tradition Modes 107
      2. Camoruco Tradition Modes 127
      3. Arauquinoid Series Modes 135
      4. Nondecorative Modes of Shape 146
   D. Distribution of Modes in the Traditions and Phases 149
      1. The Camoruco Tradition 149
      2. The Corozal Tradition 151
4. CONCLUSIONS 155
   A. Interpretation of the Parmana Sequence 155
      1. The Stability of the La Gruta Tradition 155
      2. Complexity and Change in the Corozal Tradition 156

    3. Corozal Tradition as a Transition 158
    4. The Development of Camoruco Pottery 162
    5. Interpretation of Iconographic Change 165
 B. Long-Distance Relationships 170
    1. The Saladoid and Barrancoid Series 171
    2. Incised and Punctate Horizon 174
 C. The Significance of Corozal for Future Research 177
REFERENCES 351

ACKNOWLEDGMENT

THE PUBLICATION OF THIS MONOGRAPH WAS MADE POSSIBLE BY A GRANT FROM THE WENNER-GREN FOUNDATION FOR ANTHROPOLOGICAL RESEARCH.

Tables

1. Chronological chart for Parmana region phases 185
2. Phase and stratigraphic identifications and provenience numbers of the levels of Excavation 2 186
3. Phase and stratigraphic identifications and provenience numbers of the levels of Excavation 3 187
4. Areal extent and approximate depths of the levels of Excavation 2 188
5. Location and approximate depths of the features of Excavation 2 189
6. Areal extent and approximate depths of the levels of Excavation 3 190
7. Location and approximate depths of the features of Excavation 3 195
8. Radiocarbon dates from the Middle Orinoco 196
9. Sherd totals per level, Excavation 2 210
10. Sherd totals per level, Excavation 3 211
11. Frequency of mode #135, Corozal sherdware, Excavation 2 212
12. Percentages of mode #135, Corozal sherdware, Excavation 2 214
13. Frequency of mode #135, Corozal sherdware, Excavation 3 216
14. Percentages of mode #135, Corozal sherdware, Excavation 3 217
15. Frequency of mode #140, Corozal gritware, Excavation 2 219
16. Percentages of mode #140, Corozal gritware, Excavation 2 221
17. Frequency of mode #140, Corozal gritware, Excavation 3 223
18. Percentages of mode #140, Corozal gritware, Excavation 3 225
19. Frequency of mode #204, Corozal Saladoid-Barrancoid decoration, Excavation 2 227
20. Percentages of mode #204, Corozal Saladoid-Barrancoid decoration, Excavation 2 229
21. Frequency of mode #204, Corozal Saladoid-Barrancoid decoration, Excavation 3 231
22. Percentages of mode #204, Corozal Saladoid-Barrancoid decoration, Excavation 3 232
23. Frequency of mode #5, Saladoid paint, Excavation 2 234
24. Percentages of mode #5, Saladoid paint, Excavation 2 235
25. Frequency of mode #5, Saladoid paint, Excavation 3 237
26. Percentages of mode #5, Saladoid paint, Excavation 3 238
27. Frequency of mode #134, Corozal curvilinear incision, Excavation 3 240
28. Percentages of mode #134, Corozal curvilinear incision, Excavation 2 242
29. Frequency of mode #134, Corozal curvilinear incision, Excavation 3 244
30. Percentages of mode #134, Corozal curvilinear incision, Excavation 3 245

Tables Cont'd

31. Frequency of mode #132, Corozal rectilinear incision, Excavation 2 247
32. Percentages of mode #132, Corozal rectilinear incision, Excavation 2 248
33. Frequency of mode #132, Corozal rectilinear incision, Excavation 3 250
34. Percentages of mode #132, Corozal rectilinear incision, Excavation 3 251
35. Frequency of mode #18, Corozal red-and-white paint, Excavation 2 253
36. Percentages of mode #18, Corozal red-and-white paint, Excavation 2 255
37. Frequency of mode #18, Corozal red-and-white paint, Excavation 3 257
38. Percentages of mode #18, Corozal red-and-white paint, Excavation 3 258
39. Frequency of mode #126, Corozal bowl rim strap handles, Excavation 2 260
40. Percentages of mode #126, Corozal bowl rim strap handles,
    Excavation 2 261
41. Frequency of mode #126, Corozal bowl rim strap handles,
    Excavation 3 263
42. Percentages of mode #126, Corozal bowl rim strap handles,
    Excavation 3 264
43. Frequency of mode #209, spongeware animal-effigy bowls,
    Excavation 2 266
44. Percentages of mode #209, spongeware animal-effigy bowls,
    Excavation 2 267
45. Frequency of mode #209, spongeware animal-effigy bowls,
    Excavation 3 269
46. Percentages of mode #209, spongeware animal-effigy bowls,
    Excavation 3 271
47. Frequency of mode #152, Camoruco mauve paint, Excavation 2 273
48. Percentages of mode #152, Camoruco mauve paint, Excavation 2 275
49. Frequency of mode #152, Camoruco mauve paint, Excavation 3 277
50. Percentages of mode #152, Camoruco mauve paint, Excavation 3 279
51. Frequency of mode #14, Arauquinoid maroon paint, Excavation 2 281
52. Percentages of mode #14, Arauquinoid maroon paint, Excavation 2 283
53. Frequency of mode #14, Arauquinoid maroon paint, Excavation 3 285
54. Frequency of mode #14, Arauquinoid maroon paint, Excavation 3 287
55. Frequency of mode #19, Arauquinoid rectilinear incision, Excavation 2 289
56. Percentages of mode #19, Arauquinoid rectilinear incision, Excavation 2 291
57. Frequency of mode #19, Arauquinoid rectilinear incision, Excavation 3 293
58. Percentages of mode #19, Arauquinoid rectilinear incision,
    Excavation 3 294
59. Frequency of mode #160, circle-stamp motif, Excavation 2 296
60. Percentages of mode 160, circle-stamp motif, Excavation 2 297
61. Frequency of mode #160, circle-stamp motif, Excavation 3 299
62. Percentages of mode 160, circle-stamp motif, Excavation 3 301
63. Frequency of mode #40, Arauquinoid large human-effigy jars,
    Excavation 2 303

Tables Cont'd

64. Percentages of mode #40, Arauquinoid large human-effigy jars, Excavation 2 304
65. Frequency of mode #40, Arauquinoid large human-effigy jars, Excavation 3 306
66. Percentages of mode #40, Arauquinoid large human-effigy jars, Excavation 3 308
67. Frequency of mode #32, Arauquinoid small human-effigy jars, Excavation 2 310
68. Percentages of mode #32, Arauquinoid small human-effigy jars, Excavation 2 311
69. Frequency of mode #32, Arauquinoid small human-effigy jars, Excavation 3 313
70. Percentages of mode #32, Arauquinoid small human-effigy jars, Excavation 3 314
71. Frequency of mode #136, Arauquinoid human bowl rim lugs, Excavation 2 316
72. Percentages of mode #136, Arauquinoid human bowl rim lugs, Excavation 2 317
73. Frequency of mode #136, Arauquinoid human bowl rim lugs, Excavation 3 319
74. Percentages of mode #136, Arauquinoid human bowl rim lugs, Excavation 3 320
75. Frequency of Mode #57, Modeled Limbs, Excavation 2 322
76. Percentages of mode #57, modeled limbs, Excavation 2 323
77. Frequency of mode #57, modeled limbs, Excavation 3 325
78. Percentages of mode #57, modeled limbs, Excavation 3 326
79. Frequency of mode #212, everted and/or beveled open bowl rims, Excavation 2 328
80. Percentages of mode #212, everted and/or beveled open bowl rims, Excavation 2 330
81. Frequency of mode #212, everted and/or beveled open bowl rims, Excavation 3 332
82. Percentages of mode #212, everted and/or beveled open bowl rims, Excavation 3 334
83. Frequency of mode #213, flat, angled bowl bases, Excavation 2 336
84. Percentages of mode #213, flat, angled bowl bases, Excavation 2 337
85. Frequency of mode #213, flat, angled bowl bases, Excavation 3 339
86. Percentages of mode #213, flat, angled bowl bases, Excavation 3 341
87. Frequency of mode #214, round bowl bases, Excavation 2 343
88. Percentages of mode #214, round bowl bases, Excavation 2 344
89. Frequency of mode #214, round bowl bases, Excavation 3 346
90. Percentages of mode 214, round bowl bases, Excavation 3 348

Figures

1. Map of northeastern South America... x
2. Map of northern Venezuela xiii
3. Map of localities in the Parmana region.. xiv
4. Map of Parmana environments.. 22
5. Map of the excavations at Corozal 25
6. Stratigraphic profile of Excavations 2 and 3 42
   Stratigraphic profile of Excavation 2.. 43
7. Plan of ashy soil patch in Stratum M, Excavation 2, Level 7.......................... 50
8. Plan of reddish soil feature at juncture of Strata H and G, Excavation 2,
   Levels 11 and 12... 50
9. Successive plans of the soil feature over Skeletons 2, 3 and 4–5,
   Excavation 3 55
10. Plan of Skeletons 1, 2, 3, and 4–5, Excavation 3, Levels 18–21 58
11. Plan of charcoal and clay lenses at juncture of Strata F and E,
    Excavation 2, Levels 13 and 14... 60
12. Plan of soil features at the top of Stratum C, over the flexed burials in
    Excavation 2, Level 16, and Excavation 3, Level 25.................................... 64
13. Plan of burial pits in Stratum C 65
14. Plan of child burial in Strata A and B, Excavation 2, Levels 18 and 19.......... 68
15. Rim and base sherd profiles, mode #135: Corozal sherdware 108
16. Rim and base sherd profiles, mode #140: Corozal gritware with
    Saladoid-Barrancoid decoration.. 112
17. Rim sherd profiles, mode #130: Corozal curvilinear incision.......................... 118
18. Rim and base sherd profiles, mode #132: Corozal rectilinear incision 120
19. Base sherd profiles, mode #18: Corozal red-and-white, and mode
    #20: polychrome paint... 122
20. Rim and base sherd profiles, mode #126: Corozal bowls with vertical
    rim strap handles 125
21. Rim and base sherd profiles, mode #209: Animal-effigy bowls...................... 127
22. Rim and base sherd profiles, mode #152: Camoruco mauve paint 131
23. Rim and base sherd profiles, mode #14: Arauquinoid maroon paint 137
24. Rim sherd profiles, mode #19: Arauquinoid rectilinear incision and
    punctation 138
25. Rim sherd profiles, modes #32 and 40: Arauquinoid human-effigy jars.......... 141
26. Rim sherd profiles, mode #136: Arauquinoid human bowl rim lugs 144

Plates

1. False-color infrared image of the Middle Orinoco, 1986 369
2. The Corozal site 371
3. Excavations 2 and 3 at Corozal after excavation 373
4. Artifact features during excavation 375
5. Human skeletons uncovered in Excavation 3 377
6. Human skeletons uncovered in Excavation 2 379
7. Corozal sherdware and gritware decorated sherds 381
8. Sherds of Corozal curvilinear and rectilinear incision 383
9. Sherds of Corozal red-and-white paint, polychrome, and vertical rim strap handles 385
10. Sherds of animal-effigy bowls and Camoruco mauve paint 387
11. Sherds of Arauquinoid maroon paint and rectilinear incision and punctation 389
12. Sherds of Arauquinoid human-effigy jars and human bowl rim lugs 391
13. Fragments of human-effigy jars 393

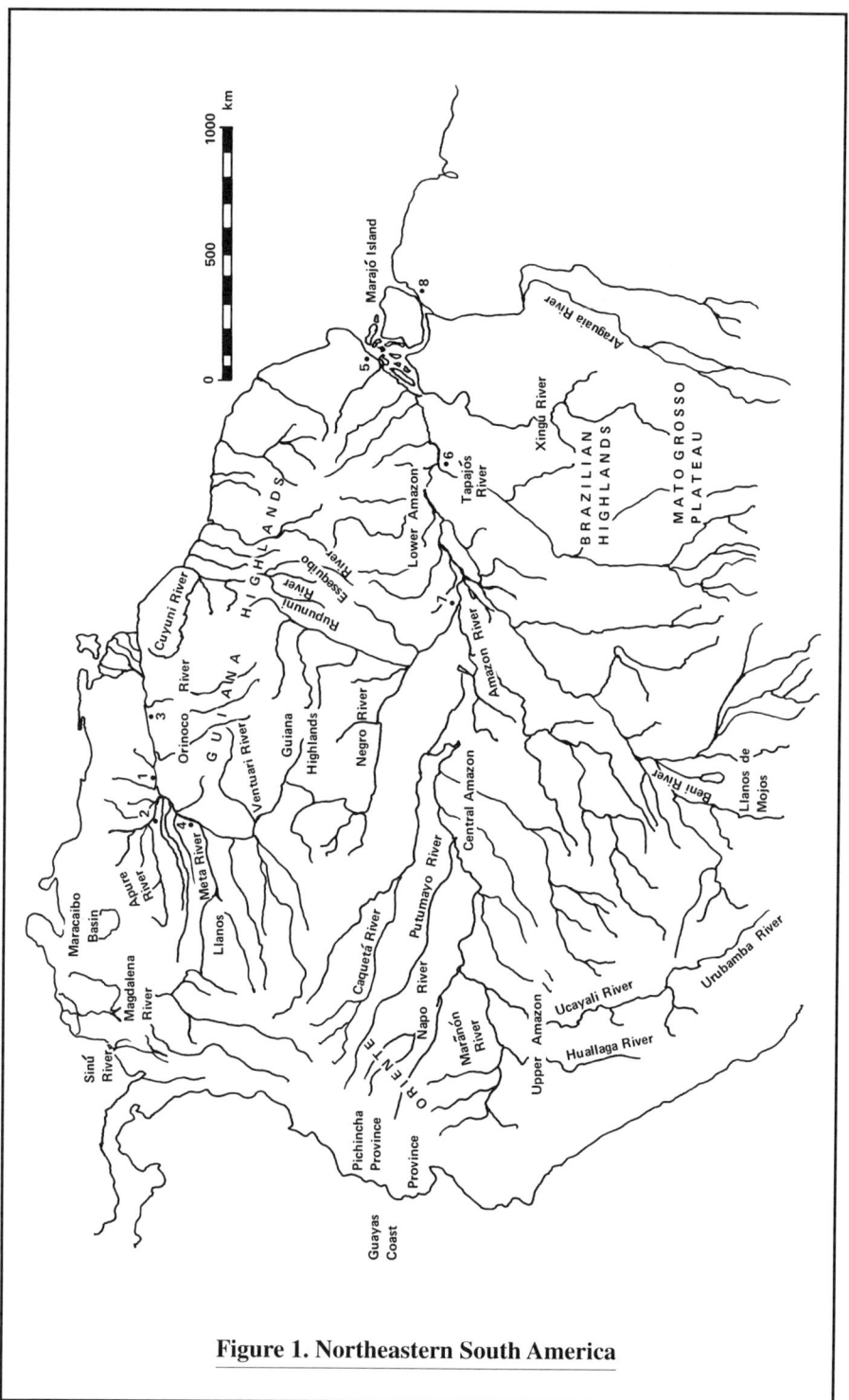

Figure 1. Northeastern South America

Preface

This monograph is based on fieldwork carried out with the encouragement of Irving Rouse of the Department of Anthropology of Yale University and José Cruxent of the Department of Anthropology of the Instituto Venezolano de Investigaciónes Científicas, Caracas, Venezuela. My initial trip to the Parmana region in 1974 was taken with Rouse and Cruxent, and I have benefited greatly from collaboration and discussions with them all along the way.

The purpose of my research in Parmana was to investigate the history of maize cultivation in relation to human population growth in the prehistory of the region. An explanation of the theoretical rationale of the research was presented in the book *Parmana: Prehistoric Maize and Manioc Subsistence along the Amazon and Orinoco* (Roosevelt 1980). Specifics of different facets of my research can be found in that book and in several articles and reports (Roosevelt 1978, 1984a, 1989; Smith and Roosevelt ms; van der Merwe, Roosevelt, and Vogel 1981; Wing, Garzon, and Simon MS). This monograph in the Yale University Publications in Anthropology series presents in detail the data on the Corozal site that provided the crucial temporal framework for the research project.

Central to our research in Parmana was the definition of a detailed regional chronology against which to chart the prehistoric sequence of economic and demographic changes. Working together, Rouse, Cruxent, and I constructed a chronology by amplifying and subdividing the two-part Ronquin sequence originally established by Charles Osgood and George Howard, whose papers were published earlier in the Yale series (Osgood and Howard 1943; Howard 1943, 1947), and later redefined by Cruxent and Rouse (1958–59). We also identified the new La Gruta phase as an ancestor of Osgood and Howard's early Ronquin phases and identified the earliest known ceramic style in the Parmana area (Rouse, Cruxent, Olsen, and Roosevelt 1976; Roosevelt 1978; Rouse et al. 1975; Rouse 1978; Rouse and Allaire 1978). Rouse and Cruxent recognized the chronological distinction between the successive Ronquin and Ronquin Sombra phases in the early Ronquin material they excavated in the lower-lying strata of the Ronquin site (Rouse et al. 1975), and my excavations at that site documented the two phases' stratigraphic superposition. Later, I encountered further chronological distinctions, defining the Corozal and Camoruco phases within Osgood and Howard's late Ronquin material. This Yale monograph presents the basic stratigraphic and ceramic evidence for the Corozal and Camoruco phases, based on my excavations at the type site, Corozal.

I have already thanked the many who participated in the Parmana project in the preface to my 1980 book. Here I would like to thank Shira Birnbaum, John Willis, and Melinda Cahill, who helped in the final preparation of the Corozal material for publication by re-counting all the sherds and sorting the diagnostic rim and base sherds for classification. At the time, Ms. Birnbaum and Mr. Willis were graduate students at New York University and Hunter College, respectively. Ms. Birnbaum served as laboratory supervisor during 1985 and 1986, Mr. Willis was research assistant during 1986 and 1987, and Ms. Cahill was research assistant during 1987. Thanks are also due to Mary Jane Lenz for her important contributions during many years as laboratory supervisor for the Parmana project at the Museum of the American Indian, during the earlier part of the work, while I was curator at the museum, 1976–1985. I also thank Craig Morris, chair of the Department of Anthropology at the American Museum of Natural History, for his help with the arrangements for laboratory facilities and support personnel while I was research associate and guest curator there during the latter part of the work in 1986–1987. Thanks to Linda Brown and Abe Jaffe, who advised on and checked the statistical calculations. I also want to thank Ellen Quinn, graduate student at the University of Illinois, Chicago, and research assistant at the Field Museum, for meticulously checking sherd catalogue numbers; and thanks to Stephen Mayer for copyediting; Dora Chun, Amjad Ali, and Ruth Buck for proofreading; and Pegasus for preparing the camera-ready book. Publication was greatly delayed by the loss in 1995 of the entire hard-disk version when Brock Editorial Associates had a disk crash without having backed up their work.

I would like to thank especially Lita Osmundsen for her continuing support for the Parmana project while president and director for research at the Wenner-Gren Foundation for Anthropological Research. Without this support, both intellectual and financial, this work could not have been done. Wenner-Gren supplied funds both for the analysis of the material from the excavations and for the publication of this monograph. Additional funds for analysis came in an advanced research grant from the Social Science Research Council (1979), and accelerator radiocarbon dates were supplied free by Rupert Housley of the Oxford University Accelerator Radiocarbon Laboratory. My comparative study of lowland museum collections was funded by a fellowship (1981–1982) from the National Endowment for the Arts. My work on the final manuscript was aided by a John D. and Catherine C. MacArthur Foundation fellowship award (in 1988), and I obtained other comparative material in two excavation projects in the Brazilian Amazon with funding from the National Science Foundation and the National Endowment for the Humanities.

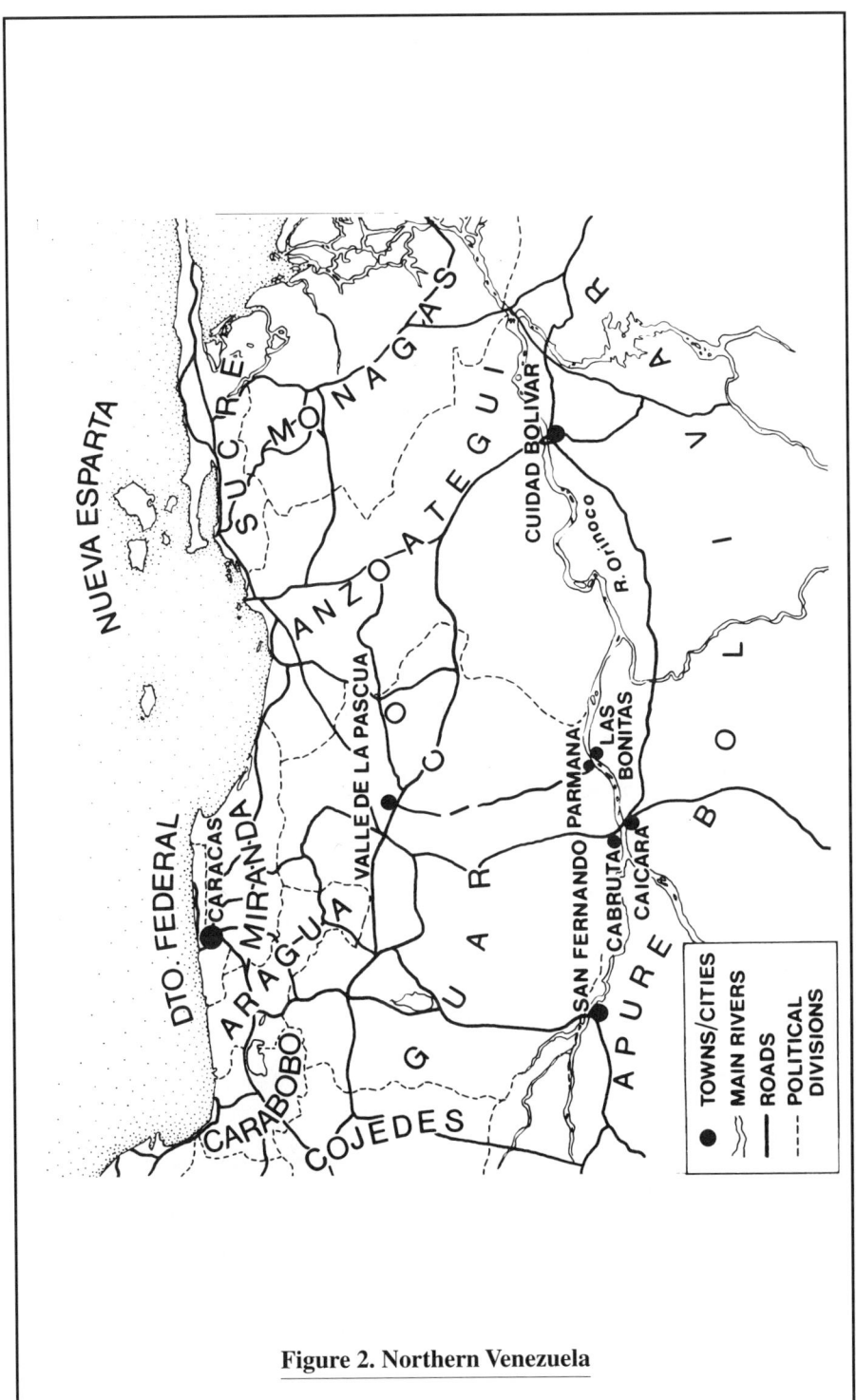

Figure 2. Northern Venezuela

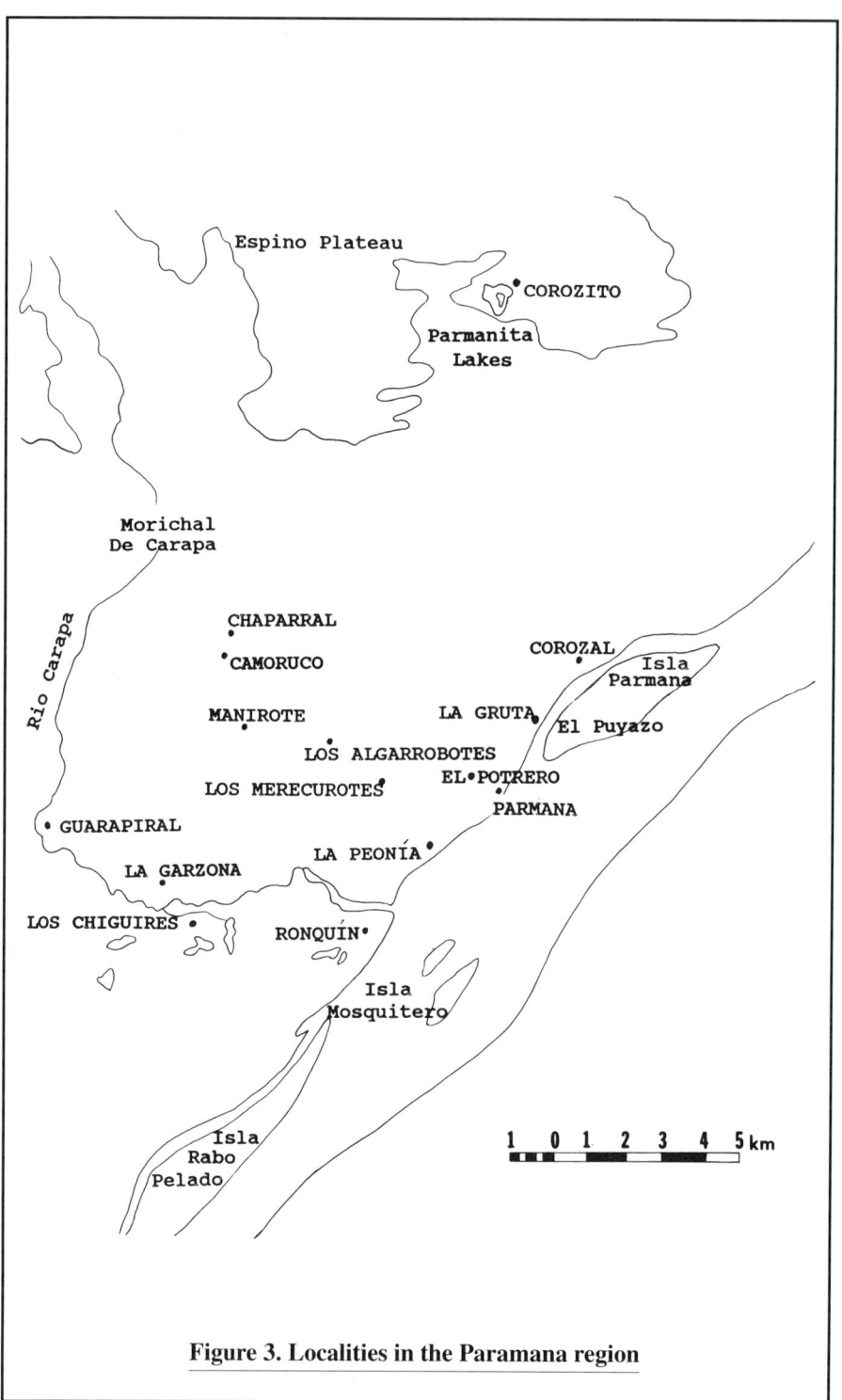

Figure 3. Localities in the Paramana region

1. Introduction

A. Background of the Research

During the fall of 1974 and spring of 1975, I carried out an archaeological research project in the Parmana region of the Middle Orinoco River in Guarico State, Venezuela (Figs. 1–3). The research involved surface surveys and stratigraphic excavations at thirteen sites, the largest of which was the Corozal site. My research in Parmana was one of several loosely collaborative projects being pursued by archaeologists in the Middle Orinoco Basin at the time (Rouse et al. 1976; Rouse and Allaire 1978). The collaborations were initiated by J. Cruxent and I. Rouse, who, with F. Olsen, invited me to go to Parmana with them for about a month in August 1974 to begin my dissertation project there. Their purpose in going to Parmana was to excavate samples of charcoal from the site of Ronquin for radiocarbon dating. I was interested in carrying out research on prehistoric cultural ecology in the region. Just before and after the 1974 field trip, we reviewed together the existing museum collections of archaeological material from the Orinoco region to lay the groundwork for a detailed chronology for the area. Then, I returned to Parmana the next year and carried out the main part of my fieldwork during approximately four months from February through May.

My fieldwork in the Orinoco was aimed at tracing the temporal relationships between changes in prehistoric subsistence and population growth in the region. I had become interested in the role of maize cultivation in the cultural history of the tropical lowlands of the Americas. My review of the archaeology and ethnohistory of lowland South America had turned up evidence that this cereal crop might have become a staple food in some areas during the development of populous complex societies in late prehistoric times. The evidence from agronomy suggested that such a crop could have been used for intensive cultivation of river floodplain soils and that its cultivation could have expanded the land's carrying capacity above that possible with other indigenous crops or with foraging alone. There was thus a possibility that the taking up of intensive maize cultivation supported the sizable population increase that occurred in many lowland river basins simultaneous with the development of complex chiefdoms, between about 500 B.C. and the invasion of Europeans in the sixteenth century A.D.

To investigate the correlation of subsistence and population change in prehistoric Parmana, I needed to construct a detailed ceramic sequence that could provide a relative temporal framework for archaeological data on diet and population size. For this purpose I carried out stratigraphic excavations at each of the thirteen archaeological sites discovered in Parmana and analyzed the distribution of ceramics in their stratigraphy. As a result of this and others' work on the ceramic sequence and a large suite of radiocarbon dates (Roosevelt 1980; Rouse and Allaire 1978), Parmana is now thought to have a prehistoric sequence of more than 5,000 years. Of the ten phases of occupation now recognized, the Corozal site represents the last six phases, a span of more than 1,500 years (*see* Table 1). The specific purpose of the excavations at the Corozal site was to define the ceramic sequence of the site occupation as a type chronology for the later part of the prehistoric sequence and to collect carbonized plant remains in chronological, stratigraphic, and cultural context. At Corozal, abundant cultural and biological material of the last two major prehistoric phases of the region lay in vertically superimposed layers in an approximately 4 m deep deposit; an ideal situation for chronological ceramic seriation and study of subsistence change. On the basis of my study of the stratification and ceramic patterning of the archaeological deposit at Corozal, I established the Corozal and Camoruco phases for the later prehistoric occupation of the Parmana region. The ceramic sequence at Corozal as a regional type sequence allowed the dating of components at other sites in the region by ceramic comparisons. This monograph presents in detail the stratigraphy and seriation of the pottery from excavations at Corozal so that the sequence can be evaluated and used by other archaeologists.

Before the Parmana project, the regional sequence had been classified into two very complex multicomponent assemblages called early and late Ronquin, based on George Howard's (1943) excavations at the site of Ronquin, a small village about 5 km upstream from Parmana village. The combination of chronologically distinct materials in the same strata may have happened because they had been mixed together at the site through natural or human disturbances and/or through the then-standard procedure of digging by artificial level excavations carried out by large crews of unskilled laborers using heavy tools such as picks and shovels. Howard was aware that his excavation levels contained pottery of several distinct styles, and he recognized that different pottery styles predominated at different depths in the deposit. However, he assumed that most of the different styles were made and used during the entire prehistoric period and changed only in frequency through time. My excavations at Corozal demonstrated that many of the different styles and wares found together at Ronquin were not contemporary and had been recovered from the same levels only because noncontemporaneous material had become mixed in the archaeological deposit. The Corozal stratigraphic excavations and ceramic seriation give both qualitative and quantitative evidence that Howard's late Ronquin phase included two superimposed, chronologically distinct major pottery complexes and that each was characterized by several chronological subdivisions.

The sequence represented at Corozal has importance beyond the regional ceramic framework because it apparently was the time of some significant cultural-ecological changes: a radical shift in basic food economy, a rapid expansion of human population, and the appearance of complex societies in the region. The results from archaeobotanical (Roosevelt 1980; Smith and Roosevelt MS) and bone isotope studies (van der Merwe, Roosevelt, and Vogel 1981; Roosevelt, Krueger, and Sullivan MSb) and radiocarbon dating (Rouse and Allaire 1978; *see* Table 2 in this volume) at this site and others indicate that maize first appeared as a crop in the Parmana region during the Corozal phase and had become the primary staple food by the beginning of the Camoruco phase. This economic shift was accompanied by a relatively rapid increase in the sizes and numbers of archaeological sites and by the addition of several new ceramic styles and new iconographies to preexisting ceramic complexes. During the Camoruco phase, site size and density reached the prehistoric maximum in the region, and a ceramic complex related to the widespread late-prehistoric Arauquinoid horizon of ceramics developed. The Arauquinoid horizon has been identified with the expansion of a series of indigenous chiefdoms in the Orinoco and Amazon regions (Lathrap 1970). Its spread seems to be associated with significant economic, demographic, and organizational changes, although the causality of the changes has yet to be determined (Roosevelt 1987a). The main problem for assessing causality is that we still lack systematic information about the characteristics and timing of such changes in different lowland regions. Progress in understanding the nature and causes of these archaeological developments will be limited until there are more regional chronologies and more comprehensive information about archaeological cultures in the lowlands. Recent archaeological research in the Barinas region of the Orinoco Basin (Garson 1980; Spencer and Redmond 1991) and the Beni drainage in the Bolivian Amazon (Erickson 1980) promises to produce some of the type of regional information that is needed.

B. Tropical Lowland Archaeology in South America

It has been difficult to gather data on the nature of prehistoric occupations in the tropical lowlands east of the Andes in South America, a vast area of rivers, forests, savannas, and low mountain ranges. In contrast to the central Andes, only a few archaeologists have worked in the lowlands. Due to aspects of the history and environment of the area, distances between urban centers today are great, transportation is slow, difficult, and expensive, and support services are scarce. This situation may have discouraged some archaeologists from working in the lowlands.

In addition, the lowland region has often been viewed in terms of the popular model of the hot, continuously rainy Amazonian tropical rain forest. Many have assumed that lowland prehistoric sites would be shallow, unstructured, and poorly preserved, due to the adverse environment. Influential anthropologists interested in human cultural evolution have declared that tropical lowland environments in the Americas presented a hindrance to substantial, long-term indigenous human occupations and cultural development (Meggers 1954, 1971; Sanders and Price 1968; Steward 1949). On analogy with the lifeways of living Amazonian Indians, these theorists initially concluded that the tropical lowland area had a slight prehistoric occupation by small groups of people living in temporary villages and nomadic bands. In this view the area's cultural history was largely attributed to invasions and migrations from the outside, and the major prehistoric technological innovations, such as the development of pottery and agriculture, were considered to have been introductions to the lowlands from centers of civilization in the central Andes and Mesoamerica. Large-scale, native complex societies were not expected in the tropical lowlands (Kidder 1964), and those that turned up in the archaeological record were attributed to invasions from the outside (Evans and Meggers 1968; Meggers 1954; Meggers and Evans 1961, 1957; Sanders and Price 1968). These ideas about lowland archaeology were debated on environmental and archaeological grounds (Lathrap 1970; Rouse 1953), but definitive empirical work to settle the question did not emerge. Leading scholars working mainly in the Amazon lowlands became engaged in feuds over access to research areas, and scholarship in the lowlands became polarized and oppositional (Lathrap and Oliver 1980; Roosevelt 1991a; Sanoja 1980). Students and protégés were drawn into the battles and recruited into cliques that tended to perpetuate the theories and methods of their mentors in opposition to those of the mentors' rivals and to ignore alternative theories and methods for research in the lowlands.

Perhaps because of the paucity of data and the combative scholarly politics, archaeology east of the Andes has until recently been relatively stagnant methodologically. Lowland archaeologists have usually carried out research by means of informal reconnaissance site surveys, artificial levels excavations, and pottery typology by modal or type variety—methods that were standards in American archaeology in the middle of this century. They have rarely incorporated newer archaeological approaches such as systematic settlement survey and stratigraphic excavation, quantified functional and statistical analysis of pottery and lithics, or geoarchaeological and bioarchaeological studies, which have become routine in the practice of archaeology in many areas outside the eastern lowlands.

Through the research of pioneering archaeologists such as Rouse and Cruxent, the research of those that they recruited, and that of others, we now know that archaeological practice in the tropical lowlands east of the Andes need not be so different from that in other areas of the world. As elsewhere, most prehistoric sites in the lowlands contain abundant observable features and strata of occupation, activity areas, domestic and monumental structures, numerous diverse artifacts, human and animal bone, and abundant ancient carbonized plant remains (Garson 1980; Roosevelt 1980, 1984a, 1991a). As in other areas, even preserved wood and other organic materials can be recovered from waterlogged archaeological sites and sites in dry caves (Roosevelt 1991c, 1991d; Roosevelt et al. MS).

Far from the slight occupation envisioned by the evolutionists, the magnitude of the ancient occupation of the lowlands is now known to be much greater than archaeologists had suspected. Archaeological sites are numerous, complexly patterned, and sometimes of very large size, with extensive prehistoric monumental earthworks and midden deposits recorded in several areas (e.g., Boomert 1976, 1980a; Denevan 1966; Denevan and Zucchi 1978; Erickson 1980; Meggers and Evans 1957; Porras 1987; Roosevelt 1991a; Roosevelt et al. 1991; Smith 1980). Further, the sequence of prehistoric cultures turns out to be much longer and much more complex than previously thought, including a number of different preceramic and early ceramic stage occupations (Barse 1990; Boomert 1980b; Roosevelt 1986, 1987c, 1989, 1991c, 1991d; Roosevelt et al. 1991, 1996) and diverse later prehistoric complex cultures (Roosevelt 1990b, 1991a, 1991c, 1991d; Roosevelt et al. MSa).

This substantial archaeological resource clearly merits intensive and comprehensive investigation in the future, with more effective archaeological methods than traditional lowland methods. It is worth investigating because such environments appear to have been important arenas for human biological and cultural evolution. In Africa, research on early human ecology and evolution has focused on the role of tropical and subtropical savanna regions, and the equatorial tropical rain forests have been treated as if they were peripheral to the process (as pointed out by A. Brooks, personal communication, and as exemplified by Phillipson [1985]). In South America, the tropical environment of theoretical interest for prehistoric human ecology has been defined as the tropical rain forest, and the evolutionary role of seasonal tropical savanna environments has been neglected by theorists (as Garson [1980] points out). Seasonal tropical lowland biomes are much more extensive in South America than the literature suggests (Roosevelt 1990a) and seem to have been even more widespread in prehistoric times (Prance 1982, 1985). In fact, much of the archaeological and ethnographic research on "tropical rain forest" peoples in South America has actually taken place in seasonally dry areas, and the available archaeological evidence suggests that such habitats may have been important foci of early prehistoric cultural development. With fertile alluvial and residual soils, abundant water, high solar radiation, and high renewable plant and animal biomass, these were a rich and reliable resource base for exploitation by preindustrial humans. Substantial archaeological sites and elaborate material culture have also been found in areas with uniformly high rainfall combined with good alluvial or residual soils (Herrera et al. 1983; Porras 1987), but less work has been done in that climate zone.

The patterns of eastern lowland prehistory discernible in available data (Brochado 1980; Lathrap 1970, 1974; Brochado and Lathrap MS; Meggers and Evans 1978, 1983; Roosevelt 1980, 1989, 1991a, 1991c, 1991d; Roosevelt, Krueger, and Sullivan MSa; Roosevelt et al. 1991, MS) give a picture of indigenous cultural evolution quite different from what the theorists expected. The evidence suggests that people have been living in the tropical lowlands as long as in any other area of the hemisphere, certainly as early as 11,500 B.P. The late Pleistocene and early Holocene occupations of the area have been defined for only a few places, but the sites that have been systematically excavated and dated do not fit consensual ideas about the development of cultures in the Americas. Early preceramic cultures in the lowlands are much more diverse than those that have been defined in other American regions. Although Paleoindian specialists have tended to assume that the early preceramic lifestyles were adapted to the large game of temperate climate regions, the presence of Paleoindians in the Amazon has been confirmed by the finds of bifacial pressure-flaked lithics and twelfth-millennium radiocarbon dates in a painted cave near Monte Alegre (Roosevelt 1991d; Roosevelt et al. MS). This and the other early preceramic cultures make up several different regional complexes of elaborate rock art, a variety of distinctive lithic complexes, including fine, pressure-flaking as well as crude, percussion-flaking, and a variety of bifacial and unifacial forms (Boomert 1980b; Roosevelt 1991c, 1991d; Roosevelt et al. 1991, 1992; Schmitz 1991; Simoes 1976). Far from being culturally retarded due to the tropical environment, early Holocene foragers in the lowlands produced the earliest pottery found so far in the hemisphere (Harris 1973; Hartt 1883, 1885; Roosevelt 1986, 1991c, 1991d, 1995; Roosevelt et al. 1991; Simoes 1981; Lopes, Imazio da Silveira, and Magalhaes 1989). The tools and faunal and floral assemblages of the preceramic and early ceramic cultures indicate a range of ecological adaptations and settlement patterns among the early foragers, from nomadic large-game hunting and broad-spectrum foraging to intensive sedentary fishing and collecting. So far early Holocene sites have produced only noncultivated plant remains, and the economic focus of the early pottery cultures is riverine foraging. Perhaps because of the lack of interest by temperate-zone archaeologists in tropical archaeology and because of language and cultural barriers among archaeologists, the important preceramic and early ceramic lowland complexes are not mentioned in hemispheric or continent-wide surveys of early American cultures (Fagan 1987; Feidel 1987; Lynch 1983, 1990; Willey 1971).

In later prehistoric times in the tropical lowlands there was a cultural florescence and population expansion similar in some ways to the early and middle Formative developments of Mesoamerica and the central Andes. Between 3000 and 1000 B.C., northern lowland cultures with elaborate supraregional pottery styles established a network of substantial villages with subsistence based on horticulture and fishing (Cruxent and Rouse 1958–59; Lathrap 1970; Meggers and Evans 1983; Roosevelt 1978, 1980; van der Merwe et al. 1981). By the time of Christ, many lowland peoples had large and numerous settlements and were building artificial earth mounds for habitation, ceremonies, urn cemeteries, and cultivation. These later prehistoric sites give evidence for the economies of intensive food production and foraging, large-scale craft production, and long-distance trade and communication. The scale and patterning of sites indicate the achievement of considerable sociopolitical complexity and cultural elaboration with time. During the first millennium A.D., a few internally differentiated and densely occupied settlements from 5 to 20 sq. km in area appeared in a number of regions (Athens 1989; Dougherty and Calandra 1981–82; Farabee MS; Hartt 1883, 1885; Porras 1987; Roosevelt 1991a). The deep and extensive midden deposits and the complex patterning of the archaeological remains suggest that such sites had both the scale and function of urban centers (Roosevelt 1987a, 1990b, 1991a, 1991d; Spencer and Redmond 1991). Literacy, hyperdense urban complexes, coercive state bureaucratic systems, and extensive monumental stone constructions apparently were absent in the lowlands. The lack of such developments may be due to the fact that the large area of productive land in the lowlands could absorb population growth for a long time, thus delaying the interregional conflict that may have stimulated the formation of large administrative states in the circumscribed valleys of the Andes and Mesoamerican highlands (Carneiro 1970).

The timing of the formation of complex societies in the tropical lowlands is not yet established. They may have developed later in lowland prehistoric sequences than in the nuclear areas of Mesoamerica and the Andes, or there may have been too little research that could uncover them in the lowlands. Although 4,500-year-old cultures with nucleated settlements with monumental architecture and elaborate art have been uncovered in the Andes (Keatinge 1988), archaeologists have yet to find firm evidence of such sites before about 1000 B.C. in the lowlands. Some have argued that complex cultures arose very early in tropical lowland sequences and strongly influenced early Andean complex cultures (Lathrap 1970, 1971, 1975). The influence of lowlands on the Andes has been confirmed many times over (Burger 1984); and permanent villages, well-developed horizons of elaborate ceramics, and horticulture are apparently earlier in Amazonia than in the Andes (Brochado and Lathrap MS; Hartt 1883, 1885; Lathrap 1970; Roosevelt 1980, 1987c, 1989, 1991d; Roosevelt et al. 1991; Simoes 1981). However, it is difficult as yet to find conclusive evidence for complex social and political organization in the lowlands until the millennium before Christ.

A number of Andean scholars have come to doubt that the existence of elaborate art and architecture in early Andean communities necessarily means that the ancient cultures were socioeconomically complex, and they do not see the development of complex organization much before the first millennium B.C. So, at the same time that some developments are turning up earlier in the lowlands than we expected, some developments in the nuclear areas are being placed later in date. The chronologies of cultural development are thus converging across regions in certain ways.

Not only the history of the development of cultures in the New World, but also the role of agriculture in cultural development has been brought into question by recent research. During the rise of complex cultures in the lowlands, cultivation patterns seem to vary greatly from region to region, in some cases emphasizing local seed crops, in others, root crops. The first intensive agriculture in the lowlands may have developed during the first millennium B.C., based on a suite of indigenous lowland seed crops that were later superseded by maize (Brochado 1980; Roosevelt 1984a, 1989, 1991a). Scholars have claimed evidence for staple maize cultivation in the Andean drainage of the Amazon as early as 6000 B.P., based on finds of several maize-like phytoliths and pollen grains dated by extrapolated radiocarbon dates (Bush et al.

1989). However, the number of identified specimens involved is statistically insignificant; no maize remains in the lowlands have been securely dated before the first millennium B.C., either by association or by direct radiocarbon accelerator mass spectrometry; and human bone chemistry in the lowlands attains maize-like patterns only after about A.D. 500 (Roosevelt 1980; van der Merwe, Roosevelt, and Vogel 1981; Roosevelt 1989, 1991a; *see also* Chap. 2, G, *below*). Ten years ago, we would have considered this to be a comparatively late start for maize cultivation because we assumed that the maize came into the intermediate area from Mesoamerica or the central Andes, where maize was dated to about 5000 B.C. and considered a staple by 1000 B.C. However, the early Mexican and Andean maize specimens and wood associated with maize from Tehucan and Guitarrero Cave have now been directly dated by accelerator mass spectrometry to an age of only about 2,000 to 4,000 years (Gowlett and Hedges 1985; Long et al. 1989). This surprising "up-dating" of early maize is a salutary lesson to archaeologists that pollen, phytoliths, and even maize macrospecimens can and do move downward in stratigraphic profiles (Doolittle and Frederick 1991). This revision in the dating of early maize cultivation is supported by the results of stable isotope analysis of human bones in many regions, which show that throughout most of the Americas, intensive agriculture based on maize as a staple rarely predates the first millennium B.C. and often occurs much later (Burger and van der Merwe 1990; Ericson et al. 1989; Norr 1984; Price 1989; Roosevelt 1989; van der Merwe, Lee-Thorp, and Raymond MS). Thus intensive maize agriculture, assumed by the evidence of contact-period peoples to have been the economic precondition for the formative stages of civilization, was not apparently a staff of life either for early pottery cultures or for early complex societies. Although it is likely that primitive maize was in widespread use in South and Central America long before it reached the status of a staple, so far no specimens earlier than the first millennium B.C. have actually been directly dated. Morphologically primitive maize is known from early caves and rock shelters in many regions of the Americas other than the Andes and Mesoamerica (for South American instances, *see* Fernandez Distel 1978; Miller 1987; Roosevelt et al. MS). Until such finds are directly dated by the radiocarbon accelerator, the geographic origins and spread of maize cultivation in the Western Hemisphere will remain in doubt.

The specific history of subsistence and population in the lowlands and the role of these factors in cultural development have only been investigated in a few places. Few lowland sites dating between 3000 and 1000 B.C., when complex cultures first appear in South America, have been investigated; and the nature of socioeconomic differentiation among later prehistoric lowland societies has been studied in only a few places. The earliest periods of occupation of the lowlands, when the first colonists arrived and then settled down to make pottery and cultivate, constitute the greatest gaps in our knowledge because their existence has been recognized only recently. But the later periods when socioculturally complex cultures come into being are also poorly known. Because knowledge exists for only a few isolated points in time and space, overall patterns of cultural change and interregional relationships in South America are not well documented. More comprehensive research is needed to reveal the nature of ecological adaptation and cultural development in the different regions at different times. Explaining the trajectory and interactions of cultures and populations in lowland South America can provide many fascinating research topics for the future. It is the general problem that originally drew me into field research in the Orinoco.

C. Parmana Archaeological Project

The main purpose of the Parmana archaeological project (Roosevelt 1980) was to investigate prehistoric cultural change in a tropical lowland floodplain region east of the Andes. Because of their possible importance in stimulating organizational changes, I focused the research on the sequence of prehistoric population growth and subsistence change.

The research plan was aimed at evaluating two hypotheses about the relationship between agricultural food economy and population growth in the region. One was the manioc hypothesis, which had been more or less implicitly accepted by scholars specializing in the South American lowland region; the other was the maize hypothesis, which I suggested as an alternative. The manioc hypothesis holds that the subsistence of prehistoric eastern lowland Indians was provided by calories from starchy manioc roots and protein from fish and game. This manioc–fish–game economy is the most common indigenous system today in Greater Amazonia, and many scholars had projected it back into the preconquest period as a matter of course.

The hypothetical rationale for the manioc economy is its adaptiveness for tropical rain forest areas of presumed low subsistence potential. The plant does comparatively well in poor soils and furnishes abundant calories so that scarce faunal resources can be conserved for filling protein needs. This system would be expected to support more people than animal capture alone, because it exploits the energy available from food at a lower trophic level. Support for the manioc hypothesis can be found in the economy's widespread use among indigenous groups in lowland South America and in finds of prehistoric ceramic griddles in some areas. However, in indigenous America griddles were used for many crops other than manioc (DeBoer 1975), and there was and still is no direct prehistoric botanical evidence for manioc. The abundant evidence for post-conquest changes in culture in the area suggested to me that the manioc hypothesis ought not be assumed a priori.

In the alternative hypothesis, manioc was the staple plant food only in earlier prehistoric times, when human population density was relatively low and protein needs could be met by the products of animal capture. The starchy root crop would have been supplanted as the major staple by maize in the floodplain regions of Amazonia during the population maximum of the last two millennia before the European conquest. According to this interpretation, the subsistence of the populous late prehistoric riverine chiefdoms described in the early European accounts of the Amazon and Orinoco would have been based primarily on maize cultivation, rather than on manioc, fish, and game. The rationale for this system would have been the need for more intensive exploitation of fertile floodplain alluvium under pressure of growing populations. In such a demographic context, maize would have been a more efficient staple food than either faunal staples or fauna and manioc because it could fill much of peoples' protein and calorie needs on a lower trophic level, with abundant storable seed protein. Manioc would have become dominant again among indigenous cultigens when the effects of conquest disruption and disease had decimated the sedentary populations of the floodplains of Amazonia and relegated Indians to the resource-poor interfluves. The initial evidence for this thesis lay in frequent finds of grinding stones in the later prehistoric complexes and in numerous ethnohistoric accounts of intensive maize cultivation along the Amazon and Orinoco mainstreams.

The archaeological test of the two subsistence hypotheses in Parmana was designed to recover archaeological data regarding changes in settlement and subsistence through time. For practical reasons having to do with the lack of basic archaeological information on the region and the usual limitations of funds and personnel in dissertation fieldwork projects, I focused data collecting in a few key areas. The most important aspect of settlement seemed the pattern of change in overall size of human population through time. The survey and excavations in Parmana traced changes in population size from the evidence of changes in the sizes and numbers of occupation sites through time. A program of transect survey, test pitting, and large-scale excavation was implemented to construct the ceramic sequence and estimate the numbers of sites and extent of the prehistoric occupation at each site through time. For establishing the minimum number of sites at different times, we carried out a site survey somewhat different from both traditional tropical lowland surveys and North American and Mesoamerican archaeologists' systematic surface surveys. In informal reconnaissance site survey, the most common method currently used in the tropical lowlands, archaeological sites are located by interviewing local people. This method alone could not serve my purposes because the land is not examined in any specified manner, and therefore it is difficult to know how the sites found compare to those that may exist in the part of the land not examined. In addition, local people, however observant, are likely to produce an unrepresentative sample skewed toward those sites that happen to lie in locations frequented by them. Those sites lying in areas that current inhabitants do not use have little chance of being discovered.

In systematic site survey, a specified proportion of the land is examined, by either total transect survey, random sampling, or some other approach. Most systematic settlement surveys estimate changes in site size through time by study of ground surfaces on the premise that most sites will be exposed on the surface and that most components of a site are reflected in the surface remains. However, many archaeological sites in the Parmana region were partly or wholly buried, and this pattern was more common with the earlier sites. (My later research in the Brazilian Amazon has shown, for example, that preceramic sites rarely are exposed at the surface [Roosevelt 1991d; Roosevelt et al. 1991, MS].) In Parmana, sites exposed on the surface usually turned out to have more components than the remains on the surface indicated. In such situations, conventional surface survey would greatly underestimate the representation of earlier sites and components. This is probably true for all but some desert regions where rates of deposition may be slow, depending on soil texture and wind patterns. Indeed, when archaeologists test the representation of material in surface remains compared to subsequently excavated material, they have found that surface remains do not reflect the abundance and time range of the material underground (e.g., Burger 1984). Accordingly, it is more practical to use some kind of systematic subsurface sampling to allow buried sites and components a better chance to appear in the sample. This can be done by machine-aided or labor-intensive test-pitting in transects or by random sampling of selected "strata." Although earlier periods of occupation will always be subject to bias compared to later periods in settlement surveys because of the increasing chances for site destruction through time, the strategy of intensive subsurface sampling at least eliminates the bias due to site concealment.

Since I was a graduate student at the time, neither the mechanized method nor intensive region-wide test-pitting was possible, because of the costs. However, I observed that the 15-kilometer-long Orinoco main river channel was like a transect cut of the region. Although some sites in Parmana had absolutely no visible archaeological material at their upper surfaces, many had a broad band of material exposed by erosion on the side facing the river channel. This cut would not expose sites that were not located on the bank of the Orinoco, but the regional topography, climate, and hydrology determine that this elevated bank is the main place where permanent settlement is possible. Most high ground north of the Orinoco overflow plain (except near permanent lakes) is inappropriate for permanent habitation because there is no water for the many months of the dry season. Therefore, it seemed likely to me that most permanent ancient settlements would have been located along the main channel banks. To locate prehistoric sites of possible permanent human occupation in the Parmana region, I surveyed the entire length of the Orinoco levee and bank on foot, focusing on the cross section of strata exposed at its river face as a view into the archaeological stratigraphy of the region. To correct partially for bias against sites not at the riverbank, I also excavated at all other sites known to archaeologists and to local people. My approach to survey still skewed against the earliest prehistoric sites, as all methods will, but that was an acceptable defect for me because my focus of interest was on later prehistoric occupations.

In the research, change through time in the size of sites was identified and dated by the distribution of pottery of different phases within the sites. The number and size of components present at sites were determined from the character of ceramics in the scraped cross sections of the riverbank exposures and from the test-pits and larger excavations placed at each site. Changes in human population through time were represented by relative changes in the summed total area of the archaeological components. Absolute population figures were calculated on the basis of population/site ratios at contemporary Amazonian villages and on archaeologists' estimates from sites in other regions, but I felt that the relative population growth curve was best used directly as a proxy for magnitude of population because of all the uncertainties deriving from absolute estimates made without unitary evidence, such as hearth counts (Roosevelt 1991a). Changes in density of cultural material per unit soil and per unit time indicated that density of occupation had increased through time as the number and size of sites increased.

The other objective of the project was to investigate the temporal relationship of changes in subsistence to changes in the size of population. The most important aspect of ancient subsistence in terms of the two hypotheses was the history of maize cultivation. The theory predicted that the introduction of maize would be correlated with an increase in population size and that population would continue to increase as maize increased in use. The theory would be falsified if the patterns of maize occurrence through time were unrelated to changes in population. The manioc hypothesis could not be proved, but corroboration of the maize hypothesis would constitute falsification of it. Then as now, secure identification of archaeological manioc remains was difficult (although future work focused on the identification of diagnostic Euphorbiaceae family wood structures may prove successful). I therefore focused the fieldwork on determining the presence or absence of maize in the ancient site components. For this purpose, I carried out one or more large excavations of about 2 x 4 m at each site to get a stratigraphic column of food remains in association with pottery. Standard archaeobotanical collection methods of wet and dry soil processing and sieving with fine-mesh screens were used to recover macrobotanical remains, and soil samples were collected for extraction of pollen and phytoliths. Most of the carbonized plant remains were recovered in the 1/8" mesh screens. The carbonized plant remains recovered were originally dated by association with the pottery sherds. Because archaeologists have learned since the 1970s that such archaeological associations can be unreliable due to taphonomic processes, this dating by association was later corrected with accelerator dates determined directly on the botanical and sherd specimens, as explained below.

This strategy for testing the maize hypothesis required a relatively detailed ceramic sequence against which to chart changes in subsistence and settlement. Finding that the methods of artificial levels excavation and type-variety ceramic classification used previously in the region had not been able to define a sufficiently detailed ceramic sequence to control for changes in subsistence and settlement, I used instead methods of excavation keyed to stratigraphic layering and ceramic analysis by attributes. In the section on method (*see* Chap. 2, C), I explain what I see as the problems of the artificial-levels–type-variety method and the advantages of the stratigraphic-levels–attribute-analysis method for determining chronology. As applied in Parmana, these methods produced a detailed ceramic sequence, comprised, as well as we know now (*see* Table 1), of a little-known preceramic archaic phase and nine ceramic phases of three traditions–the La Gruta tradition (ca. 2500–1000 B.C., all dates uncalibrated), the Corozal tradition (ca. 1000 B.C.–A.D. 800), and the Camoruco tradition (ca. A.D. 800–1550). (The archaic phase was tentatively identified ex post facto from aceramic lithic material excavated from the base of one site, Manirote.)

The results of the Parmana project tend to support the maize hypothesis and not the manioc hypothesis. The basic supporting evidence lies in the distribution of carbonized plant remains in the excavations and the isotopic ratio of carbon in pottery and the collagen of human bone from the excavations (Roosevelt 1980; Smith and Roosevelt MS; van der Merwe, Roosevelt, and Vogel 1981; Roosevelt, Krueger, and Sullivan MS; Table 8). The results are consistent with but not limited to a La Gruta tradition subsistence adaptation similar to the manioc-fish-game system found today among indigenous Amazonians. Maize is detectable in the sequence for the first time in the Corozal 1 phase, about 1000 B.C.–A.D. 500, and the isotopic analyses suggest that it became the major article of food by the Corozal 3 phase or Camoruco 1 phase, about A.D. 700–1000. As the staple food, the isotopic chemistry of maize dominates both the protein and mineral portions of the prehistoric bone samples analyzed, indicating that about 70% of the food consumed came from maize. In Parmana the maize was supplemented more by fish protein than by legume protein, although legumes were also consumed. This pattern contrasts with some inland New World areas today, but is one found in other parts of Greater Amazonia (Roosevelt 1989) and some lowland Mayan regions that have been sampled (Roosevelt, Krueger, and Sullivan MSb.) To some who believed that aquatic fauna would have been the main protein supply in prehistoric times as it is today, the maize hypothesis has been hard to accept (Carneiro 1995). However, the many nitrogen and carbon isotopic measurements on both human and faunal bones from late prehistoric sites in the lowlands yielded results that could not have been produced by a food economy whose staple protein source was faunal.

According to the results of the settlement survey, the patterning of site size and number through time indicates that regional population density was relatively low and stable from the beginning of the La Gruta tradition phases until the introduction of maize during the early Corozal phase. The regional population increased rapidly during the Corozal phase and peaked during the following Camoruco phase, when maize became a staple food. The settlement results thus accorded roughly with the expectations of the maize hypothesis and were not consistent with the manioc hypothesis. So, although the results of the Parmana project could reconstruct only some bare bones of a developmental sequence for the region, they were sufficiently definitive to allow me to choose between the two hypotheses.

These findings were important because they established that prehistoric subsistence in the northern lowland floodplain had changed substantially through time and may have varied through space in the different biomes of the lowlands, contradicting the common assumption that one particular indigenous subsistence system had prevailed throughout Greater Amazonia.

The archaeological results showed that the late prehistoric subsistence system of an important floodplain region was quite different from widely accepted reconstructions based on ethnographic subsistence in nonriverine areas. This difference between prehistoric and ethnographic subsistence turned out to have implications for our understanding of the rationale for the ethnographic subsistence adaptation and raised the question of how the current indigenous subsistence system could be considered the optimal adaptation to the environment if a very different adaptation had existed in the area shortly before. The results suggested that the manioc–fish–game system typical of ethnographic people had been replaced by intensive maize cultivation in the floodplain before the time of Christ. The correlation of subsistence change with population change suggested further that contact period reduction in indigenous populations and increase in settlement mobility may have been stimuli to a return to the earlier subsistence adaptation based on manioc. Thus, in a switch from the usual ethnoarchaeological line of reasoning, the archaeological research served to raise questions about the validity of consensual interpretations of the ethnographic situation, and by revealing a correlation of subsistence and demographic change through time, the research furnished preliminary evidence of the nature of causality in the indigenous history of Amazonia.

D. Research on the Ceramic Sequence

One important goal of the Parmana project, as mentioned, was to create a detailed ceramic sequence against which to map changes in subsistence and population through time. In the research strategy, subsistence change would be revealed in changes in the representation of biological remains and food-processing tools associated with sequential pottery complexes. History of the population would be charted by changes in the size and number of archaeological site components as identified by their content of pottery. The ceramic sequence would be created by comparison of the pottery in the different layers of the archaeological sites.

The current version of the ceramic sequence for Parmana is based on the results of many excavations, both those of my project and those of others. Of all the archaeological sites excavated by the Parmana project, La Gruta and Ronquin were the most important for establishing the first third of the ceramic sequence. The excavations at Corozal furnished the basic evidence for the last two-thirds of the sequence. Among the thirteen archaeological sites now known in Parmana, four were excavated by George Howard, the earliest scientific investigator to carry out intensive investigations in the region. Howard, with the collaboration of Charles Osgood, constructed the first prehistoric chronology for the region (Osgood and Howard 1943; Howard 1943). He excavated at Ronquin, Camoruco, Parmana, and Corozal, but it was primarily from the style and technology of about 10,000 pottery sherds recovered from a 4 x 11 m section of his 60 x 4 m trench at Ronquin that he defined a two-part division of the prehistoric time sequence in Parmana. The earlier of his two periods, early Ronquin, was characterized mainly by oxidized, grit-tempered pottery, which predominated in the lower levels of his Ronquin excavations. The later period, late Ronquin, was characterized by buff, sponge-spicule tempered pottery that was concentrated in the upper levels of the site. There was also a rare fine-paste pottery with both sponge and sand temper that peaked just after the grit-tempered pottery did, and Howard included this pottery in early Ronquin. All of the levels in his excavations at the site contained pottery from all three groups, and Howard believed that the styles had coexisted, although he acknowledged the possibility that artificial and natural disturbance might have combined different pottery styles that had originally been chronologically and stratigraphically distinct.

After the first season of excavation in Parmana, during which I excavated test pits at the site of Ronquin, I reviewed again with Rouse the Yale Peabody Museum collection of unpublished pottery that Howard excavated from the 60 x 4 m trench at Ronquin. It appeared to me that there might be more chronological phases represented than Howard had defined for the region, because the material seemed too varied to represent only two chronological complexes. I felt that the 6% sample of sherds that he studied, coming from only a small section of the large trench, might not have been of sufficient size to be representative. Also, our preliminary studies at the site of Ronquin suggested that the loose, sandy deposit there had been disturbed, and it seemed to me that the artificial-levels excavation technique that Howard used, carried out by a large team of laborers, could have resulted in the mixture of chronologically distinct materials. The published photographs of Howard's excavations at Ronquin illustrated very poorly controlled excavation methods highly likely to result in mixture of material from different cultural layers (Howard 1943, Pl. 1). Howard, of course, was not at fault to use then-current methods—indeed, he was a pioneer whose project was exemplary by the standards of the day—but since then methods of excavation and pottery classification have been developed that make it possible to discover the finer stratigraphic and chronological distinctions that earlier methods obscured. The broad, 25-cm-thick artificial levels of Howard's excavations tended to obscure smaller-scale chronologically and functionally distinct layers and features, and his classificatory emphasis on major types and wares tended to group together material that was actually chronologically distinct.

In his analysis, Howard had discerned three possible major stylistic complexes of pottery at Ronquin, the Y-group, the X-group, and the Z-group. The Y-group was composed of the early grit-tempered pottery of oxidized reddish color and well-finished surfaces. It bore sophisticated red-and-white painted designs and/or carefully executed grooved and modeled decoration of geometric and zoomorphic motifs (Howard 1943, Pl. 3–5, A–M). The common vessel shape of the group was a bowl with incised rim and zoomorphic rim adorno. This main complex of Howard's early Ronquin has close affiliation with the styles of two chronologically early stylistic series of Venezuela and the nations of the Guianas. Those two series are the Saladoid and Barrancoid series first defined for the Lower Orinoco in the late fifties (Cruxent and Rouse 1958–59; Rouse and Cruxent 1963; Sanoja and Vargas 1978).

In addition to the grit-tempered pottery, Howard had included in the Y-group some sherds that he realized were "atypical" in shape and decoration (Howard 1943, Pl. 4, C). These were thick sherds with simple incision in parallel lines or basketry patterns. I found, by examination at 20X under a binocular microscope, that these sherds had abundant sherd and vegetal fiber temper and lacked the abundant grit typical of the Y-group. The main thing that this pottery had in common with the Y-group pottery was that both were concentrated in the lower levels of the excavation. There were few resemblances in decoration, shape, or technology between "typical" and "atypical" Y-group pottery.

The other major early Ronquin pottery complex, Howard's Z-group, was light gray to buff in color and lightly tempered with sponge spicules and sometimes a little fine sand, and had simple, incised and appliquéd decoration in geometric and zoomorphic designs and crude bichrome or trichrome painting in geometric motifs (Howard 1943, Pl. 5, N). This complex has some vague stylistic affinities with the Saladoid and Barrancoid series but also some resemblances to late Ronquin pottery, which belongs to the late prehistoric Arauquinoid series defined by Cruxent and Rouse (1958–59). I saw in this Z-group pottery the possibility of the existence of a chronologically separate phase between Howard's early and late Ronquin.

Howard's early Ronquin complex has now been divided into two phases, Ronquin and Ronquin Sombra, on the basis of stylistic variation within the assemblage of pottery excavated by Rouse, Cruxent, and Olsen at Ronquin, and stratigraphic differences in the distribution of pottery styles in my excavations at Ronquin. La Gruta, a third, earlier complex also related to the Saladoid and Barrancoid ceramic series, was excavated from the site of La Gruta in 1974 by

Mario Sanoja and Iraida Vargas (Vargas 1981), and by Rouse and Cruxent in the same year (Rouse, Cruxent, Olsen, and Roosevelt 1976), and by me in 1975 (Roosevelt 1978, 1980). (For the temporal placement of the complexes, see chronological chart, Table 1.) All the components of the La Gruta tradition in the Parmana region have Howard's typical (grit-tempered) and atypical (sherd- and fiber-tempered) Y-group pottery in the same levels. The tradition, therefore, appears to be stylistically complex or, as Rouse (1985) has termed it, stylistically plural, in that it has at least two major contemporary styles of pottery with very different technology, shape, and decoration.

The late Ronquin complex, Howard's X-group, was even grayer buff in color than the Z-group and had a rather harsh and porous texture, due to the abundant sponge-spicule temper. The decoration consisted of sharp, dense, deep, sloppy geometric incisions and punctations in textile or basketlike motifs and crude appliqué modeling representing zoomorphic and human forms. There were also traces of dark red paint in an overall wash or geometric patterns on many of the vessels. This X-group pottery complex may have its distant origins in styles of the Saladoid and Barrancoid series, with which it shares a predominance of the incised adorno bowl, but its styles, iconography, and technology are very different from that of those series. Instead, the X-group pottery is very similar to the Arauquin style previously described for the Apure Delta area of the Middle Orinoco (Petrullo 1939), the type style for the important late prehistoric northern lowland horizon, the Arauquinoid series (Cruxent and Rouse 1958–59).

Howard also excavated two test pits at Corozal and found abundant pottery of the X-group in the upper levels of the deposit and Y-group pottery in the lower levels. Because he found X-group pottery unaccompanied by Y-group pottery in the upper levels of the site, he hypothesized that Corozal must be a later site than Ronquin, where he had found the X- and Y-groups together in the same levels. In 1974, Cruxent dug an artificial-levels test pit at Corozal, with results similar to Howard's. Because the X-group pottery from Howard's Corozal excavations was identical to that from Ronquin, I thought it more likely that the X- and Y-group pottery associated with one another at Ronquin had probably been combined in the deposit by mechanical mixture, either during excavation or before. In that case, the X-group pottery at Corozal would be contemporary with the X-group pottery from Ronquin, not later in date. I also hypothesized that Howard's late Ronquin complex included at least two chronologically distinct styles, a rich later style of rather gross, complex incision and appliqué modeling (Howard 1943, Pl. 2, B,C,D,G,J,K,N,Q) and an earlier style of shallower, simpler incision and simpler modeled-appliqué shapes (Howard 1943, Pl. 2, E,F,H,M,O,P,R). As mentioned, I suspected that the Z-group pottery that he included in early Ronquin might be a phase that postdated his early Ronquin and predated his late Ronquin.

The possibility that the Ronquin sequence was chronologically subdivisible in this way was confirmed by my stratigraphic excavations at Corozal. I excavated about 64 cubic meters at the site by stratigraphic methods in 1974 in hopes of getting a good stratigraphic sequence of ceramics associated with plant remains. These excavations indeed showed that some ceramic complexes that were combined in levels of Howard's Ronquin excavations occurred separately in distinct, superimposed layers at Corozal. The results indicate that there is a stylistically, stratigraphically, and chronologically distinct phase sandwiched between earlier and later phases characterized primarily by classic Y-group and X-group pottery, respectively. The pottery of this phase, called Corozal after the site, is culturally transitional between earlier and later pottery. It includes the Z-group pottery, simpler, finer examples of X-group pottery (Howard 1943, Pl. 2, M,P,R), and some rather crude, simple examples of the grit-tempered pottery that predominates in Howard's Y-group (Pl. 3, I–L) and in the pottery from La Gruta (Roosevelt 1978, 1980). The Corozal phase examples of the grit-tempered pottery style, however, lack the elaborate modeling, incisions, and red-and-white painting of pottery found at the earlier sites. The Corozal phase also includes numerous examples of Howard's "atypical" incised Y-group pottery. Statistically significant differences in the distribution of pottery of these various styles in the layers of the Corozal site allowed me to define three chronological subdivisions of the Corozal phase, which I will discuss and illustrate below. The Y-group pottery frequencies decline sharply with time, indicating, along with the radiocarbon results, that early Corozal was the final phase in the region to have La Gruta tradition pottery.

Stratigraphically above the Corozal phase layers in the site were layers distinguished by an abundance of Howard's classic X-group pottery. Rouse and Cruxent have suggested that this phase be named after Camoruco, a site that has produced an abundance of such pottery. Statistically significant changes in frequency of different stylistic attributes of Camoruco pottery in the layers of Corozal allowed me to distinguish three subphases in the material, and I will treat these in detail below. The dark red paint and sharp, rectilinear incision styles that are related to the Arauquinoid series (Howard 1943, Pl. 2, D,N,Q, Pl. 6, E,P) were markers for the last of the subphases, and vessels of the two first subphases differed from those of the later subphase in having simpler plastic decoration and somewhat different vessel shapes (Howard 1943, Pl. 2, E,F,I, Pl. 6, I,O).

These findings confirmed that the earlier classification of Parmana pottery had combined some pottery styles that were actually distinct chronologically and separated some that were contemporary. That is, the typological separation of pottery groups from one another on the basis of ware and of basic decorative style had separated some pottery that was contemporaneous, and the integration of pottery of similar style had combined pottery that was in fact not contemporary. My excavations and seriation showed the chronological distinctions by clear stratigraphic superposition of layers containing pottery with different microstylistic attributes. The results show that the Corozal phase ceramics were very complex and include several different contemporary wares and styles. That this diversity of the phase was contemporanous and not the product of mechanical mixture is confirmed by the existence of stylistic crossovers between the different wares. In terms of ceramic history, the diversity seems to have been the product of the integration of several new wares and styles into a ceramic complex of the La Gruta tradition.

In this monograph I describe the sedimentary and cultural stratification at Corozal and chart and analyze the distribution of chronologically significant pottery attributes in the excavation levels, in order to illustrate the temporal distinctiveness of the material of these two late prehistoric phases.

My excavations at other sites in Parmana show stratigraphic superpositions of ceramics similar to those I found at Corozal, but the sequence is best illustrated at Corozal, where pottery is very abundant and the stratigraphic column is deep and well preserved. The general characteristics of the pottery of each of the nine ceramic phases in the Parmana sequence will be described below, and then the pottery of the Corozal and Camoruco phases will be discussed in detail and illustrated. First, however, I will introduce the Corozal site and describe the stratigraphy as revealed by the excavations.

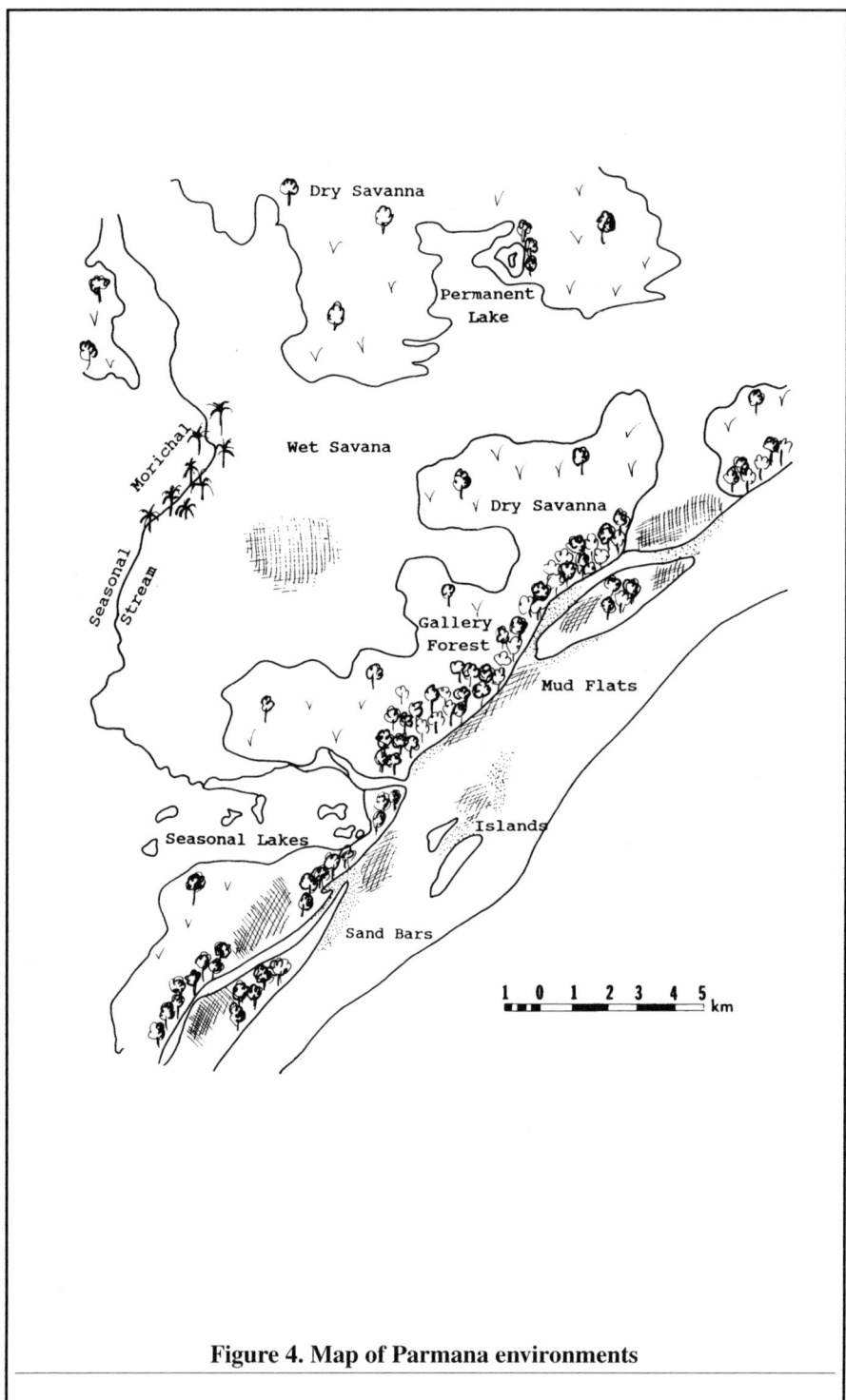

Figure 4. Map of Parmana environments

2. The Excavations at Corozal

In this chapter, the Corozal site and its region are introduced, excavation and mapping procedures are outlined, and then the stratigraphic evidence from the excavations is presented and discussed.

A. The Site and Its Region

The Parmana region, in which Corozal lies, is an area of about 500 sq. km on the left bank of the Middle Orinoco River in Venezuela (Figs. 1–4). (General references on the characteristics of the region are summarized in Roosevelt 1980.) Parmana, like many other areas of the Orinoco, Amazon, and Guiana coasts, has a seasonal tropical savanna climate.[1] Typically, the Middle Orinoco climate is highly seasonal, with about 1,500 mm of rain a year, falling mainly in the six-month rainy season, the time of highest solar radiation. The dry season is a time of drought, strong winds, dust storms, and high rates of evapotranspiration. Many lakes and streams dry up entirely, and surface sediments concentrate salts in some areas. Only the Orinoco main channel and certain lakes and swamps retain water in the dry season. In the rainy season, there is extensive flooding because the topography is very flat and basal sediments are clayey and impermeable. At this time of year in the floodplains only the levees escape flooding, and the dry land becomes a series of long islands in a large, shallow lake. North of the Orinoco floodplain, the land is higher and escapes flooding. However, such areas lack drinking water in the dry season, except at the rare permanent lakes.

The vegetation on nonflooded land in Parmana is a mosaic of gallery forests and savanna woodland or "dry savanna," and seasonally flooded land has grassland savanna or "wet savanna" gallery forests, and floating meadows (Fig. 4). There is no tropical rain forest per se in the region. Much of the vegetation is deciduous and becomes dry, barren, and brown in the dry season. The vegetation on the river levees and bottomlands stays greener in the dry season than the vegetation away from the floodplain, because of the abundant moisture available in the main channel of the Orinoco. However, from half to two-thirds of the gallery forest along the main channel loses its leaves and stops photosynthesizing in the advanced dry season, according to Landsat multispectral data that I classified by false-color infrared (Pl. 1) at the Boston University Center for Remote Sensing (with the help of Scott Madry of the NASA Space Remote Sensing Center). When the gallery forest on the floodplain gets flooded for weeks or months during the rainy season, the trees drop leaves and suspend growth temporarily, forming annual growth rings. Seeds and fruits from savanna or dry-forest trees are found in archaeological deposits of all Parmana phases, suggesting that the climate remained seasonally dry during the prehistoric occupation (Smith and Roosevelt MS). Many species of savanna-woodland and dry-forest trees bear edible fruits, berries, and seeds, but only the large palm groves are considered a substantial potential source of plant food. The other trees would have been valuable as sources of vitamins, medicines, and raw materials. All the vegetation in the area today must be considered anthropogenic, for it has been much modified by human activity, both past and present.

Much of the higher-lying land in the Middle Orinoco floodplain is sandy, leached, droughty, and poor for agriculture, but the river bottomlands are filled with fine, rich silt that is the product of erosion in the Andes and Caribbean coastal ranges. Suitable for intensive annual cropping during the dry season, the higher of these alluvial lands are used today for cultivating cash crops of beans or cotton and small subsistence crops of corn and manioc. The small local population of the region subsists mainly on imported store-bought maize flour, garden produce, and occasional supplements of meat from domestic fowl or beef from cattle raised primarily for export. During the dry season, fish is an important protein supplement.

Although rich in species, the population of indigenous mammals and land vertebrates in the area is not an abundant source of food for very large populations, because of its relatively low biomass and slow rate of turnover. The native terrestrial game is probably somewhat impoverished today in comparison with prehistoric times, due to disturbances caused by the long-standing cattle industry. The rich grasses of the floodplains are at present used for raising beef cattle, but cattle mortality rates are high because of water supply problems in the seasonal habitat. The abundant river fish and other aquatic fauna are an important seasonal resource, and the prehistoric faunal record from Parmana sites (Wing, Garson, and Simons MS; Roosevelt 1989) not surprisingly shows a heavy reliance on aquatic rather than terrestrial fauna. Cabruta and Caicara to the west of Parmana and Ciudad Bolivar to the east have productive dry-season fisheries, but fishing is not a reliable source of food through much of the rainy season, when the fish are scarce and dispersed in the high, turbid waters.

The main channel of the Orinoco is lined with relict rock outliers of the Guiana Shield and high natural levees built up of sand, silt, and gravel. In the interior overflow plain, there are small fossil levees by the channels of extinct streams that still serve as aquifers in the dry season. All the higher-lying, well-drained places appear to have been the focus of year-round habitation for

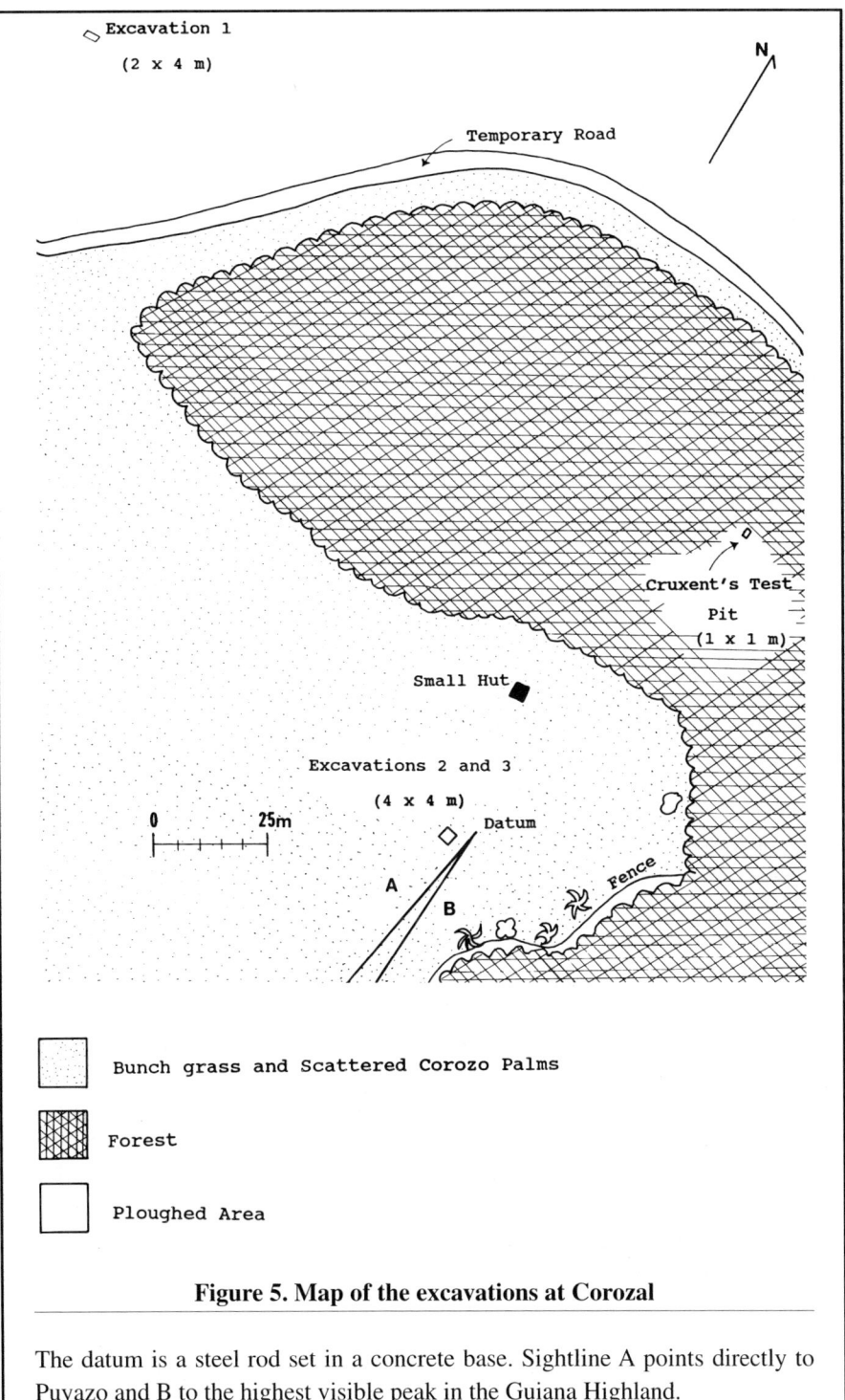

Figure 5. Map of the excavations at Corozal

The datum is a steel rod set in a concrete base. Sightline A points directly to Puyazo and B to the highest visible peak in the Guiana Highland.

many thousands of years. Large, deeply stratified prehistoric habitation sites, such as Corozal, lie on the highest parts of the channel levee system. The Orinoco floodplain proper is low and very flat, heavily flooded in the rainy season and bone dry in many places in the dry season. As yet no large, deep sites rich in prehistoric remains have been found down in the bottoms, although next to some low seasonal streams, small thin archaeological sites have been found, and a small artificial mound, Camoruco, is located near the village of Chaparral on a large stretch of grassy floodplain (Fig. 3). At present, there are no year-round settlements located directly on the floodplain except those on archaeological mounds or ancient or modern levees. All permanent habitations today are on elevations, but people move around a lot during the year, visiting their shacks in the bottomlands for several weeks during harvest time and congregating near the large corrals in the pastures for annual roundups and cheese making. Many people take fishing trips of several days to dry-season pools in the floodplain north of Parmana village. The archaeological habitation sites on the levees are situated in patches of gallery-forest and savanna-woodland vegetation overlooking large expanses of silt banks and islands, which were presumably used for seasonal cultivation in prehistoric times. Corozal, the largest archaeological site in Parmana, overlooks one of the largest expanses of such land (Pl. 2, *bottom*).

Corozal is a large, deeply stratified archaeological habitation site containing numerous object-rich strata of ancient refuse, features, and burials. Perhaps due to its considerable elevation 20 to 50m above the water table in the Orinoco channel below, the site bears dry savanna woodland vegetation of Corozo palms (*Acrocomia sclerocarpa*) and high bunchgrass, in addition to patches of gallery forest (Pl. 2). The soil over much of the surface of the site is sandy, fine, and dark with powdered charcoal from prehistoric cooking fires and modern swiddens. In his book on the Parmana region, Howard (1943) calls this soil "black sand." The surface and upper layers of this archaeological site belong to the famous "black Indian soils" of Greater Amazonia. It has been demonstrated that these extensive soils, much valued for commercial agriculture, are actually the middens of prehistoric archaeological sites (Falesi 1974; Smith 1980; Sternberg 1960). Since these deposits constitute topographic, mineral, and albedo anomalies of considerable magnitude in their regions, someday it will be possible to ascertain their remote-sensing signature for the purpose of mapping sites from the air.

Below Corozal the river bottom consists of expanses of dark, clayey, element-rich silt. The higher portions of the bottomland are called "islands" locally. They are flooded only briefly in the wet season and support low trees and shrubs. The lower floodlands are beaches and mud flats. They are deeply flooded for many months and bear only grass and other low annuals. There are, then, at least two kinds of "black soils" in these regions: those created in late prehistoric times by the accumulation of habitation refuse stained by the cook fires of large villages and towns, and those created by the river's deposition of dark, montmorillonitic sediments from mountain drainages. Together these two black soil types make up the primary local agricultural resource in Parmana.

Like many lowland archaeological sites, the Corozal site extends over a considerable area, at least 16 ha. It is bounded by the Orinoco to the southeast and by low, thorny scrub forest on the northwest. Most of the upper surface of the site lacks identifiable sherds or other archaeological objects, though it is colored black with soot in some places. Howard excavated somewhere near a hut at the southwest extremity of the site and found his late Ronquin material in a black-soil deposit approximately 2.50 m deep. Below that he found orange sand with pottery that he related to his early Ronquin material. Howard also dug at a ravine at the northeast edge of the site and found similar material there. (It was not possible to relocate Howard's excavations because they had disappeared, and there were no fixed points at the site that the location of those excavations could be measured from.) When I worked at the site, the part along the northwest edge had been plowed for cultivation, and there I could follow the extent of the prehistoric deposit in the dark color of the soil and the numerous ceramic sherds and carbonized plant remains littering the plowed surface. The first excavation I attempted at the site, Excavation 1, was located just northwest of the plowed area (Fig. 5). I also found sherds eroding out of the sloping edges of the site toward the river channel to the southeast. Only Camoruco-phase ceramics were found at the top surface and eroding edges of the site, and it thus appears that the site grew to its greatest extent during that phase. Corozal-phase material did not occur on the surface and was found only in the deepest part of the deposit at the center of the site, where Cruxent and later I excavated, indicating that the habitation area was smaller during that earlier period. Cruxent kindly gave me the material from his test pit to analyze with the material from my excavations, and it turned out to have all the phases that I excavated except Corozal 1. I was able to relocate Cruxent's excavation to map it because it was still visible as a shallow depression. The location that I finally chose for a deep stratigraphic cut was the high-lying central portion of the site that had not yet been plowed for cultivation. It lay to the south of Cruxent's test pit. Here, in Excavations 2 and 3, I found about 4 m of archaeological deposit, about 1.5 m deeper than the deposit at the locations where Howard excavated.

This archaeological site, with its extensive, deep, stratified multicomponent deposit full of sherds, lithics, bone, and carbonized plant remains, seemed ideal for my goal of defining a ceramic sequence by which to chart changes in site size and subsistence remains through the later part of the region's prehistory. Accordingly, I used it as the type site for the Corozal and Camoruco phases.

In the next section, the specific purpose and placement of my excavations at Corozal are explained.

Note 1

This climate type is designated Aw in the Koeppen classification: tropical savanna climate with dry "winter." Other important archaeological regions with the seasonal tropical climate are Marajo Island at the mouth of the Amazon, Santarem at the mouth of the Tapajos River in the Lower Amazon, Monte Alegre opposite Santarem, the Upper Xingu Basin in the South Central Amazon, Yarinacocha in the Ucayali Basin of the Upper Amazon in Peru, the Llanos of Mojos and Chiquitos of the Beni River drainage in the Bolivian Amazon, the plains of Caribbean Colombia, and the Yucatan Peninsula. Such areas have often been called humid or evergreen tropical rain forests by both social and natural scientists, but studies of rainfall and vegetation have shown that such terms are not appropriate for them (Roosevelt 1990a, 1991a). Unlike classic tropical rain forests, they have a distinct dry season of four to six months and often drop leaves for long periods in the dry season.

B. The 1975 Excavations

In his earlier work, Howard had encountered areas of sherd-rich black soil at the site and sampled them with a test pit. I had to reexcavate the deposit to obtain additional information and objects that could not be collected at the time of the last excavations because the methods to do so were not yet in use. Although Howard had noted perspicaciously that the archaeological soil at Corozal was black and full of carbonized plant remains, he did not collect any because at the time most archaeologists did not realize how important carbonized plant remains are for the reconstruction of ancient diet and environment or how best to recover them from the soil. Therefore, to find out about the distribution of carbonized plant remains in the strata, I had to resample the site. In addition, I needed to try to collect material from the different soil strata of the deposit, in order to recover as detailed a chronological sequence as possible while avoiding mechanical mixture. Other reasons to reexcavate the site were that Howard felt that his two 1 x 1 m excavations might have been too small to sample adequately the deposit and that there was some confusion about the provenience of his material from Corozal, because termites had eaten the labels of several of his levels from the site.

As mentioned, I made three excavations at Corozal. Excavation 1 was a 2 x 4 m rectangular excavation aligned east-west at the highest part of the site, at the northern end. This location turned out to have late-Camoruco-phase material only and to lack the black, garbage-laden soil deposits that I sought for their abundant ceramic sherds and biological remains. Therefore, Excavation 1 was discontinued after the second level in favor of Excavations 2 and 3, which were characterized by the black sandy soil that Howard had described. The deposit at Excavation 1 was light-colored, clayey, and very poor in objects, although the objects, mainly broken cooking bowls, were in good condition, often whole or nearly whole. In retrospect, comparing the evidence from my excavations at Teso dos Bichos and Guajara on Marajo Island (Roosevelt 1990b, 1991a), I believe that the deposit at Excavation 1 may represent prepared floors of dwellings. At sites on Marajo, the prepared house floors were light-colored, clayey, and poor in objects, except for cracked or nearly whole cooking bowls associated with hearths. There, the garbage areas outside the houses were similar stratigraphically to much of the deposit sampled by Excavations 2 and 3 at Corozal—sooty soil full of small sherds, bones, and carbonized plant remains, ideal for deriving chronology and food remains. Excavation of house floors can yield information about architecture and the nature of households, among other things, and it will be important for someone to excavate them someday at sites such as Corozal. For the purposes of creating a chronology for the Parmana project, however, it seemed more important to me at the time to spend a month at Corozal excavating a stratigraphic column for information with which to build a regional chronological framework than to excavate and map a single dwelling. Our discovery that prepared floors are associated with numerous features and objects in place suggest that it will be possible to extract useful information from such contexts in the future through horizontally extensive, rather than vertical, excavations.

The important excavations at Corozal for chronology were Excavations 2 and 3, which sampled the deep black-soil garbage deposit discovered by Howard. The ceramic seriation described in this monograph was based on the material from these excavations, which I placed downhill from Excavation 1 across a temporary road. Two adjacent rectangular 2 x 4 m cuts placed alongside one another, together they made a 4 x 4 m hole in the ground. Excavation 2 was placed first, with its long sides facing north and south. To facilitate stratigraphic excavation, Excavation 3 was placed directly adjacent to and north of Excavation 2 after the latter had been completed, so that layers exposed in the sidewalls of Excavation 2 could be used to guide work in Excavation 3. This strategy, used by Junius Bird (1943) in northern Chile and on the north coast of Peru at Huaca Prieta, helped the process of stratigraphic excavation, making it possible to isolate more individual layers and features in Excavation 3 than in 2. Often I found that a layer defined in Excavation 2 could be separated into two or more distinct layers and features in Excavation 3, because the knowledge of the stratigraphic profile provided by the prior excavation made it easier to recognize layers and features. Excavation 2 was carried down to soil sterile of cultural remains at about 375 to 400 cm, but Excavation 3 was discontinued between about 315 and 320 cm because the heavy seasonal rains began and prevented further work at the site by starting to wash out the excavation walls. So, while Excavation 2's lowest level relates to early Corozal 1, Excavation 3's lowest level relates to late Corozal 1.

The next section summarizes the field methods that I used at the site.

C. Mapping and Excavation Methods

I worked at the site of Corozal for about one month. Because the Parmana project field staff consisted of only five or six local men and me most of the time, and because there were about twenty linear km of riverbank to survey and thirteen sites to sample in about five months, it was not possible to do extensive instrument mapping at each site. I set a permanent steel-and-concrete datum about a meter into the ground at each archaeological site and used a self-indexing telescopic alidade with plane table to map the distance and elevation of the excavations, significant surface remains, and prominent environmental features in relation to the datum. Unlike the sketch maps previously published by archaeologists working in the region, my site maps, although simple, were made from surveying-instrument readings, and the permanent datums embedded at the sites allow future researchers to relocate the excavations and landmarks. The telescopic surveying instruments available in 1975 were slow and inaccurate in comparison with the electronic distance-measuring devices available today. Then, a detailed topographic map of a 16-ha site like Corozal would have taken a surveyor several months, and instrument topographic maps of all the thirteen sites that I excavated in the region would have taken more than a year. Now, with computerized infrared laser instruments it is possible to map the entire surface of a site like Corozal in a couple of weeks and also make all the necessary measurements and maps of features and layers within the excavations. The new instruments are many times more rapid and precise than the older ones, and their readings can be recorded directly on computer media so that publishable maps can be produced automatically with battery-driven portable printers or copied onto a disk for safekeeping. Such maps are extremely valuable for study in the field in advance of excavation. If Corozal is excavated more extensively someday for information about within-site patterning, the instruments are available for good ground control.

The method that I chose for digging the fifty excavations placed at Parmana-region sites differed somewhat from that used previously in the area. Other excavators who have worked in Parmana have used "artificial" excavation levels about 25 cm thick. For several reasons I decided to try to excavate by "natural" stratigraphic layers instead of artificial levels.

Field methods vary in their suitability in different situations. A particular method is best used in those situations for which it is especially appropriate. Other methods can be used for situations where it is not appropriate. The most sensible use of the artificial horizontal excavation layers is to divide up the soil mass of those parts of a site that, like areas of Ronquin, have few or no discernible natural or cultural layers or features. For such sites, this method achieves some chronological information, because the superposition of depositional units through time tends to result in the more recent layers being higher up in the ground than earlier ones. (There are special cases of "reversed stratigraphy" in archaeological deposits, which can be caused by large-scale earth moving or severe erosion and redeposition, but these are not very common.) Ordinarily, each successive horizontal excavation level dug down into a site will have greater percentages of the earlier pottery, and the changing percentages of the different styles and types will provide a rough sort of sequential dating. However, the material in such artificial levels cannot be considered "true" to a single period because such levels (being 25 cm thick and at least 16 sq. m in area) invariably combine material of several periods. This is not usually taken into account when artificial levels are used routinely for excavation, and the assemblages of objects recovered for analysis are often conceived of by archaeologists as representing integral time periods.

Artificial-levels excavations are not appropriate for excavating deposits in which there are discernible layering and features. The layering or stratification of archaeological sites and the distribution of objects in strata are related to depositional processes that include human behavior through time. Thus, the patterning of the strata and objects can in principle inform about ancient human behavior. In contrast to the optimum use of the artificial-levels method, in Amazon and Orinoco archaeology levels are customarily cut across excavations in set metric increments without regard for the horizontal and vertical patterning of objects and soil characteristics. Sometimes the stratigraphic patterns visible in the sidewalls of deposits after excavation are recorded graphically or photographically. Howard, for example, recorded that the Ronquin site had several layers and hypothesized that certain styles of pottery were concentrated in certain of the layers. However, it is difficult to use this stratigraphic information for detailed chronologies unless the objects were actually excavated, collected, and recorded with reference to those soil layers so that the different layers' contents can be compared. That way the layers and features can be interpreted and dated according to the objects that they contained in addition to the associations between the soil layers and features.

Strictly artificial levels tend to cross-cut and combine soil and objects from more than one chronologically and functionally distinct layer or feature, blurring temporal distinctions and destroying the associations of soils and objects. This happens because the deposits resulting from prehistoric human activities are usually not broad and neatly horizontal like the metric levels but rather are discontinuous, of variable thickness, and sloping. Archaeological features, particularly, are difficult to deal with by artificial levels, because they are usually smaller in horizontal extent than the artificial excavation levels, and they often have deeper vertical dimensions. For example, features such as ancient pits were dug down from a surface into deposits of earlier date. When filled back in, they received material from several different periods all mixed up together. If the material that fills a pit feature is included with the undisturbed surrounding soil at the same level, then material from several distinct time periods will be combined to the detriment of both chronological clarity and functional interpretation. The timing of the creation of a feature and its relationship to other features and layers cannot be determined if the interfaces between them are not traced during excavation. Information about activity areas and ancient and modern disturbances cannot be obtained by the artificial-levels method, because the levels combine material from the small features or layers related to activities and disturbances along with a lot of other unrelated material. Radiocarbon samples taken throughout artificial levels rather than from specific stratigraphic units are likely to be faulty or misleading, because they combine charcoal from different periods (Hedges and Gowlett 1986), and the lack of recorded in situ associations between pottery, charcoal, and particular soil layers means that there may be no way to tell to which of the pottery styles a carbon date relates. When artificial levels, rather than strata, are used to collect pottery for seriation, chronological and functional distinctions are obscured by the merging of stratigraphically distinct material in the collection units.

In order to derive basic archaeological information from sites, it is necessary to excavate strata and features separately, trace their spatial relationships, and record objects with reference to the stratigraphic units in which they lie. Since I was primarily interested in obtaining a detailed sequence, it seemed appropriate to try to obtain unmixed samples of objects and soil from different periods. In order to recover soil and archaeological objects according to the layers in which they were deposited, I excavated Corozal by the observable individual stratigraphic layers, where possible, rather than by artificial metric levels. The goal was to excavate each distinguishable layer or patch of soil or cluster of objects separately and record its spatial dimensions. The natural stratigraphic units by which I dug were distinguished by contrasts in texture, color, particle size, hardness, moisture, or contents of the soil; and their soil was screened and sampled separately. Thus each sample of soil, charcoal, or ceramics pertained to one of these layers or features and did not include stratigraphically distinct material unless I erred during excavation or the material had become mixed previously through ancient or modern disturbances. Significant artifact and ecofact clusters or soil features were recorded according to their position in space and their relationship to other observable strata or object clusters. As described below (Chap. 3, B), the attributes of ceramics from each stratigraphic entity were tabulated separately, and the layers were dated in a relative sense by the chronologically significant ceramics that they contained.

As described below, Corozal, like most other tropical sites, had distinct stratigraphic and object patterning that could be followed during excavation. Although I was sometimes unable to follow a particular layer successfully during excavation because of errors in perception or unclear stratigraphic patterning, the evidence of the stratigraphy and seriation seems to show that most of my excavation levels removed distinct chronological-cultural units. In the patterns of distribution in the tables of the ceramic seriation (Tables 11–90), there is much less spread of different wares, types, and styles through the stratigraphy than in the tables for excavations made by artificial levels (e.g., Howard 1943; Cruxent and Rouse 1958–59; Zucchi, Tarble, and Vaz 1984). The presence of stray sherds and radiocarbon samples out of chronological order in the stratigraphic columns at Corozal (Tables 8, 11–18, 39–42) suggests that there must have been small disturbances that I could not recognize, such as animal burrows. These disturbances did not confuse the ceramic seriation, however, because the intruded sherds usually were present in statistically insignificant frequencies.

I carried out the excavations at Corozal with the help of a group of men from Parmana. In the division of labor, I excavated, sorted the screen contents, collected and labeled samples, and took notes; and the men collected the excavated soil, carried it to the screen, shook the screen, brushed down excavation surfaces, and held meter tapes. They also shared the heavy work of picking through the occasional indurated layer and of filling in finished excavations. The men were meticulous, indefatigable workers. Several times, colleagues and students visiting Parmana lent their assistance with the work for a week or two. In particular, Karen Mulder, then a senior in the International High School in Caracas, gave substantial help in the excavations at Corozal for several weeks.

My excavation procedure at Corozal was to begin by scraping and brushing the area to be excavated, looking for differences in soil color, texture, hardness, moisture, and contents. If differences could be distinguished, each different horizontal area was given a unique provenience designation and was excavated separately. Trowels were used for soft soils, but awls, knives, machetes, and picks were needed for cutting indurated soils. Horizontally extensive stratigraphic entities were usually assigned level numbers. If an area under excavation had two or three large, distinct soil areas, the same level number was given to each, but each was separately excavated and recorded under a different letter designation with the level number. So, for example, a dark layer in the eastern half of an excavation might be named Level 11A, while a yellowish layer uncovered elsewhere in the excavation at more or less the same elevation would be called 11B, and so on. Excavation levels were numbered and lettered sequentially, so the next one encountered or recognized would get the next number or letter, regardless of the sequence of deposition, which often was not determinable until later when the stratigraphy of the whole section had been reviewed. Features were named for the levels in which they first appeared, and multiple features in a level were given sequential numbers in order of encounter. The first feature recognized in Level 5 would thus be named Feature 1, Level 5; and the second would be Feature 2, Level 5. If a feature seemed to continue down through several larger layers, its designation could be changed as excavation proceeded downward in order to provide for the possibility that the feature had several different component parts.

Since the contents of each excavation level were registered with reference to the stratum or feature from which the soil came, objects could be analyzed in cultural and chronological context. We maximized recovery of objects by intensively screening and floating the soil. The soil from the Corozal excavations was dry-screened through 1/8" mesh, except for 15-lb. bags of soil that were later water-separated with 1/16" mesh. (Since our excavation layers tended to be thinner and smaller than usual, and because we were trying to isolate functional or chronological stratigraphic units, our flotation samples would be comparable to 30–40 lb. samples from standard excavation levels.) In our water flotation procedure, dry soil was agitated in water, the material that floated was scooped off with a strainer of 1/16" mesh, and the heavy fraction was caught in a screen of the same mesh. Observable sherds, lithics, and botanical remains were collected during excavation, but by far the largest number of small objects were recovered from the 1/8" screens through which all the excavated soil except the flotation samples was passed. Those objects recognized in the earth during excavation were the larger, rarer specimens. The smaller objects predominated both by weight and by number. Mass fine-screening greatly increases the number of small seeds, small fauna such as fish, diagnostic sherds, lithic debitage, and small artifacts such as beads and microliths. If only the specimens visible during excavation had been collected, the quantitative representation of different types of objects would have been very different. The representation of faunal species, for example, would have been greatly skewed toward large vertebrate terrestrial species, which, however, represented only a small proportion of the fauna by weight (Elizabeth Wing, personal communication). Further, many of the very small sherds recovered in the 1/8" screens were diagnostic or decorated, and the seriation would often have run into the difficulty of inadequate samples for statistical analysis if they had not been collected.

Many excavators working in Latin American sites do not use screens to process the excavated soil, or they use only 1/4" or 1/2" mesh screens that let through most of the ancient food remains. By using finer screens and by processing all the soil excavated, we were able to recover more material, and more kinds of material, than other excavators, including thousands of carbonized plant remains and animal bones from sites where few or none had been recovered in earlier work (Roosevelt 1989; Smith and Roosevelt MS; Wing, Garson, and Simon MS). For example, while our 4 sq. m pit in the Corozal and Camoruco phase deposit at Corozal yielded almost 30,000 sherds, Howard's 11 x 4 excavation at Ronquin, representing seven of the Parmana region phases, yielded only ten thousand. Thus our excavations, by using intensive soil processing, were more cost-effective and conserved site material. Although time-consuming and unglamorous, the fine-screening and flotation were the most valuable of the data-gathering techniques used in the project.

What sieving procedures an excavator chooses will depend on the purpose of the excavations and the nature of the sites and their environments. Fine-mesh dry-screening is not practical in sites with damp soil or in sites with fine, clayey, compact soil, because these soils will not pass through screens dry. In the five- to six-month dry season on the Orinoco banks, the sandy soil of the archaeological sites is loose and friable and drops easily through screens. However, in the rainy season the soil is too damp to pass through fine dry-screens, and soil-flotation samples do not dry out sufficiently in the wet weather to be processed in the field. In August–September, for example, my test pit at Ronquin produced few carbonized plant remains in the screens due to the clumping effect of rain on the soil, although during the dry season I recovered numerous plant specimens from the site. Damp soil is best screened entirely with water, as Wing has recommended (Wing and Brown 1979). Lacking running water or electricity, this could be done most cheaply and easily in the Orinoco with Struever's original method, taking the soil to the river and washing it in screen-bottom buckets or basins (Struever 1968).

Archaeological soil-processing procedures have been expanded and improved since the Corozal excavations. We now know that even 1/8" screen mesh is too coarse to produce quantitatively reliable samples of biota of different size classes. It was adequate for collecting the carbonized maize and sherds that were important for my research problem, but the informative small seeds and faunal specimens, which we have found in large numbers in the excavations on Marajo Island, would not have been adequately sampled in the 1/8" dry screens. Only the 1/16" flotation screens that we used in Parmana caught such material, and they let through the many 1-mm-sized specimens that many archaeological soils have, including identifiable fish teeth and catfish spines. In my present excavations in the Brazilian Amazon, the bulk dry-screening of the soil from excavations is augmented with a final wet-screening of all lumps that would not pass through the dry screen, and we use paper filters or 1-micron mesh cloth for the final straining of both the heavy and light fractions of the flotation samples.

The sherds recovered from the excavations in Parmana were placed in doubled plastic bags, and two strong Manila luggage labels with metal ties were affixed, one placed between the two bags and the other tied around the mouth of the bags, to hold them shut. Two labels were necessary because sometimes the outer label was lost through being torn off by mistake or eaten by termites and some of the inner labels became illegible from mildew. Howard lost many of the labels of his specimens from Corozal. Precautions to protect labels are necessary to preserve basic documentation. Alternative precautions might be to use inscribable plastic or nylon labels or specimen bags. The carbonized plant remains from Parmana sites were wrapped individually in cotton balls and placed in corrugated cardboard boxes able to withstand 200 lb. psi.

Samples of charcoal for radiocarbon dating were protected from contamination by dust or handling with wrappings of metal foil and then two plastic bags. Because accelerator mass spectrometry (AMS) radiocarbon dating, which allows analysis of very small samples, was not yet available for archaeology, we often had to collect charcoal from throughout entire levels to get enough for dating. This procedure risks dating error because of the possibility that the composite samples include charcoal of different periods, and our subsequent project of accelerator dating shows that composite samples are indeed much less precise than individual samples. As dating methods have improved since 1975, we have been able to date some individual samples from Corozal, such as single seeds, single carbonized wood chunks, and charcoal in the fabric of single sherds. These dates have in some cases clarified chronological issues by documenting the presence of intrusive modern charcoal in some samples and verifying the antiquity of other samples. However, since much of this material was not originally collected for radiocarbon dating, there is a danger that our handling, washing, packaging, and storage procedures may have introduced recent carbon to those samples. Because accelerator dating has made almost all archaeological objects potentially datable, to avoid such contamination we now collect most material from the excavations with clean tools, such as tweezers or scoops, rather than picking it up with our hands.

Not prepared by the existing literature for the abundance of faunal bones and human skeletons that turned up in my excavations at Corozal, I was not able to package adequately the bones from the site, and many suffered breakage in transit. Also, I did not know at the time how harmful it is to expose skeletons to the sun and air while drawing and photographing them in the then-standard archaeological procedure, and the skeletons suffered severely from exfoliation of surface bone due to uneven drying and heating after exposure. In order to preserve morphologically significant features of the skeletons excavated at Corozal, we coated the crania with polyvinyl acetate (PVA) consolidant. When some of the human bones were later analyzed for stable carbon isotope ratios in a paleodietary study (van der Merwe, Roosevelt, and Vogel 1981), we chose for analysis specimens that had not been consolidated with PVA. The experience with bone conservation problems at Corozal has shown us that skeletons must be kept covered during excavation to prevent rapid drying and heating, packed individually with tissue and fiber padding, and transported in separate corrugated paper boxes of appropriate sizes. If handled properly, most bones do not require PVA consolidation treatment, which creates problems later for chemical analysis, and, in fact, creates eventual conservation problems by itself deteriorating through time.

The results of the excavation methods were generally better than expected, in terms of both stratigraphic control and yield of material. As described below, types of features and strata were found that had never been recorded at sites in the area. Distinct patterns of object distribution not described before were also recovered. Although less soil was excavated overall, the intensive processing produced more objects, and more varied objects, than before. The collections from our excavations at Corozal included abundant material of categories not usually recovered from sites in Greater Amazonia, such as the numerous plant, animal, and human remains. Many species of plants and animals were identified, so that in an area where there had been no identifications of prehistoric biota, suddenly there were hundreds. These results should not be considered unique or anomalous, but merely the product of the use of standard archaeological collection and recording methods in an area where such methods had seldom been applied. Anyone who used such methods would probably have obtained the same results, and the results of other similar work elsewhere in the Orinoco (Garson 1980) and Amazon (Roosevelt et al. 1991) tend to parallel or surpass our findings in Parmana. Though low-budget, the field methods were quite effective at achieving the goals of the project.

D. Introduction to the Stratigraphy

The archaeological sites in the Parmana region vary considerably in their cultural and natural stratigraphy. Some, such as Los Algarrobotes, have a series of living floors with well-defined artifact features and minor and major soil layers with discernible color-texture differences, but such deposits are relatively scarce in artifacts and ecofacts overall and have relatively shallow stratigraphic columns. Floors unfortunately were often kept quite clean of refuse by the ancient people, as is the practice of many present-day Indians in Amazonia (DeBoer and Lathrap 1979; Siegel and Roe 1986). Thus, despite their stratigraphic clarity and superposition, prepared house or formal plaza floors may not be desirable locations to obtain a chronological sequence of artifacts, for there may be too few artifacts to fulfill statistical tests of significance, and the artifacts may be restricted to rare, special-purpose types. Our subsequent excavations at prehistoric mounds on Marajo Island revealed that dwellings, although informative about household organization and residence stability, are not as useful for seriation as artifact-rich, deeply stratified refuse middens (Roosevelt 1991a).

Parmana sites like Ronquin and Los Mangos/Parmana have deep, sooty garbage deposits rich in objects, but these lack clear color-texture differences within the deposits, and their loose, sandy soils have undergone considerable disturbance by humans and natural agents. These problems stem from particular processes of natural deposition and post-depositional disturbance at the archaeological sites. Los Mangos/Parmana and Ronquin are dune sites subject to periodic deflation by the wind, erosion by rain and flooding, and easy penetration by roots or burrows into the friable soils. Such sites are not the best ones for definition of ceramic or radiocarbon chronology, because material of different periods has been extensively mixed and may appear contemporaneous when it is not. It is important to recognize that these deposits are extensively disturbed; otherwise the distribution of artifacts in the stratigraphy might mistakenly be assumed to be representative of the ceramic chronology, and artifacts that date to different periods might be considered contemporary.

Corozal was chosen as the type site for the Corozal and Camoruco phases because it seemed likely to have the kind of deposits useful for ceramic seriation and archaeobotany. My primary reason for excavating there was to sample a garbage midden in order to recover abundant food remains and pottery in stratigraphic sequence. Preindustrial domestic garbage is usually colored dark with soot from cooking fires, and objects are abundant, though often broken in small pieces. According to Howard's and Cruxent's descriptions, Corozal had a blackish garbage deposit of great depth, with numerous well-defined layers and features and great density of sherds and biological remains in the soil. Howard also noted that the pottery changed somewhat from the lower to upper parts of the stratigraphic column and that the black-soil deposit was underlain by an orangey-yellow sandy layer with material that was rarer than and different in style from what lay above it. This information suggested that the stratigraphy at the site was particularly apt for excavating to obtain the information needed for framing the chronological-developmental sequence for Parmana. The natural and cultural stratigraphy at the site indeed turned out to be quite well defined, richly endowed with decorated and diagnostic pottery and biological remains. The area where I excavated had not been plowed within the memories of present Parmana inhabitants and did not have the rich surface deposit of sherds that the plowed area showed. The soil seemed to be harder and more clayey overall than that at sites like Ronquin and Los Mangos/Parmana, and so the deposit would be expected to be somewhat less disturbed by deflation and animal burrows. As mentioned above, the stratigraphic separation of pottery attributes was much clearer at Corozal than at Ronquin, although the widely varying radiocarbon dates on charcoal, carbonized seeds, and sherds indicate that some objects had indeed been displaced by disturbances.

There were twenty-three different major soil strata recognizable in the part of the deposit sampled by Excavations 2 and 3. The appearance of the strata in the cross sections of the excavations is illustrated in Figure 6 and Plate 13. During excavation, the levels used to excavate the layers were numbered in the sequence of our recognizing the layers, starting at the top of the deposit and ending at the base. Each excavation had a separate suite of numbered levels. After excavation, the levels and their contents were studied in relation to the stratigraphic profile, and a chronological sequence of strata and features was defined in probable order of deposition and given letter designations starting from the bottom of the site and going to the top. The metric horizontal and vertical extent of the layers is indicated in the following sections and illustrated in the stratigraphic drawings, and the correspondence of levels and strata is given in the text and in Tables 2–6. Each excavation collection entity was given a provenience catalogue number, and these are listed in Tables 2 and 3.

The overall texture of the soil of the deposit, though described by Howard as sand, is actually a mixture of sand, silt, and clay. There was obvious variation in the gross patterning of soil coloration, texture, hardness, and contents from the top of the excavations to the bottom, and we recorded these characteristics of the soil for each stratum during excavation. Texture varied from fine and clayey-silty in prepared floors to coarse and sandy in the lower layers. Hardness varied from powdery soft in some features to rock hard at the base of the deposit, and contents varied from sparse in some prepared floors to rich in hearth features and garbage fill. The soil colors, classified by the Munsell Soil Color Charts (Munsell 1975) and also described with vernacular color names, ranged from sooty black and pale beige in the upper column to bright orange at the base of the column.

The overall patterning of the stratigraphy was characterized by generally horizontal, thick, extensive layers of from 5 to 25 cm in thickness extending over much of the 16 sq. m of excavated surface, interspersed occasionally with very thin layers and features of relatively small areal extent. There were also systematic differences in stratigraphy between the upper and lower parts of the excavated column. The upper and middle part of the stratigraphy, from the surface down to about 3 m deep, was composed of a block of blackish-stained soil subdivided clearly into layers that were more or less sandy and clayey and more or less dark or light in color and varying among hues of black, brown, red, or yellow. These would correspond to Howard's "black sands." The uppermost layers in this block of the stratigraphic column were a group of strata (W–S) whose soil was very dark gray-brown. Then came a group of soil layers (R–J) that was a lighter-colored gray-brown. The final group of layers (I–G) in the upper block of stratigraphy was a somewhat darker, redder gray-brown. Overall, the texture of this part of the column, although sandy, was more silty and clayey than that of the strata below.

The lower block of strata in the profile was for the most part harder, poorer in objects, redder, and lighter in color than the upper block. The first group of these (F–E) was a tannish brown color. Then came a single darker, redder brown stratum (D), the only possible "Black Indian Soil" in the lower stratigraphy. The final group of layers in the lower block of stratigraphy was a much lighter orangey red (C–A), similar to that encountered by Howard in the base of his test pit.

E. Description of the Strata

Next, I will describe the individual layers of the deposit in the order in which I excavated them. Each of the twenty-three layers is briefly characterized below, starting with the uppermost stratum, designated W, and ending with the lowest stratum, designated A. According to the ceramic seriation, the strata date primarily to the following phases: Corozal 1: A–D; Corozal 2: E–F; Corozal 3: G; Camoruco 1: H–J; Camoruco 2: K–O; Camoruco 3: P–V or W. For each stratum, the Munsell soil color code is given, the approximate depths, the relationship to other strata, the relationship to my excavation levels, any radiocarbon dates, and the chronological phase. (The radiocarbon dates are discussed further in Sec. G, *below*.) As mentioned above, in Tables 2–7 the excavation levels and features are listed with reference to the strata, phases, and provenience numbers, and the approximate depths of the levels from the surface are noted. During excavation, I measured the depths from a fixed datum on the ground surface down to the upper and lower surfaces of the levels, usually taking measurements at the center and corners of the layers and features exposed in the excavation. If all measurements of a surface's depth were approximately the same, only one figure is listed for it. Plan drawings and photographs of strata and features are included in the illustrations.

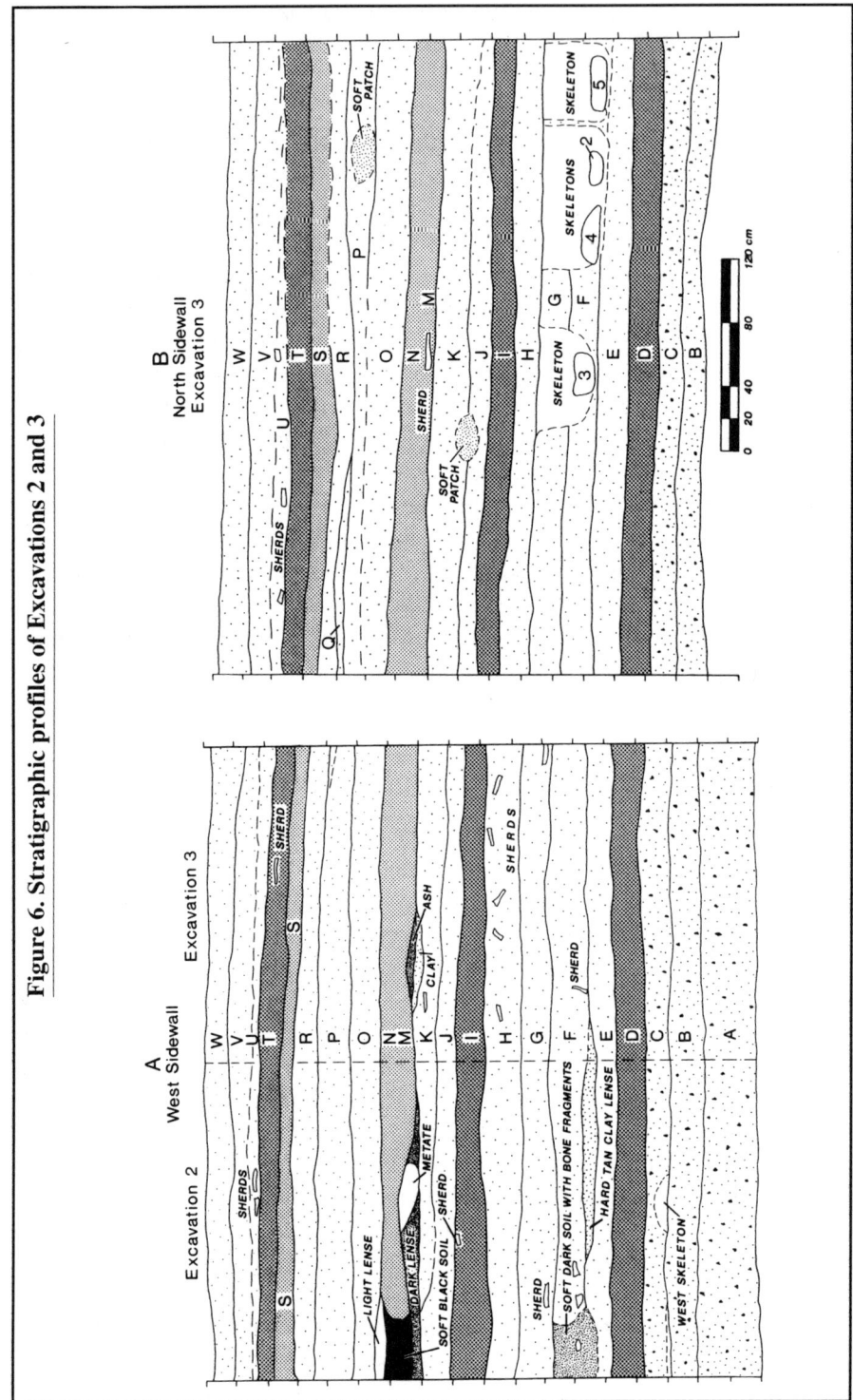

Figure 6. Stratigraphic profiles of Excavations 2 and 3

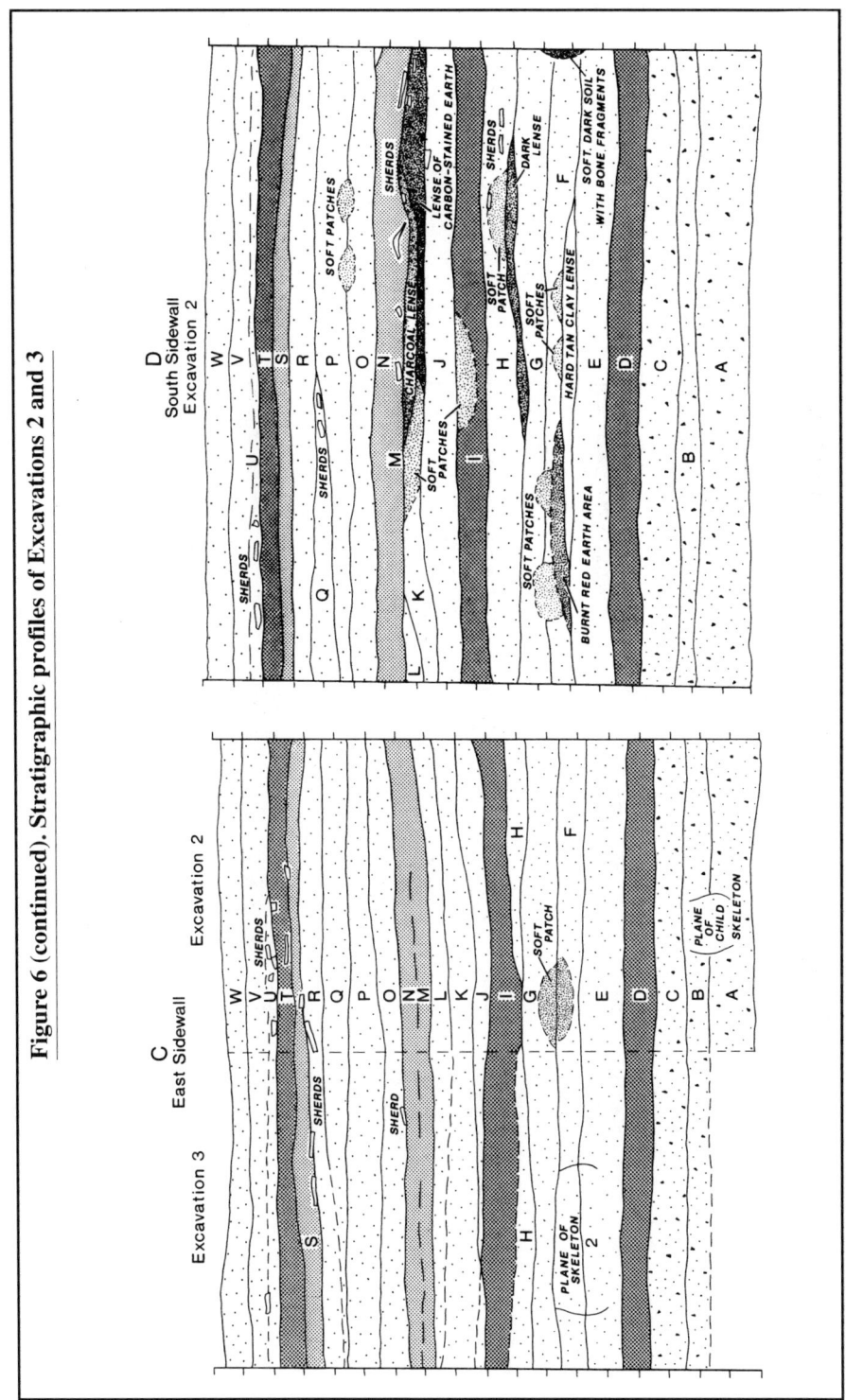

Figure 6 (continued). Stratigraphic profiles of Excavations 2 and 3

Figure 6 (continued). Stratigraphic profiles of Excavation 2

STRATUM W. Stratum W was a thick, blackish layer extending from the surface of the site down to a depth of about 19 cm. The universal color class of this black soil was Munsell dark grayish brown (10YR 4/2) (all Munsell readings were carried out on dry soil). The soil was dry and had a fine, sandy, silty texture with enough clay to make it hard in situ, although it was powdery when crushed. The black color probably derives from several factors: the abundant finely divided charcoal from modern and ancient burning, the organic matter from decayed garbage, and the thin surface layer of humus and litter produced by the local savanna-woodland vegetation.

Stratum W appears to have accumulated by natural deposition after the last prehistoric occupation at the site, for it contained few artifacts. The major processes of deposition involved are likely to have been aeolian and colluvial deposition, both of which are occurring today. Stratum W undulates slightly and intersects uncomfortably with the underlying Stratum V, the latest prehistoric cultural layer at the site, which contained numerous Camoruco 3 phase artifacts, a few of which were excavated from Stratum W. It is also possible that Stratum W may have incorporated a small amount of Camoruco material by way of natural processes of disturbance-erosion from upslope, redeposition, root penetration, and animal burrowing.

Stratum W was removed by Level 1 of Excavation 2 and Level 1 of Excavation 3. The base of Level 1, Excavation 2, went slightly deeper than the bottom of Stratum W, scraping up a few centimeters of the rich cultural deposit of Stratum V.

STRATA U AND V. Strata U and V were made up of a hard gray-brown soil with a slight red tinge. The color of this soil was lighter than that of Stratum W. The texture of the soil of Strata U and V was less sandy and more compact than that of Stratum W. The Munsell soil color is reddish brown (5YR 4/3). The pair of layers was between 20 and 40 cm from the surface. They contained numerous ceramic sherds, stone artifacts, carbonized plant remains, and animal bone. Although the strata were very similar, it was possible to discern two distinct layers in the excavation profiles after Excavation 2 had been dug. The lower one, Stratum U, 5 to 15 cm thick, was slightly lighter in color and slightly harder than Stratum V and contained many large sherds lying flat. Stratum U appears to be a layer of alluvial soil that was plastered on the ground to prepare an occupation surface. Stratum V appears to have been an accumulation of refuse in the top of the surface, possibly after the structure had been abandoned. Stratum U is probably made up of several successive prepared floors, and the large sherds in it probably relate to activities that took place on the different floor surfaces. Stratum V was thicker than U, varying from approximately 10 to 20 cm in thickness. Stratum U ranged between approximately 5 and 10 cm in thickness. Stratum U lay on top of Stratum T, and in the eastern part of the north wall of Excavation 3 there is a blurring of the juncture between them, probably because of a disconformity, where part of the surface of Stratum T seems to have been removed before or during the occupation of Stratum U.

Strata V and U were removed together in the upper part of Level 2 of Excavation 2. In Excavation 3, V was removed as Level 2 and U as Level 3. As mentioned above, Level 1 of Excavation 2 scraped the top of Stratum V. All these levels had numerous examples of pottery with Camoruco 3 modes. The two strata thus both date to Camoruco 3 phase. Two radiocarbon dates for Level 2 of Excavation 2 were A.D. 1475 and 1560, based on the carbon from the fabric and surface of a pottery sherd, respectively. The carbon in and on the pottery had a stable carbon isotope ratio close to that of wood charcoal.

STRATA T AND S. Strata T and S lay about 40 to 60 cm from the surface, dipping down 5 cm or more toward the north. Strata T and S were composed of a grayish brown soil discernibly softer and darker than the soil in Strata V and U and rich in artifacts, charcoal, and carbonized seeds. The Munsell color for Stratum T was dark grayish brown (10YR 4/2) and for Stratum S was dark brown (7.5YR 4/2). The two strata were similar in soil texture, but Stratum S was slightly lighter and grayer in color, harder, and sparser in artifacts than Stratum T, except in the southeast corner of Excavation 3, where there was a darkish artifact and hearth feature rich in finely divided charcoal. Stratum T seems to comprise softer, richer occupation debris that was deposited on top of S, a possible living floor hardened by trampling and/or the addition of a layer of clayey alluvium to prepare the floor. Both strata contained a number of large sherds lying flat. Strata S and T varied in thickness, ranging from about 8 to 15 cm. The top of T undulated and bore a clear disconformity in the northeast.

The fireplace feature referred to in the previous paragraph extended down into Stratum R apparently from the top of Stratum S, from about 54 to 70 cm in depth. This hearth area was littered with stone tools, pottery vessels, carbonized firewood, and carbonized maize cobs and kernels (Pl. 4, *top*). The feature was located in the southeast corner of Excavation 3 and can be seen in the profile drawing of the east sidewall of the excavation (Fig. 6). The hearth and associated objects were excavated in situ separately from the rest of Stratum S, in which the feature lay. At the base of the hearth feature, which was also the base of Stratum S, there were a few sherds in a patch of soft, darker soil, apparently a firepit extending down into Stratum R. The firepit contained numerous broken corncobs with kernels still attached. The base of Stratum S was blurred in the northeast of Excavation 3 by a disconformity of some kind, perhaps functionally associated with the hearth feature in the southeast.

The base of Level 2 of Excavation 2 removed most of Stratum T, and Level 3 removed Stratum S. In Excavation 3 I was able to remove most of Stratum T in Level 4 and most of Stratum S in Level 5. The hearth feature in Excavation 3 lay in Level 5. It turned up near the top of the level and continued down through the base of the level, with a firepit at its base extending into Level 6. The feature seems to have been dug down from a surface that lay at the juncture between Levels 4 and 5.

The excavation levels related to Stratum T, Stratum S, and the hearth feature all contained sherds of pottery with Camoruco 3 chronological modes and thus are assigned to this period. Level 4 of Excavation 3 produced two radiocarbon dates: A.D. 1090 and 1530, the latter an accelerator date on maize from the hearth feature. The earlier date on wood suggests the inclusion of some earlier charcoal in the Camoruco 3 layer through some kind of disturbance or use of a tree several hundred years old.

STRATUM R. Stratum R was a layer of harder, yellower soil extending from roughly 60 to 75 cm in depth from the surface. It was rich in maize and other carbonized plant remains and had a hand-grinding stone lying at its base at the north sidewall of Excavation 2. The color of the stratum was Munsell dark grayish brown (10YR 4/2), slightly grayer than the soil of Strata Q and P, which underlay Stratum R.

Stratum R ranged from 10 to 20 cm thick and undulated somewhat, dipping down in the north part of Excavation 3. It lay on top of Strata P and Q and intersected unconformably with Strata Q and P in the east of Excavation 3. This layer might possibly be that part of a prepared floor surface on which food preparation took place.

Stratum R was excavated by Level 4 of Excavation 2 and Level 6 of Excavation 3, which also scraped up part of the top surfaces of Strata P and Q. These levels contained pottery with Camoruco 3 modes. Stratum R therefore is dated to the Camoruco 3 phase. Excavation 2, Level 4, produced an accelerator radiocarbon date of A.D. 1340 on a maize specimen.

STRATA P AND Q. Composed of somewhat lighter-colored yellow, hard soil similar to that of Stratum R, these two strata were discontinuous, undulating occupation layers of uneven thickness lying between roughly 75 and 95 cm in depth from the surface. During excavation it was not possible to follow the juncture between the two, but it seems clear that Q was laid down on top of P and intruded down into it in places, which would have presumably mixed material from both strata into Stratum Q. As mentioned above, Stratum R seems to have lain unconformably on both Q and P in places, so presumably, material from these two layers was included in the soil of Stratum R.

Most of the soil of these two layers was removed by Level 5 of Excavation 2 and the lower parts of Level 6 and Level 7 of Excavation 3.

Strata P and Q were relatively low in artifact density. Stratum Q seems to date to Camoruco 3, and Stratum P seems to date to the Camoruco 2 phase. The levels contained ceramics with modes characteristic of both subphases. Level 5–6 of Excavation 2 contains more Camoruco 3 material than Level 7 of Excavation 3, possibly because Stratum Q is thicker in the southeast of the excavated area. A small amount of the Camoruco 2 phase pottery in the levels may derive from the inclusion in Stratum P of some material from Stratum O, due to the disturbance at the juncture between them, which can be seen in the northwest profile of Excavation 3. This situation is an example that supports an interpretation of mechanical mixture with evidence from both stratigraphy and ceramic seriation. The lighter color of the soil of these layers, the scarcity of artifacts, and the presence of an intrusive feature suggest that the layers represent occupation surfaces prepared for use by the addition of mud plaster.

STRATUM O. This was a thick layer of soil lying between 95 and 120 cm in depth. The soil was yellower in color and less sandy in texture than the layers overlying it, and it was relatively poor in artifacts, except for one large sherd lying flat. The Munsell color was dark brown (10YR 4/3, 4/4). As noted above, the interface of this stratum with the overlying Stratum P was not intact in the western part of the north side of Excavation 3. The color and the presence of intrusions suggest that Stratum O may possibly be the remains of a prepared floor.

Stratum O probably dates to the late Camoruco 2 phase. The layer was excavated by Level 6 of Excavation 2 and Level 8 of Excavation 3. The sherds from Level 6 were combined by registration error with those of Level 5, and the modes show a combination of Camoruco 3 and Camoruco 2. In Excavation 3, Level 8, which represents unmixed cultural material from Stratum O, sherds with Camoruco 3 modes are almost entirely absent. This distribution of modes tends to support the interpretation of the stratum as Camoruco 2 phase. (Level 6 of Excavation 2 may also include a small amount of soil from the base of Stratum Q.)

STRATA N AND M. These are two darkish soil layers lying between about 120 cm and 143 cm in depth. The Munsell color of Strata N and M was dark yellowish brown (10YR 4/4 and 4/3, respectively). Stratum N was dark and rather soft, a carbon-stained layer rich in carbonized maize and sherds. Stratum M was a dark-blotched layer with numerous large sherds lying flat and partial vessels sitting upright (see photos of the sherd feature in the course of excavation, Pl. 4, *center and bottom*), abundant carbonized plant remains, animal bone, and some lenses of ash and powdered charcoal. The pair of strata dip and thicken to the east and north. At their base is a complex of carbonaceous and clayey lenses that interleave with one another. One of the lenses contained a large grinding stone that can be seen in the west sidewall of Excavation 2 (Fig. 6A). Also visible in the sidewalls of the excavation are in situ sherds and carbonized plant remains. The color and contents of the layers suggest that they represent primary garbage. The layers beneath them looked like prepared house floors. It is possible, therefore, that the large sherds and the features relate to the occupation of the floors, and the rest of the material is garbage that accumulated at the location after the structure was abandoned.

Level 7 of Excavation 2 took Strata N and M and the lens system out together, but in Excavation 3 it was possible to separate Strata N and M into Levels 9 and 10 and the underlying lenses into Levels 11A and 12A. Level 11A removed the complex of lenses in the center and southeast of the excavation, and Level 12A is the complex of lenses that lay directly below the other lenses and on top of Strata K, L, and J. The lens system had a humped upper surface that projected up into M in some places. During the excavation of Level 7, Excavation 2, it was possible to map an ashy patch at about 138 cm in depth (Fig. 7) that matches a concentration of ash and carbonized plant remains in the lower part of Stratum M in the south sidewall of that excavation (Fig. 6D). There is another, possibly related, carbonaceous patch visible in the layers of the sidewall of the southwest corner of Excavation 2 (Fig. 6A).

The modes of the pottery in the levels were mainly of the Camoruco 2 phase. Level 7 had a radiocarbon date of around A.D. 1235, from an aggregate charcoal sample. A pottery sherd from that level had two accelerator radiocarbon dates: A.D. 930 from carbon inside the sherd and A.D. 1400 from carbon crusted on its surface. Interestingly, both the carbon on the sherd and the carbon in the sherd had stable isotope ratios close to that expected for Carbon 4 plants such as maize, suggesting that maize had been cooked in the pot from which the sherd came and that material from maize plants may have been used to temper and/or fire the vessel. Level 10 of Excavation 3 had aggregate mean charcoal dates of A.D. 1440 and 1540. These may be derived partly from anachronous charcoal, since they are stratigraphically inconsistent, but their 2-sigma ranges overlap with the other dates, in any case. On pooled charcoal, Level 11A of Excavation 3, had a date of A.D. 1490, and Level 12A had one of A.D. 1120.

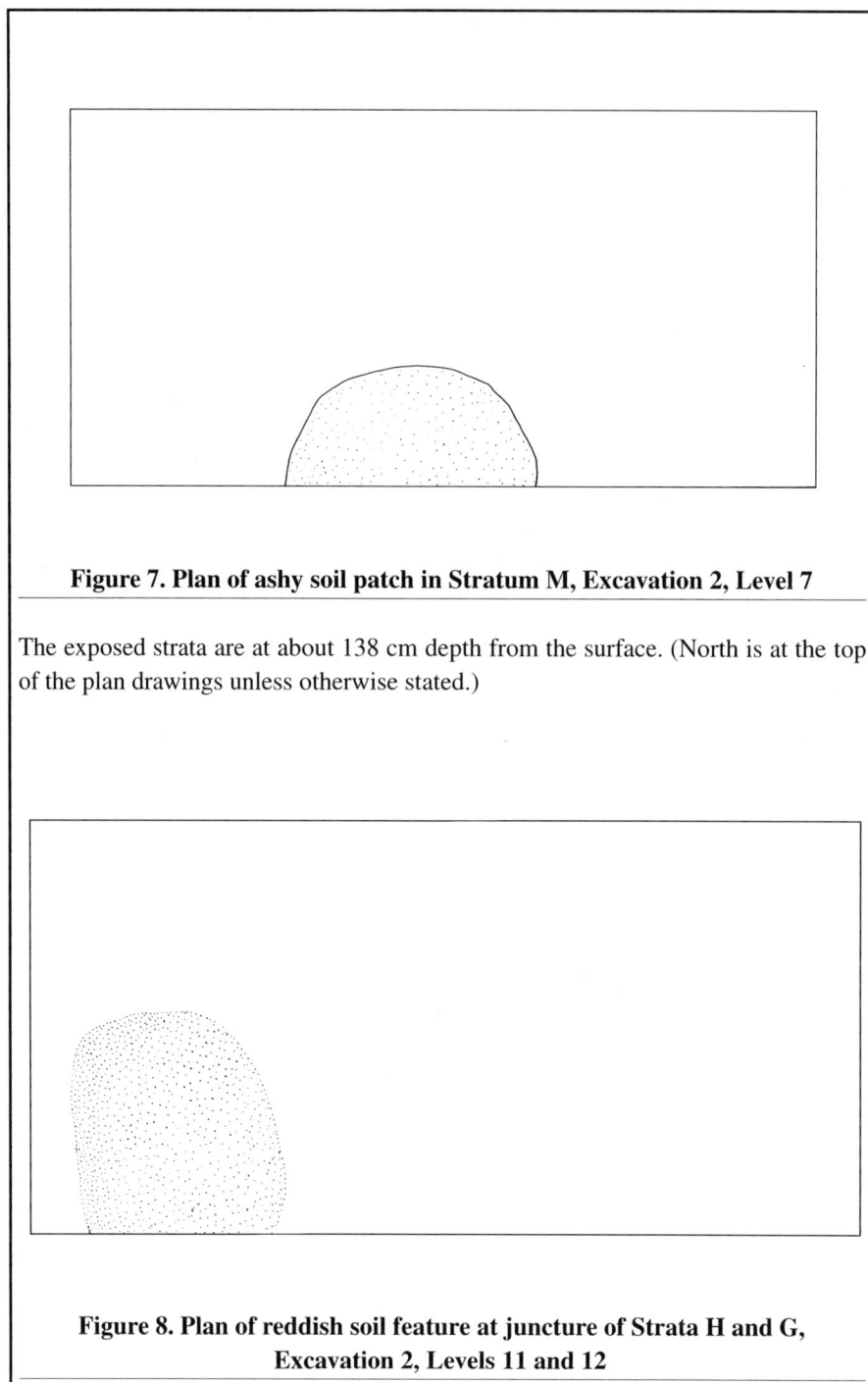

Figure 7. Plan of ashy soil patch in Stratum M, Excavation 2, Level 7

The exposed strata are at about 138 cm depth from the surface. (North is at the top of the plan drawings unless otherwise stated.)

Figure 8. Plan of reddish soil feature at juncture of Strata H and G, Excavation 2, Levels 11 and 12

About 210 cm in depth

The assemblage of sherds, partial vessels, and other objects in Stratum M seems to represent a distinctive activity area functionally somewhat different from that of other deposits in the excavations. Activities that took place there seem to include food preparation, cooking, and eating and also possibly some kind of fertility ritual. Several unique objects were found in this feature, including three female figurines. Two of the figurines are erotic in that their genitals are displayed or emphasized by the position of the hands, and one is obviously pregnant, with her hands placed on either side of the belly (Roosevelt 1980, Fig. 92). The imagery of such figurines has been hypothesized to relate to cults for enhancing female fertility and health (Roosevelt 1987b). The cults often revolve around elaborate rituals of female initiation and sometimes compose a ritual cycle separate from men's ceremonies. Cross-culturally, figurines are often found in domestic deposits rather than in temples or high ceremonial deposits, but it is rare for them to be recovered with stratigraphic documentation, as these were.

Other artifact distributions in the strata are also unusual and show statistically significant differences in frequency compared to other strata. Both Strata M and N had a relative lack of examples of the major Camoruco phase decorated animal-effigy cooking bowl (mode #209) and an important Camoruco phase mode, mauve paint (#152). In contrast, they had a greater percentage of human-effigy jars (mode #40) than that occurring in other Camoruco 2 phase levels. The pottery bearing the mauve paint (Fig. 22; Pl. 10B) tends to occur in shapes interpretable as special service wares for eating and drinking. Use of such service wares is often the exclusive prerogative of men in Amazonia, and they are often used during periodic feasts that include visitors. Women usually do not take part, except to prepare food and serve (Roosevelt 1991a). Anthropomorphic jars for brewing and serving beer are commonly used today by the Indians of the Upper Amazon, though their ritual gender associations and emic characterizations are not recorded. The presence of a grinding stone and the evidence for the cooking of maize near the feature suggest that the particular location is likely to have been a domestic female work area. The whole assemblage, then, might be interpreted as representing ritual activity that took place in female work areas apart from areas where men held ceremonies.

Because female imagery is often employed for general community ceremonial purposes and because the spatial patterning of men's and women's activities varies greatly from society to society (Roosevelt 1991a), the judgment that the feature under discussion may be an area of female activities and ceremonies requires independent evidence over and above the unique iconography and tool distributions. In any case, it is of interest that functional aspects of deposition, rather than chronological ones, may sometimes significantly affect the frequencies and percentages of decorative modes.

Strata L and K. These strata lay between about 140 and 165 cm in depth. They were discontinuous layers of soil, lighter colored and yellower than the overlying strata. The soil in these layers was stained dark in places from contact with the carbonaceous lens that lay at the base of Stratum M. The nature of the soil and its contents suggest that Strata L and K were prepared floors on which the activities represented by Stratum M took place. There were many fewer artifacts and plant remains in these layers than in those immediately above.

The strata were harder in the east, perhaps a section of prepared occupation surface, and softer and sootier in the central and eastern portion of Excavation 3. The lowest of the large sherds and vessels in the overlying Stratum M had their bases near the top of Strata L and K, suggesting that the top surface of the latter strata constituted the ground when the vessels were deposited. Stratum L overlay Stratum K and dipped down into it at the eastern sides of the excavations. The interface between the two strata is blurred and probably unconformable in places. Both layers seem to have been leveled and cut into just before the deposition of the layers of the overlying lens system, which was followed immediately by the deposition of Stratum M. Perhaps an uneven surface had developed during a less intensive occupation, and this surface may have been partially leveled for use as an occupation surface during the deposition of Stratum M.

The color of the soil in the layers was Munsell brown-dark brown (10YR 5/3, 4/3, and 3/3). Due to their spatial complexity and similarity in color and texture, it was impossible to remove L and K separately from each other and from the underlying Stratum J. Stratum L and the upper part of K were removed in Level 8 of Excavation 2 along with a small area of the upper part of Stratum J. Some soil in Stratum K may derive from Stratum J, which was intruded into immediately before K was deposited onto Stratum J. The unconformity between K and J can be seen in the northeast sidewall of Excavation 3. Levels 11B and 12B of Excavation 3 relate to Strata L and K respectively. Small amounts of Stratum K were probably included in Level 9 of Excavation 2 and Level 13 of Excavation 3, where the layer dipped downward into Stratum J.

Chronologically, Level 8 seems to relate to Camoruco 2, and Levels 11B and 12B seem to be transitional between Camoruco 2 and 1. It is probable that Strata K and L date to Camoruco 2 and Level J to Camoruco 1, but this is not possible to demonstrate conclusively by the statistics of pottery distribution. Level 8 of Excavation 2 had a radiocarbon date of A.D. 1690 on pooled charcoal and an accelerator date of A.D. 1130 directly on a maize specimen. The varying results of the dates suggest varying degrees of contamination of samples with historic-period carbon, with the second and fourth dates probably nearest to the actual radiocarbon age of most of the material in the stratum.

STRATUM J. This is a partly discontinuous, undulating layer of tan, hard, somewhat sandy soil flecked with charcoal. The color of the soil was not very different from that of Stratum K above, which led to difficulties in separating the two during excavation. Carbonized plant remains were less abundant in Stratum J than in the overlying strata. Stratum J extended between about 145 and 170 cm in depth. It was overlain by Stratum K, and the interface was unconformable. Apparently J was originally thicker, as indicated in the south sidewall of Excavation 2, but large amounts of the stratum seem to have been removed just before Stratum K was laid down.

Stratum J was mainly excavated in Level 9 of Excavation 2 and Level 13 of Excavation 3. Probably these levels included a small amount of soil from the overlying Stratum K, which dipped down into J in places, and a little from Stratum I below. Some soft patches possibly produced by Stratum K's intrusion were noted in the otherwise hardish soil of Stratum J during excavation.

Stratum J dates to Camoruco 1 times, based on the distribution of ceramic modes. Level 9 of Excavation 2 had a pooled charcoal radiocarbon date of about A.D. 1540, a sample probably contaminated by some anachronous carbon, considering its overlap with dates associated with Camoruco 3 pottery in strata lying above this depth. A sherd from Level 9 was dated by accelerator to A.D. 1035 for carbon found in its fabric, and A.D. 1255 for charcoal on its surface. The carbon on the sherd's surface included a considerable amount from a Carbon 4 plant, such as maize, according to its stable isotope ratio, although the carbon from the pottery fabric seems mainly derived from Carbon 3 plants.

It is not clear whether this stratum should be interpreted as a prepared floor. Like some of the others, it has a lower percentage of elaborate decorative modes, such as mauve paint and animal-effigy bowls with vestigial handles, than was found in most of the garbage layers. This pattern is consonant with an interpretation of it as a domestic floor, since the pottery of other house-floor excavations at sites in Amazonia has tended to lack high proportions of fancy cooking and service wares (Roosevelt 1987b, 1991a).

STRATUM I. This soil layer was darker than the overlying strata. It was a hard, brown layer of relatively sandy soil with many large charcoal chunks, much animal bone, and abundant sherds. The Munsell soil color was dark brown or brown to dark brown (7.5 YR 4/2 or 4/4). Stratum I extended between about

160 and 180 cm in depth. It had more regular dimensions and was less disturbed than the overlying layers, but in several places its top surface bore softish areas that may represent shallow intrusions from above. The juncture between Stratum I and the underlying Stratum H is well marked, except for a blurred area in the east sidewall of the profile of Excavation 3.

The layer was excavated by Level 10 of Excavation 2 and by Level 14 of Excavation 3. Small scrapings of the stratum may also have got into Levels 9 and 13 of Excavations 2 and 3 respectively. An accelerator radiocarbon date of A.D. 1085 was derived from a specimen of maize from Level 14 of Excavation 3.

This stratum dates to Camoruco 1 times, acording to the distribution of modes in the levels. Its color and rich contents suggest that it is made up of garbage deposits.

STRATUM H. Stratum H was composed of a somewhat lighter colored brown soil containing some charcoal and beads, and abundant well-preserved animal bone, but relatively little carbonized maize compared to other layers. There are several large sherds in the south and west sidewalls, but they are not consistently oriented or grouped. The Munsell color of the stratum is dark brown (7.5 YR 4/2).

Stratum H was the layer deposited over the surface from which the pits for Skeletons 2, 3, and 4-5 seem to have been dug and then filled. These skeletons were three extended burials, of which 4-5 had been partly disturbed when the pit was dug for Skeletons 2 and 3 (Fig. 10). The disturbed part of the skeleton was given the designation 4 and the in situ part was designated Skeleton 5. The three skeletons lay between 225 and 255 cm in depth, and Stratum H extended from about 185 to 215 cm in depth. In Excavation 3, Stratum H lay upon a slight pile of excess soil remaining from the burial-pit area after back-filling (see below). This soil was mottled reddish brown and brown, because it contained a combination of soil from all the different layers which were intruded by the burial pits. Traces of this mottled soil were also found in Excavation 2 at the juncture between Levels 11 and 12 (Fig. 8). It can be seen as the darker soil lens at the base of Stratum H in the south sidewall of Excavation 2. The interface between Strata H and G was apparently part of the land surface from which the pits for the skeletons were dug in Excavation 3. That interface lay at about 200 to 215 cm in depth.

Stratum H was excavated in Level 11 of Excavation 2 and Level 15 of Excavation 3. The feature of mottled reddish-brownish disturbed soil (Fig. 9) remaining from the burial pits was excavated with the base of Stratum H by the base of Level 11 of Excavation 2 and of Level 15 of Excavation 3. We were able to excavate it separately as Level 16 of Excavation 3 (see below).

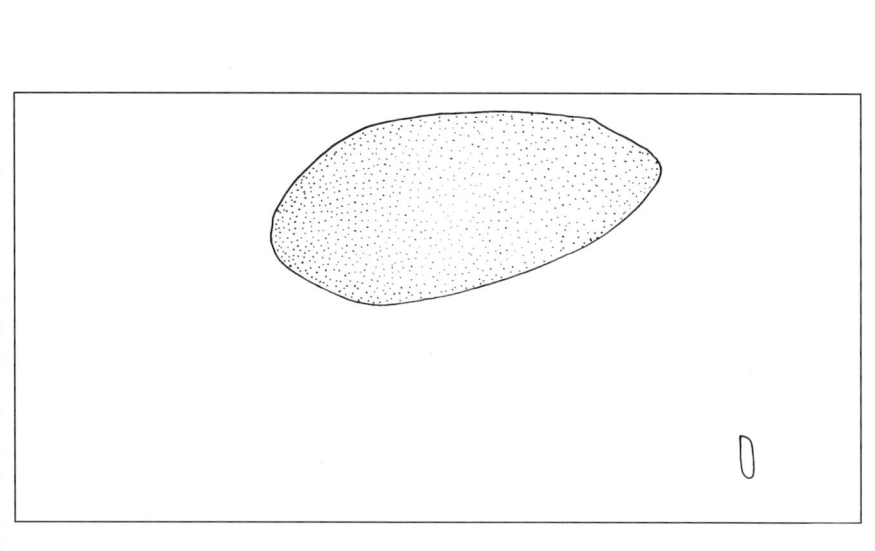

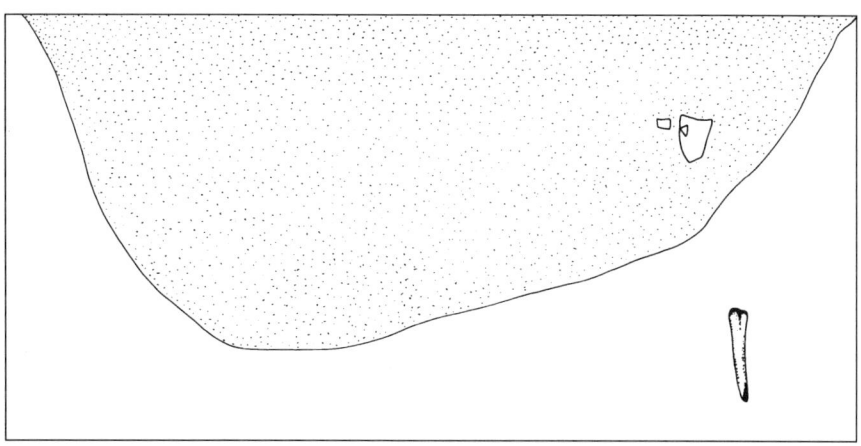

Figure 9. Successive plans of the soil feature over Skeletons 2, 3, and 4–5, Excavation 3

Top, about 215 cm depth at the base of Level 15. *Bottom,* about 220 cm depth at the base of Level 16. The mottled soil feature lay over the burial pits of the skeletons. The bone at lower right in the drawings is designated Skeleton 1. The sherds in the bottom drawing are those in the top of the broken vessel feature found with Skeleton 2.

The stratum is Camoruco 1 in date, and the mottled soil feature is mainly Corozal 3. Level 15 of Excavation 3 gave a pooled charcoal radiocarbon date of A.D. 750.

STRATUM G. This was a stratum of hard tan-colored soil with somewhat sandy texture. Its similarity to Stratum F, below, made the boundary between them unclear during excavation. Stratum G extended between 210 and 225 cm in depth, except where it was removed by the excavations for the burial pits. The layer was not very rich in contents, having some animal bone but not very much pottery or carbon. Once apparently continuous, this stratum was invaded by the burial pits for Skeletons 2, 3, and 4–5 of Excavation 3, and its soil became mixed with that of Stratum F and possibly with a small amount of Stratum E. From Stratum G downward in the deposit, the soil became sandier in texture and less sooty than the strata above. The reason for this may lie in drier climatic conditions, which might have increased aeolian sand deposition, or different cultural patterns, in which few or no clayey prepared floors were made. The relative lack of soot could be the product of a lower rate of hearth use due to less intensive or permanent habitation or to a smaller, more dispersed site population.

Stratum G was excavated by Level 12 of Excavation 2 and Level 17 of Excavation 3. Level 17 also included some soil from the burial pits of Skeletons 1, 2, 3, and 4–5, because the distinction between them and the stratum was not at first apparent during excavation of the layer.

The stratum dates to the Corozal 3 phase, as does most of the material in the burial pits. Level 12 of Excavation 2 had a pooled charcoal radiocarbon date of around A.D. 1130 and an accelerator date of about A.D. 1340 on a maize specimen. The pooled date falls close to the expected date range of material of the subphase but may have been slightly skewed by the admixture of a small amount of more recent carbon. The accelerator date falls closer to the Camoruco 2–3 boundary rather than to Corozal 3 and could indicate the intrusion of anachronistic maize from slightly more recent strata, but the 2-sigma range of the maize date is in any case close to the date expected for Corozal 3. Moreover, maize dates would always be younger than associated wood dates, because maize is harvested in its first year, whereas trees are often several hundred years old when cut for firewood or construction.

BURIAL-PIT FEATURE FOR EXTENDED SKELETONS 2–5, EXCAVATION 3. When the burial pits were filled in after the deposition of Skeletons 2, 3, and 4, a pile and layer of soil were left on the surface from which the pits were originally excavated. This may have happened because the soil from the pits had swelled slightly in volume through the incorporation of air and through the displacement of soil by the bulk of the bodies and their accoutrements. The soil layer over the pits extended from about 200 cm down to about 220 cm in depth from the surface. This soil feature of mixed and disturbed soil lay between Strata H and G and projected up slightly into Stratum H. The spatial relationship between the layers can be seen in the successive plan drawings of this soil feature as it was uncovered (Fig. 9). In the first plan, the patch of soil near the north side of Excavation 3 represents the top of the pile of soil over the pits. The lens grew larger as one excavated because its upper surface was convex. At its greatest horizontal extent, the earth lens extended over the north and central parts of Excavation 3 in a thin layer about 5 cm thick. It was invisible in the cross sections except as a dark lens between Strata H and G in the south sidewall of Excavation 2 (Fig. 6D).

I excavated the top of the mottled earth lens as the base of Level 15 and the whole of Level 16 of Excavation 3. I arbitrarily discontinued excavating the mottled soil feature when the pottery feature placed above Skeleton 2 was reached, for at that point I realized that I was dealing with a burial. A mottled soil similar to the earth lens in color and texture continued down into the burial pits.

It was in the upper part of this soil lens while excavating Levels 16 and 17 that I encountered Skeleton 1, a single humerus that heralded the appearance of Skeletons 2, 3, and 4–5 lower down. This bone came from Skeleton 4–5 and was accompanied by a large La Gruta tradition, grit-tempered animal-head lug and a large, poorly preserved freshwater mussel shell. The animal lug is an anachronistic specimen that may have been picked up from an earlier deposit, perhaps from the Corozal 1 or 2 phase layers that the burials intruded down into. The bone lay at about 212 cm in depth (*see* Fig. 10), and the other objects lay a few centimeters lower. The shell and lug may have been grave goods originally placed for Skeleton 4–5 and then dislodged when Skeletons 2 and/or 3 were buried, but they also could have been placed on the ground as an offering for Skeletons 2 and/or 3 when their burial pit was filled in.

When I first encountered the mottled soil lens and the features at the base of Level 11 in Excavation 2, they appeared to be hearth deposits, because the mottled reddish and blackish color of the soil made it look like burnt soil. My interpretation in retrospect is that the mottling probably resulted from a mixture of soil of the different strata intruded upon by the burials. Nonetheless, it is still possible that some of the patches do represent the remains of a celebratory bonfire built over the burials, for they contain patches of charcoal.

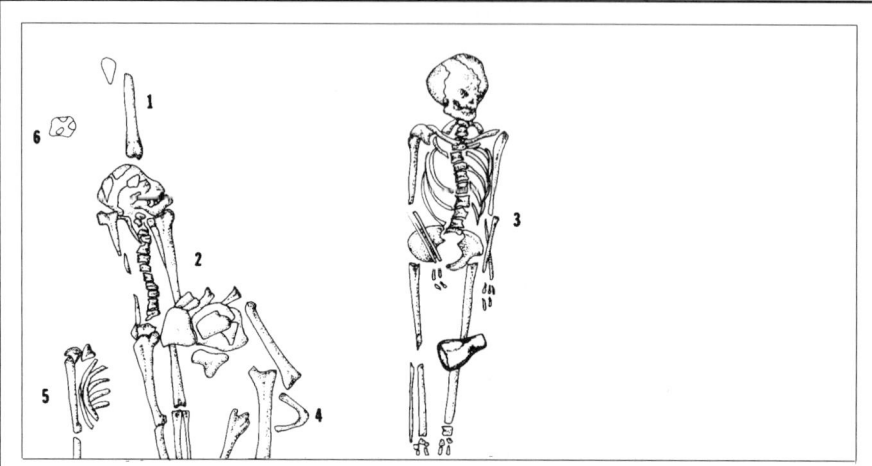

Figure 10. Plan of Skeletons 1, 2, 3, and 4–5, Excavation 3, Levels 18–21

Object #6 in the drawing is a grit-tempered animal-head lug (provenience #56–29), possibly an offering. The sherds accompanying Skeleton 2 are classified as mode #209, animal-effigy vessels. (See Plate 5)

The soil from the heap over the burials and the soil from the upper part of the burial pits was similar in color and texture to that from lower down in the burial pits, but a little redder in color and richer in charcoal. The former had a Munsell soil color of *dark brown* (10 YR 3/3), and the latter had a Munsell soil color of *dark brown* (7.5 YR 3/2).

The ceramic seriation indicates that most of the sherds in the soil of the pits have Corozal 3 phase modes. The burials thus seem to date to the transition of Corozal 3 to Camoruco 1. It is also possible, however, that they date purely to early Camoruco 1. There are stray sherds with diagnostic Corozal 1 and 2 modes in the Corozal 3 and early Camoruco 1 strata in both excavations, but it is difficult to tell whether they should be interpreted as the product of disturbance by the burial pits or merely as rare survivals of early modes in the Corozal ceramic tradition.

Extended Skeletons 1, 2, 3, and 4–5 of Excavation 3. Below the disturbed soil feature lay Skeletons 2, 3, and 4–5, three mostly complete adult skeletons. Two complete skeletons were lying extended on their backs next to one partly disarticulated skeleton that had originally been buried extended on its back and then was disturbed during the excavation of the burial pit for the other skeletons (*see* plan, Fig. 10, and photograph, Pl. 5). It was not possible to tell whether there was one large pit or two individual pits for Skeletons 2 and 3 that would have been separated by remnants of Strata G and F, the strata that were intruded into by the burials. Skeleton 1, mentioned above, was an isolated long bone found in the fill of the burial pit over Skeleton 2. This bone came from burial Skeleton 4–5, which was disturbed by the pit for Skeleton 2. The majority of bones dislodged from Skeleton 4–5 seem to have been put down in a jumble in the pit next to Skeleton 2.

Skeleton 2 was an adult female (J. Buikstra, personal communication). It lay oriented with the head pointing a few degrees east of south in the eastern third of Excavation 3, at a depth between about 225 and 250 cm from the surface. Its grave goods were large sherds from animal-effigy cooking bowls placed in a group over its left elbow (*see* Fig. 21A). The head was turned slightly to the west. Skeleton 3 was an adult male (Steinhart MS), oriented with the head pointing north, lying between about 240 and 250 cm in depth. Its offering was a unique human-effigy bottle placed on top of the knees, and there was a bone toggle between the right arm and the rib cage and a stone bead at the left wrist (Roosevelt 1980, 268–269, Figs. 91, 97, *middle,* 100, *left*). Skeleton 4–5 (two numbers were given because during excavation it was not clear at first whether one or two bodies were present) was an adult male. As mentioned above, Skeleton 4 is the disturbed portion of the skeleton and Skeleton 5 the part that was still in situ when uncovered by excavation. It was only after the bones of 4–5 had been cleared of the earth above them that it became apparent that Skeleton 4 was the disturbed, redeposited bones of Skeleton 5, whose right shoulder and chest bones still lay articulated in the ground. Skeleton 5 had originally been buried with the head pointing slightly east of south, in the northwest corner of Excavation 3. The bones of this individual lay between about 235 and 255 cm in depth from the surface.

Samples of bone from the three skeletons were submitted for stable isotope analysis of the collagen (van der Merwe, Roosevelt, and Vogel 1981) to determine the quantity of Carbon 4 plants such as maize in the diet. The results indicated that maize made up at least 70 percent of the protein in the diet. The teeth of all three adults were substantially worn down and there were signs of periodontal disease, possibly as a result of the effects of chewing gritty maize ground up on stones. These skeletons, then, constitute the earliest secure quantitative evidence that maize had become an important staple food in the Parmana region.

Levels 18 and 19 of Excavation 3 were assigned to the skeletons and their burial pits. The Munsell soil colors of the burial pits were brown to dark brown (10 YR 4/3 or 3/3). The dark yellowish brown of the burial pits contrasted with the tanner color of the Strata F and G into which they intruded. The burials appear to have been dug down from the juncture between Stratum G and Stratum H, which seems to represent the transition between Corozal 3 and Camoruco 2.

Since the modes represented by the ceramic grave goods occur from Corozal 3 through Camoruco 2, the stratigraphic evidence that the top of the burial pit occurred between Stratum G and Stratum H suggests that the skeletons may date to the transition between Corozal 3 (Stratum G) and Camoruco 1 (Stratum H).

STRATUM F. Stratum F consisted of quite sandy, hard soil with much animal bone and a few charcoal chunks. Carbonized plant remains were not very abundant in this stratum. The soil was a little darker than either Stratum E or Stratum G, but none of the three seemed dark enough to be considered "black Indian soils." The Munsell soil colors for Stratum F are brown to dark brown (YR 5/3, 4/3). Stratum F lay between approximately 230 and 250 cm in depth from the surface. At the juncture of this stratum with the underlying Stratum E were several lighter colored, clayey lenses lying under patches of burnt red earth, charcoal-rich earth, and concentrations of animal bone. The clay had a Munsell color of pale brown and light yellowish brown (10 YR 6/3, 6/4). The lenses can be seen in the south and west sidewalls of Excavation 2 in the profile drawings, and the one found in the southeast of Excavation 2 at the juncture of Levels 13 and 14 is shown in a plan drawing (Fig. 11). There also was a patch of dark soil with bone fragments visible in the southwest corner of Excavation 2, but it was not apparent as a definable feature during excavation.

Figure 11. Plan of charcoal and clay lenses at juncture of Strata F and E, Excavation 2, Levels 13 and 14

About 250 cm depth from surface. The charcoal lens, shown black in the drawing, overlies the clay lens, shown stippled.

Stratum F was excavated by Level 13 of Excavation 2 and Level 21 of Excavation 3. Level 21 also removed remnants of the burial pits of the skeletons, which combined soil from both Strata G and F. Stratum F extended over the entire surface of Excavation 2. In Excavation 3 the bones of Skeletons 2, 3, and 4–5 lay mainly at the level of Stratum F, which was thus disturbed over a large area of the excavation by intrusion of the burial pits. Stratum F, apparently, was found intact only in Excavation 2 and in the western part of Excavation 3.

The stratum is late Corozal 2 in date, according to the seriation of ceramic modes. A carbonized berry of the Malpighiaceae family excavated from Level 13 of Excavation 2 was dated by accelerator to modern times, documenting a very recent intrusion into this level. Intrusive carbonized plant remains of recent age were found in archaeological deposits at Corozal and at other sites. Presumably they descend into prehistoric layers by means of human disturbances, animal or insect burrows, or root instrusions.

STRATUM E. This thick, slightly undulating stratum consisted of hard tan soil with sandy texture, very dense in sherds, with much animal bone and little charcoal. The Munsell soil color for the stratum is dark yellowish brown (10 YR 4/4 and 7.5 YR 4/2).

Stratum E lies between about 250 and 275 cm in depth. It is lighter and grayer in color than the underlying Stratum D and redder and darker than the overlying Stratum F. In Excavation 3, the burial pits of the three skeletons lying mainly in Strata F and G grazed the upper part of Stratum E. The soil of these pits showed up grayer and a bit lighter than Stratum E, and a little of their soil may have become mixed in the stratum.

This layer was removed in Level 14 of Excavation 2 and Levels 22 and 23 in Excavation 3. Levels 14 and 23 may have also scraped up a little of Stratum D below, but the soil colors do not reflect this possibility.

Stratum E dates to Corozal 2. This layer had a pooled radiocarbon date of about A.D. 210 and an accelerator date of about A.D. 910 on palm seed fragments, both from Level 14, Excavation 2. The seven hundred years difference between these two dates indicates the presence of some anachronistic charcoal in the level.

STRATUM D. This stratum was a layer of very hard, dark brown, sandy soil that contrasted sharply in color with the underlying orangey soil of Stratum C. The soil of Stratum D was much grayer than Stratum C below and more intense and darker in color than the overlying Stratum E. Munsell soil colors for Stratum D are brown to dark brown (7.5 YR 4/2, 4/4, or 3/4). There were numerous sherds and an abundance of animal bone preserved in the soil. Stratum D lay between approximately 265 and 285 cm in depth and thinned and dipped more than 5 cm toward the center of the excavated area from the sidewalls. It varied considerably in thickness over its extent, from about 10 cm to more than 20 cm. From near the base of this stratum, the burial pits for several flexed burials (Figs. 12 and 13) were dug.

Stratum D was mainly excavated in Excavation 2 by Level 15 and in Excavation 3 by Level 24. The lower portions of this stratum were presumably mixed with the underlying Stratum C when the burial pits were sunk from the base of Stratum D down into C for the west, center, and north wall skeletons of Level 16 in Excavation 2 and Skeletons 2 and 3 of Level 25 of Excavation 3 (*see below*). Thus Levels 16 and 16W of Excavation 2 and the mottled soil feature of Level 25, Excavation 3, presumably include soil from both Stratum C and Stratum D that was mixed in the fill of the burial pits.

Stratum D falls into the Corozal 1 phase, according to the distribution of ceramic modes. This stratum was the earliest dark, object-rich stratum in the excavations. Those below were orange in color and relatively poor in pottery. It may be that Stratum D represents an increase in the density or size of population at the site related to the initial expansion of the economy with maize cultivation. The fact that this layer and Stratum E were richer in faunal bone than the layers above suggests that fauna may have been more important in the diet during late Corozal 1 and 2 than it was in Corozal 3 and Camoruco times. An alternative explanation might be that the high-lying layers were subject to more intense weathering and therefore had less faunal bone preserved. In the later periods, the human bone chemistry, discussed above, indicates substantial reliance on plant protein from a species like maize. The bone chemistry of the Corozal 1 skeletons, discussed below, had patterns that suggested the dominance of faunal protein over plant protein in the diet (van der Merwe, Roosevelt, and Vogel 1981).

Level 15 of Excavation 2 has accelerator dates of A.D. 630 and 700 from the carbon inside and outside a pottery sherd, respectively. The stable carbon isotope ratios of the carbon inside the pottery suggest that it derived almost entirely from a carbon 4 plant, probably maize, and the ratios from outside the pottery appear substantially influenced by carbon from such a plant. A third date a. d. 995 was on pooled charcoal fragments.

STRATUM C. With Stratum C, the soil became appreciably sandier and more orange in color, a pattern that intensified toward the base of the deposit. This thick layer was composed of extremely hard, orangey soil with very sandy texture, solidified with indurated clay, possibly translocated from the upper stratigraphic block by tropical weathering processes. The intense color probably was due to the advanced weathering of the soil plus a lack of soot compared to the dark strata higher up in the profile. The soil in Stratum C was poorer in artifacts, charcoal, and bone than that of Stratum D. Munsell soil colors are strong brown (7.5YR 4/6) or dark brown (7.5YR 4/2). The darker patches in this soil are probably the result of the deposition of soil intruded from Stratum D when the pits for the late Corozal 1 phase burials were dug down from its base. Stratum C lay from approximately 285 to 310 cm in depth.

Stratum C was excavated by Level 16 East and Level 17 of Excavation 2 and Level 25 of Excavation 3. Levels 16 and 16 West of Excavation 2 contained mostly the darker brown soil of the burial pits of the skeletons lying in Stratum C, whereas 16 East of Excavation 2 was confined to the undisturbed orangey soil of Stratum C. Level 25 of Excavation 3 seems to have included mostly soil from Stratum C, but apparently also a small amount of soil from the intrusive burial pits of Skeletons 1, 2, and 3. The mottled soil feature in Level 25 and the top of 26 is probably soil intruded from the burial pits of Skeletons 1 and 3 (see Figs. 12 and 13). The bases of the burial pits in both excavations lay near the base of Stratum C.

According to the ceramic modes, this layer dates to the early years of late Corozal 1. The stratigraphy suggests that the skeletons date to middle-late Corozal 1 times. Level 17 of Excavation 2 has a late Corozal 1 accelerator radiocarbon date of A.D. 500 on a charcoal fragment.

THE FLEXED ADULT SKELETONS IN EXCAVATIONS 2 AND 3. Four adult flexed burials intruded into Stratum C from Stratum D between 280 and 310 cm in depth. They included, in Excavation 2, the center, north wall, and west wall skeletons. In Excavation 3, we uncovered Skeletons 1, 2, and 3. The legs of the north wall skeleton in Excavation 2 turned up as Skeleton 2 in the southwest of Level 25 of Excavation 3, and the legs of the center skeleton of Excavation 2 turned up as Skeleton 1 of Excavation 3. The soil of the fill of the pits was a dark brown mottled with orange, very hard in places but slightly softer than the rocklike undisturbed soil. The burial pit Munsell soil colors are: for 16 and 16 West, 7.5YR 4/4, dark brown; for north burial, center burial, and west burial, 10YR 4/3, brown to dark brown. The skeletons were encased in very hard soil and were highly compressed vertically (Pl. 6, *top*), presumably by the weight of the approximately 3 m of soil overburden. The extreme hardness of the soil and the soft, leached state of the skeletons meant that the skeletons could not be removed except by cutting large blocks out of the soil, a procedure that was damaging to the bones and made in-place drawings of these particular skeletons impossible (*see* Fig. 13 for plans of the location of the skeletons' burial pits). For this reason, and because early rains began to destroy Excavation 3 soon after the burials were found, Skeletons 1, 2, and 3 were sampled and then reburied.

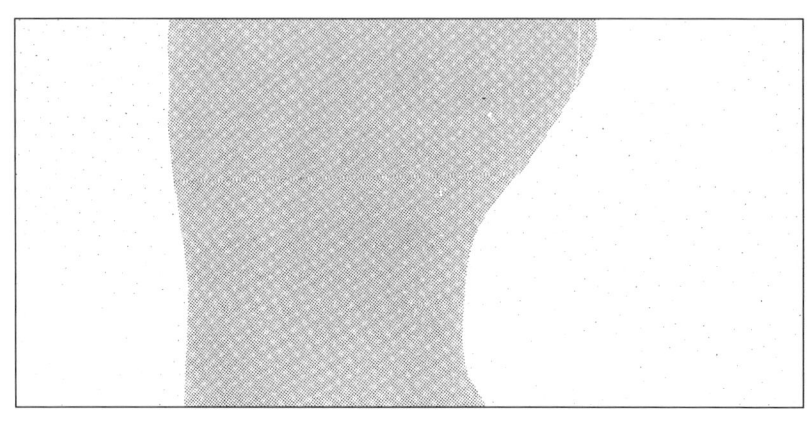

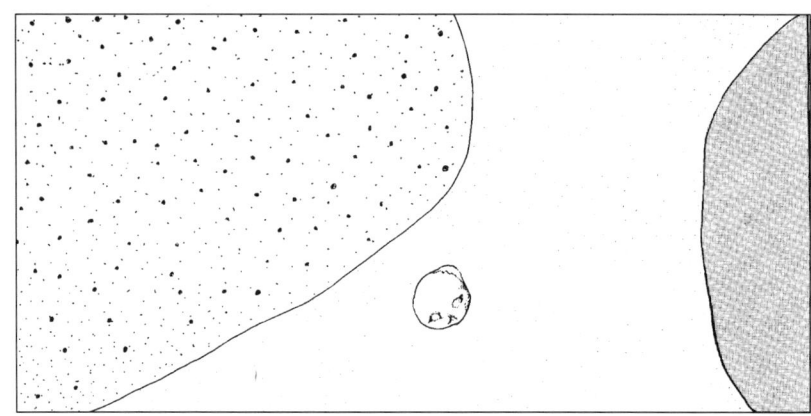

Figure 12. Plan of soil features at the top of Stratum C, over the flexed burials, Excavation 2, Level 16, and Excavation 3, Level 25

The mottled soil features lay about 290 cm in depth over the burial pits of the skeletons. Excavation 3 is at the top, and Excavation 2 is at the bottom. In Excavation 3, the mottled soil feature is shaded, and undisturbed sandy soil is stippled. In Excavation 2, the mottled soil feature of Level 16 is lightly stippled, and the undisturbed sandy soil of Level 16 East is heavily stippled; the dark mottled soil of Level 16 West is shaded. The top of the skull of Center Skeleton (Pl. 6, top) can be seen in the north center of Excavation 2.

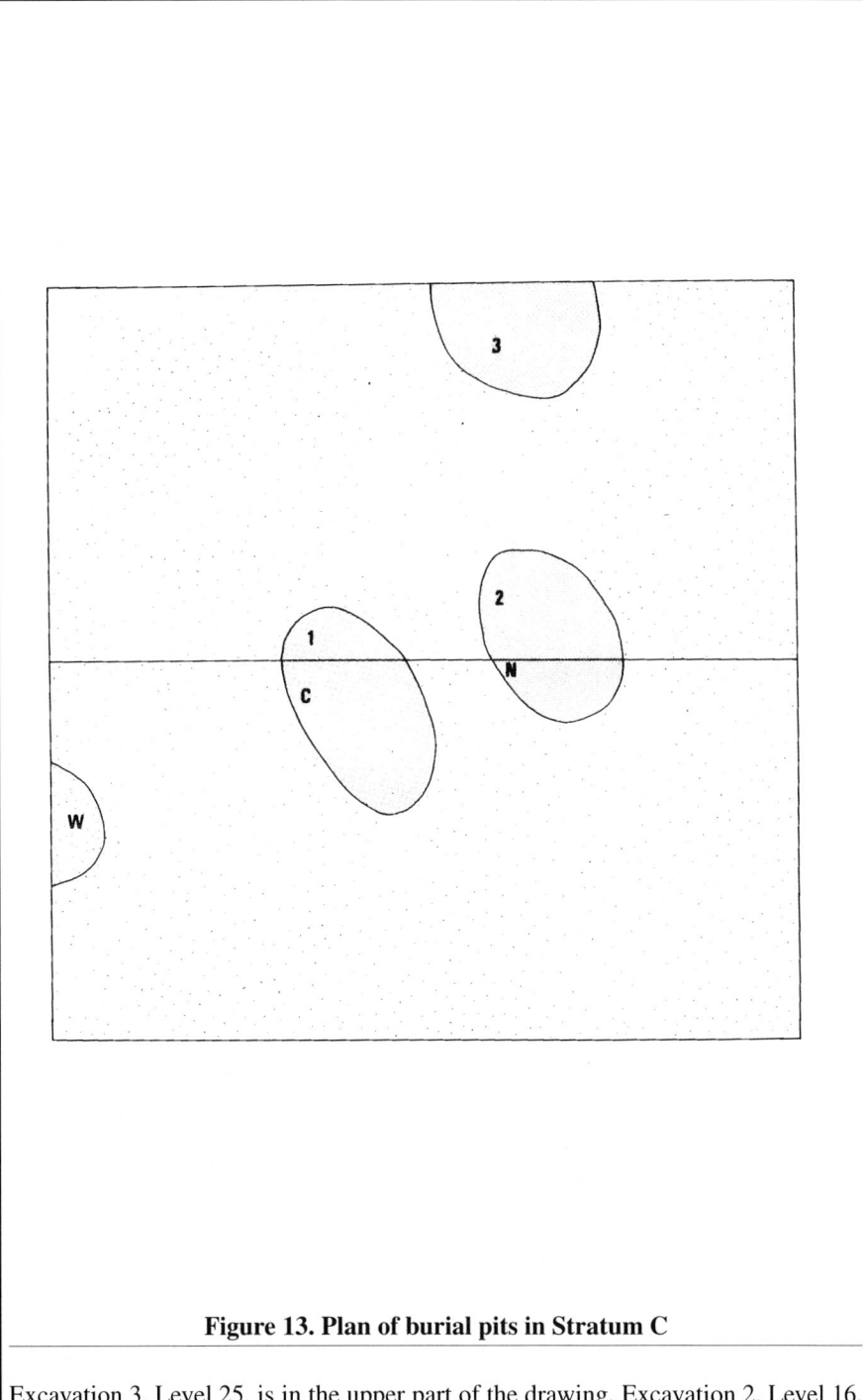

Figure 13. Plan of burial pits in Stratum C

Excavation 3, Level 25, is in the upper part of the drawing, Excavation 2, Level 16, in the lower part.

No attempt was made to clear the hard soil from them. Only the center skeleton could be tentatively sexed, as a female. The center and north wall skeletons were oriented with the crania facing southeast, but the orientations of the west wall skeleton and Skeleton 3 were not clear. It is noteworthy that these early Corozal phase skeletons are all tightly flexed and placed in small, oval pits just big enough to hold them, whereas the late Corozal—early Camoruco ones were all extended and placed in spacious pits with room for offerings.

The burial pits of the early Corozal skeletons were visibly browner than the matrix of the level. The intrusive soil mixture of the burial pits appeared mottled red and brown during excavation, leading to a mistaken preliminary identification as a fireplace, as with the later skeletons. Upon reaching the flexed skeletons, I realized that the overlying reddish patches probably derived not from fire oxidation but from the mixture of the orange soil of Stratum C with the browner soil from Stratum D. The mixed soil of the burial pits was excavated primarily by Levels 16 and 16 West of Excavation 2 and by the mottled soil feature in Level 25 of Excavation 3, as mentioned. Level 16 West has an accelerator radiocarbon date of A.D. 580 on a piece of wood charcoal.

According to the stratigraphy and seriation, the skeletons date approximately to the middle part of the Corozal 1 phase. The sherds associated directly with the skeletons were too few to seriate with statistical validity, and too few both for chi-square calculations and for quantified percentage comparisons. However, because the skeletons were deposited from near the interface of Strata C and D, which are securely dated by statistically significant mode distributions to the early and late Corozal 1 phase, respectively, the skeletons presumably date near the middle of the Corozal 1 phase.

The stable carbon isotope ratio of collagen from the bone of the four individuals was analyzed as part of the experiment mentioned above (van der Merwe, Roosevelt and Vogel 1981) and other research (Roosevelt, Krueger, and Sullivan MSa) and the results indicated a diet based primarily on carbon 3 plants, such as manioc, and game and fish. According to the bone results, maize or other carbon 4 plants could have been consumed at levels of fifteen percent or less. According to the results of stable isotope analysis of carbonized food from sherds, maize was actually being eaten and used as pottery-tempering material during late Corozal 1 times. But it seems that maize, which appeared for the first time in sites of the region during the Corozal 1 phase, had not yet become the major staple in the diet. Even without being consumed in large quantities, the plant could have had a substantial economic and demographic impact if added to the protein-poor rainy-season diet, when fish, the major source of faunal protein available in the region, were scarce.

STRATUM B. This was a thick layer of hard, sandy clay soil with bright reddish orange color, poorer in artifacts and charcoal than Stratum C. The soil contained patches of tan clay and was stained near the east sidewall of Excavation 2 by the burial pit of the child skeleton (*see below*). The overall color of Stratum B was a much more intense reddish orange than that of Stratum C above it. The soil of Stratum B was Munsell color yellowish red (5YR 5/6). This stratum lay between about 305 and 325 cm in depth.

Stratum B corresponds with Level 18 of Excavation 2 and Level 26 of Excavation 3. Level 18 has accelerator radiocarbon dates of A.D. 570 on a charcoal fragment and A.D. 1265 on a fragment of maize. Obviously, judging from the disparity of the two samples, it appears that there has been intrusion of Camoruco phase carbonized maize into these layers.

Stratum B dates to early Corozal 1, according to the distribution of modes. Though low in total number, the stratum still had more than the one hundred necessary for valid statistical comparisons.

THE FLEXED CHILD BURIAL IN EXCAVATION 2. Lying in Stratum B in Excavation 2 was the skull of the child burial: a flexed supine burial lying between 310 and 340 cm in depth and oriented with the feet facing southwest (*see* plan and photographs, Fig. 14 and Pl.6, *center* and *bottom*). The child appears to have been about nine years old at the time of death. The postcranial part of the child's skeleton lay in Stratum A, below Stratum B. The burial seems to have been dug down from Stratum C into Strata A and B, but the outline of its burial pit was not sharp enough above the body to tell for certain. The pit contained soil that was browner than that of the matrix of Strata A and B but not as dark as that of the other skeletons, which lay about 40 cm higher than the child. This intermediate color presumably derived from the fact that the burial pit contained a mixture of soil from several strata. The Munsell color of the soil of the burial pit was brown/dark brown (7.5 YR 4/4) inside the skull and strong brown (7.5 YR 4/3), at the shoulder. This soil would presumably include soil from the various strata into which the pit intruded.

As noted, the postcranial part of the child's skeleton lay in the upper part of Stratum A, surrounded by an area of soil darker and browner in color than Stratum A. This lower part of the burial pit for the skeleton contained a mixture of soil from Strata A, B, and C and also presumably was tinged with organic matter from the decay of the flesh of the corpse. The pit's Munsell color was closer to the color of Stratum C than to that of Stratum A.

STRATUM A. This thick stratum had very orange, extremely hard, sandy clay soil with very few artifacts. Vigorous excavation with heavy picks had little effect on the soil, other than dislodging small chips of material. The soil con-

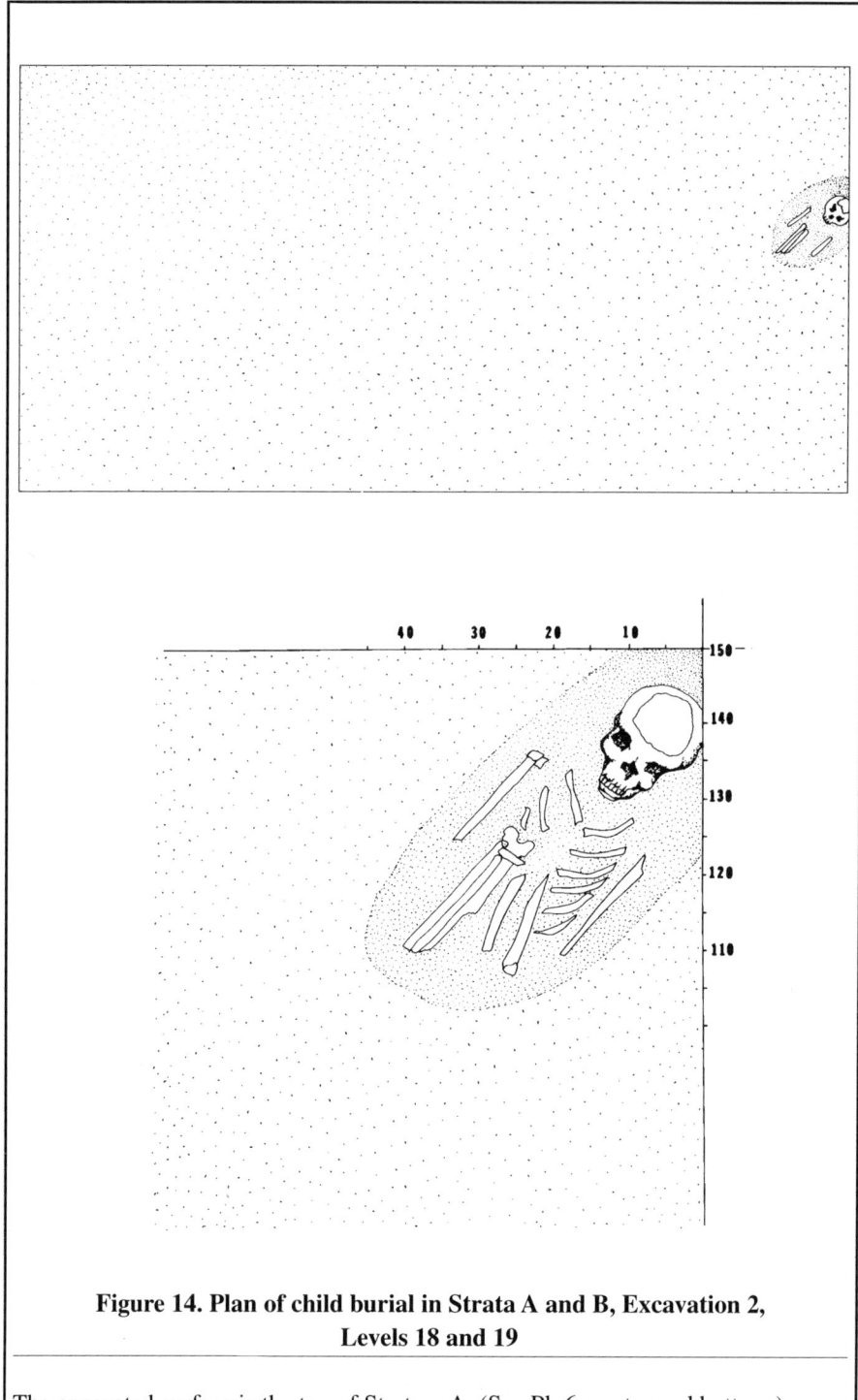

Figure 14. Plan of child burial in Strata A and B, Excavation 2, Levels 18 and 19

The excavated surface is the top of Stratum A. (See Pl. 6, center and bottom.)

tained patches of very indurated lignite. Stratum A is markedly more orange in hue than Stratum B. The Munsell color designation for A is yellowish red (5YR 5/8). The stratum lies between 320 and 400 cm, and its upper part was sampled by Levels 19, 20, and 21 of Excavation 2. Levels 19 and 20 had fewer than one hundred sherds each, and 21 was apparently barren. I excavated a shovel test below Stratum 21 with a pick into the lower part of Stratum A and found no pottery. The archaeological deposit may extend down somewhat farther at various places in the site, but the soil in the bottom of the excavation had become too hard to excavate without machine tools, and there were no more observable cultural remains.

Stratum A dates to the beginning of Corozal 1 and is differentiated from Strata C and B by its intensely orange color, extreme hardness, and the very small number of sherds found in it. Excavation 2, Level 19, produced an accelerator radiocarbon date of A.D. 1610 on the carbonized shell of a palm seed, which therefore appears to be an intrusion of historic-age plant material into the prehistoric layers.

F. Interpretation of the Stratigraphy

The major layering patterns of the soil in the Corozal deposit probably derive from both natural and cultural factors. The possible causes of the stratigraphic patterning at the site are several, including changes through time in climate, vegetation, hydrography, density of occupation, and nature and intensity of human activity.

One factor that contributed to the layering patterns was the ancient people's practice of alternating use of the location for garbage dumping and houses. The thick, horizontal black layers at the Corozal site seem to derive in part from regular dumping of refuse removed from living areas presumably located outside the immediate area of the dumping. This garbage was clearly secondary, not a primary deposit. Garbage had apparently been swept regularly from living areas and carried away to be dumped. The secondary garbage had broad, horizontal layers rich in soot, fragmentary artifacts, and food remains. The objects were turned every which way and scattered through the soil. There were few or no features in these particular layers, although they did have some burials extending down from them.

At many levels in the upper part of the stratigraphic column there were, in addition, slightly undulating layers that looked like plastered clay house floors or platforms. These layers were light in color and hard, and they had the finer texture of river bottom alluvium, in contrast to the coarser soils that compose the elevated levee and dune system in Parmana. The finer-textured soils may have been mined from the river bottomlands for use in preparing dwelling sites. They differ from in-place river alluvium in being more oxidized by weathering.

The soil of the probable prepared floors lacked the secondary garbage's richness in objects and was much less stained with soot. On and extending down from the floors was a variety of discrete features of more restricted horizontal extent, possibly the products of activities carried out on the prepared surfaces. The apparent floors had relatively sharp stratigraphic interfaces, and soot or ash lenses and object-rich patches and layers, such as clusters of broken pots, grinding stones, patches of carbonized plant remains, and ash pits. These features seem to represent primary refuse from different domestic activities. Such refuse would have been swept up from floors during occupation but left in place when structures were rebuilt or abandoned. The primary cultural deposits on top of the floors often had a higher proportion of ordinary cooking wares and fewer examples of highly decorated service or cooking wares than the secondary garbage layers did. Possibly those decorated wares were for ceremonial use in feasts held away from houses out in the open or in exiguous shed-like ritual structures. Our excavations at mounds on Marajo Island have revealed that highly decorated pottery is rare in the pottery assemblages associated with domestic house floors but is common in garbage and predominant in special caches (Roosevelt 1990b, 1991a). Since our excavations at Corozal were columnar cuts, they only could reveal possible functional distinctions in activities through time. Further excavation at Corozal would be necessary to reveal spatial patterning in the distribution of objects of different functions.

The pattern of major horizontal layering at the Corozal site may thus derive in part from superposition of ruined earthen buildings, as in Near Eastern tells. The thickness of the upper layers of the site would have been increased by the accumulation of material from decayed earth or wattle-and-daub structures. Fragments of burnt or unburnt clay with vegetal impressions were common finds in the Orinoco sites (Roosevelt 1980, 269, Fig. 99), and earth and/or wattle-and-daub structures are commonly used for dwellings in the Orinoco and Amazon regions today. The excavations on Marajo Island in the Lower Amazon produced evidence of debris from thatched earthen dwellings (Roosevelt 1990b, 1991a), although the Marajo structures have floors made up of narrow laminations from repeated replastering and also baked clay hearths, both of which appear to be lacking in the Parmana sites.

The lower part of the stratigraphic column at Corozal lacked the pattern of alternation between garbage and possible floors, and a series of sandier layers occurred that were for the most part not dark and sooty enough to be considered black Indian soils. This lower block of strata seems to represent occupations that lacked the high rate of garbage production and the building activity characteristic of the occupations that produced the upper block of stratigraphy.

In addition to the buildup of soil by garbage dumping and building, the pattern of thick, horizontal layering at Corozal may in part be a product of the aeolian soil deposition characteristic of the region. There is a substantial accretion of windblown sand and silt over the land during the dry season when the river bottoms are exposed to erosion. This aeolian material builds up rapidly in the cultural deposits and creates layers that may be thicker for their time spans than those at sites in other regions. For example, the site of Corozal has deposits approximately 4 m deep for an occupation of about thirteen hundred years, whereas some sites away from the sand and silt banks had only one meter of soil deposit or less for that time period. (However, some dune sites with very loose sand, like Ronquin, had only a meter of archaeological deposit for a period of about three thousand years, probably due to site deflation by wind or rain.) The sandier texture of the basal layers in the stratigraphy at Corozal may relate to drier time periods or periods of deforestation when there was more aeolian deposition, less vegetation cover, and, consequently, more erosion throughout the region. At such times, wind-blown deposits would be coarser in texture. Alternatively, these layers may be sandier simply because they lack the thick, clayey debris from prepared floors and earthen structures and the abundant decayed organic matter that the more intense later occupation added to the soil. Though sandier, the lower layers in the deposit are much harder than the later ones. This hardness may be the result of translocation of fine clay particles downward through the soil profile during weathering by rain. Because of their generally coarse sandy texture, the soils of terra firme sites in the Middle Orinoco region are better drained and more leached than those in lowland regions with finer-textured upland soils. Nonetheless, faunal remains and skeletal remains are preserved in abundance in the archaeological deposits at some sites, such as Corozal.

The characteristics of the botanical remains in the Corozal stratigraphic column changed considerably through time. The distribution of maize, particularly, varies through the stratigraphy (Roosevelt 1980, 138, Table 20). As mentioned in the introduction, maize seems to come into use in the region during the Corozal 1 phase. The earliest evidence for maize consists of the maizelike stable isotope ratios of carbon on and in Corozal 1 phase pottery sherds (Table 8). The rare maize kernels that we excavated from Corozal phase layers, when assessed by AMS radiocarbon dating, turned out to date to the Camoruco phase. The early Camoruco phase maize is morphologically different from later maize, with hard, small kernels and larger row numbers. In the Camoruco 3 phase layers, maize is very abundant, and the race is a tropical lowland flour corn, similar to the modern race Chandelle (Roosevelt 1980; Walton Galinat, personal communication). The increase in abundance suggests that maize increased in importance in the diet through time, and the results of the bone-chemistry studies on a total of ten individuals document its importance in late prehistoric times (van der Merwe, Roosevelt, and Vogel 1981; Roosevelt, Krueger, and Sullivan MSa). The stable carbon isotope ratios of the human bones from Corozal show a shift from little or no consumption of maize in Corozal 1 to consumption at high levels as a staple food in late Corozal or early Camoruco times.

There are also shifts in the distribution of faunal remains through the stratigraphy (Wing, Garson, and Simon MS). Some of the Corozal phase layers are much richer in fauna than the Camoruco layers. It seems unlikely that this pattern is the result of differential preservation, because the Corozal layers have sandier soil that is usually less favorable to bone preservation than more clayey soils characteristic of the Camoruco layers. A possible explanation is that fauna were more important per capita in the diet during the Corozal phase, when maize was first entering the diet. During that time, starchy roots such as manioc or Xanthosoma could have been staple foods, and so fauna would have been the major source of protein in the diet. Later, when maize rose to about 70% or more of the diet, its protein would perforce have become the major source, and faunal food would have become only a protein supplement, as explained above.

The distribution of archaeological objects in the Corozal stratigraphy tends to add evidence for an increase in human population during the Corozal phase. The site survey showed that there was a marked increase in the sizes and number of archaeological sites in the Parmana region during the transition to intensive maize cultivation. The stratigraphic column at Corozal seems to give corroborative evidence for this population increase by showing an increase in overall density of artifacts and carbonized plants in the layers during the periods when the number and sizes of sites increased. The number of objects recovered from strata increases rapidly during the Corozal phase, which is when the most rapid increase in number and sizes of sites in the region occurs. Thereafter, during the Camoruco phase, when the increase in number of sites slows, the distribution of archaeological objects stays quite stable at a high level of density.

Settlements in the Parmana region may have changed in character as well as in magnitude during this time. As mentioned, the earlier Corozal phase layers at Corozal lacked evidence of the clayey prepared-floor layers that occurred in the Camoruco phase levels. Earlier deposits at other sites, such as La Gruta and Ronquin, also appear to lack the prepared clay floors. This difference between the earlier phases and Camoruco is difficult to interpret without more information about the layout of settlements and the range of facilities present. However, the lack of prepared floors could be interpreted as evidence that Corozal phase structures were built primarily of perishable materials, rather than earth. If so, then the phases contrast in the amount of investment in permanent buildings at the site. In Parmana today, perishable thatch-and-pole structures without earthen floors are commonly used at very small permanent sites or at seasonally occupied sites for harvesting crops, and more permanent earthen structures with prepared floors are more common in the larger villages, such as Parmana. Perhaps the lack of earthen structures in the Corozal levels could be taken as an indication of smaller site population or less permanent patterns of habitation in earlier times.

Understanding the possible cultural, behavioral, and environmental significance of the stratigraphic patterning will require additional information about the history of the climate and the nature of the occupation at the site. For example, study of the ecological significance of the temporal shifts in the forest species represented in the carbonized plant remains (Smith and Roosevelt MS) may give evidence of climate changes that may correlate with the increase in sandiness of the strata with depth. Since pollen and phytoliths were not reliably preserved in the generally coarse, oxidized soil, that obvious source of information about the environment cannot help us in the Parmana region. To understand the implications of the stratigraphy for settlement organization and permanence, it would be necessary to excavate at the site more extensively, to uncover floor plans and learn more about changes through time in the site layout as a whole. Corozal would be a good site to study more extensively, being large, deep, complexly stratified, and rich in both artifacts and biological remains. Such work could be expected to yield much information about ancient environment and the characteristics of prehistoric settlement through time.

G. The Dating Problem

The main purpose of the chronological work in Parmana was to gain an ordering in time of strata and of objects in a relative ceramic sequence. As such, the work had satisfactory results, producing a sequence of nine major temporal units for the prehistoric period. The research at Corozal in particular established six temporal units for the late prehistoric part of the sequence, a period that earlier had been defined as a single temporal unit. The absolute dating of the occupational phases in the region has not been as conclusive. (All dates mentioned in this volume are quoted in uncalibrated radiocarbon years.) Absolute dating in the lowlands is important for establishing how developmental changes in one region compare to those in another and evaluating the direction and significance of interregional influence and communication.

1. Relative Dating

The relative dating of the layers at Corozal was arrived at by study of their spatial and physical relationships and their contents (Harris 1979). In the stratigraphic work, interfaces and soil characteristics and the distribution of chronologically distinctive ceramic attributes in the layers were studied for information about the sequence of deposition and disturbance. The layering of the stratigraphy was the primary guide for the collection of material, and the material remains were the key to the definition of chronological subdivisions. Usually, I have established a major chronological boundary between levels where there was a statistically significant change in both the absolute frequency and percentages of several modes from one level to the other. Levels considered within the same temporal unit usually have fewer significant differences in frequencies and percentages of chronological modes than levels considered to be in different time units. In a few cases, there were significant shifts within the lesser time units, permitting subdivisions into early and late. This, for example, was the case with early and terminal Corozal 1 and early and late Corozal 2. For the most part, divisions in the ceramic sequence occur at stratigraphic divisions, although stratigraphic divisions also occur within chronological units. In a few cases, ceramic transitions occur without apparent stratigraphic change. (The changes in the distribution of ceramics through time are described and discussed in Chap. 3 of this volume.)

The nature of the stratigraphy at the site helped the effort to create a relative chronology. Most of the deposit was composed of discernibly contrasting layers, as described above, and for the most part the layers contained sufficient quantities of artifacts for statistical analysis, ranging from over one hundred to over seventeen hundred total sherds per level, except for the three lowest levels of the site, which contained fewer than 50 total sherds each. The combination of information from the studies of stratigraphy and artifact distribution, therefore, yielded relative archaeological time units of considerable precision for some phases. These in turn provided evidence of the sequence of cultural evolutionary changes on which the research was focused.

Most of the major layers at Corozal seemed to be relatively free of massive disturbance and mixture of pottery from different layers, but it is routine for an archaeological deposit to have disturbances of various kinds. Both ancient and modern people and animals are likely to have intruded into earlier deposits by digging pits and holes. The disturbed soil in or near such intrusive features may contain material from two or more periods: the period when the disturbance occurred as well as the periods of the deposits that were disturbed. As mentioned in the stratigraphic discussion, there are several apparent unconformities in the stratigraphy at Corozal, where people seem to have scraped the surface of an earlier deposit or dug into it and then deposited material. These disturbances were often confirmed by the seriation, which showed instances of a layer or feature containing modes of more than one phase.

There was also indirect ceramic evidence of small disturbances that we could not discern stratigraphically, possibly postholes, small pits, root intrusions, or burrows. These are indicated by out-of-order radiocarbon dates and numerous historic or modern radiocarbon dates on charcoal from prehistoric strata. Probably also related to such disturbances are the rare examples of sherds of styles particular to one temporal unit that turned up in layers of much earlier or later periods (see Tables 11–14 for examples of these). In addition, there were several cases where sherds of one vessel turned up in two adjacent layers or even in layers that were separated by yet another layer. In some instances anachronistic sherds seem to have been curated "found" objects, such as the early, grit-tempered zoomorphic lug (56–29) placed as an offering in the pit (Level 17) of Skeleton 2 of Level 18 in Excavation 3 (Fig. 10, object #6). At the time this lug was deposited, such lugs were no longer manufactured, so its presence is interpreted as reuse of an earlier object perhaps collected during the excavation of the burial pit, which intruded into earlier layers. The rare anomalous sherds in the stratigraphy do not obscure the patterns of ceramic mode distribution in the excavations because they occur at significantly lower frequencies than in their "home" layers. Thus, although the strayed sherds are a warning that some kind of intrusion seems to have taken place, their localized occurrence does not significantly alter the patterns of ceramic distribution on which the relative chronology is based.

2. Absolute Dating

Our first attempt at assigning years for the prehistoric phases of the region was based on the first regional sequence of sixteen radiocarbon dates, which were run in the late 1970s. These dates have been discussed in detail in several works, and along with all other known radiocarbon dates from the Middle Orinoco they are reproduced here in Table 8 (Roosevelt 1978, 1980; Rouse 1978; Rouse, Cruxent, Olsen, and Roosevelt 1976; Rouse and Allaire 1978;

Rouse, Allaire, and Boomert MS; Vargas 1981; Zucchi, Tarble, and Vaz 1984). In creating our first chronological chart (Roosevelt 1980, Table 1), we accepted radiocarbon dates that fell between about 2100 B.P. and A.D. 1500, and we rejected modern dates and any prehistoric dates that seemed stratigraphically inconsistent. Where radiocarbon dates were lacking to provide details for a temporal unit, approximately equal time spans were provisionally assigned to units until further dates allowed their length to be corrected. Since 1980, 60 additional radiocarbon dates have been run (Table 8), and these extend the beginning date of the sequence somewhat and require adjustments in the estimated length of its subunits.

At the time the "long" chronology was created, an alternative "short" chronology was suggested for the region based on acceptance of late prehistoric dates and rejection of both early prehistoric and modern dates. The underlying theoretical rationale for the short chronology was an evolutionary one. Its proponents believed that the tropical lowlands east of the Andes did not have early pottery-age occupations (Meggers and Evans 1957; Meggers 1954; Hilbert 1955, 1959a; Hilbert and Hilbert 1980; Simoes 1969; Sanoja and Vargas 1978; Vargas 1981). The assumption was that pottery was not made in the eastern tropical lowlands until the craft diffused into the area from the Andes around 1000 B.C., relatively late in the Formative developmental period. The "short" chronologists put the date of the introduction of the white-and-red painting complex to the lowlands from Peru even later—between about 200 B.C. and A.D. 200. The proposed reason for the comparative retardation of culture in the lowlands was that the resources there were too poor to permit the development of intensive subsistence economies that would support the indigenous development of the craft of pottery.

The short chronology for the eastern lowlands was bolstered by the fact that most of the dates in the Parmana sequence were, in fact, late prehistoric, as were most published dates from other eastern lowland sites at that time. The La Gruta and Los Merecurotes sites in the Parmana region were among the first pottery sites in the eastern lowlands to produce dates before 1000 B.C. Sites in northern lowland South America had already produced dates between 3000 and 1000 B.C. for Initial and early Formative pottery, but in the late 1970s east of the Andes there were few dates from stratified ceramic sites and no published dates for Initial pottery. Some scholars had claimed that people in the lowlands already had pottery by 2000 B.C. (Lathrap 1970), but until the excavations at Parmana no dates of this age from the eastern lowlands had been published. Interestingly, archaeologists had by then excavated several sites that later proved to have early prehistoric pottery, but either they did not have the sites dated (Evans and Meggers 1960) or they rejected early radiocarbon dates for pottery and withheld them from publication because they did not fit the short chronology (Smithsonian Anthropology Archives 1965–85; Roosevelt 1995). Thus, at the time of the Parmana project there was little published evidence for Initial or early Formative pottery east of the Andes.

Given its premises, the short chronology required some reason for the occurrence of early prehistoric dates in the late prehistoric archaeological sites. The explanation offered was that the charcoal samples that produced early dates had become contaminated by very ancient carbon from lignite or similar coal-like substances, which occur in many tropical regions, including the Orinoco. We submitted a piece of lignite from Corozal to the Queens College Radiocarbon Laboratory for dating, and, as expected, it gave a geological time-scale date of about 23,000 B.C. (R. Pardi, personal communication). Contamination of aggregate radiocarbon samples by this material would definitely give dates that were erroneously early by several thousand years (Tankersley, Munson, and Smith 1987), and contamination of individual charcoal specimens by small amounts of dissolved or powdered geological carbon could presumably yield dates that were several hundred years too old. However, lignite has a specific gravity and spectrographic index different from charcoal, so doubtful charcoal samples can be tested for the presence of lignite before dating. Karl Turekian of the Yale Radiocarbon Laboratory and Rupert Housley of the Oxford University Radiocarbon Accelerator Laboratory examined Parmana charcoal samples that gave early radiocarbon dates, prior to dating, and found no lignite in them. Further, no anomalously early radiocarbon dates have come from the upper levels of the stratigraphy of any sites, whether the sites had lignite or not; no sites that produced specimens of lignite (Los Mangos, Corozal, and Ronquin) have produced too-early dates; and to our knowledge, no layers that produced early prehistoric dates have as yet produced specimens of lignite. To the "long" chronology archaeologists, although the possibility of lignite contamination could not be eliminated, it seemed that lignite contamination alone could not explain all the early radiocarbon dates.

The long chronology is supported by several additional considerations. The forces expected to produce erroneous archaeological dates are considered more likely to produce too recent than too early dates, as explained below and documented in texts on radiocarbon dating (Gowlett and Hedges 1985; Hedges and Gowlett 1986; Taylor 1987). The long chronology also seems a more economical hypothesis than the short chronology because it allows acceptance of more radiocarbon dates than the short. In Parmana the short chronology requires across-the-board rejection of the majority of radiocarbon dates—all the early ones because they are considered too ancient, and all the modern and post-conquest ones because they are not prehistoric. Even series of early dates that occur in stratigraphic order with no inconsistencies, such as those for the early Corozal 1 phase at the Parmana site (Table 8), must be rejected in the short chronology. Only the later prehistoric dates are acceptable, and all these are accepted at face value, even though the presence of modern-age charcoal in prehistoric layers indicates that the age of aggregate samples is likely to be skewed toward the modern era, to some degree, due to the admixture of modern charcoal with prehistoric.

Even more important, when the early prehistoric dates are removed from the chronology, the remaining prehistoric dates do not produce an intelligible sequence but cluster in the late prehistoric era. Thus, acceptance of all the recent prehistoric dates makes most of the phases of the region contemporary, leaving the region with negligible cultural history, in contrast to adjacent regions. The extensive phase overlap has been explained by the "short" chronologists as the product of synchronous ethnic diversity, but this explanation is falsified by the cultural stratigraphy in the region, which shows that pottery of the three traditions lies in superimposed layers at Corozal and other well-preserved multi-component sites in the Parmana region. Material that is contemporary in the short chronology, in fact, is separated vertically by more than a meter of strata at Corozal, a situation difficult to account for by stratigraphic principles. The short chronology also required that the artifact-rich four meters of deposit at Corozal had accrued in only a few hundred years, an unlikely eventuality, even taking into account the soil-forming processes characteristic of the habitat.

The long chronology is now also supported by the finding that Initial pottery in the tropical lowlands substantially predates Andean and northern South American pottery. The theoretical premise of the short chronology—that pottery developed in the Andean region and subsequently spread to the lowlands—is therefore no longer valid. A large series of early Holocene dates from ceramic sites in the eastern tropical lowlands has established that the ceramic period in the region began much earlier than archaeologists realized twenty years ago. This pottery is dated radiometrically between about 5,500 and 2,000 B.C. (Roosevelt et al. 1991; Roosevelt 1995; Simoes 1981; Smithsonian Anthropology Archives 1965–85; Williams 1981). Specifically, pottery-age shell middens at the mouth of the Amazon near Bélem (Simoes 1981), at Santarem, 900 km upriver in the Amazon (Roosevelt et al. 1991), and in coastal Guyana (Williams 1981) have produced thirty-nine radiometric dates between 5000 and 2500 B.C. on pottery, shell, and charcoal. These dates seem conclusive evidence for the age of the pottery because they were run directly on the pottery itself by the methods of accelerator radiocarbon dating and thermoluminescence, as well on a wide variety of materials including carbonized botanical remains and fauna, all associated with the pottery in the stratigraphy. The dates on the different materials fall in the same time ranges and are quite consistent stratigraphically.

The early Formative dates in the Parmana long chronology overlap neatly with the dates of the terminal phase of Initial pottery, and the early Formative pottery from Parmana bears some technical and stylistic similarities to some of the Initial pottery. For example, the Initial pottery from Santarem and Guyana, like La Gruta tradition pottery, is of oxidized, grit-tempered paste, and the Formative pottery from Santarem includes decoration by shallow broad-line incision and sherds of thick griddles, like La Gruta tradition pottery. The short chronology, in contrast, leaves an inexplicable gap of three thousand years between Initial and Formative pottery phases in eastern South America.

Further, sites in neighboring regions have produced radiocarbon dates and pottery that are comparable to the long chronology but not to the short chronology. The sequence in the Lower Orinoco parallels the Parmana long chronology in having a transition from grit-tempered Saladoid-Barrancoid styles to sponge-tempered Arauquinoid styles during the period 1000 B.C. to A.D. 1000. A suite of radiocarbon dates has also come from Aguerito, a site several hundred miles upriver from Parmana, where the ceramic phases closely parallel the Parmana phases stylistically. The dates for the early Corozal-like pottery from Aguerito are nearly identical with the radiocarbon dates for the early part of the tradition in the Parmana region (Zucchi, Tarble, and Vaz 1984). These similarities have not been recognized because the excavators of Aguerito aligned their Corozal 1—like phase with the Ronquin Sombra phase, although that phase is not comparable to the Aguerito phase. (The pottery attributes of the Corozal phase are compared to those in other South American regions in Chapter 3.) Finally, the dates of the early Formative Mabaruma Phase of Guyana, 2000–1500 B.C., are identical to the early La Gruta dates (Williams 1992).

Other evidence relevant to the question of the dating of the early phases of the Parmana sequence has come from the Antilles. In the late 1970s and 1980s, it was assumed that red-and-white painted Saladoid pottery had arrived in the islands from the Orinoco and coasts of the Caribbean mainland several hundred years after Christ (Rouse and Allaire 1978). Since then, numerous radiocarbon dates have documented that such pottery arrived in the Antilles by at least 500 B.C. (Siegel 1992). In the Parmana long chronology, such pottery dates between approximately 2500 B.C. and A.D. 500. The short chronology for mainland Saladoid pottery, however, means that the Saladoid style would have to have been introduced from the islands to the mainland, an intriguing reversal of prior interpretations but certainly one not accepted by most archaeologists, due to the lack of evidence for earlier pottery in the Antilles.

3. Accelerator and Thermoluminescence Dating Program

Additional chronological evidence for the Parmana ceramic sequence has come from an experimental program of accelerator and thermoluminescence dating on archaeological materials from the region. In order to try to straighten out the prehistoric lowland chronological sequence, we contracted with Rupert Housley of the Radiocarbon Accelerator Laboratory of Oxford University and James Feathers of the Luminescence Laboratory of the University of Washington to date a wide range of samples from the excavations at La Gruta, Ronquin, Parmana, and Corozal. The results of this program of research—a series of twenty-six accelerator and thermoluminescence dates—tend to confirm the basic framework of the long chronology but suggest the need to adjust the estimated lengths of individual phases of the sequence.

Definitive absolute dating has been a problem at many tropical lowland sites, which often yield a contradictory suite of dates ranging from obviously modern to several millennia B.C. Generally, radiocarbon specialists hold that contamination of dated material by more recent carbon is much more common than the reverse. Thus, a likely explanation for the occurrence of unexpectedly recent dates is the contamination of archaeological deposits by soil organic matter and by soot and charcoal from modern burning, washed down the soil profile by rain or introduced by soil disturbances. Many Orinoco archaeological sites are still occupied today, and the inhabitants dig pits and postholes into the deposits and, as at La Gruta, dig into the sites to make charcoal ovens. Also, sandy dune sites such as Ronquin, La Gruta, and Aguerito are especially subject to aeolian deflation and invasion by burrowing animals. In the tropical lowlands, also, ant nests are a common kind of disturbance that moves material downward (Roosevelt 1984a), and snakes and rodents burrow into sites. Because of the multitude of such taphonomic factors working to introduce recent carbon into the archaeological sites in Parmana, erroneously early dates are less likely than erroneously late dates.

Despite this intrusion of modern material into prehistoric sites, in the 1970s it was routine for archaeologists to date samples made up of charcoal that had been dispersed throughout broad excavation levels, rather than samples from a restricted, controlled location within a layer. The reason for this procedure was that, before accelerator radiocarbon dating, such aggregate radiocarbon samples were often the only samples large enough to date. Because aggregate samples commonly combine charcoal from several different ages, the resulting dates are averages of the dates of charcoal from various temporal contexts. Given the operation of the force of gravity, such dates from mixed samples are usually more recent than radiocarbon samples "true" to a specific, temporally limited context. Accordingly, radiocarbon specialists highly recommend that charcoal for dates be collected only as individual unitary samples from specific, stratigraphically controlled layers and features, rather than from material scattered through broad levels (Hedges and Gowlett 1986; Taylor 1987). Many of the first set of early prehistoric dates in the Parmana sequence were from localized contexts under good stratigraphic control, such as floors or hearths (Roosevelt 1978; Rouse 1978; Rouse, Allaire, and Boomert MS; Vargas 1981), but these still were aggregate samples because such narrowly defined contexts do not usually yield enough charcoal for conventional dating. Therefore, contamination by unseen disturbances could not be eliminated, despite the good stratigraphic control.

Accelerator dating, unlike conventional radiocarbon dating, can date single objects directly because it requires only small amounts of carbon. In this way, heterogeneous aggregate samples can be avoided, and specific objects of interest, such as pottery sherds or corn kernels, can be dated directly. In an attempt to get uncontaminated radiocarbon dates for the Parmana sequence, Housley dated a number of sherds with organic inclusions and samples of burnt food stuck to sizeable sherds less likely than small charcoal chunks to have been moved by minor intrusions. We also selected for accelerator dating several charcoal pieces from the same block of stratigraphy, to see what the pattern of age variation in aggregate samples would be. According to the reasoning behind the long chronology, aggregate samples combine early prehistoric cultural material and intrusive modern material. According to the short chronology, in contrast, the aggregate samples would contain late prehistoric cultural material, too-ancient geological carbon, but no recent carbon.

The accelerator results on the sherds and carbonized plant specimens present some interpretive uncertainties deriving from object-handling procedures customary in the 1970s. Because the Parmana project took place before accelerator dating was available to archaeologists, the sherds from the Parmana excavations were treated in the then-standard manner: they were washed in water, dried in the open under the sun, and handled during excavation and sorting. They were not treated as radiocarbon samples, which should be kept clean from dust and other contaminants. Therefore, sherds had ample opportunity to pick up extraneous modern carbon in their fabric or on their surfaces. Carbonized plant specimens also were subject to contamination by carbon in the dust and water and on people's hands, because such specimens were much too small to date by the methods available in the 1970s. Further, the project botanist placed the carbonized plant material in gel capsules and cellophane envelopes that became dry, brittle, powdery, and broken after about five years. When I received the samples back for accelerator dating, some seeds had fallen out of their containers, confusing the provenience, and all were coated with powdered cellophane, gelatin, and other fine-grained debris. Such contamination factors would generally be expected to have the effect of producing dates that were slightly younger than the true age of the object. The specimens dated by Oxford were cleaned rigorously with standard procedures, but particulate insoluble carbon lodged in the structure of a specimen is probably impossible to remove. The accelerator dates, therefore, are not necessarily definitive because the samples dated could not be protected from contamination. Nevertheless, in certain ways they have clarified the Parmana sequence.

First, the accelerator dating of individual carbon chunks and seeds did document, precisely as predicted by the long chronology, that aggregate charcoal samples undoubtedly contain carbon specimens of different ages due to mechanical mixture of prehistoric and modern charcoal in the ground. Most interesting, our accelerator dates on individual carbonized seeds such as maize, palm seed shells, and the seeds of tree fruits show that postconquest or terminal prehistoric specimens have undoubtedly intruded deeply into the archaeological sites in some cases. In the case of the La Gruta phase, the samples gave two types of dates—recent and early Formative—as predicted by the long chronology. They did not give the geological and late prehistoric ages predicted by the short chronology. For example, *Sterculia* seeds from La Gruta deposits about 2 m below the surface gave a historic-epoch radiocarbon date of A.D. 1720, while a charcoal chunk (verified as charcoal, not lignite) from the assemblage gave a date of 2840 B.C. Aggregate samples from these depths gave a range of dates indicating a range of levels of contamination with recent carbon: 2140 B.C., 1585 B.C., A.D. 720, and A.D. 1660.

Like the *Sterculia* and palm seeds dated, two of the dated maize kernels from the Corozal site were found to be out of stratigraphic order, illustrating again how individual seeds can move downward in archaeological sites. It is important to reiterate that when the introduction or use of a particular plant is important in an archaeological theory, it is absolutely necessary to date specimens of the plant directly, not just the accompanying charcoal or pottery, because of the likelihood of spurious associations due to taphonomic processes. In the case of the few anachronistic maize specimens at Corozal, the stratigraphic displacement was slight and does not alter the finding that the first documented maize in Parmana occurs in the Corozal phase. The accelerator radiocarbon results also show a difference of as much as five hundred years between the dated maize kernels from Corozal levels and the carbon in or on sherds from the same Corozal levels. This difference is an expected one since wood for fuel may come from trees several hundred years old at the time of cutting, whereas a corn kernel is likely to have been formed in the actual year it was burned. Despite the updating of some Corozal maize kernels to Camoruco phases, isotopic evidence for maize occurs as early as A.D. 630 in the ratios of carbon in and on dated sherds. Thus, by late Corozal 1 or Corozal 2 times, maize was common enough as food at the site to be detectable archaeologically in several contexts. Maize had become the staple food in the diet by Corozal 3 or Camoruco 3 times, as the isotopic results on human bone have shown (van der Merwe, Roosevelt, and Vogel 1981; Roosevelt, Krueger, and Sullivan MSa).

Our experiment in accelerator dating of individual specimens demonstrates that recent and early prehistoric charcoal pieces are found together in the stratigraphy of sites and confirms that combined samples will produce radiocarbon dates much more recent than the archaeological context. This finding strongly supports the long chronology and is not accounted for by the short chronology, which treats the aggregate samples as representing the true date of the archaeological context. The accelerator dating program did not support the prediction of the "short" chronologists that geological-age carbon would be found mixed in with late prehistoric charcoal. None of the accelerator-dated samples had dates in the range of lignite or other types of ancient carbonaceous material.

In a parallel effort to verify the length of the chronological sequence, luminescence dating was carried out on pottery from Parmana. When the first set of radiocarbon dates had been run, Karl Turekian of Yale University carried out thermoluminescence (TL) measurements on three sherds from La Gruta. Dosimetry was estimated from analysis of soil samples from the site. The resulting dates were of modern age. There was a possibility that the TL of the sherds had been reset, because, after washing, the pottery had been dried outdoors in the bright sun and heat characteristic of the Middle Orinoco.

More recently, James Feathers of the Luminescence Laboratory of the University of Washington, Seattle, and Peter Clark and Gillian Carr of Oxford University have carried out further luminescence-dating tests on pottery from the region, to evaluate the reason for earlier problems with TL dating and to check the radiocarbon dates.

The Luminescence Laboratory of the University of Washington studied five sherds from La Gruta tradition phases in Parmana: one from La Gruta, two from lower levels of Ronquin Sombra, and two from Corozal 1 phase levels at Corozal. The results of the research revealed disequilibrium in the U–238 decay chain for large quartz inclusions and unusual dose-induced sensitivity changes with the fine-grain technique that prevented a linear fit of TL curves to the additive dose curve. As yet, then, the OSL and TL dating of La Gruta tradition pottery remains too problematic technically to clarify the absolute dating of the tradition's phases in Parmana.

To verify the later part of the sequence, Oxford ran TL dates on two of the Corozal site sherds that had been dated by AMS with dual measurements on charcoal adhering to the surface and on carbon in the fabric of the sherd. The AMS had showed that the surface carbon was younger than the carbon in the pottery fabric. Possible reasons for the difference were because sherd surfaces were contaminated with more recent carbon from groundwater or museum dust or because the pottery clay contained old carbon. The Oxford TL results on the sherds fit the former interpretation, rather than the latter. The TL ages were close to the radiocarbon ages of the carbon within the pottery sherds, when calibrated to calendar years, but older than the calibrated radiocarbon ages of their surfaces. Camoruco 3 sherd 32–355 gave a TL of 535 ± 77, compared with the one-sigma calibrated radiocarbon range of 495–545 (Ox2488) for the fabric and 320–515 (Ox2487) for surface carbon. Camoruco 2 sherd 43–35 gave a TL of 794 ± 97, compared with a calibrated radiocarbon date range of 735–925 (OxA2492) for fabric and 575–685 (OxA2491) for surface carbon. (See Table 8 for the uncalibrated dates for these samples.) Thus the carbon within the pottery fabric was close in age to the TL date for the firing of the pot, but the carbon on the surface of the pottery was younger. These results tend to accord better with the hypothesis of a long chronology than with the short chronology.

The new dates that have been run on Middle Orinoco material since 1980 tend to confirm the early prehistoric beginning of the ceramic sequence, but they reveal great variation in the length of phases and several substantial temporal gaps in the sequence. Some of the earlier phases appear to have been quite long-lived, and some of the later phases appear to have been comparatively short-lived. According to the new dates, the beginning of the ceramic sequence in this part of the Orinoco is as early as, or earlier than, the date provided for in the long chronology. The early Formative age of La Gruta phase pottery is confirmed by the new dates and its beginning extended back to about 2500 B.C. The early dates for the beginning of the La Gruta phase make it a very long phase, lasting about eight hundred years, followed by a chronological gap containing only one date until the cluster of dates for the beginning of the Corozal tradition around 1000 B.C. The early beginning of the Corozal tradition was confirmed by the accelerator dates, which show that the dates of both aggregate charcoal samples and individual charcoal pieces from early Corozal 1 levels at Parmana fall in the early years of the first millennium B.C. Confirmation of the early beginning of early Corozal 1 and the ending of late Corozal 1 at A.D. 500 make Corozal 1 a very long phase with a long dateless gap in the middle, as was the case for its counterpart at Aguerito. The apparent length of the phase accords with the evidence in the seriation for significant ceramic change from early, to middle, to late Corozal 1 times. In contrast to these early phases, the later phases in the sequence, Corozal 2 through Camoruco 3, are much shorter, ranging from about one hundred to three hundred years in duration. The new sequence suggests, consequently, that the pace of cultural change varied greatly with time, being slow during the early part of the occupation and generally speeding up in later prehistory.

Despite the need to verify the absolute dating of the Parmana sequence with further research, obtaining a relative chronology for studying prehistoric evolutionary change was the main goal and achievement of the Corozal excavations and ceramic analysis. In Chapter 3, I summarize the characteristics of the Parmana ceramic sequence and then present in detail the ceramic data for the Corozal and Camoruco traditions from the excavations at Corozal.

3. The Ceramic Seriation

Having described the stratigraphy at Corozal and related it to the excavation levels and chronology, I will now summarize the ceramic sequence that our research produced. Then, I will explain the method of the ceramic analysis and describe each of the seriated ceramic modes.

A. The Parmana Ceramic Sequence

Based on the results of our excavations, the Parmana sequence has been divided into three major chronological divisions called *traditions,* each in turn divided into three parts called *phases* (Table 1). The traditions, in turn, are related to several supraregional ceramic entities called *horizons* or *series*.

My terminology for archaeological categories in the sequence has the following rationale. A phase, in my use of the word, is a regional–temporal occupational entity that represents a group of people with a particular lifeway and material culture living in a specific region at a specific time. The term *complex,* as used in northern lowland archaeology (Cruxent and Rouse 1958–59; Willey 1971), is more or less synonymous with the term *phase.* I use it to refer specifically to the collection of material on which the definition of a phase is based. The meaning of the term *assemblage* is different, for it is a more preliminary analytical entity of the material found associated in an excavation level or series of levels. Due to taphonomic processes, the assemblage may include material from several different phases, which would then be analytically separated through comparison with the materials in other stratigraphic units. Traditions are regional–temporal sequences composed of a succession of related phases of occupation. Earlier in our analysis we used the term *phase* for the larger grouping and *subphase* for the smaller units (Roosevelt 1980). Here, we term the longer-lasting entity *tradition* and the subunits *phases,* in order to avoid the cumbersome term *subphase.* Often, archaeological phases can be defined by one or more integral styles of ceramics, because the abundance and ubiquity of ceramic material make it a good index fossil or identifier for particular occupations. For me, a style in art history is characterized by a particular iconography and mode of representation or decoration, usually focused on ceramics though it may appear in other media. The greater abundance of ceramics in comparison with other types of material in the lowlands makes it the most desirable material for stylistic seriation. The technology of the pottery of related styles, in terms of firing conditions and temper, may or may not be similar, so it sometimes may be useful for chronological analysis to distinguish art style from the technological aspects of ceramics. In other cases, an integral style may be executed in a particular pottery technology. The ceramic styles of phases and traditions may be related to supraregional ceramic-stylistic groupings, called *horizons* or *series* (Cruxent and Rouse 1958–59). I prefer to use Rouse and Cruxent's term *series* in some cases, rather than *horizon,* because it does not have the chronological implications of horizon. Some of the lowland long-lived ceramic series are more like widespread traditions than like synchronous, temporally limited horizons. The ceramic styles of a series are considered to be historically related to one another, either because they share a common origin or because they influence one another. Phases, traditions, horizons, and series are usually arbitrarily named after the first site where they were recognized (Lanning 1967), and use of the site's name for a ceramic entity should not be taken to imply that the entity originated at that site or even in its region. Geographic origins of styles often take years of comparative cultural historical research to establish and are rarely evident at the time of first definition of the entity (Rouse 1986). In many cases the geographic origin of a series of styles is never settled to everyone's satisfaction. Therefore, the supraregional ceramic entities cannot practically be named according to their hypothetical origins, for that would result in constant renaming and in the use of different names by scholars of different opinions about origins.

LA GRUTA TRADITION. The La Gruta tradition is the earliest major division yet defined in the Parmana regional sequence. It is comprised of the sequential La Gruta, Ronquin, and Ronquin Sombra phases. These three early phases of prehistoric occupation in the Parmana region primarily belong stylistically with the Saladoid and Barrancoid series, defined first from complexes of the Lower Orinoco (Cruxent and Rouse 1958–59; Rouse and Cruxent 1963; Vargas 1976; Roosevelt 1978, 1980; Sanoja 1979). Although they were first defined dichotomously as two series of styles—one with plastic decoration and one with red-and-white painting—further excavations and stylistic study show that most of the mainland styles of these series have both kinds of decoration, often on the same piece. Therefore, I use the term *Saladoid-Barrancoid series* to refer to pottery complexes characterized by both the painted and plastic decorative styles. The Saladoid and Barrancoid series have been found primarily in the Middle and Lower Orinoco, the Caribbean coasts and islands, and the Guianas, although preliminary research in the Amazon mainstreams in Brazil and Bolivia suggests the existence of related styles there also (Boomert 1983; Dougherty and Calandra 1981–82; Hilbert 1959b, 1968; Roosevelt et al. M.S.). Barrancoid pottery styles, apparently without Saladoid components, have been excavated from sites in Peru (Lathrap 1970).

The La Gruta tradition phases of Parmana share a predominant pottery fabric of reddish orange to pinkish buff color and abundant grit temper. The nature of the grit varies a good deal, but most seems to be variegated crushed rock, not sand as it is often called. The paste color is quite uniform, with only a slight gray or buff core, and the contour of outer surfaces is very even and smooth. Most of this pottery is richly decorated with well-executed and sophisticated modeled-carved animal lug handles, sidewall bosses, or vessel necks (Roosevelt 1980, 200–202, Figs. 52–54) and broad-line incision in panels on or below rims (Roosevelt 1980, 197–200, Figs. 49–51). This style of plastic decoration was first defined by Rouse and Cruxent at the sites of Barrancas and Los Barrancos, hence the adjective *Barrancoid*. Also characteristic of the La Gruta tradition grit-tempered ware pottery is elaborate decoration of red-and-white Saladoid-style paint (Roosevelt 1980, 204–205, Fig. 55; described *below,* Sec. C, 1), first defined by these scholars at the site of Saladero in the Lower Orinoco. The Saladoid paint occurs either by itself or together with the Barrancoid plastic decoration. The basic shapes of the grit-tempered pottery include very common round or oval open bowls and plain griddles, asymmetrical animal-effigy vessels, and composite silhouette bottles. The bottles, bowls, and effigy vessels commonly bear modeled-incised and/or painted animal-shape figures on their handles or rims. Most vessel rims are slightly squared or triangular, and there are distinctive thickened and/or flanged rims. The round base predominates, but there are also slightly flattened, recessed, and ring bases.

A contrasting minority ware in the La Gruta phases, rare but ever present, is dark tan in surface color and densely sherd-tempered, often with an admixture of some kind of partly fugitive vegetal material. The sherd temper can be observed as small, lighter-colored square chunks within the paste, often with the original smoothed, slipped outer vessel surfaces still visible. The cross sections of vessel walls are usually dark gray-brown in color, indicating incomplete oxidation and/or incomplete combustion of organic matter. The absence of abrasive sand or sponge temper in this ware makes it feel softer to the touch than the other wares. Like the temper and color, the shape and style of this pottery are very different from the Saladoid and Barrancoid styles. The sherd-tempered paste was shaped most commonly into thick-walled, large bowls, basins, and jars. Rims are primarily simple and round, squared or beveled, or tapered and out-turned, a range of shapes different from those of the gritwares. Only very rarely are there flanged or thickened rims similar to those characteristic of the grit-tempered pottery. The sherd-tempered pottery is often incised with simple, geometric, basketlike patterns on the tops of rims and sides of vessels (Roosevelt 1980, 206, Fig. 56). The incisions often were filled with red pigment, and there are very rare examples of polychrome paint or Saladoid paint on sherds without incised decoration. This sherd-tempered ceramic style, which was first described for the Parmana region, is named the Parmana style, and, since pottery with similar decoration has been found on other parts of the Orinoco and possibly beyond, it is thought of, preliminarily, as part of a Parmanoid series. Howard called this pottery style "atypical" Y–group pottery.

The grit-tempered pottery styles of the La Gruta tradition phases are distinguished from one another by differing color and hardness of the pottery paste, characteristics of the grit temper, and differential distribution of certain modes of shape and decoration. For example, La Gruta grit-tempered pottery is friable and light orange in color and lacks flanged bowl rims. Being the oldest pottery complex of the tradition, it has begun to undergo rehydration and disintegration, like Initial pottery from the Lower Amazon. Although La Gruta phase grit-tempered pottery is aesthetically of the highest quality, it is so fragile that it might be considered less technically accomplished than that of the other La Gruta tradition complexes. Ronquin and Ronquin Sombra gritware pottery is darker, harder, and smoother; and the Ronquin Sombra pottery has an abundance of flanged rims.

The early part of the La Gruta tradition is dated between about 2500 and 1600 B.C. by six radiocarbon dates from excavations in the lower strata at La Gruta (Table 8). (*See* Chapter 2, G.) The five dates from our excavations derive from features such as hearths or floors, and their 2-sigma ranges are consistent with the order of superposition of the frequently sloping strata. Numerous dates from my and others' excavations in disturbed or superficial strata at the site are not consistent with the stratigraphy and cluster in the circumconquest era (Rouse and Allaire 1978; Rouse, Allaire, and Boomert M.S.). Our dating of different individual specimens from La Gruta strata demonstrated that the prehistoric charcoal is mixed with historic and modern charcoal. One anomalous date of 6260 B.C. was measured on a sample that was not checked before dating for the presence of carbonaceous contaminants (Vargas 1981). The third and early second millennium dates for the La Gruta phase are paralleled by similar dates for material in basal strata at Aguerito in another region of the Middle Orinoco (Table 8; Zucchi, Tarble, and Vaz 1984).

The Ronquin phase has no reliable absolute dates, due to a lack of sufficient prehistoric charcoal in the relevant strata of the Ronquin site, and the subsequent Ronquin Sombra phase is dated by only one radiocarbon measurement from the Ronquin Sombra component at Los Merecurotes site, around 1020

B.C. In addition to these dates, there are numerous anomalous dates from measurements on apparently contaminated aggregate carbon samples from Ronquin (listed here in Table 8 and in Rouse 1978, Rouse and Allaire 1978, and Rouse, Allaire, and Boomert M.S.). These latter problematical dates range from 50 B.C.. to modern times. The disturbed condition of the sand-dune archaeological sites, described above, is the reason that charcoal of recent date occurs in the archaeological deposits.

At present, La Gruta is the earliest known phase of the Saladoid-Barrancoid series in South America, but few regions have been investigated by professional archaeologists, so we expect that future work will reveal related phases both earlier and later.

COROZAL TRADITION. In the following Corozal tradition, a new tempering agent, sponge spicules, is introduced and replaces the earlier kinds as the predominant temper. Technologically and stylistically, this is a period of transition, and the pottery complex is characterized by rapid change and the co-occurrence of several different wares with different combinations of sponge-spicule, sherd, clay, and sand tempering. At this time, decorative styles cross over ware groups, and several distinctive new pottery styles appear in the region with new forms of modeling, incision, and painting.

Most of the Corozal tradition pottery is beige to light buff-gray in color, tempered with moderate to relatively abundant amounts of sponge spicules, a moderate amount of sherd and/or clay bit temper, and rare, waterworn sand particles. The color is very variable, both between vessels and within vessels. Thus firing seems not to have been very carefully controlled, and finished surfaces are not very even in contour. This sponge-spicule-tempered ware bears a wide range of decoration (Figs. 17–20; Pl. 8 and 9) and, as a ware, seems to be new to the region. Howard included it in his Z–group pottery.

A much smaller proportion of the Corozal complex pottery is the thick, Parmana-ware sherd-and-fiber-tempered ware (Pl. 7, *top;* Fig. 15; Tables 11–14) of the incised style that Howard included as atypical Y–group pottery. This pottery ware begins at a percentage of 40% at the beginning of Corozal and quickly drops to 20% and then 3% before the end of the first Corozal phase. An even smaller proportion of the Corozal phase pottery is reddish, grit-tempered pottery related to the predominant Saladoid-Barrancoid wares of the earlier La Gruta tradition, with occasional additions of small amounts of sherd temper (Pl. 7, *bottom;* Fig. 16; Tables 15–18, 23–26). This pottery ware begins at about 17% at the beginning of the phase and drops rapidly to about 1% by the end of Corozal 1. Howard included this in his Y–group pottery. The least abundant ware (fewer than 50 sherds overall and therefore too rare to be seriated) is a fine-paste incised style with only small amounts of very finely ground temper, which includes varying amounts of sponge, sand, sherd, and shell. This pottery bears a variety of decoration ranging from motifs of the earlier Saladoid-Barrancoid styles to new motifs introduced with the sponge-tempered ware.

Some of the Corozal phase sherds bear classic Saladoid-Barrancoid series decoration. These decorative holdovers from the La Gruta tradition occur mainly in the grit-tempered ware and include rare examples of both Barrancoid modeled-incised decoration and Saladoid red-and-white paint. In addition, some Barrancoid modeling and incision also occurs in Corozal sponge-tempered wares (Pl. 8, *top;* Fig. 17). In contrast to their abundance in La Gruta tradition phases, the Barrancoid modeling and grooving and Saladoid painting are extremely rare during the Corozal phase and much less elaborate. La Gruta tradition components of only a few thousand sherds have produced hundreds of decorated sherds with elaborate red-and-white painting and/or modeled-carved zoomorphic decoration, whereas the large Corozal site assemblage of about thirty thousand sherds includes fewer than 50 grit-tempered sherds decorated with the Saladoid paint, zoomorphic adornos, or Barrancoid incision. In addition, the Saladoid and classic Barrancoid decoration of Corozal gritware pottery is for the most part much simpler and cruder than it is in the La Gruta tradition gritwares. All these differences make it easy to distinguish Corozal phase gritware from the La Gruta tradition phases gritwares.

During the Corozal tradition, while vessels of older wares and styles continue to be made of their characteristic traditional grit- or sherd-tempered paste, there are also in each style a few examples of sherds tempered with either a mixture of the old and new tempers or solely the new sponge temper. Also, as mentioned above, there is a new Barrancoid decorative type with modeled-grooved decoration ultimately derived from the La Gruta tradition but executed on sponge-tempered pottery (Pl. 8, *top;* Fig. 17; Tables 27–30). This style resembles styles found in the Barrancas and Los Barrancos sites in the Lower Amazon more than it resembles the pottery of the La Gruta tradition in Parmana. In addition to the Barrancoid sponge-tempered adaptations, the shapes and decorative motifs typical of the Parmana ware are transferred to new shapes in the new sponge-tempered pottery (Fig. 18; Pl. 8, *bottom;* Tables 31–34).

The new sponge-tempered wares of the Corozal tradition include several distinct decorated types, some of them differing slightly in the use of temper. All the types have a little sherd temper or clay and sparse inclusions of waterworn sand in addition to the sponge temper. One decorated sponge-tempered type, mentioned above, has shallow curvilinear incised designs related to Barrancoid styles, occasionally accompanied by hemispherical nubbins related to animal imagery such as eyes or ears (Fig. 17; Pl. 8, *top;* Tables 27–30). This type has many diverse shapes, most of which stem from the La Gruta tradition or from a similar tradition in another region. Its rare painting, however, is entirely new to the region and includes powdery, fugitive pinkish mauve and yellowish pigments. Another common type with relatively abundant sponge temper has simple, crude, rectilinear incised decoration in geometric patterns on the rims and sides of bowls (Fig.18; Pl. 8, *bottom;* Tables 31–34) and appears distantly related to the incised Parmana sherd-and-fiber-tempered ware of the La Gruta tradition phases, as mentioned above. As in the case of the sherd-ware, there is often red pigment rubbed in the rectilinear incisions, but this new sponge-tempered version has sharper incisions and much thinner and more curving vessel walls than the Parmana ware. Its rims, in addition, are much more tapering than most Parmana ware rims.

Another sponge-tempered decorated taxon is a distinctive type comprising asymmetrical slightly closed bowls with tapering rims adorned with vertical rim strap handles often decorated on top with small nubbins or modeled animal-head ornaments executed in crude modeling and punctation (Fig. 20; Pl. 9, *bottom;* Tables 39–42). These may be crude descendants of the famous La Gruta tradition asymmetrical bowls with D-shaped handles with animal lugs on top, but unlike the La Gruta tradition bowls, the sponge-tempered bowls have two handles and do not have any incision or modeling on the rims or sides. The nubbins and rare animal heads on the handles are the only decoration. This crude decorative type seems to be of an early style related to the widespread Incised and Punctate Horizon of the tropical lowlands (Meggers and Evans 1961), of which the Arauquinoid series is a later member. Another Corozal tradition decorated vessel type related to the later Incised and Punctate Horizon includes animal- or human-effigy jars, mostly very simple in iconography and extremely rare (Pl. 13, *bottom*). There are also rare examples of crudely executed animal-effigy bowls that change rim shape and become quite common in Camoruco times. These effigy jars and bowls appear to have no close relatives in the La Gruta tradition and seem to have come in as part of the decorative complex associated with sponge tempering.

There are also in the Corozal tradition several new painted styles on sponge-tempered pottery, a banded red-and-white one being the most common phase-wide one (Fig. 19; Pl. 9, *top;* Tables 35–38). This kind of paint is new to the region. As mentioned above, the Corozal tradition rectilinear incision on spongewares occasionally has red pigment rubbed into the incisions, which is a trait also characteristic of the Parmanoid sherdwares. The shallow curvilinear incised pottery of sponge-tempered paste, mentioned above, sometimes bears traces of overall or zoned mauve and/or yellow post-fired paint. There are also a few sponge-tempered white-painted sherds, though these seem to have been part of vessels bearing the red-and-white banded decoration. A few sherds of sponge-tempered pottery and fine-paste ware bear Saladoid-style red-and-white paint, but this painting style is more common on the grit-tempered ware mentioned above. The Saladoid paint, in any case, is extremely rare in the Corozal tradition, in contrast to its abundance in La Gruta tradition phases.

A very rare new painted ware that appears for the first time in the Corozal tradition has a geometric linear polychrome decoration of red, black, and brown on white or buff (Pl. 9, *top,* N–R). This decoration occurs with a variety of light-colored pastes, either sponge temper combined with sherds or fine paste with no observable inclusions. The number of sherds is too few to reveal characteristic shapes. The polychrome seems similar to a rare linear polychrome style found on Parmanoid ware sherds in earlier phases.

The Corozal tradition has thirteen radiocarbon dates on charcoal, carbonized seeds, and pottery. Four dates between about 1000 B.C. and 700 B.C. were run by different laboratories on charcoal collected from features at the Parmana site for the beginning of the phase, early Corozal 1. From the Corozal site there are eight dates on charcoal and pottery between about A.D. 500 and 800 for the later part of the phase, late Corozal 1 through Corozal 3, leaving a gap of twelve hundred years between the early and late parts of the phase. As in the levels of other traditions in the region, in Corozal 2 and 3 levels at Corozal there were other dates that fell one to three hundred years too early or too late for their stratigraphic position (Table 8, dates with asterisks), presumably because of disturbances in the archaeological deposit. In early Corozal 1 levels at Parmana, however, all dates were consistent and without anomalies, so there is no indication in the radiocarbon evidence for any taphonomic or technical problem with the dating of the early part of the phase.

CAMORUCO TRADITION. Camoruco tradition pottery is made mainly in a ware with heavy sponge temper and sparse clay temper. Minor wares of extremely rare occurrence include a coarse, grit-tempered pottery and pottery tempered with caraipe, a siliceous wood ash. The sponge-tempered pottery tends to be thick, heavy, and poorly smoothed, of a buff color more gray than that of Corozal tradition sponge-tempered wares. The most common phase-wide decoration is complex modeled, appliqué, incised, and punctate decoration, representing geometrics and humans or animals (Figs. 24–26; Pl. 10–12). Such decoration first appears during the Corozal tradition and becomes the dominant plastic decoration during Camoruco times. Human-effigy jars and bowl rim adornos are common. The most common tradition-wide painted ware is a powdery mauve and/or yellow, post-fired painted pottery that occasionally has tempering by caraipe instead of sponge spicules (Pl. 10, *bottom;* Fig. 22; Tables 47–50). Primarily restricted to the latest phase of the tradition are a very common maroon paint (Pl. 11, *top;* Fig. 23; Tables 51–54) and a complex type of rectilinear incision and fine punctation (Fig. 24; Pl. 11, *bottom;* Tables 55–58). The maroon paint, rectilinear incision, and modeled-incised lugs of the tradition are very similar to those of archaeological phases identified in the environs of Arauquin, and the name of this site has been assigned to a horizon of similar styles in the Orinoco called the Arauquinoid series (Cruxent and Rouse 1958–59). This series is considered a member of the widespread, late-prehistoric Incised and Punctate horizon of the lowlands (Lathrap 1970).

There are twenty-nine dates for the Camoruco phase, which range from about A.D. 800 through 1550. This is the final prehistoric phase in the Parmana region, and later archaeological deposits are characterized primarily by the presence of pieces of thick, coarse oxidized earthenwares, glass, iron, rare soft-paste glazed pottery, and glazed, transfer-printed English ironstone ceramics.

B. Method of Ceramic Analysis

The following sections describe the seriation of the pottery from the site of Corozal, which served as the type site for the Corozal and Camoruco traditions. Before describing the pottery according to the seriation, I will first describe the methods of the seriation.

The purpose of a classification determines the kinds of traits the classifier chooses to observe and analyze. The purpose of the Corozal ceramic analysis presented here was basically chronological: to find out how ceramics had changed through time so that this information could be used to establish a sequence to cross-date the layers and components of other sites. Accordingly, the pottery was classified primarily in terms of its temporal qualities, as determined by changes in its frequency and proportions through the strata of the deposit. The fact that other factors, such as chance, functional distinctions, and disturbance, can also cause variation in the distribution of pottery in archaeological deposits was taken into consideration in the analysis, and the possible effects of such factors will be mentioned in the discussion of the seriation, where appropriate.

1. Procedures

The following procedures were used to process and analyze the pottery from Corozal. About thirty thousand sherds were recovered from the two deep excavations, Excavations 2 and 3 at Corozal. All of the sherds recovered were retained for analysis. The laboratory workers washed them and wrote on each sherd the catalogue number assigned to the provenience unit, such as #49 for Excavation 2, Level 1. Each of the "body" sherds with no observable diagnostic shape or decorative attributes was then examined and classified by gross paste characteristics and color. A selection of about one-fifth of the body sherds from each unit was chosen at random for examination by me under 30-power magnification with a binocular Bausch and Lomb Stereo Zoom 7 microscope to observe details of paste characteristics and especially temper, since temper was already known to vary considerably through time in lowland pottery. All of the "diagnostic" sherds, with rims, bases, or other nondecorative shape attributes, were given subnumbers to distinguish each sherd from the others. So, for example, the first sherd subnumbered for the level provenience number 49 would be subnumber 1 and bear the number 49–1; the second would bear 49–2, and so on. The paste of all the diagnostic sherds was studied for temper in the same fashion as the body sherds, but in addition their rim or base shapes were recorded by scale profile drawings made with a formigage. Assisted by Mary Jane Lenz, the laboratory supervisor, I checked and corrected all the profiles. The decorated sherds were treated similarly to the diagnostic sherds, except that I studied all of the decorated sherds under the microscope for temper information, rather than just a 20% sample of them.

The temper and shape studies turned out to be important for the success of the classification, for these traits were important distinguishing characteristics between styles in many cases and turned out to vary significantly with time, when their distribution was tabulated and analyzed statistically. In analyses where each decorated sherd is not examined under the microscope for temper and is not studied for shape, useful typological distinctions and chronological modes can go unrecognized. For example, Howard realized that the atypical Y–group pottery was different in decoration from the pottery typical for the group but did not separate it out typologically because he did not realize that it was also very different in shape and temper. As another example, certain

Aguerito pottery was misequated with Ronquin phase pottery because the shapes and microscopic tempering were not compared.

2. Defining Modes

For the seriation, the attributes of temper, shape, surface treatment, and decoration of the pottery from excavations at the type site were reviewed to find out how they varied through time so that the variations could be used to construct a chronological sequence. Each discernible attribute or mode (significant cluster of attributes) was examined for this purpose by checking its distribution in the excavation levels. I followed the suggestions of Rouse (1960) and Gary Vescelius (personal communication) about the preliminary analysis of ceramic attributes. Tables were made listing the number of examples of each mode in the excavation levels. If examples of the mode were relatively abundant but confined to a relatively small number of adjacent levels, the mode was judged good for defining periods and for separating the levels of different periods. The seriation thus was a study of the distribution of different pottery modes in the excavation levels for the purpose of defining chronological change.

Tables 9 and 10 list the total number of pottery sherds in Corozal Excavations 2 and 3 by excavation and level. In Tables 11 through 90, each of the twenty important chronological modes defined in the seriation is listed by excavation and level. The tables published here present both the absolute numbers of occurrences of the modes and the percentages that the modes constitute of the total number of sherds in each level or feature. The frequencies of a mode in an excavation are presented in the first table for each mode, placed in the third column, after the level and phase columns. The percentages for the mode are presented in the second table, placed in the same column location as the frequencies in the preceding table. So that quantitative similarities and differences in distributions of modes through the levels can be more easily grasped visually, I have also plotted the frequencies and percentages for each level as rows of Xs in the fourth column of each table—one X for each occurrence of a sherd with the mode in the frequency tables and one X for each 0.1% in the percentage tables. (In Tables 9 and 10, which give the total number of sherds in the levels, each X signifies one hundred sherds, which we considered the minimum number of total sherds for a seriatable level.)

For purposes of the seriation, a mode was a cluster of chronologically significant attributes. These chronological modes can be more or less inclusive than types and wares. A type in the Parmana pottery corpus might be the sponge-tempered cooking bowls with animal lugs decorated with modeled appliqué, incision, and punctation. Within that type, however, several chronological modes might be defined, because the attributes of the bowls changed through time although they continued to be part of an integral type. So, for example, the lugs of the earlier animal-effigy bowls have a tiny vestigial handle attached under the lug, whereas later bowls lack this feature. For chronological analysis, it can be useful to distinguish such stylistic variation within types as a temporal mode and analyze its distribution in the stratigraphy. Other motifs, such as circle stamps, crosscut types within a ware and were good for linking the phases of a tradition and setting the tradition off from other phases. Some modes were styles of decoration that crosscut wares as well as types, such as the Camoruco mauve paint or the Saladoid-Barrancoid decoration. Such styles were useful for chronology because examples of them were more numerous than each type that comprised them and because they linked the levels of an entire phase.

Our detailed study of stylistic and iconographic features was an important aid to seriation, and the stratigraphic segregation of the pottery during excavation was very important initially to help sort out chronological units of style. Each microstylistic mode then could be evaluated for possible statistical and chronological significance by the tabular distributions. This information about stratigraphic distribution helped to distinguish superficial stylistic similarities from chronologically meaningful ones. Our study of shape, temper, and micro-stylistic differences led to the separation of distinct styles that had previously been classified together. An example of this is the differentiation of Corozal (#132) and Arauquinoid rectilinear incision (#19), types which are only superficially similar and are distinct in style, morphology, technology, stratigraphic distribution, and chronology. In other classifications (Howard 1943; Vargas 1981; Zucchi, Tarble, and Vaz 1984), these two quite unrelated types have been classified as one type. Our study of the temper, shapes, and motifs in conjunction with the tabular distributions revealed the distinct difference between the types and their stratigraphic separation (Pl. 8, *bottom,* and 11, *bottom;* Figs. 18 and 24; Tables 31–34, 55–58). As another example, Corozal rectilinear incision, which has been conflated with the incision found on Parmana softwares (Zucchi, Tarble, and Vaz 1984), is easy to distinguish from the softwares when one compares vessel shapes, temper, incision forms, and stratigraphic distributions (Pl. 7, *top,* and 8, *bottom;* Figs. 15 and 18; Tables 11–14, 31–34).

The patterns of change in mode frequencies through the stratigraphic column are assumed to be a product of change through time in the rate of production and use of the modes. Another possible cause of mode-frequency differences, however, is function. For example, variation in the distribution of objects in stratigraphy can be caused by change through time in the kinds of activities carried out at the location being excavated or at the location from which refuse was collected in order to be thrown away at the location under excavation. As another example, different wares or types may be used for different tasks that may customarily be carried out in different parts of settlements. Through time, the use of space at a site may vary, so that the frequencies of the different wares or types may change through the stratigraphic column. In this way, the frequency of functionally different but contemporary pottery entities may vary stratigraphically independently of the chronology of their manufacture. This explanation is not so likely for directional changes in frequency, such as the majority of changes illustrated in the seriation. However, some of the differences in temper, shape, and decoration of pottery from Corozal are quite likely to represent differences in the function of the pottery. For example, some of the pottery has the shape and decorative characteristics of service ware, and other pottery seems more likely to be cooking pottery. Among the possible cooking pottery, in addition, there seems to be special, decorated cooking pottery and ordinary, undecorated cooking pottery. Some nondirectional fluctuations in the frequency of various modes in the Corozal stratigraphy do seem possibly attributable to such functional differences. An example would be the fluctuations in percentages of mauve-painted ware, which seems to have been a special service and cooking pottery. The mauve sherds seem more abundant in the garbage layers than in the layers representing prepared floors, in contrast to ordinary service and culinary wares. This pattern parallels the distribution of fancy service and cooking pottery in comparison to ordinary service and culinary pottery at Marajoara phase sites at the mouth of the Amazon and may represent gender contrasts in access to material culture (Roosevelt 1990b, 1991a). Such fluctuations are difficult to interpret in a columnar excavation intended for chronological seriation but may be useful and illuminating in a context of broad-area excavation.

A number of different kinds of modes were charted in the seriation, including modes of shape and decoration. The decorative modes turned out to be very useful for seriation, being relatively short-lived but also quite abundantly represented, since much of the pottery was originally decorated. However, some fugitive modes of decoration, such as Corozal polychrome or Saladoid red-and-white paint (#5), had too few examples for the distributions to be valid statistically. Major modes of shape or temper tended to be fewer in number than the decorative modes and to change more slowly through time. They were thus somewhat less useful for fine-grained chronological distinctions than the modes of decoration. Such modes, however, were sometimes represented in large quantities of sherds and could be used to define important phase boundaries, particularly between Corozal 3 and Camoruco 1. Temper definitely changed through time and distinguished some subphase boundaries, but some paste changes, such as the increase in quantity of sponge temper and in the grayness of pottery from Corozal to Camoruco, took place so gradually that no boundary could be drawn between the two groups and they could not be seriated. Thus shape differences were more useful than most temper differences, despite the fact that shapes did not change as much through time as decoration did. Although I will summarize, interpret, and tabulate certain information about ceramic vessel shapes in my discussion of the Corozal seriation, nondecorative shape distinctions will be discussed more fully in a separate article focused on vessel function and techniques of manufacture. Discussion of the time-sensitive decorative modes is sufficient to define the chronology and is all that can conveniently be fitted into this publication.

In addition to other time-sensitive attributes, I sometimes used for seriation small differences that developed within long-lasting types. If I had used only inclusive types for classification, the Corozal sequence would not have been reliably divisible into phases. By concentrating on less inclusive units of ceramic analysis, I was able to define six phases, some of which can be subdivided even further. I looked for subtype variation of sufficient quantity for analysis and then plotted the distribution of the examples to see if it had chronological significance. Sometimes it became clear during the research that two separate decorative modes different in iconography and shape were part of the same motif. Thus the animal-effigy bowls (#209) were originally classified into two modes—the animal lugs with vestigial handles and the incised and punctate tabs. It later became clear from study of large sherds and whole vessels that the tabs were from the effigy bowls. They constituted the paws or wings of the animals whose heads bore the vestigial handles. Combining the two into mode #209 was a logical step in terms of morphological unity and also gave me a larger quantity of examples and charted exactly the same chronological change.

For purposes of seriation, it was desirable to have modes that existed in moderately abundant quantities. If they were too rare, statistical comparisons could not be made with chi-squares, because cell numbers were too small. Also, when level sherd totals were less than one hundred, the percentage differences became more likely the product of chance than of changes in popularity or rate of use of the mode, and the statistical tests of the significance of percentage differences of such small totals are not reliable. With very abundant modes, such as sponge temper or round rims from hemispherical bowls, both of which make up a large proportion of the sherds of most levels, there is in addition a purely probabilistic increase in the likelihood of statistically significant differences in frequencies occurring, a pattern that can obscure the chronological similarities and differences between distributions (A. Jaffe, personal communication).

The modes varied a good deal in their patterns of distribution. Some were confined to two or three phases; other modes were longer lasting, and statistically significant changes in their frequencies relative to total sherds in each level furnished definitive chronological information. The levels where a mode first appeared, peaked, or disappeared were very valuable for defining subphase boundaries. The subphase boundaries were drawn at junctures where several significant changes occurred. Within phases, changes in frequency of very abundant modes were not necessarily considered boundaries, because of the effect of large numbers in creating spurious frequency changes. If several modes changed within a phase, then I felt a subdivision was indicated.

There were many different chronologically useful modes discerned in the Corozal pottery, and these are presented in twelve graphic figures, seven photographic plates, and eighty seriation tables. The discussion focuses on the modes that were sufficiently abundant and changeable through time to help create the ceramic sequence, but I mention all modes that we recognized, whether or not they were useful for seriation. Those modes that occurred in fewer than twenty examples per excavation are not tabulated here (except for the Saladoid red-and-white paint, which had less than twenty examples in Excavation 3 because that excavation was suspended before reaching the base of the deposit). The very rare modes are less reliable chronological indicators due to the greater likelihood of statistical error in their presence-absence distribution. Many of the modes tabulated here were present in adequate numbers and varied significantly in their distribution. However, I also illustrate and tabulate here abundant modes that did not vary significantly in the stratigraphic column.

Out of 220 modes analyzed for possible chronological significance, twenty were present in adequate numbers to seriate. I will discuss each mode in turn, illustrate it in photographs and morphological drawings where appropriate, and present tables of the numerical and percentage distribution in the levels of Excavations 2 and 3. (In the illustrations, all sherd examples that expressed the mode visually are included. As is customary in archaeological monographs, only those sherds or vessels that could not be "read" photographically or graphically are not illustrated, but these are included in the tabulations.) The results of the statistical tests of the significance of the differences in mode distribution between levels and clusters of levels are presented at the foot of each mode table.

3. Statistical Tests of Significance

In order to evaluate the significance of the patterns of distribution of modes in the Corozal excavations, I carried out two types of statistical tests on the quantitative distributions of modes. I carried out the analysis with the advice of Linda Brown, a physical anthropologist at the University of Montana, of A. Jaffe, a statistician-sociologist at Columbia University, and of Stan Freed, an ethnologist, and David Thomas, an archaeologist, both at the American Museum of Natural History. The purpose of my analysis was to determine what modes were nonrandomly distributed in the levels of excavations and thus might be used for chronological seriation. Specifically, I wished to find out if the variation between phases or levels in the distribution of frequencies or percentages of modes was statistically significantly different from the distribution expected for random or chance variation. I used the modes that had statistically significant variation in stratigraphic distribution to make chronological distinctions among levels.

The tests that I used were the chi-square calculation and the test of proportions. The test results were important evidence that corrected for distortions in the mode frequency distributions caused by fluctuations in totals of sherds in the levels. For example, two adjacent levels might contrast in absolute frequency of a mode, with one having ten examples of mauve paint and the other having one example. Whether or not this difference might be significant in terms of chronological change in use of the mode depends on the relationship of the two frequencies to the total number of sherds in each level. Thus if level one has one hundred sherds in it and level 2 has ten, the absolute frequencies would not be considered significantly different for chronological purposes, because they each amount to 10% of the total in each level, and the probable cause of the difference in absolute frequency is the difference in total number of sherds. The differences in absolute frequencies could thus be a product of the differences in overall numbers of sherds in the levels. Although there were some repetitive and progressive differences through time in the density of sherds in the archaeological deposit, such as those between floors and garbage and between Corozal and Camoruco levels, nonetheless, the excavation levels mainly varied in total number of sherds because some layers were thin or small in area and thus had fewer sherds, and some were broad and thick and had many sherds. Thus the pattern of variation in the absolute frequencies of modes per level needed to be corrected by comparing mode frequencies to the totals of sherds in each level. Most published pottery seriations from the lowlands present absolute frequencies without statistical comparisons, so it is difficult to assess the chronological significance of variations in frequency.

In the first part of the statistical analysis, I set up tables of the frequencies of different modes and calculated chi-squares to assess the significance of variation in the distribution of each mode in the stratigraphic column of each excavation. The following was the procedure that I used. The levels of each hypothetical subphase were grouped by mode in a column of cells, and the number of examples of the mode in each group of levels was summed. A second column of the sherd totals in each level, less the number of modal sherds, was then filled in. The number of expected examples for a random distribution was calculated for each cell as the total number of examples in the column times the total number of sherds in each group of levels, divided by the total number of sherds in the excavation. Only modes with expected cell frequencies greater than five in 75% or more of the cells could be analyzed in this way, because of the statistical requirements of chi-square calculations, but most modes had more than the necessary number. In the few cases where an excavation level had too few examples of modes for the excavation to be analyzed by itself, I combined it with an adjacent level in the calculations. The chi-square value was calculated as follows: chi-square equals the square of the difference between the observed numbers in each cell and the expected number for the cell, divided by the expected number for the cell, summed. The degrees of freedom equal the number of rows, which would be 6 in the case of comparisons among phases, less 1, times the number of columns, which was 2, less 1, yielding 5, which gives a critical value of 11.07 at a .05 level of confidence, which the chi-squares must be equal to or greater than in order for the distribution to be significant, not random. For most of the modes presented in the tables, the distributions in the excavations did not fulfill the null hypothesis and differed significantly from randomness in their distribution in the stratigraphic column. The results of the calculations are entered after the symbol X^2 at the foot of the distribution tables for the modes.

If the chi-square results did not fulfill the null hypothesis that the distribution was likely to be caused by chance alone, then I calculated a further set of chi-squares comparing the levels of successive phases. Using the chi-square equation with one degree of freedom, I compared pairs of stratigraphically adjacent levels or groups of levels near possible phase boundaries with each other in order to determine whether they varied significantly from each other in mode frequencies. In this equation, 0.5 is subtracted from the difference between the observed and expected frequencies in each cell before squaring, in order to correct for continuity (Young and Veldman 1965; Senders 1958). The critical value for these results is 3.84. The results of these calculations are entered at the foot of the mode distribution tables after the symbol X^2c.

A further statistical procedure was used to evaluate the significance of the percentage differences in the distribution of the modes between levels. This is the test of proportions, which compares modes in terms of their percentages. Its advantage over the chi-square test, whose uses are similar, is that it can analyze the statistical significance of distribution differences between levels that have occurrences of a mode and those that do not.

After tabulating and analyzing the absolute frequencies and calculating the chi-squares, I tabulated the percentages of examples of each mode per level and then compared levels with each other. To determine if the differences were statistically significant, I first calculated the standard deviation for the two proportions using the formula:

$$S = \sqrt{PQ \left(\frac{N_1 + N_2}{N_1 \times N_2} \right)}$$

To determine S, N_1 equals the sample size in the first level and N_2 equals the sample size of the second level. In this test, P equals the probability of an event occurring and Q (or $1 - P$) equals the probability of the event not occurring. The procedure for calculations is as follows. To get the probability of the mode occurring in the two levels (P), the sum of the examples of the mode in both levels is divided by the sum of the total number of sherds in both levels. To get the probability of the mode not occurring (Q), this ratio is subtracted from 1 ($Q = 1 - P$). The standard deviation is equal to the square root of the product of these two results multiplied by a value computed by dividing the total number of sherds from both levels ($N_1 + N_2$) by the product of the number of sherds from each level ($N_1 \times N_2$).

Once the standard deviation is computed, it is a simple matter to test the difference between the two proportions as follows:

$$Z = \frac{P_1 - P_2}{S}$$

Here, the proportion of the mode in one level is P_1; and the proportion of the mode in the second level is P_2. The procedure is to subtract one proportion from the other and to divide this value by the standard deviation. For the difference between two percentages to be statistically significant and not the product of chance, the result of this equation has to be 2 or greater than 2.

Results of less than 2 support the null hypothesis that the percentage difference could be the result of random error. Results of 2 are significant at about a 95% confidence level, and results of 4 or over, at a confidence level of 99% or more. The results of these calculations are presented for each comparison of level pairs at the foot of each percentage table.

According to probability laws, percentages of total lots of fewer than one hundred tend to be subject to skewing from small numbers, so I did not draw conclusions about chronology from the percentages of modes for levels or features with fewer than one hundred seriatable sherds. The two levels at the bottom of Excavation 2 and the bottom level of Excavation 3 had sherd totals of fewer than fifty, so their percentages and frequencies of modes could not be used for seriation purposes. Nonetheless, their frequencies and percentages are included in the tables, so that the reader can review them. (The percentages of levels with fewer than one hundred sherds total are given in parentheses in the tables.) In accord with the prediction on statistical grounds that their percentage distributions would not be reliable indicators of mode distributions, it can be seen that the percentages of these levels with few total sherds are often sharply divergent from the percentages in the adjacent levels. It is important to recognize the percentage distortions that low total sherd frequencies can cause, when one is characterizing significant changes in pottery frequencies through time. For example, a hypothetical new phase was defined at the site of Aguerito (Zucchi, Tarble, and Vaz 1984, 165–66, Tables 1–4) primarily on the basis of percentage patterns in levels having fewer than fifty sherds overall. Statistical considerations suggest that these percentage differences are more likely to be the product of chance than of chronological differences in the use of pottery. By using the two statistical tests to analyze the frequency and percentage distributions, I have attempted to base the Corozal site chronology only on distributions that had a good possibility of being the product of some kind of human behavior, rather than chance occurrences.

4. Cross-Regional Ceramic Comparisons

As I describe the ceramic modes in the next section, I will note specific relationships of the pottery with pottery phases elsewhere. At present, because the cultural history of most lowland regions has never been studied by professional archaeologists, it seems premature to draw firm conclusions about the significance of similarities and differences among ceramic styles in lowland South America. Although it may be possible to show that pottery in different regions is related, unless both regions have reliable sequences of absolute dates, it is not possible to know which region may have influenced the other. Therefore, I will assess the possible relationships of Parmana pottery with that of other regions in order to prepare for the time in the future when enough lowland cultural history is known for these similarities and differences to be interpreted meaningfully.

Several authors have made exhaustive summaries of the relationships among the ceramics of lowland archaeological phases (Osgood and Howard 1943; Howard 1947; Cruxent and Rouse 1958–59; Rouse and Cruxent 1963; Brochado and Lathrap M.S.; Foster and Lathrap 1973; Meggers and Evans 1983; Willey 1971). These studies were the basis for my general understanding of lowland ceramic affinities and guided me in making comparisons. However, it is often difficult to grasp accurately the exact similarities and differences among regional pottery styles without actually examining the pottery in question, seeing the surface, looking at the paste with a binocular microscope, recording rim angles, drawing profiles, and making measurements. Assessment of similarities and differences from literature is difficult, because illustrations are selective and cannot usually reveal the diagnostic-level characteristics of the pottery. This is particularly true for evaluating the existence of trade wares. Often mere visual examination of pottery with the naked eye reveals that two complexes hypothetically linked as trade wares obviously could not be, because of gross differences in paste and style characteristics between the complexes.

Therefore, to better assess the geographic relationships of the pottery from Corozal, I have compared Parmana pottery directly with particular examples in collections of pottery from lowland and highland South America. This work was done during a review of lowland collections funded by a National Endowment for the Arts fellowship (1981–86) for preparation of a survey of Amazonian archaeology. The study included the following lowland pottery collections: The Yale University Peabody Museum collections from Parmana (Howard 1943, 1947), Saladero, and Barrancas (Cruxent and Rouse 1958–59); the collections from the Valencia Basin (Kidder 1944), Santarem region, and Marajo region (Hartt 1883, 1885) in the Harvard University Peabody Museum; the pottery from Valencia (Bennett 1937), the Bolivian Amazon (Bennett 1936), Marajo (Lange 1914), and the Guianas (Evans and Meggers 1960) in the American Museum of Natural History; the Santarem, Marajo (Farabee M.S.), and

Arauquin (Petrullo 1939) collections in the University of Pennsylvania Museum; various collections from the Amazon in the Musˇ82e de L'Homme; the pottery from Santarem (Nimuendaju M.S.), Marajo, and the Bolivian Amazon in the Gˇ94teborg Ethnographic Museum (Nordenskiold 1930); the pottery from Tobago in the Cambridge University and British Museums; the pottery from Valencia, Santarem, and Marajo in the Museum of the American Indian; the pottery from the Santarem area, the vicinity of Manaus, and Marajo in the National Museum in Rio de Janeiro, the University of São Paulo Museums (Palmatary 1950, 1960; Bezerra de Meneses 1972), and the Goeldi Museum (Netto 1885; Ferreira Penna 1877); and the pottery from the Yarinacocha area (Lathrap 1970) in the National Museum of Anthropology and Archaeology in Lima and the American Museum of Natural History in New York. I also compared the Parmana pottery with pottery from the Andes, lower Central America, and Mesoamerica in the Museum of the American Indian.

The possible similarities among the Corozal site pottery and pottery of other lowland regions are noted in the sections on each ceramic mode, in the following section describing the distribution of modes in the Corozal sequence.

C. Description of the Ceramic Modes

The description of the modes will start with the earliest modes and end with the most recent, beginning with Corozal 1 and ending with Camoruco 3, the last phase of prehistoric occupation at the site. As discussed above, the modes range from inclusive units such as wares, through types and styles, down to clusters of decorative, technical, or shape attributes that may crosscut or subdivide wares, types, or styles. In order to help the reader to make sense of the pottery at the various levels, as I proceed I will try to show how the modes are linked to each other and to nonseriated ceramic entities. I will also mention the pottery's specific similarities to that of other regions in South America. After describing the modes and their occurrence in the traditions and phases, I will summarize the distribution of modes in the Corozal ceramic sequence.

1. Corozal Tradition Modes

Corozal sherdware, mode #135 *(Pl. 7, top; Fig. 15; Tables 11–14)*. This first important Corozal mode is a sherd-and-fiber-tempered ware closely related to, if not indistinguishable from, a minor but persistent La Gruta tradition ware named after Parmana (Roosevelt 1980, 209, Fig. 63; Vargas 1981, Lam. 15, G, H; 20, C–E). The primary decoration is simple rectilinear incision on vessel

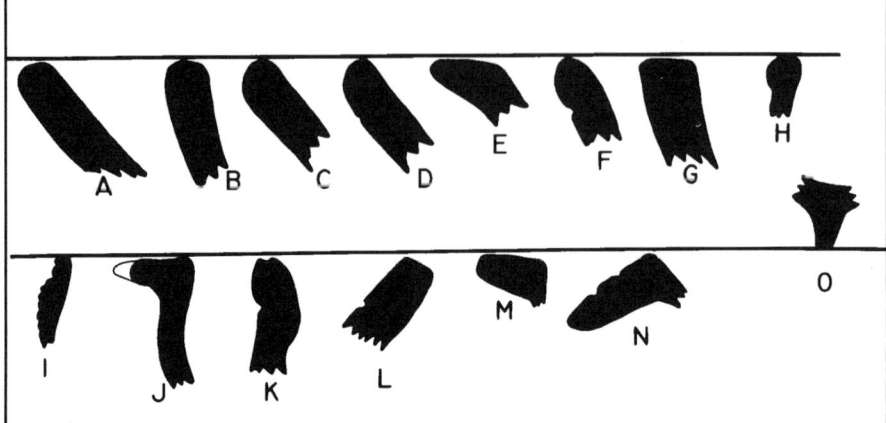

Figure 15. Rim and base sherd profiles, mode #135: Corozal sherdware

Provenience numbers and diameters: A: 45–11, d. 36 cm; B: 31–51, d. 26 cm; C: 27–12, d. 45 cm; D: 22–16, d. 52 cm; E: 8–25, d. 45–50 cm; F: 8–27, d. 54 cm; G: 27–16, d. 70 cm; H: 54–6, d. 12 cm; I: 21–64, d. 42 cm; J: 37–13, d. 20 cm; K: 40–1, d. 41 cm; L: 46–6 and 46–11, d. 28 cm; M: 48–192, d. 36 cm; N: 27–11, d. ? cm. O: 8–68, d. 68 cm. (The interior of vessels faces to the right in the sherd profile illustrations. When a sherd is too irregular or too incomplete for diameter measurements, a question mark is entered.)

rims and walls. Parmanoid decorative types of somewhat different temper (sand, fiber, and clay bits) have been found outside the Parmana region near Caicara on the right bank of the Orinoco to the west, at Aguerito (Zucchi, Tarble, and Vaz 1984, Fig. 4 A–F, ware B). Sherdwares possibly distantly related to Parmanoid styles have also been found in pottery of the Ananatuba phase (1500–500 B.C.) of Marajo Island at the mouth of the Amazon (Meggers and Evans 1957, Pl. 36; Meggers and Evans 1983). Otherwise, the Parmana ware does not seem to have close relatives among known pottery phases outside the Middle Orinoco region, although future work may discover some. The Parmana region sherdware has characteristic paste, thickness, shape, and decoration that differentiate it clearly from other pottery wares and styles in the Parmana sequence. The ware is very rare at the beginning of the regional sequence, peaks sharply in the beginning of the Corozal 1 phase, and then tapers off rapidly at the end of Corozal 1. The peak during Corozal 1 parallels a peak in the frequency of the related ware during the earliest occupation of Aguerito, the site upstream from Parmana on the other side of the Orinoco river.

Like the La Gruta, Ronquin, and Ronquin Sombra phase sherdwares, this Corozal phase ware is always very densely tempered with crumbled pottery sherds and usually tempered with a dark, fine, fibrous vegetal temper that has sometimes disappeared, leaving holes and spaces in the paste. The sherd temper in the pottery is from ground-up sherdware, and we have not observed pieces of other wares in the paste of the sherdware. Many Parmana region wares contain sherd or clay-bit temper, but this one is distinctive in that the sherd temper is very abundant and is the primary temper of the ware. To the naked eye the paste of this ware appears chunky from the close-spaced, abundant, squarish sherd bits. The sherdware feels soft and smooth to the touch in comparison to the other wares, in which sharp rock or sand particles or abrasive sponge spicules abound. In terms of actual hardness, this ware, like most Parmana region pottery, is between 2 and 3 on the Moh's hardness scale. The surfaces are dull but smooth and bear an even self-slip. The core of sherds tends to be gray and darkish (ranging between Munsell colors dark grayish brown [10YR 4/2], dark brown [10 YR 4/3], and brown [10 YR 5/3]), and the surface a light gray, brown (Munsell colors pale brown [10 YR 6/3], brown [10YR 5/3]), and light yellowish brown [10 YR 6/4]. There are rare examples of sherds with the shapes and decoration of the Parmanoid sherdwares but with a combination of tempers, including sherds, fiber, sponge, and grit. These are interesting as examples of the apparent technical interchange that took place among makers of distinct wares and styles during the Corozal phase.

In addition to its distinctive sherd-and-fiber temper, this ware has distinctive shapes that contrast with those of other wares. The vessels are large and thick-walled (Fig. 15). (Sherds in the illustrations are reproduced at 77% reduction, unless otherwise noted.) Three shapes predominate: a large, shallow hemispherical bowl, a constricted-neck jar, wand a basin with angled sides. Most rims are simple, round, or square, but there are rare flanged rims also (Fig. 15, M–N). Basins have round, beveled, or square rims; bowls have round or beveled rims; and jars have tapered, everted rims. Bases are predominantly round, but two examples of ring bases exist (Fig. 15, O). There are a few other shapes that occur in exceedingly small frequencies, such as small bowls and cups. The shapes expressed in the ware are few, and other shapes found in other contemporary Corozal wares, such as bottles, griddles, handles, and adornos, are never found in this ware. These great differences in shape suggest that the ware may have had a different function from other wares.

The ware's decoration is mainly simple, shallow, parallel, rectilinear incisions, but rare sherds have simple versions of Barrancoid modeled and grooved motifs (Fig. 15, N) as was the case with earlier sherdwares (Roosevelt 1980, 206, Fig. 56). The Parmanoid incisions are narrower than the usual Barrancoid broad-line incision, but wider and shallower than the incision of Corozal spongewares or the sharp, Arauquinoid incision of Camoruco times.

Like the incision of Corozal spongewares but unlike the incision of La Gruta tradition gritwares, the incisions on the sherdwares often are filled with red paint. The basic incised motif on sherdware basins is a band of repeated parallel lines below a horizontal line just below the rim. The parallel lines are sometimes vertical, sometimes diagonal, and occasionally zoned in basketlike patterns at an angle to one another. Rarely are the lines curved. Most basins seem to have been treated with this type of decoration, for there are few undecorated basin rims. Not all bowls are decorated, but those that are bear short, parallel diagonal slashes on top of the rim. This simple but ancient lowland rim motif first appears on sherds of the eighth millennium from Taperinha in the Brazilian Amazon, some of the earliest pottery in the Americas (Roosevelt et al. 1991; Roosevelt 1995). About one-fifth of all Corozal sherdware sherds bear incised decoration. A few, otherwise plain, sherds bear a thin, red wash of paint. Very rarely, a sherdware sherd will borrow decoration from other wares. For example, one sherdware rim from Corozal has the La Gruta tradition incised circle-and-punch motif (Pl. 7, *top*, L), and another has an incised flange (Pl. 7, *top*, M), like many gritware sherds.

At Corozal, the sherdware occurs mainly in Corozal 1, tapering off to small quantities in Corozal 2. It is quite abundant in the lower levels of the site, making up about 41% of all sherds in Corozal 1. Its frequency varies significantly among early, middle, and late Corozal 1 and between Corozal 1 and Corozal 2. It is therefore a good marker for the internal divisions of the Corozal phase. Outside of the Corozal levels, the ware has rare occurrences probably associated with minor disturbances. Its pattern of proportional occurrence through time is a sharp curve from high percentages at the start of Corozal 1 at the site, dropping rapidly to a low percentage by the end of the phase. It is worth noting that the absolute frequencies conceal this curve, because they are diminished in the earliest seriatable Corozal 1 levels by the lower overall frequency of pottery in those levels.

Aside from its value as a chronological indicator for Corozal 1, this ware is interesting because of its persistence in the Parmana sequence. It is so different in paste, shape, decoration, and frequency from the other wares of its period of existence that it has been suggested that it is chronologically and ethnically distinct (Zucchi, Tarble, and Vaz 1984) and, due to its relatively crude decoration, possibly a very early ware that preceded the grit-tempered Saladoid-Barrancoid wares. However, the distribution of this pottery in the stratigraphy of several Parmana region sites shows that it has never been found alone in any layer or level of any site but always co-occurs with other wares, such as the La Gruta tradition or Corozal gritwares and Corozal spongewares. In addition, the gritwares have never been found unaccompanied by sherdwares in any component in Parmana, and rare examples of the sherdware incorporate shapes or decorative motifs from decorative types of the other contemporary wares. Therefore, the reasonable conclusion seems to be that the sherdware is contemporary with the other wares with which it consistently has been found.

The possibility that the sherdwares were used for a function different from that of other wares has been mentioned, and another possibility is that the distinctive ware was an import, made in an adjacent region by people of a different cultural tradition. Trace-element analysis of the clays might reveal that its geographic origin is different from the gritwares, though the technical temper differences might be difficult to distinguish from differences in geographic origin. Even if an import, the ware still might be a special-function ware. Soot is rare on the outside of sherdware vessels, although common on gritwares and spongewares, but this could be because of some physical characteristic of the clay that prevents soot from clinging. The interior surfaces of sherdware sherds usually are much darker and grayer than the exterior, presumably a product of firing practices. These vessels may have been for use away from the fire, as buck pots for catching manioc juice or bowls for preparing palm-fruit drinks or foods. As mentioned in the section on iconography at the conclusion of this work (Chap. 4, A, 5), identifiable zoomorphic motifs, common in other wares, have not been identified in this ware, and this difference in subject matter may relate to differences in function between the wares. The sherdwares might have been used for vegetal foods. Possible functional differences could be elucidated by future research investigating the nature of occupation features at sites and the distribution in them of pottery of the different wares.

COROZAL GRIT-TEMPERED WARE, MODE #140 *(Pl. 7, bottom; Fig. 16; Tables 15–18)*. Another ware mode for the Corozal phase is Corozal grit-tempered pottery (Howard's Y–group). Though grit-tempered pottery was the predominant ware in the La Gruta, Ronquin, and Ronquin Sombra sites, it is less frequent than the sherd-tempered wares and sponge-tempered wares in Corozal tradition levels. The ware has its greatest frequency (about 17%) at the beginning of Corozal 1, decreases gradually during the middle of the phase, and then drops sharply to a lower percentage (about 4%) at the end of the subphase. The ware continues in extremely low frequencies during later phases, possibly due to movement of sherds in disturbances or mistakes in our separation of the Corozal gritware and the rare Camoruco style gritware.

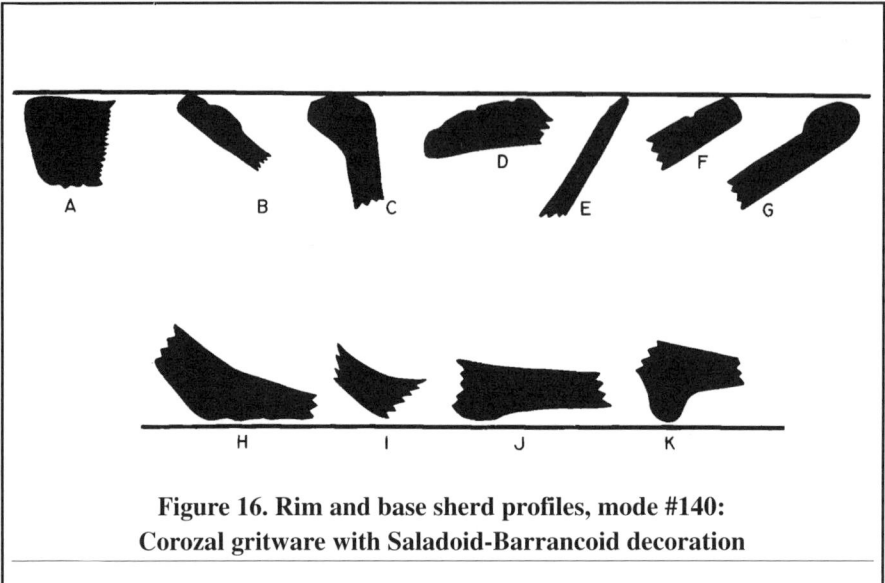

Figure 16. Rim and base sherd profiles, mode #140: Corozal gritware with Saladoid-Barrancoid decoration

Provenience numbers and diameters: A: 27–19, d. 46 cm; B: 37–25, d. 44 cm; C: 42–28, d. 29 cm; D: 8–10, d. 42 cm; E: 62–6, d. ? cm; F: 37–35, d. 22 cm; G: 31–59, d. 18 cm; H: 46–4, d. 32 cm; I: 27–23, d. ? cm; J: 8–67, d. ? cm; K: 2–238 d. 8 cm.

The decoration of the Corozal gritware, though clearly derived from the La Gruta tradition gritwares, is highly impoverished and crudely executed in comparison. For this reason, the ware is given the new name of Corozal gritware, rather than La Gruta tradition gritware, to make clear that the Corozal ware, though presumably derived from the earlier gritwares, is quite different and easily distinguishable from those. It is important to emphasize this fact, because at the site of Aguerito a gritware parallel with Corozal's was misaligned with that of the Ronquin Sombra phase, from which it is quite different, as explained below.

The tempering of the Corozal gritwares varies a great deal. It is primarily crushed or ground rock, not sand. The rock types include variegated grains from granites, sharp gray crystals, and white limey chunks. The degree of integration of the paste also varies, from dense, hard pottery to porous, friable pottery. The core of the paste is slightly grayer than the surface, which is oxidized in color—red, orange, or pink-buff—as in the La Gruta tradition gritware examples (Munsell colors yellowish red [5 YR 5/8, 4/6], brown [7.5 YR 5/4], and red [2.5 YR 5/6]).

The shapes of this ware are similar to those of the grit-tempered wares of the earlier La Gruta, Ronquin, and Ronquin Sombra phases, but fewer and much less elaborate. Open bowls are the most common shape, but there are also thick griddles (Fig. 16, A) and bottles. The bowls often bear soot on the outside, evidence of a culinary function. Rims are usually squarish and slightly tapered; some are thickened on the outside, others thickened on the inside and often flanged (Fig. 16, B, E, F). Bases are round, angled, flat and plain, flat and thickened, flat and pedestaled, recessed (H–J), or ringed (K). Open bowls with out-turned sides and with broad rims thickened on the interior are decorated with shallow grooving (B). There are also rare bowls with animal rim lugs (Pl. 7, *bottom,* E) and rare asymmetrical gritware animal-effigy bowls with D-shaped handles adorned with animal heads (D, F–I). Lacking are some of the more elaborate shapes of La Gruta tradition gritwares, such as boat-shaped bowls, bowls with elaborately lobed rims, and composite silhouette bottles with face-necks.

The decoration of the Corozal gritware clearly is related to the La Gruta tradition gritwares' Saladoid paint and Barrancoid carving, grooving, and modeling. The Saladoid paint (Pl. 7, *bottom,* J–O) is found primarily on sherds of closed vessels, possibly bottles, as in the La Gruta tradition phases. As earlier, the identity of painted images is difficult to resolve from the fragmentary, eroded examples. Motifs include curved negative lines, areas of red outlined with a narrow white line, and areas of white. The plastic imagery of the Corozal gritware seems to function iconographically as in the La Gruta tradition phases. It has animal images and geometric motifs that often seem to depict animals' eyebrows, eyes, ears, and so forth. A characteristic motif is the small, round, shallow dot found inside circles and on nubbins (Pl. 7, *bottom,* D–I). This motif is most commonly used for animal eyes or ears in naturalistic designs, and it also appears alone on rims and vessel walls. For eyes, the motif is placed on a small hemispherical modeled mound with a shallow groove encircling its base.

Although closely related to the earlier grit-tempered decorated pottery, the Corozal grit-tempered decorated pottery is clearly distinguishable from the earlier material in its simplicity and rarity. Comparison of the examples illustrated here (which are the best-preserved and most elaborate decorated specimens of the ware from Corozal) with those from La Gruta and Ronquin shows that the Corozal phase ware lacks the distinctive abundance and elaboration of the earlier decoration. The elaborate modeled-grooved animal adornos and the wide, elaborately modeled and carved rims of La Gruta, Ronquin, and Ronquin Sombra simply do not exist in the Corozal gritwares. Curiously, the Barrancoid incised decoration on sherds of the Corozal grit-tempered ware is simple in comparison with the richly patterned incised designs on the contemporary sponge-tempered Barrancoid ware at Corozal (mode #134, *below*).

The elaborate traditional incised Barrancoid decoration seems to have moved over to the new sponge-tempered ware, and the remaining decorative types of the grit-tempered ware seem few and impoverished. A parallel stylistic-technical transition appears to have taken place in the Barrancoid tradition of the Lower Orinoco at the same time as the Corozal phase. There, during the period from about 1000 B.C. to A.D. 500, Barrancoid and Saladoid decoration changed over from grit-tempered to sponge-tempered wares (Cruxent and Rouse 1958–59).

Most of the Corozal grit-tempered pottery in the Corozal excavations is found in early and middle Corozal 1 phase levels, which are significantly different from other levels in frequency and percentages of the ware. However, both the ware and the decoration continue in very scarce quantities into the Camoruco phase. This later distribution may be the result of disturbances and/or confusion with the later Camoruco gritware. If not, this distribution makes the Corozal gritware the longest lasting of the pottery wares derived from the La Gruta tradition.

At the end of the existence of Corozal gritware, during Camoruco 1 and 2, a very rare new form of grit-tempered pottery with a brown core (#203) appears, often with temper of very coarse gray rock crystals and with crude appliqué and punctate decoration in Arauquinoid style (Howard 1943, 5–O). This later ware has also been found at Aguerito (Zucchi, Tarble, and Vaz 1984, Fig. 6, L–S). Except for decorated pieces, sherds of the two gritwares could not always be distinguished reliably from each other because the paste characteristics intergrade. The low-frequency persistence of gritware sherds in Camoruco phase levels in the Corozal gritware tables can probably be at least partly attributed to the presence of examples of plain Camoruco gritware.

Grit-tempered ware parallel to the Corozal phase gritware is also found at Aguerito (Zucchi, Tarble, and Vaz 1984, Fig. 3, A–M). The Aguerito ware, termed Ware A, shares the Corozal phase gritware's differences from the gritwares of the La Gruta, Ronquin, and Ronquin Sombra phases, as can be seen by comparing the Aguerito pottery to that in the illustrations of the La Gruta tradition gritware pottery (Roosevelt 1980, Fig. 50–54). The alignment by the excavators of the Aguerito gritwares with the Ronquin Sombra phase is unjustifiable in terms of style and technology, for the Corozal and early Aguerito gritwares both lack the fine, hard paste, smooth vessel contours, and highly elaborate decoration of Ronquin Sombra pottery. The radiocarbon dates for the Aguerito sequence put this Corozal-related pottery in the Corozal range of dates, and the pattern of association of wares and styles at Aguerito also matches the patterns of the Corozal phase complex, rather than the Ronquin Sombra complex. The Aguerito gritwares should, therefore, be realigned with the Corozal phase, rather than with Ronquin Sombra. Another region where gritwares similar to those of the La Gruta tradition have been found is Santarem. There, oxidized, reddish orange wares with decorative grooving, red-and-white painting, and thick griddle sherds appear to come after Initial pottery and before polychrome pottery (Roosevelt et al. M.S.). (See Oliver 1989 for further commentary on the problems with the Aguerito sequence as defined by the excavators.)

SALADOID-BARRANCOID DECORATION, MODE #204 (Pl. 7, *top*, L; Pl. 7, *bottom*; Pl. 8, *top*; Tables 19–22). This is an example of a decorative mode that crosscuts wares, types, and styles. Under this mode are included all the examples of Saladoid or Barrancoid decoration, regardless of paste type and temper. This mode was found on sherds of the decorated grit-tempered wares, rare examples of decorated sherdwares, the curvilinear incised and the rare Saladoid painted sponge-tempered wares, and the extremely rare fine-paste wares.

The mode is a good marker for the Corozal tradition and helps to distinguish subdivisions within the tradition. This mode is very common in Corozal 1, is much less common in Corozal 2, and drops to low percentages in Corozal 3. Its highest percentage (about 11%) occurs at the very beginning of Corozal 1, and it drops abruptly to about 4 to 5%, remaining at that level until the end of Corozal 1. The percentage of the decoration in Corozal 2 (about 1 to 2%) is significantly different from that of Corozal 1 and Corozal 3 (about 4 to 5%). The stray sherds with this decoration in Camoruco phase levels are present in insignificant percentages and may represent stratigraphic mixture by minor intrusions from those levels into Corozal phase layers. An alternative explanation is that people continued to use small quantities of this pottery with this style of decoration in the early part of the Camoruco tradition. This mode's decorative inventory in Corozal tradition levels includes all the typical motifs of the Saladoid and Barrancoid styles: Saladoid red-and-white paint, Barrancoid broad-line incision, modeled-groved zoomorphic adornos, and so forth. The most common motifs are the grooved lines that run along rims, either on the rim or below (Pl. 7, *top*, L; Pl. 7, *bottom*, A, C; Pl. 8, *top*, A, D, E–G, I, J). The styles and placement of motifs vary greatly within the mode. For example, the Barrancoid broad-line incision on spongewares (see mode #134) is shallower than on the gritwares and often extends over the entire outside surface of vessels, rather than only on rims or modeled animal lugs. In addition, the Corozal spongewares lack the La Gruta tradition zoomorphic adornos and effigy vessels found in the gritware. There are occasional zoomorphic adornos in the curvilinear grooved spongewares (Pl. 8, *top,* B), but these are executed by modeling techniques that resemble those of the Arauquinoid series styles more than the Saladoid-Barrancoid series styles. Shapes of vessels that bear decoration of the mode also vary a great deal and include triangular rims, flanged rims, carinas, recessed bases, and ring bases, as well as simpler forms, such as tapered and squared rims (Figs. 15, J, N–O; 16, B, D–F, J, K; 17, B–F, H).

The fact that this style of decoration is found on so many different pastes and in so many different forms during the Corozal tradition is one of the characteristics that seem to reflect the tradition's complex, transitional nature.

MODE #5 SALADOID PAINT *(Pl. 7, bottom, J–O; Tables 23–26).* The sophisticated red-and-white painting style so distinctive and common in the La Gruta tradition (Roosevelt 1978, 1980) continues into the Corozal phase as a minor attribute and dies there. It is executed mainly in the grit-tempered wares, but a few sponge-tempered sherds also bear it. This mode, tabulated as Saladoid paint, occurs mainly in the early Corozal phase, with only rare sherds found thereafter. Sherds of spongewares with this paint are too rare to analyze separately for seriation and are included in the table with the gritware examples. Even combining examples of the paint in different wares yields a small total number of thirty-three for the site. Though the number was too small for an excavation chi-square to be calculated, the calculations comparing early and late Corozal 1 levels and Corozal 1 and 2 show significant differences in occurrence of the pottery. Like other pottery traits of La Gruta tradition origin, this decorative style has its highest percentage in the earlier part of Corozal 1.

As in earlier La Gruta tradition forms of the Saladoid paint, the best-developed examples have "negative" patterns executed by rubbing away the thick, shimmering white paint to form fine curved (Pl. 7, *bottom,* L) or straight lines. Other common motifs are areas of red paint bordered with a narrow white line (M). Sometimes the red-and-white paint is found on modeled sherds (E), and it is zoned to complement the images of the plastic decoration. Although the white paint is very thick and somewhat resistant to weathering, the red paint is highly water soluble and fugitive. The designs on sherds consequently are very damaged. It is doubtful that any of this paint is a fired, ceramic type of paint. The red paint is Munsell red (10 R 4/6), and the white is pinkish white (7.5 YR 8/2).

This style of red-and-white paint, though clearly related to that of the La Gruta tradition phases, is much less elaborate and abundant than the paint style of those phases. There are, for example, no Corozal phase painted sherds with complex figural designs and no elaborately painted, wide, thickened rims characteristic of the La Gruta tradition phases. Although the La Gruta tradition phases each have produced numerous modeled-incised animal effigies and adornos decorated with the paint, Corozal has produced only one example with the combined decoration (sherd E in Pl. 7, *bottom*). The best Corozal phase examples of the paint are illustrated in the plates, and these make a poor showing indeed when compared with the many examples recovered from the sites of La Gruta and Ronquin (Roosevelt 1978; 1980, Fig. 55).

This distinctive style of painting has numerous relatives elsewhere in the lowlands of South America, although I have never seen similar examples from the Andes or Central America. The style most closely similar to the rather degraded Corozal phase version of this paint is found at Aguerito (Zucchi, Tarble, and Vaz 1984, Fig. 3, J–M). More distantly related phases with more elaborate Saladoid paint include the earlier Saladero phase, the contemporary Barrancas phase (Cruxent and Rouse 1958–59), several phases in northern Venezuela (e.g., Vargas 1979) and the Wonotobo phase of Surinam (Boomert 1983). There also are sherds of red-and-white paint somewhat similar to the Saladoid paint, in collections of pottery from Lower and Middle Amazon sites (Hilbert 1955, 1959a, 1968; Hilbert and Hilbert 1980; Palmatary 1960, Pl. 85).

COROZAL CURVILINEAR INCISION, MODE #133 *(Pl. 8, top; Fig. 17; Tables 27–30)*.
One of the important Corozal tradition diagnostics is a type of shallow, primarily curvilinear incision on spongeware bowls—a style of decoration related to Barrancoid styles—such as the Barrancas and Los Barrancos phases of the Lower Orinoco (Cruxent and Rouse 1958–59). Some of this curvilinear-incised pottery found at Ronquin was included among the Z–group pottery defined by Howard (1943), and a similar style was found at Aguerito (Zucchi, Tarble, and Vaz 1984, Fig. 4, N,S). In both cases, the curvilinear-incised pottery was classified together with other chronologically, technically, and stylistically distinct material. At Corozal, it was possible to isolate this pottery stratigraphically from the other styles and show that it is a good chronological marker for the Corozal tradition. It is relatively abundant. One hundred twenty-five examples were recovered from the two main excavations at the Corozal site.

Most of the sherds with this style of decoration are tempered with moderate to abundant amounts of sponge spicules and a few crushed sherds and contain rare inclusions of waterworn sand and clay bits. The core of sherds is often slightly grayer than the buff surface, which is Munsell pink (7.5 YR 7/4), light brown (7.5 YR 6/4), light reddish brown (5 YR 6/4), or reddish yellow (5 YR 6/4). The bowls are neatly and elaborately decorated on the outside and/or top of the rim and occasionally bear a carefully modeled hemispherical nubbin on

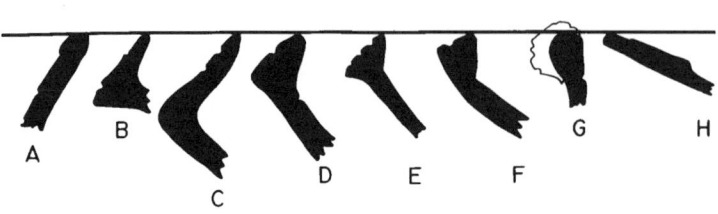

Figure 17. Rim sherd profiles, mode #133: Corozal curvilinear incision

Provenience numbers and diameters: A: 51–1, d. 21 cm; B: 152–2, d. 25 cm; C: 3–4, d. 10 cm; D: 152–1, d. 36 cm; E: 24–3, d. 19 cm; F: 26–3, d. 23 cm; G: 3–1, d. ? cm; H: 3–78, d. 30 cm. (This and the following three figures pertain to Corozal spongewares.)

the rim or a simply modeled zoomorphic ornament (Roosevelt 1980, 207, Figs. 58 and 59). As in Barrancoid pottery, shallow incised grooves are used to define the inflections of modeled forms, but similar to Arauquinoid pottery, modeling is executed by appliqué and crude manipulation, rather than by the smooth carving found in Saladoid-Barrancoid styles. Some of the Corozal curvilinear-incised sherds have small traces of yellow, red, or pinkish mauve paint on their surfaces. The mauve is Munsell pale red (10 R 6/4) and weak red (10 R 5/4), and the yellow is Munsell yellow (10 YR 8/8). Probably because the incision is rather broad and shallow and not good for holding pigment, none of the sherds with the curvilinear incision were decorated with pigment rubbed into the incisions, which is a trait confined to the Corozal sherdware and to Corozal spongeware with rectilinear incision. (*See* mode #132.)

The open bowls bearing the curvilinear decoration vary in rim and base form (Fig. 17). Shapes include triangular rims, upright squared rims, out-turned squared rims thickened on the inside, tapered rims thickened on the outside, rounded rims thickened on the top, carinated bases, and round bases. Many but not all of these shapes seem to derive from those characteristic of the earlier La Gruta tradition decorated gritware pottery.

Sherds from spongeware vessels decorated with Corozal curvilinear incision are almost entirely restricted to Corozal levels, first appearing in middle Corozal 1 times. Percentages peak at about 2% in late Corozal 1 and early

Corozal 2 levels, and taper off sharply during Corozal 3. The mode helps divide early and middle Corozal 1, links late Corozal 1 with Corozal 2, and distinguishes Corozal 2 from 3 and Corozal 3 from Camoruco 1. The differences in the frequencies and proportions of the mode are statistically significant between middle and late Corozal 1, early and late Corozal 2, Corozal 2 and 3, and Corozal 3 and Camoruco 1, and not significant between late Corozal 1 and 2.

This decorative type has been found at many Parmana region sites and has contemporary relatives in the Barrancas, Los Barrancos, and Guarguapo phases of the Lower Orinoco (Cruxent and Rouse 1958–59, Pl. 92, 94:3–7, 96:10, 100:12–14, 101:10,12,14), La Cabrera in the Valencia Basin (Cruxent and Rouse 1958–59, Pl. 66:8, 9, 15), and the Aruka incised style of British Guiana (Evans and Meggers 1960). In the Middle Orinoco, sherds of a very similar ware have been found upriver in Aguerito, near Caicara (Zucchi, Tarble, and Vaz 1984, Fig. 4l, M–O,S). As at the Ronquin site in Parmana, at the Aguerito site the stratigraphy was not sufficiently intact (and the excavation levels too arbitrary) to reveal the distinct chronological placement of this mode, and it was classified with sherds of sponge-tempered decorative modes that are not contemporary with it. For example, the Corozal tables show clearly that this Corozal tradition mode has a different stratigraphic distribution from that of the animal-effigy bowls (mode #209) with which it had been classified by Howard at Ronquin and by Zucchi and Tarble at Aguerito, for the animal-effigy bowls are abundant only from Corozal 3 through Camoruco 2. Although the styles both have sponge temper, the animal-effigy bowls are stylistically and technologically totally different from the vessels with the curvilinear style—in shape, color, nature and abundance of temper, type of incision, and motifs. By separating the two types of bowls on the grounds of style, temper, and stratigraphic distribution, it was possible to gain a more refined chronology for the periods involved. The definition of Corozal curvilinear incision as a time marker is an example of the effectiveness of combining stratigraphic excavation with non-inclusive micro-stylistic classification for purposes of chronology.

COROZAL RECTILINEAR INCISION, MODE #132 *(Pl. 8, bottom; Fig. 18; Tables 31–34)*. Another very important Corozal diagnostic is a spongeware decorative type that seems to be distantly related to the simple, incised decoration of the Corozal sherdwares. This is Corozal rectilinear incision on bowls. It consists mainly of crude, parallel, diagonal incisions usually arranged around the upper sides of simple bowls with upright or inturned sides. The band of parallel lines is usually set off from the rim by a single horizontal line beneath the rim and a row of repeated nicks on the top or side of the rim. These lines are

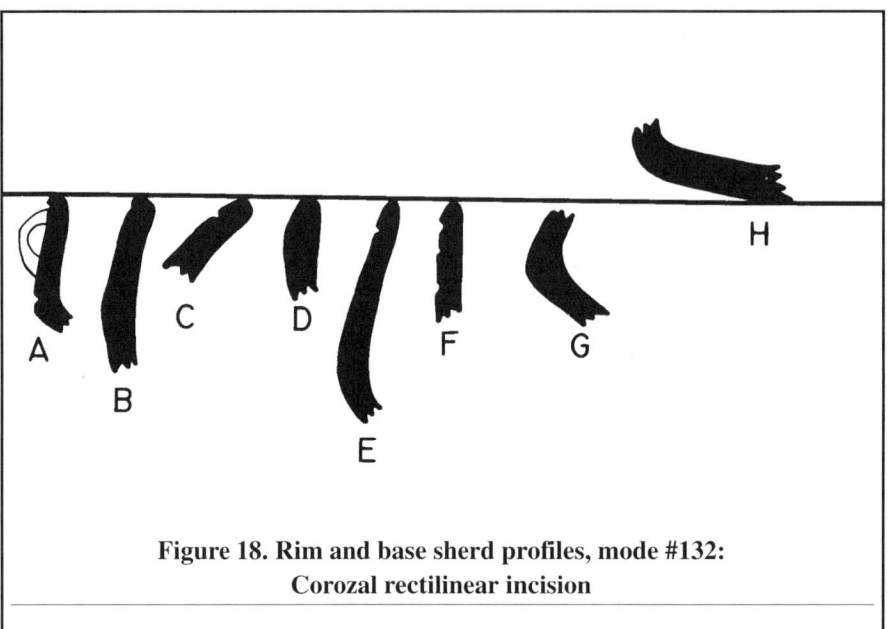

Figure 18. Rim and base sherd profiles, mode #132: Corozal rectilinear incision

Provenience numbers and diameters: A: 2–67, d. 11 cm; B: 2–70, d. 19 cm; C: 7–12, d. 14 cm; D: 8–16, d. 19 cm; E: 8–17 and 8–18, d. 14 cm; F: 37–8, d. 16 cm; G: 31–52, d. 18 cm; H: 2–49, d. 18 cm.

for the most part narrower and deeper than the incisions in the sherdwares, and the sherdwares for the most part lack the nicks on the rim. Often the Corozal rectilinear incisions and nicks are filled with red pigment, just as are the incisions in sherdwares. The pigment is Munsell red (10 R 4/8). Paint is not usually found on the surface of the rectilinear-incised vessels. It seems to have been applied exclusively as filling in the incisions.

Despite some decorative parallels, the shapes of this type are quite different from the sherdwares' shapes, and vessel walls are much thinner. The predominant shape is the bowl with simple rounded, slightly squared, or tapered rim and with curving walls, gently carinated sides, and round bottom. The sides of vessels are usually upright or slightly inturned and slightly curved. There is no decorative or morphological similarity to the Corozal curvilinear-incised bowl type despite its contemporaneity. The two types have incised decoration of very different quality and content, and the Corozal rectilinear-incised pottery's shapes lack the complexity of rim treatment characteristic of vessels of the curvilinear-incised type.

The temper of this decorative type is very different from that of the sherdwares and similar to that of Corozal curvilinear-decorated spongeware, consisting of moderate to abundant amounts of sponge and sparse sherd temper, with rare waterworn sand inclusions. Although usually not very large in diameter, these bowls seem to have been used over the fire, for they are often crusted on the outside with soot. The pottery is buff in color, with the core of sherds often slightly grayer and more brown than the surface. The surface ranges among Munsell light brown (7.5 YR 6/4), reddish yellow (5 YR 6/6), red (2.5 YR 5/6), and dark gray (5 YR 4/1).

The rectilinear-incised pottery makes a good chronological mode because it is present in adequate quantities for statistical analysis (seventy-nine examples) and very short-lived, beginning in late Corozal 1 and dropping out in Corozal 3. The mode has a somewhat similar distribution to that of the curvilinear-incised pottery mode, differentiating early and late Corozal 1 and Corozal 2 and 3 by statistically significant differences in proportions. The peak percentage is in late Corozal 1 (1.5%).

Sherds of this style were found by us at most of the sites in Parmana, by Howard at Ronquin, and by Vargas and her colleagues at various sites (Vargas 1981, 550; Lam. A,D). Vargas includes it in her type Ronquin zoned-incised with spicules, but this latter type (our mode #19, Arauquinoid rectilinear incision; *see* Tables 55–58) is a late Camoruco mode that is stylistically and stratigraphically totally distinct, with no distributional overlap with the Corozal rectilinear incision in the strata of the site. In fact, a full three strata without any sherds of either of the two different styles intervene between them in the stratigraphic column. To equate the two styles simply because they both have straight-line motifs, disregarding their stylistic and chronological separateness, makes no classificatory sense and does injustice to the archaeological sequence, collapsing its phases of temporal development and obscuring real and substantial cultural change. Styles that really are closely similar to Corozal rectilinear-incised pottery also existed elsewhere in the Orinoco. The site of Aguerito has sherds that are decoratively identical (Zucchi, Tarble, and Vaz 1984, Fig. 3, O–Q), but the temper is defined as sand rather than sponge. In the Yale University Peabody Museum collections from Los Barrancos there are a few sherds with decoration and shape very similar to the Corozal rectilinear-incised sherds. Sherds with similar decoration are included in Osgood and Howard's (1943, Fig. 23,D) treatise as one of the "unclassified" types from Orinoco sites.

COROZAL RED-AND-WHITE PAINT, MODE #18 *(Pl. 9, top, A–M; Fig. 19; Tables 35–38).* Another outstanding Corozal diagnostic decorative type is mode #18, Corozal red-and-white paint in bands. This mode is abundant (146 examples) and entirely restricted to Corozal levels. Like Corozal curvilinear and rectilinear incision, it is most common in late Corozal 1 and early Corozal two levels. The statistics show that these two levels have significantly more examples of

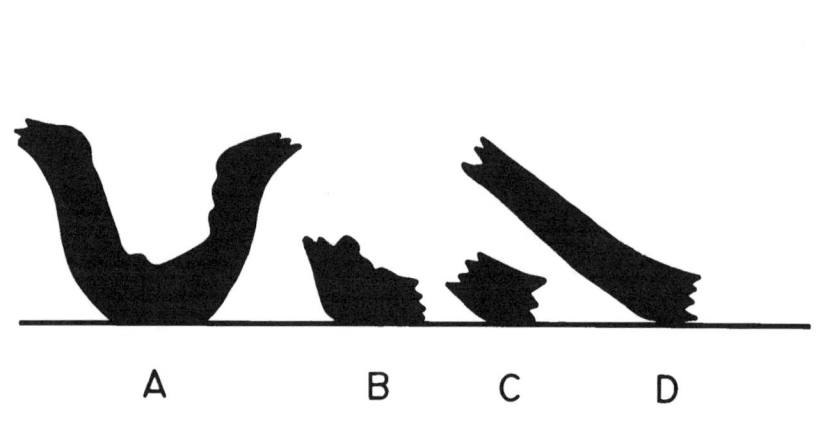

Figure 19. Base sherd profiles, mode #18: Corozal red-and-white, and mode #20: polychrome paint

Provenience numbers and diameters: A: 2–75, d. ? cm; B: 24–8, d. 20 cm; C: 21–21, d. 12 cm; D: 2–73, d. ? cm.

mode #18 than other Corozal levels. Thus the mode is a good diagnostic for distinguishing certain time periods within the Corozal phase. The differences in frequencies and percentages of the pottery between Corozal 1 and 2 are statistically insignificant.

This paint is found almost always on the outside of sherds. The motifs are simple bands, most commonly alternating wide red-and-white bands, less commonly with white parallel lines on red or red bands on white or plain. Occasionally the parallel bands diverge or merge. Handles and spouts are commonly plain white. The painted lines are straight or slightly curved and vary from about 5 mm to 1.5 cm in width. The red paint is Munsell red (10 YR 5/6) and light red (2.5 YR 6/6) and turns brown when heated. The white is Munsell white (2.5 YR 8/3, 8/2) and pale brown (10 YR 8/3).

The painted sherds derive from closed vessels that seem to be small to medium-sized bottles. A few of the sherds with the paint were characterized by a large spout with thickened rim, a crude appliqué band or nubbin, large, stocky feet, wide strap handles, or flat bases (Fig. 19). The majority of the sherds with the paint were body sherds with no diagnostic morphological characteristics. The inner surface of the sherds is almost always deeply striated with wipe marks from a cloth. The paste and temper characteristics are the same as those of Corozal rectilinear-incised pottery.

This decorative paint mode is common in Corozal tradition components in the Parmana region. As a painting style, it has no known antecedents in the La Gruta tradition phases or any other tradition that we know of. Paint in banded patterns is found in the Andes region of Venezuela and Colombia, the northwestern Orinoco, and the vicinity of Santarem in the Lower Amazon in Brazil, associated with pottery of the Incised and Punctate Horizon. However, the bands in the other styles are usually much narrower and the motifs more complex than those characteristic of the Corozal red-and-white paint. It is intriguing that Saladoid red-and-white paint, though stylistically entirely different from Corozal red-and-white paint, also occurs frequently on closed vessels during the Corozal phase and the La Gruta tradition phases. It is unclear what significance red-and-white decoration may have had in connection with the use of the bottles or their contents in the perceptions of the makers and users of the pottery.

COROZAL POLYCHROME PAINT, MODE #20 *(Pl. 9, top, N–R)*. Mode #20 is a rare style of water-soluble polychrome paint executed in geometric patterns on buff or white. The patterns are usually linear, including repeated crosshatching and parallel bands or lines, but occasionally curvilinear lines appear (Pl. 9, *top*, Q, R), in scrolls or parallel curves. The colors are red, black, and/or brown on white or cream. This rare paint was applied on a number of different pottery fabrics. A few sherds have a very fine white paste with no observable temper. Most others have moderate amounts of sponge temper, like the majority of Corozal phase pottery. A few have sherd-and-fiber temper, a few have caraipe, and a few have very abundant sponge temper. Perhaps analysis of trace elements could in the future be applied to the question of whether the fine-tempered polychrome ware might be a foreign trade ware and coarser ones local copies. There are too few sherds to reconstruct many shapes, but at least some sherds come from vessels that seem to be bottles, jars, and open bowls. Due to the comparative rarity of examples of the polychrome paint (thirty-four examples), it could not be meaningfully tabulated or analyzed statistically. The decorative style appears confined to the Corozal phase, but the sample is too small to determine for certain.

This mode, which occurs at many sites in Parmana, has no antecedents in Saladoid and Barrancoid styles. (In the Lower Orinoco, Saladoid paint sometimes has black designs along with the red-and-white, but the style of paint does not resemble mode #20.) It is found at Aguerito (Zucchi, Tarble, and Vaz 1984, Fig. 4, G–K) and vaguely resembles polychrome paint from the Venezuelan Andes and northwestern Orinoco (Kidder 1944). More distantly, it could be said to resemble the painted styles of northeastern Colombia (Reichel-

Dolmatoff 1965b, Pl. 40). The Colombian stylistic connection is interesting, for the early Corozal corn resembles the Pollo maize race of the northern Andes and Caribbean Colombia (Walton Galinat, personal communication). There is also a similarity between the Corozal polychromes and the polychromes of the sponge-tempered pottery in Santarem phase collections from the mouth of the Tapajos River in the Lower Amazon in Brazil. (Numerous examples are illustrated in Palmatary 1960.) The Santarem polychromes are more elaborate in motifs but have a stylistic context somewhat similar to that of the Corozal polychromes, being associated in sites with majority wares bearing plastic decoration.

COROZAL VERTICAL RIM STRAP HANDLES, MODE #126 (Pl. 9, bottom; Fig. 20; Tables 39–42). Another Corozal diagnostic type is mode #126, which comprises the sponge-tempered bowls with decorated and undecorated vertical rim strap handles (Roosevelt 1980, 207, Fig. 59). These are relatively abundant (ninety-nine examples) and predominate in Corozal levels. There are a few anachronistic examples in Camoruco levels, probably from animal-burrow or posthole type disturbances or curation of found objects. The handles first appear late in Corozal 1 and peak soon after at around 1 to 2% during late Corozal 1 and Corozal 2, dropping abruptly by the end of the phase. The type is rare (about .1 to .2%) before and after these times. The changing distribution of the handles distinguishes late Corozal 1 from middle Corozal 1 and links late Corozal 1, Corozal 2, and Corozal 3.

The handles are either plain or decorated. Their orientation is always vertical, although the degree of projection of the handle above the rim varies. The decorations include one or two nubbins or simply modeled zoomorphic heads. All but one of these representational heads seem to be that of a bulbous-eyed, long-beaked bird. These representational decorations are rare (five examples), and plain examples greatly outnumber the decorated. The handles occur on unpainted bowls with tapering or rounded inturned rims and flat bases with a slight pedestal. This type of flat base (separately seriated as mode #213, Tables 83–86) is also the base type of the animal-effigy bowls (mode #209, Tables 43–46). The bowls with the rim strap handles appear to be slightly asymmetrical in circumference, so the rim diameters (Fig. 20) that we obtained from the concentric circle charts can be expected to be somewhat erroneous. The temper consists of moderate to abundant amounts of sponge spicules with some clay bits, and the paste is light buff or beige. The ware seems the same as the nearly contemporary pottery decorated with Corozal rectilinear incision, but the two types have no overlap in shape or decoration. The bowls with handles never have any incised decoration except for a few punctate or incised details

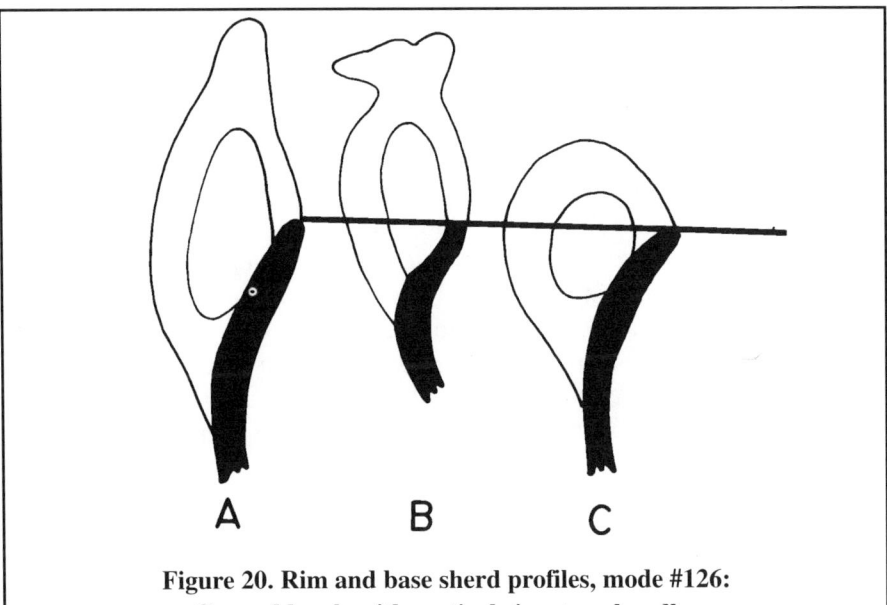

Figure 20. Rim and base sherd profiles, mode #126: Corozal bowls with vertical rim strap handles

Provenience numbers and diameters: A: 2–82, d. 16 cm; B: 3–18, d. 14 cm; C: 2–85, d. 18 cm.

on the rare zoomorphic heads, and the Corozal rectilinear-incised bowls, in turn, never have rim handles or modeled decoration. (One Corozal rectilinear sherd has a plain handle slightly below its rim: Fig. 18, A.)

The rim handles seem to hark back to the La Gruta tradition grit-tempered D-shaped rim handles with animal adornos, which occur on the asymmetrical animal-effigy bowls. If so, the animal adorno has shrunk to a small nub or disappeared, and the vessel wall modeling that represented an animal face has gone. The La Gruta and Corozal bowl types are comparable functionally, in that both commonly have sooty bases indicating use for cooking. The Corozal bowls with strap handles may be functional and stylistic precursors to the sponge-tempered animal-effigy cooking bowls (mode #209), whose simple animal-head handles often have a small vestigial strap handle luted underneath the animal head. Soot on the outside of sherds of the spongeware animal-effigy bowls indicates a cooking function also. The sponge-tempered animal-effigy bowls overlap stratigraphically with the later examples of the Corozal bowls with rim strap handles and increase in frequency as the others taper off. They might therefore be considered to have replaced the earlier bowl type functionally during the late Corozal tradition and early Camoruco tradition.

These bowls with rim strap handles, which occur in Corozal phase levels at many other sites in Parmana, do not, to my knowledge, have exact parallels in other lowland complexes, although future finds may reveal some. The style of their crude, rare adornos is, however, closely related to that of the Incised and Punctate Horizon styles of the tropical lowlands.

COROZAL AND CAMORUCO TRADITION SPONGEWARES. Although paste characteristics varied significantly in the Corozal site pottery corpus, there were more modes of decoration and shape useful for the seriation because they were more distinctive and varied than paste characteristics through time. With a couple of exceptions, temper and color of paste tended to be similar or intergrade imperceptibly between wares and styles, making it difficult to separate clearly different paste complexes. As described above, however, the Corozal tradition grit-tempered (#140) and sherd- and fiber-tempered wares (#135) were distinctive enough to be classified and abundant enough to be useful for chronological seriation. For most Corozal site levels (except for Level 18, Excavation 1, in which sherdwares are approximately equal in frequency to spongewares) the majority ware was the sponge-tempered pottery. This major ware category was not useful for seriation, for it was both too variable and too persistent, predominating during both the Corozal and Camoruco traditions. Both the paste and the color of the sponge-tempered pottery changed somewhat through time. The Corozal tradition spongeware tends to be more pink and paler than early Camoruco tradition pottery, which is more tan-gray in color, and late Camoruco tradition pottery gets lighter-toned and grayer in color. I have given the range of Munsell colors for the Corozal spongewares in the sections above. The most common colors for the Camoruco phase sponge-tempered pottery were light reddish brown (5 YR 6/3, 6/4) and light brown (7.5 YR 6/4). But all these and other similar colors were common in the pottery corpus of both traditions. Color, therefore, varied, but not abruptly enough that pottery could be separated into different, clear-cut taxonomic color groupings. The tempering showed a similarly unhelpful pattern of intergradation. Many of the Corozal tradition sponge-tempered sherds contained sparse sherd temper and rare clay bits in addition to moderate amounts of sponge temper, whereas most Camoruco tradition pottery usually had more abundant sponge temper and more clay bits than sherds. Both pottery groups had sparse sand inclusions. However, the sponge-tempered pottery in all levels is very variable in these characteristics, which exist as subtle variations rather than as separable, classifiable states. A given Corozal tradition level's pottery had many body sherds identical to those in a given Camoruco tradition level. Therefore, it has not been possible to divide the sponge-tempered pottery into distinct groupings on the basis of temper and color alone.

The Corozal tradition spongeware decorative modes have been described above. The following decorative modes primarily distinguish the Camoruco tradition and its subdivisions. Although several of the Camoruco tradition modes appear first in the Corozal tradition or even earlier, most of the others first come into use during Camoruco.

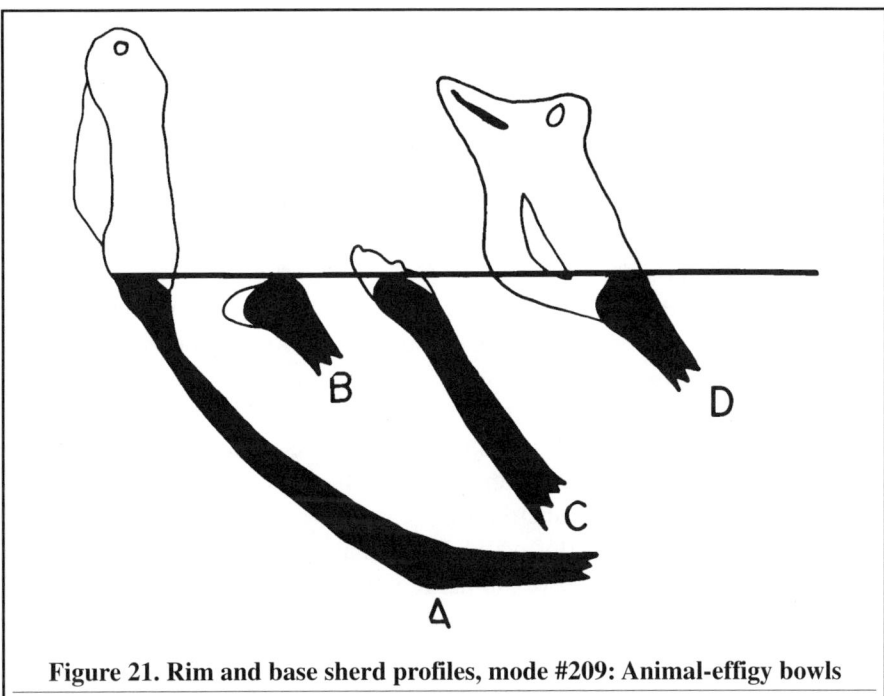

Figure 21. Rim and base sherd profiles, mode #209: Animal-effigy bowls

Provenience numbers and diameters: A: 56–17, rim d. 33 cm, base d. 14 cm; B: 23–2, d. 36 cm; C: 35–197, d. 40 cm; D: 12–87, d. 52 cm.

2. Camoruco Tradition Modes

SPONGE-TEMPERED ANIMAL-EFFIGY BOWLS, MODE #209 *(Pl. 10, top and bottom, S; Fig. 21; Tables 43–46)*. This mode refers to sponge-tempered animal-effigy bowls that were made primarily during Corozal 3, Camoruco 1, and Camoruco 2 phases. The effigy vessels consist of hemispherical bowls with crude modeled-incised animal heads and tablike paws or wings attached to the rims.

Animal-effigy bowls have a long history in the Parmana region. Animal images are the most common icons in representational imagery during the

La Gruta, Ronquin, and Ronquin Sombra phases of the La Gruta tradition, and many of the depictions suggest that the bowls and bottles with zoomorphic imagery were conceived of by their makers as effigies, that is, vessels in the shape of animals. Animals continue to be depicted in small numbers during the Corozal tradition, in both sand-tempered and sponge-tempered wares. During the Camoruco tradition, although animal images increase in abundance at first, human images, which are exceedingly rare earlier, become more common than animals by the end of the tradition, both as effigies and as figurine adornos.

At the Corozal site, there were at least three modes of animal-effigy bowls. The earliest, mode #63, is represented by rare animal-head bowl rim ornaments of the Saladoid-Barrancoid style executed in sand-tempered ware (Pl. 7, *bottom,* D, E, H; Roosevelt 1980, 209, Fig. 62, 2-92, 24-7, 8-28). These heads usually are placed on the rim or atop a D-shaped vertical rim strap handle on the bowls. These adornos are too rare to be tabulated and analyzed separately as a diagnostic chronological attribute, but as described in previous sections are seriated in the Corozal gritware mode and the mode of Saladoid-Barrancoid decoration. The adornos occur in both Corozal and Camoruco levels, possibly as anachronistic curated finds in the latter levels. In fact, one gritware animal adorno was found as an offering in one of the Corozal 3–Camoruco 1 burials (Skeleton 2, Fig. 10, sherd #6). There are too few examples of Corozal gritware zoomorphic lugs for valid functional inferences based on stratigraphic context, but this type of animal lug was a cooking-bowl handle in the earlier La Gruta tradition phases, to judge from the soot on the vessel walls and underside of the lugs of those phases.

A later effigy-bowl mode of sponge-tempered ware, #209 includes two approximately contemporary types of bowls with zoomorphic rim lugs. Both types are open bowls with outward-facing animal-head lugs and paw/wing rim tabs. The bowls have slightly thickened or occasionally beveled rims, and flat, thickened bases (Fig. 21). The vessels are made in the usual sponge-tempered Corozal and Camoruco phase wares described above.

One of these two sponge-tempered animal-effigy bowl types lumped under mode #209 is mode #8, a bowl with a crudely shaped animal- or bird-head lug on the rim (Pl. 10, A, D; Roosevelt 1980, 212, Fig. 66, 12-87 and 200-1). The crude lugs' features are executed in sloppy modeling, incision, and punctation, and neither they, or the vessels are ever painted. The animal images on the mode #8 bowls are too crude to be identified to species, although birds (Pl. 10, A) can sometimes be distinguished from mammals by their pointed beaks. These bowls with animal-head lugs occur between Corozal 2 and

Camoruco 2 phases. The lugs may have developed originally from something like the Saladoid-Barrancoid animal-head lugs, for they bear underneath a curious small, flattened, vestigial handle where the D-shaped vertical strap handle would have been attached (Fig. 21, A,D). The intermediate step in the evolution of D-shaped handles with zoomorphic lugs into these animal lugs with vestigial handles may be the Corozal bowl rim strap handles (mode #126), which occasionally are adorned with crudely modeled animal images. These Corozal rim strap handle bowls phase out as the sponge-tempered animal-effigy bowls with vestigial handles expand in numbers.

Grouped into mode #209 with the animal-lug bowls of mode #8 is another type of sponge-tempered bowl with animal-head lug, termed mode #6. Mode #6 bowls have relatively carefully made animal-head lugs attached to the rims (Pl. 10, *top*, E, J; *bottom*, S; Fig. 22, B; Roosevelt 1980, 212, Fig. 66, 43-6, 35-12, 58-10). This mode could not be tabulated separately from mode #8 because of its rarity. It exists from Camoruco 1 through Camoruco 2 times. These lugs are more standardized than those of mode #8, and the images are limited to animals with definite muzzles, such as dogs and bats. Like the lugs with the vestigial handles, these bowls with animal-head lugs were made in the primary Camoruco sponge-tempered ware. A few have a covering of mauve paint (mode #152) (Pl. 10, *bottom*, S; Fig. 22, B).

In addition to the above-mentioned animal bowl rim lugs, there are various other modeled-incised animal ornaments occurring in small numbers throughout the Corozal and Camoruco phases. They are not useful for chronological purposes because they are found in all subphases, occur only in very small numbers, and are very variable in style and iconography (one is illustrated in Pl. 8, *top*, B, and others are illustrated in Roosevelt 1980, 207, Fig. 59, 1-157, 3-18, 2-1; 212, Fig. 66, 32-109, 34-61, 76-1, 12-81). They are executed in a range of sponge-tempered pastes and occur in small numbers on various types of bowls. For these reasons, these particular animal lugs were not assigned a mode number and are not tabulated in this monograph.

From Corozal 2 through Camoruco 2 phase levels, there also occurred a number of triangular and subtriangular modeled rim tabs decorated with crude, deep, simple incised and/or punctate geometric designs (Pl. 10, *top*, K–P; Howard 1943, Pl. 2-E; Roosevelt 1980, 213, Fig. 67, all except 32-114). From study of whole or almost whole vessels it is clear that these constitute the paws or wings for the mode #6 and #8 animals and birds, and they have similar level distributions. Thus, the bowls were conceived of iconographically, as animal effigies in which the back of the animal was hollowed out as a container. (Such use of animal images for containers is common worldwide, with the large, wooden zoomorphic feast dishes of the ethnographic Northwest Coast Indians being some of the best known examples.) The tabs have the primary Camoruco sponge- and sherd-tempered paste. A few are painted with mauve, and these are the most complex in shape, apparently being the paws of the well-shaped, outward-facing animal-head lugs of mode #8.

For chronological purposes and to seriate together the parts of the same figurative vessel forms, mode #209 was established to include both sponge-tempered, outward-facing animal bowl rim lugs and the rim tabs. By combining two similar and contemporary decorated bowl types, the mode was made abundant enough (145 examples) for statistical analysis but was still relatively restricted chronologically. The sponge-tempered animal-effigy bowls occur in very low percentages in Corozal 2 (about .1 to .2%) and much higher percentages (1 to 2%) in Corozal 3 and Camoruco 1, and then drop rapidly during Camoruco 2 to very low percentages again (about .1 to .2%). Frequencies in Corozal 1 are negligible and confined to the final levels, and only two stray examples were recovered from Camoruco 3 levels. The frequencies and percentages of the mode in the Corozal 3 and early Camoruco levels did not differ statistically from each other but did differ from those in other subphases' levels. These distributions help to contrast Camoruco 2 and 3, Camoruco 1 and 2, and Corozal 2 and 3 from each other.

The animal-head lugs of mode #209 appear functionally analogous to the Camoruco 2 and 3 human rim lugs (mode #136) in their placement as lug handles on the rims of open cooking bowls. Many bear sooty crusts on their undersides. Because the majority of the soot-covered cooking bowls in Corozal 3 through Camoruco 2 levels are plain beveled or everted rim bowls, the rarer animal-lug cooking bowls may have been cooking bowls for feasts or other special occasions. Two burials, one at Ronquin and one in Excavation 3 at Corozal (Fig. 10, Skeleton #2), had offerings of the mode #8 animal-effigy bowls. At Ronquin, the animal-effigy bowl was placed upside down over the head of the individual, and at Corozal the bowls were placed at the person's side. Only at Corozal was the sex determinable, and it was female.

The animal-head and paw-wing bowl rim lugs have been found in the project excavations at other sites in Parmana, including Ronquin (Howard 1943, Pl. 2, E, F, H–J, Pl. 6, I, O; Vargas 1981, 545, Lam. 55, A–C, E, F, H, G; 546, Lam. 56, F–J; 549, Lam. 57, H, K) and Parmana-Los Mangos (Roosevelt 1980, 212, Fig. 66). They also occur in many other areas of the lowlands in styles of the Incised and Punctate Horizon. In the Orinoco, the outward-facing lugs and complex paw-wing tabs are found in the Arauquin area (Petrullo 1939, Pl. 26–28). The animal-head lugs with vestigial handles have been found at Aguerito (Zucchi, Tarble, and Vaz 1984, Fig. 4, Q and U, and 5, J).

Both at Aguerito and in Howard's analysis at Ronquin, the animal heads and tab lugs are classified with pottery with which they are not contemporary, such as the flat, highly decorated human rim adornos, Arauquinoid rectilinear incision, and maroon paint. In addition, in Vargas's classification, the animal heads and the triangular tabs were actually separately classified into different decorative types, although they are from the same vessels. Nericagua in the Upper Orinoco, also, has examples of the outward-facing lugs (Evans, Meggers, and Cruxent 1959). Animal-head lugs are common in the Valencia and La Cabrera phases of the Valencia Basin, but they lack vestigial handles and the distinctive outward-facing animals. Animal-head lugs and rim tabs quite similar to the Corozal ones are also found at the mouth of the Tapajos River in the pottery of the Santarem phase (Palmatary 1960). Animal bowl rim lugs of quite different imagery but similar modeling and incision styles have been found in the prehistoric pottery of the Upper Amazon in Bolivia and Peru.

CAMORUCO MAUVE PAINT, MODE #152 *(Pl. 10, bottom; Fig. 22; Tables 47–50).* The three subphases of Camoruco are linked by the abundant occurrence of mode #152, a particular type of overall mauve or purplish paint. The nearest

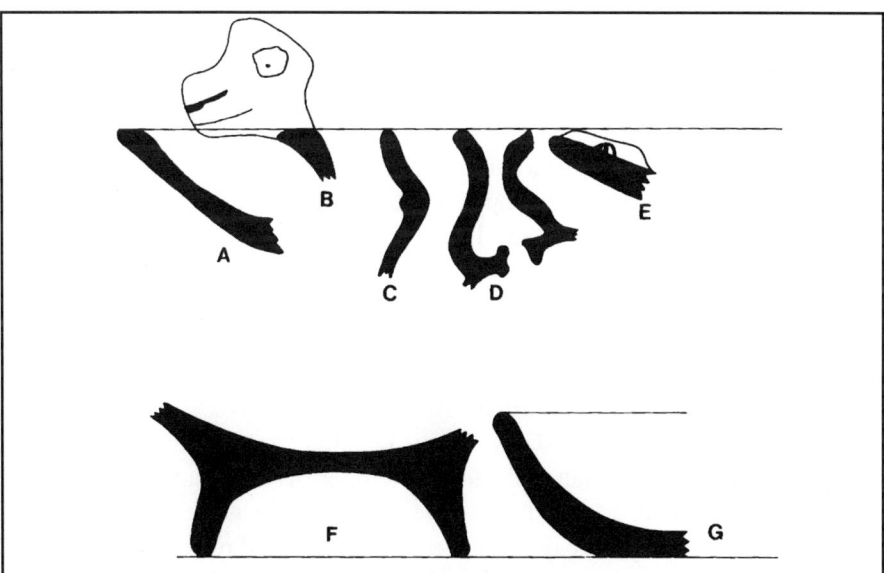

Figure 22. Rim and base sherd profiles, mode #152: Camoruco mauve paint

Provenience numbers and diameters: A: 35–17, d. 10 cm; B: 43–5, d. 26 cm; C: 4–10, d. 9 cm; D: 59–5, d. ? cm; E: 53–52, d. 20? cm; F: 39–74, d. 8 cm; G: 59–2, d. 20 cm.

colors in the Munsell Soil Color Charts are weak red (10R 5/4) and light red (10R 6/6); however, the mauve is usually more intense and pinkish than any soil color. It is a thick, powdery, water-soluble paint that was probably applied in some kind of fugitive resin that has mostly dissolved away. The composition of the paint is unknown, but probably *Bixa orellana* (*annatto, onoto,* or *urucu*) can be eliminated as a possibility because that coloring rapidly fades to brown when oxidized. The paint is delicate, and its original surface is usually not preserved. Its hardness is always less than 1, indicating that it is not a fired ceramic paint or slip.

In all cases where the original surface is preserved, the mauve paint is overlaid with white or yellow paint in minute, complex geometric designs (Munsell brownish yellow [10YR 6/6] to pale yellow [2.5Y 7/4]), which are outlined with fine, sharp incision that cuts into the paint, but not into the fired ceramic surface underneath (Fig. 33, sherds 4-10, 48-342, and 12-5; Roosevelt 1980, 213, Fig. 68; 216, Fig. 72, 4-10, 48-342, 12-5). Thus this mode actually represents a kind of complex biochrome paint with incised details, although due to its fragility, the color most apparent to the naked eye is the monochrome mauve of the base color. The few observable preserved figural motifs in white or yellow include repeated lines, zig-zags, triangles, hooks, and scrolls combined in square and triangular panels. Occasionally, the color of the paint has turned orange because the mauve and yellow have powdered and become mixed together.

The paint usually occurs as a thick overall layer on pottery without modeling or incision. Only a few examples of the paint (ten out of a total of 431) occur on modeled-incised pieces. There are four examples of a rare type of human face modeled on plate rims (Fig. 22, E; Pl. 10, *bottom,* Q), one human adorno (Fig. 22, E; Pl. 10, Q), three animal lugs (Fig. 22, B; Pl. 10, *bottom,* S), three tabs, one spout from a double-spout-and-bridge bottle (Fig. 22, D; Pl. 10, *bottom,* U), and one example of a vessel neck with modeled strip or ring around it (Fig. 22, C; Pl. 10, *bottom,* R).

The temper of most of the sherds of this decorated type is abundant sponge with much less abundant but conspicuous temper of large clay bits of orange color. A small number of the sherds have caraipe temper, a common lowland siliceous tempering agent that is believed to be burnt and pulverized tree bark. Caraipe appears, under binocular magnification of 20 to 50 times, as chunky, soft bits of white, gray, or black material organized in long, parallel cylindrical fibers. This organic vegetal temper can be dated radiometrically, and the current Parmana dating project in collaboration with the Oxford University Accelerator Laboratory includes samples of pottery of this paste.

This mauve-painted pottery seems to have functioned as both a special service ware and a special cooking ware. Many pieces are thin walled and small in capacity, with shapes including cups, small bowls, small jars, and bottles. Bowl and cup rims vary from simple tapered to beveled on the outside or inside. There are simple thickened flat (Pl. 10, *bottom*, G) and round bases and slightly out-turned ring bases (F). Fewer pieces are thick, with soot on the outside, and have thickened rims and lug handles (B). The mauve-painted ware may have had a use similar to the highly decorated polychromes of the Marajoara phase, pottery which is thought to represent a special ceremonial ware used for feasting. The Marajoara polychromes also have a great variety of shapes and include highly decorated pottery apparently used for cooking or warming food, as well as for eating and drinking. The Marajoara ware is rarely found in domestic contexts, such as house floors, but is abundant in burials and garbage fill (Roosevelt 1991a). We do not know much about the distribution of the mauve-painted pottery in different types of activity areas because of the focus of the excavations at Corozal on the stratigraphic column rather than the site layout, but this paint type is rarer in some of the putative house floors than in the garbage layers, as might be expected for a special feasting ware.

Because this mode is an integral taxon, a decorative ware with many vessel types, it is more inclusive than other modes and not confined to a single subphase or part of a subphase. Also, it is very abundant, making it likelier to have spurious changes in proportions. However, the mauve-painted ware is an excellent diagnostic of the Camoruco tradition as a whole, occurring very frequently (a total of 431 examples) in all layers of all the Camoruco phases. Its changes in percentage through the levels of the phase may help to define microchronological units. It is also a useful demarcation of the boundary between the Camoruco and Corozal phases because it begins abruptly, creating a significantly different distribution between Corozal and Camoruco 1 levels. It is absent from all Corozal levels except for two examples from the Corozal 3 levels. There is a rare mode of paint of the same color that occurs in Corozal layers, but it is a distinct mode, with paint applied thinly on the Corozal curvilinear-incised pottery (#134), which never occurs in Camoruco levels (except for one sherd found at a stratigraphic disturbance). The rare Corozal mode occasionally includes areas of bright yellow paint next to the mauve paint, a particular combination never found in the Camoruco mauve paint, where the yellow is always applied over the mauve. Possibly, a similar material is used for the two paints (this needs to be investigated by chemical analysis), but they clearly differ in their decorative use. The rapidity with which the Camoruco mauve-paint mode appears, full blown, suggests that it may have been developed in another region and introduced by trade or diffusion into Parmana. On the other hand, the existence of an earlier Corozal phase pigment that may have the same composition, though different style of use, could be taken as evidence for a local origin. Until more regional sequences are known in the Orinoco, the geographic origins and history of the different wares, types, and styles will remain obscure.

CIRCLE STAMPS, MODE #160 (Tables 59–62). The Camoruco phases are also linked by the presence of the circle-stamps motif in pottery decoration. Sherds bearing the circles are relatively abundant (198 examples in the two excavations) and occur in every Camoruco tradition level. The motif comes into the Parmana sequence in very low frequencies during Corozal 3 and then rapidly increases to abundance in Camoruco 1. The earliest circle motifs are small and seem to evolve iconographically out of a simple, medium-sized punctation, which occurs in similar iconographic contexts. The circle-stamp motif is an excellent separator of Saladoid-Barrancoid-influenced phases from Arauquinoid ones. According to the statistical tests, the differences in frequencies and percentages of the mode between early and middle Corozal levels on the one hand and those of late Corozal and Camoruco on the other hand are significant. There are also statistically significant differences in its distribution among the levels of Corozal 3 and the Camoruco phases, and these may relate to changes through time in the use of the excavation locality for activities employing plastic-decorated pottery.

The circle stamp is part of the distinctive Arauquinoid complex of decorative motifs related to the Incised and Punctate Horizon. The Arauquinoid decorative elements, which include sharp, careless incision and crude appliqué, are never used in the styles of the Saladoid-Barrancoid pottery tradition, which instead have broad-line grooving, shallow, rounded punctations, and careful three-dimensional carving and modeling. Several Orinoco ceramic complexes, such as Guarguapo (Cruxent and Rouse 1958–59, Pl. 100), seem to have sherds from both decorative styles in the same components. However, it seems possible that these may actually be multicomponent assemblages of pottery combined by mechanical mixture, rather than integral, contemporary complexes. The Guarguapo pottery was excavated in the period of archaeology when artificial-level excavation was the primary collection method, and so the process of excavation may have combined pottery of different periods. At Corozal, the vertical distribution of the two styles of decoration is virtually mutually exclusive, and the Saladoid-Barrancoid decoration has dropped to minuscule frequencies by the time the Arauquinoid decorative motifs appear.

The circle stamp is a motif executed by marking wet or leather-hard pottery with the end of a hollow reed (Howard 1943, Pl. 6, E, F, J, Pl. 7, B, F, G; Roosevelt 1980, 210, Fig. 64, 1-16, 12-73, 12-72, 34-67; 211, Fig. 65, 1-3, 12-86,

48-107; 212, Fig. 66, 12-87, 58-10; 213, Fig. 67, 32-114, 23-4, 74-1; 214, Fig. 70, 48-16, 12-74, 48-97). The circles are used extensively in the decoration of pottery throughout the Camoruco phase, crosscutting many types and styles. They appear on a variety of shapes—on the representational lugs and tabs of open cooking bowls, directly on the rims of bowls, on the necks of jars, and on the features of human-effigy jars and figurines. The motif occurs almost exclusively on sponge- and sherd-tempered wares, with a slight gray core.

Iconographically, the circles are used to delineate human and animal body parts and ornaments and as geometric patterns within the rectilinear basketlike incision of Camoruco 3 (mode #19). The circles appear as decoration on appliqué eyebrows of humans, as ear ornaments or ear holes, as nostrils, as hair or headdress ornaments or as meatuses on male genitals, as nipples on female breasts, or as decorations on human joints and on the wings or paws of birds and animals. The circle stamp is commonly used with a dot inside for animal eyes but never for human eyes. This interesting iconographic distinction suggests that people's eyes were conceived of differently from animals' eyes.

In many motifs, the circle stamp is iconographically an alternative to simple punctation or a dash, which occur in similar decorative contexts. In order to see if the two different punctation styles had chronological differences in their distribution within the sequence, I plotted their distribution in the levels and found that they had essentially the same temporal distribution. Although appearing in the same levels, however, the two motifs rarely occur together on the same piece, suggesting that some potters favored one or the other punctation style. This kind of minor stylistic distinction would be useful to follow in the broad-area sampling of a site such as Corozal, to see if the spatial distribution of the motifs differs. In this way it might be possible to trace groups of individuals working within slightly differing ceramic traditions. It has been hypothesized that different residential groups might have different ceramic traditions (Deetz 1968; Longacre 1968), and, though this has never been verified ethnographically, there is still considerable potential interest among archaeologists in the spatial patterning of microstylistic contrasts within and between sites. Comparison of stylistic variation with microgenetic patterning of associated human skeletons (Lane and Sublett 1972) would add inferential breadth and help to test hypotheses about the relationship of style, genealogy, and residence.

3. Arauquinoid Series Modes

ARAUQUINOID MAROON PAINT, MODE #14 (Tables 51–54; Fig. 23; Pl. 11, top). Perhaps the best mode for defining the Camoruco 3 phase is #14, Arauquinoid maroon paint. This is a thick, water-soluble, unfired paint. The Munsell reading for the paint is dark red, 10 YR 3/6. It usually occurs as a wash over the entire surface of a vessel, except that modeled-incised lug handles and incised and punctate decorative panels on vessels are often left free of paint, as are the insides of vessels with narrow mouths. Where not damaged by abrasion or water, the paint is glossy and even. In a few examples, it is used as a figural paint in triangular and rectangular areas and bands, lines, lines of dots, and spirals (Pl. 11, *top,* B; Howard 1943, 30, 35, Fig. 9, F, 70, Fig. 11, E; Roosevelt 1980, 211, Fig. 65, 20-4; 214, Fig. 70, 12-74; 216, Fig. 72, 1-22; Vargas 1981, 552, Lam. 60 B; 553, Lam. 61 A, B). The figural paint, which is included in mode #14, was also seriated separately as mode #31 (not tabulated here). This procedure showed that it had the same stratigraphic and chronological distribution as plain maroon paint, taking into account sampling error due to the smaller number of specimens of mode #31. Accordingly, the figural paint was considered just an elaboration of the maroon-paint mode and was tabulated and analyzed with it as mode #14.

The maroon paint occurs on many different shapes. Notable among the plastic-decorated pots that bear the paint are the open bowls with human lugs (Pl. 12, *bottom;* Fig. 26) and the narrow-necked jars with Arauquinoid incised and punctate decoration on the neck (Fig. 24, B). These bear the maroon on the body of the vessel below the plastic decoration. Certain small human-effigy jars (mode #32) also bear the paint (Fig. 25, F), as do some of the rare hollow human figurines. The rims on the painted bowls are mostly simple—rounded, beveled, or slightly squared (Fig. 23, A–C). The rims of the incised jar necks are tapered and everted (Fig. 24, B), placed above necks that are more or less vertical and too narrow to insert a hand in. Bases are slightly thickened and rounded, sometimes with a slight break in the curvature (Fig. 23, E–G). The bases usually have lost paint from abrasion on the parts where they touched the ground or table.

Mode #14 is an outstanding chronological mode because it is very abundant and almost completely confined to Camoruco 3 phase levels. The mode sets the phase off from the other Camoruco phases by statistically significant differences in both frequencies and percentages. It is present in negligible quantities in Camoruco 1 and 2, then increases suddenly to very high frequencies at the beginning of Camoruco 3, and is cut off abruptly by the end of the prehistoric occupation. There are 590 sherds bearing the maroon paint in the Camoruco levels at Corozal, and all but ten of these are confined to Camoruco 3 levels. The ten stray sherds may, in fact, represent the slippage of a few sherds down minor intrusions by animal burrows into lower levels. Apparently, a large proportion of Camoruco 3 pottery was originally covered with

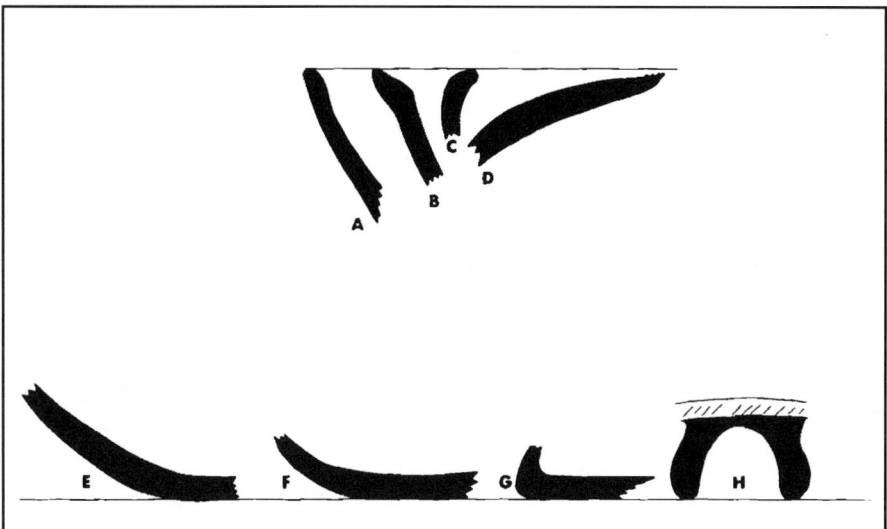

Figure 23. Rim and base sherd profiles, mode #14: Arauquinoid maroon paint

Provenience numbers and diameters: A: 30–114, d. 22 cm; B: 32–140, d. 38 cm; C: 32–145, d. 22 cm; D: 32–183, d. 7 cm; E: 34–304, d. 7 cm; F: 32–52, d. 36? cm; G: 80–135, d. 15 cm; H: 30–89, d. 5 cm.

this paint. Despite its fugitiveness, traces of the paint are preserved on a large number of sherds, and it is the most common decorative mode in the seriation. The reason so many examples were recovered from the Corozal excavations compared to the numbers from other excavations in the area is probably that we examined all sherds for paint before washing them, and did not wash the sherds with visible paint. Reversing the process would greatly lower the number of specimens recovered, since the paint is highly soluble in water.

The use of Munsell to discriminate colors helped to show that the maroon paint is very different from the Camoruco mauve paint (#152). This discrimination was important in precisely defining the mode chronologically, for the mauve paint was used for the whole of the Camoruco tradition, a much longer period of time than the time span of the maroon paint. Careful study of the physical qualities of the maroon paint also helped to distinguish it from the other paints.

Dark red, overall paint is an integral part of the Incised and Punctate Horizon and is found in most of the member styles. This kind of paint, associated with Arauquinoid series plastic decoration, has been found in several locations in the Venezuelan Orinoco, including Arauquin in the Apure Triangle (Petrullo 1939), Aguerito near Caicara (Zucchi, Tarble, and Vaz 1984), and Potrero Nuevo on the Cuchivero tributary (surface collections by Cruxent, Rouse, and me). The Valencia red type from the Valencia Basin is also related to the maroon paint of Parmana. Further afield, the Santarem style of the Lower Amazon of Brazil also has examples of dark red, overall paint on vessels stylistically related to the Horizon.

ARAUQUINOID RECTILINEAR INCISION, MODE #19 (Pl. 11, bottom; Fig. 24; Tables 55–58). Another common mode that defines the Camoruco 3 phase by setting it off from all other phases is mode #19, Arauquinoid rectilinear incision. This mode occurs mainly in Camoruco 3 levels, with negligible frequencies (five examples) in earlier Camoruco phases. It is very common, with 118 examples occurring in Camoruco 3 levels at Corozal. The frequencies and percentages of the mode in Camoruco 3 levels are significantly different statistically from those in other levels. The mode consists of complex, closely spaced geometric incisions placed in bands on the outside of the necks of jars, on the top or inside of the rims of open bowls, on handles and lugs, and, occasionally, as headbands or head decoration for human lugs (Pl. 11, *bottom*, Q, R; Petrullo

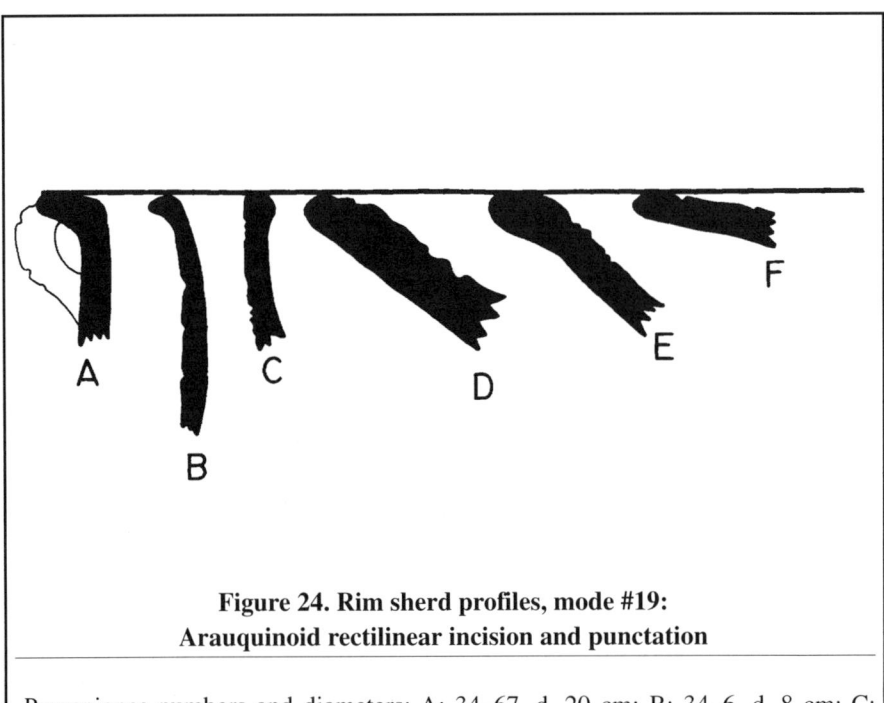

Figure 24. Rim sherd profiles, mode #19: Arauquinoid rectilinear incision and punctation

Provenience numbers and diameters: A: 34–67, d. 20 cm; B: 34–6, d. 8 cm; C: 32–2, d. 14 cm; D: 1–19, d. 26 cm; E: 25–10, d. 38 cm; F: 12–72, d. 27 cm.

1939, Pl. 30, 1; Pl. 31, 32; Howard 1943, 26, Fig. 7, E, F, I–L; 70, Fig. 11, I, Pl. 2, D, Q; Roosevelt 1980, 210, Fig. 64).

The incision was done with a narrow, sharp tool that cut deeply into the moist clay. The decorative patterns are mainly composed of repeated concentric triangles or diamonds arranged in wide horizontal bands bordered by incised lines. The incision is very sloppily and hastily done, and the motifs often have poorly closed corners. Linear motifs predominate in the patterns, but they are almost always accompanied by either punctations or circle stamps. The simple punctations occur in a single horizontal row between two incised horizontal lines at the top and bottom edges of the decorated area, and the circles appear within triangles. The incision is sometimes used on modeled elements, such as human and geometric lugs or handles (Fig. 25, F), and the style of modeling of these objects is the crude style related to the Arauquinoid style of the Incised and Punctate Horizon. The rectilinear incision often occurs on the necks of vessels that bear Arauquinoid maroon paint on their bodies, as noted in the previous section.

This rectilinear incision seems to mimic complex basketry, textile patterns, or braided hair. In this it is similar in iconographic meaning to the geometric-incised patterns of Meillacoid and Chicoid art of the Greater Antilles, style series that appear to be distantly related to the Arauquinoid series.

The Arauquinoid incision has previously been confused with Corozal rectilinear incision (mode #132) and included in the same type, Ronquin zoned incision with spicules (e.g., Vargas 1981, 550, Lam. 58, A, D [the Corozal incision]; 551, Lam. 59, A–F [the Arauquinoid incision]), but the two styles of incision are distinct technologically and stylistically and occur stratigraphically in nonoverlapping levels at this site. The Corozal incision is confined to Corozal levels, and the Arauquinoid incision is confined to Camoruco levels. The Corozal incision is found on wares with moderate sponge and rare sherd temper, with rare sand inclusions. The Arauquinoid incision occurs only on pottery that is heavily sponge tempered, with moderate accessory temper of clay bits. The Corozal rectilinear incision always occurs on the outside of bowl walls, and the Arauquinoid incision never occurs on the outside of bowl walls. Also, the Corozal incision occurs in simple patterns of well-spaced lines, while the Arauquinoid incision is usually very closely spaced and depicts complex geometric patterns. If the two styles of incision are neither contemporary nor stylistically comparable, they cannot together make up a valid type for ceramic analysis.

The Arauquinoid style of rectilinear incision was first classified in material from sites in the area of Arauquin in the Apure Delta (Petrullo 1939, 30–33). It has also been found at Guarguapo on the Lower Orinoco (Cruxent and Rouse 1958–59: Pl. 100, 4–10), Aguerito (Zucchi, Tarble, and Vaz 1984, Fig. 5, A–F). Comparative regional chronology of the Middle Orinoco is not well enough worked out to show where the incision style was first used. Perhaps because it appears rather abruptly in Parmana, it is likely to have been introduced from elsewhere. However, there is in Corozal 3 and early Camoruco a very rare, rather simple style of incision and punctation, placed on the inside of beveled open bowl rims, that could be an immediate precursor for this style of incision. The ultimate precursor of the Arauquinoid incision is the broadline paneled incision of the Saladoid and Barrancoid series, which, although very different in style and iconography, has a generally similar decorative function. Within the Middle and Lower Orinoco, the late prehistoric Arauquinoid rectilinear style of incision seems to have become part of the material cultural complex that spread rapidly during the period of the expansion of the late prehistoric chiefdoms.

The particular style of Arauquinoid incision has not been found outside the Orinoco, to my knowledge, although other styles of the Incised and Punctate Horizon, such as Santarem, have a vaguely similar style of incision. As mentioned above, the Meillacoid and the Chicoid pottery series of the Greater Antilles also have a vaguely similar type of incision. Both the Lower Amazon and Antillean styles of incision are shallower and better executed than the Arauquinoid incision, and they include more curvilinear motifs with the rectilinear. In view of these differences, the general similarity among all these distant styles may possibly derive from an ancient shared concept of iconography and stylization, rather than from contemporary communication of shared concepts about pottery decoration.

ARAUQUINOID HUMAN EFFIGIES, MODES #40 AND 32 (Tables 63–70; Fig. 25; Pl. 12, top, 13, top). These types of human effigies are composite silhouette jars and bottles in which the upper portion usually represents the head and the lower part represents the body of a human. Features and ornamentation are executed with modeled appliqué strips and nubbins (for eyebrows, limbs, genitals, and ears) decorated with incised and punctate designs. Both sexes are represented, but the frequencies of gender are not known because most examples are fragmentary and cannot be sexed. The shape of the vessels is usually globular, and the temper is primarily sponge, with rarer clay bits and sherds.

There are two types of effigies—small, relatively thin walled effigies with small faces and modeled, slitted eyes (mode #32) (Tables 67–70; Pl. 12, *top*, K–P, R–U; Fig. 25, D–F; Howard 1943, Pl. 2, B, Pl. 7, G; Vargas 1981, 546,

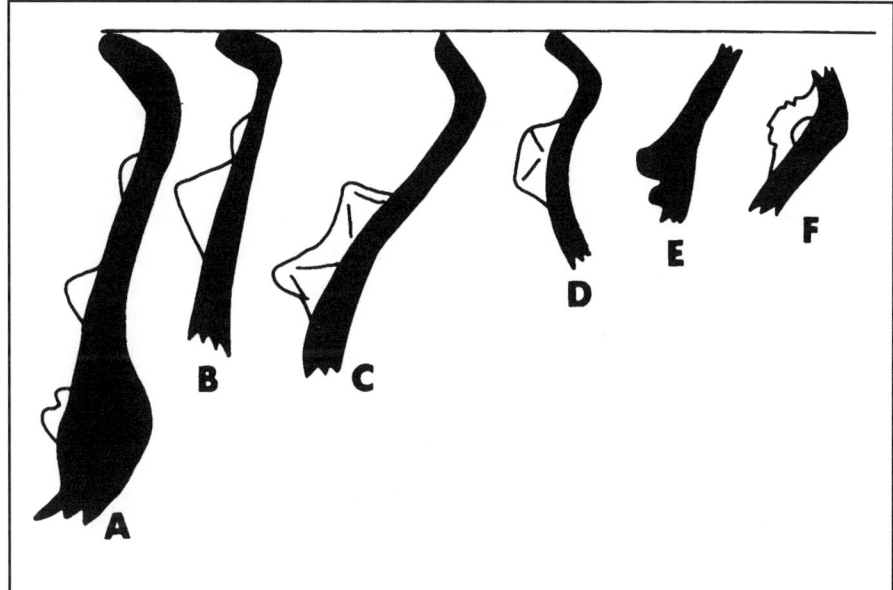

Figure 25. Rim sherd profiles, modes #32 and 40: Arauquinoid human-effigy jars

Provenience numbers and diameters: A: 48–111, d. 13 cm; B: 48–114, d. 20 cm; C: 77–2, d. 10 cm; D: 35–166, d. 12 cm; E: 63–19, d. ? cm; F: 30–4, d. 13 cm.

Lam. 54, B, E; Roosevelt 1980, 214, Fig. 69, 20-68) and larger, thicker ones with prominent coffee-bean eyes (mode #40) (Tables 63–66; Pl. 12, *top,* A–E, Q; Pl. 13, *top;* Fig. 25, A–C; Howard 1943, Pl. 2, C, K, T; Vargas 1981, 546, Lam. 54, A–C; 551, Lam. 59, F; Roosevelt 1980, 214, Fig. 69, 48-11). The former occur primarily in Camoruco 3 levels. They are often decorated with maroon paint (mode #14) and rectilinear incision (mode #19). The latter effigies appear in small numbers during late Corozal 1 and Corozal 2, become common in Camoruco 1 and 2, and last into Camoruco 3 only in small quantities. The statistical tests show that Camoruco 1 and 2 are not significantly different from one another in the occurrence of the larger effigies, but that Camoruco 2 and 3 and Camoruco 1 and Corozal 3 phases are significantly different. Only the larger human effigies are abundant enough (168 total) to make a reliable diagnostic analysis, and their temporal spread is rather long for seriation purposes. Nonetheless, they effectively distinguish Camoruco 1 and 2 from the other phases. The small effigies are sufficiently short-lived to be a useful decorated type, but they are rather rare, existing in only fifty-four examples. Still, their numbers were adequate for the statistical analyses, and their distribution differed significantly between the Camoruco 2 and 3 subphases.

The larger human effigies are all quite similar in shape and share a common type of everted rim. However, their styles of features and decoration vary a great deal. Some of the different styles of facial features and body parts (noses, arms, eyebrows, genitals, and the like) of the larger human effigies were tabulated separately to see if there were chronological distinctions among them, but none were found. For example, as mentioned above in the section on circle stamps, we studied the differences in type of punctation on the appliqué-strip eyebrows and other similar features, to see if they differed chronologically. However, they showed no statistically significant changes through time. The appliqué ridges with slashes on top extended throughout the Camoruco phase in moderate quantities, with one or two examples occurring in Corozal 3 levels. The appliqué ridges with circle stamps had a similar distribution. Such features were not useful, then, for dividing the effigies chronologically. However, since the different appliqué-strip punctation styles never occur simultaneously on the same piece, they may represent the work of different potters. This kind of variation might thus be useful for the study of activity areas and craft production, as suggested earlier. Other stylistic differences in motifs that we studied fruitlessly for chronology were nostril punctation type (circle stamp, slash, or plain punctation), mouth types, hand and foot types (appliqué and incision or just incision), and arm position (whether luted to the body or separate).

Crude modeled human limbs (mode #57) were tabulated separately from the effigies (Tables 75-78), because it is usually not possible to tell whether an example comes from a human-effigy jar or a human lug. These objects were most abundant during late Camoruco 2 and Camoruco 3, but were also present in very small numbers during the period of Corozal 3 through early Camoruco 2. They correlate better with the distribution of the human-effigy vessels than with that of the human lugs, and probably derive primarily from the former representations.

A small number of human-effigy jars of non-Arauquinoid styles were found in Corozal tradition levels. They vary a great deal in paste and style and include a grit-tempered example and several different styles of sponge-tempered effigies with extremely simplified features (Pl. 13, *top*). Unlike the Arauquinoid examples, none of the Corozal tradition ones have separately modeled limbs. These Corozal effigies may be precursors to the Arauquinoid effigies, which are both much more abundant and more conventionalized. The non-Arauquinoid human effigies were too rare to analyze quantitatively and are not tabulated here.

Among the human images there are also fifteen hollow human figurines and one solid freestanding pregnant human figurine (Roosevelt 1980, Fig. 92; similar items in Howard 1943:Pl. 2, G, and p. 31). Some of these and fragments of large human-effigy vessels (such as sherd 72-7, Pl. 13, *top*) were found in place in the broad sherd feature of Excavation 3, Level 10 (Pl. 4, *center* and *bottom*), and their context and possible function in rituals are discussed in the section on Stratum M (Chap. 2, E). The figurines are not tabulated or analyzed here due to their rarity. They all date to the Camoruco tradition. Among the Camoruco 3 examples are a few decorated with maroon paint.

Nonzoomorphic human representations such as the human-effigy vessels, figurines, and human lugs, discussed in the next section, appear to be absent from the Parmana sequence until the Corozal tradition, do not become common until the Camoruco tradition, and are abundant only in the Camoruco 3 phase. The appearance and proliferation of human iconography, then, correlate chronologically with the rise of efficient agricultural economies of seed cropping, large, dense populations, and ranked sociopolitical organization. The implications of this association of iconography and lifeway are discussed in Chapter 4, *below*. The shapes of the human-effigy vessels suggest use for liquids, with the large, open jars perhaps for brewing beer, and the smaller bottles for serving or drinking it. The bowls with human lugs, discussed in the next section, seem to be for special-purpose cooking.

The Arauquinoid human effigies are very similar to effigies found among other styles of the Incised and Punctate Horizon in other parts of the Orinoco and northern lowlands. They have been found as funerary offerings in the Valencia Basin, executed in the Valencia red ware (Kidder 1944; Bennett 1937; Osgood and Howard 1943), in the Apure Triangle of the Middle Orinoco (Petrullo 1939; Cruxent and Rouse 1958–59, Pl. 80, 6 [like mode #32], Pl. 81, 9 [like mode #40]), and on the right bank of the Orinoco, near Caicara, at Aguerito (Zucchi, Tarble, and Vaz 1984, Fig. 5, F, M, Fig. 6, S). The Aguerito versions align with mode #32 effigies rather than with the mode #40 effigies, but there are examples of both types at Arauquin. The Valencia Basin appears to have both types also (Osgood and Howard 1943, Fig. 16, C 2, B 4; Bennett 1937; Kidder 1944, Pl. 6, 14,15,16,18) and other types as well. Farther afield, there are stylistically similar human-effigy jars in northern Colombia (Reichel-Dolmatoff 1965b, Pl. 3, 35–37), which has been thought to be the origin of the type, but the chronology there is not established. Also, the function of the Colombian examples seems to be somewhat different, being funerary body containers. In the Middle and Lower Amazon, both human-effigy statues and funerary jars are also common (Nordenskiold 1930; Hilbert 1968; Palmatary 1950, 1960; Meggers and Evans 1957), but none are very close in style to the Arauquinoid types. The closest are the late prehistoric effigies of Maraca and Arua, two Incised and Punctate Horizon phases from the mouth of the Amazon.

ARAUQUINOID HUMAN BOWL RIM LUGS, MODE #136 (Tables 71–74; Fig. 26; Pl. 12, bottom). Also characteristic of the Camoruco phase is a type of special-purpose cooking bowl with a pair of human rim lug handles. The lugs are small modeled images of humans shown from either the thighs or waist up. Those whose sex is indicated are female. The lugs are crudely hand shaped, with features executed by appliquéd lumps and strips, modeling, incision, and punctation. Ears and limb joints are usually indicated by circle stamps, fingers by slashes or simple punctations. The humans are represented as if they were holding up and offering the bowl. The person faces the inside of the vessel and grasps the rim with both hands. This arrangement differs from that of the earlier animal lugs (mode #209), which are placed facing out on vessels that ap-

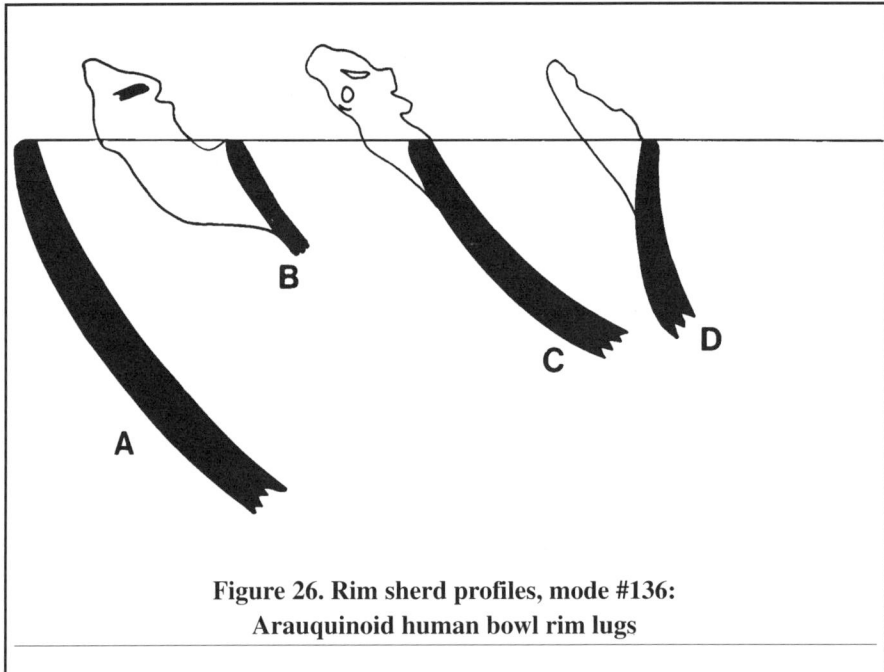

Figure 26. Rim sherd profiles, mode #136: Arauquinoid human bowl rim lugs

Provenience numbers and diameters: A: 32–51, d. 42 cm; B: 32–108, d. ? cm; C: 32–111, d. 32 cm; D: 150–60, d. 34 cm.

pear conceived as the animals' bodies. It is interesting that the human rim lugs expand in numbers just as the animal rim lugs are dropping out of the sequence, as if replacing them. Why it was thought appropriate for special cooking bowls to represent animals in earlier times and humans in later times is not clear. Perhaps the change is related to changes in food production. The changeover correlates with a trend away from reliance on animal protein and toward reliance on protein from cultivated cereal crops (Roosevelt 1987c; 1989, Table 2), as discussed in Chapter 4, A, 5 *below*.

The human lugs have a quite restricted chronological range, first appearing in very small quantities in Corozal 3 and reaching abundance only in late Camoruco 2 and Camoruco 3 levels. Most are found in Camoruco 3 levels, and their frequencies and percentages in the levels of that phase contrast significantly with their occurrence in the levels of other phases. Like the earlier Arauquinoid human-effigy vessels, the earliest of the human lugs have prominent coffee-bean eyes (mode #13) (Pl. 12, *bottom*, BB, CC; Howard 1943, Pl. 2, C, K, T, 6, B, C, 7, E, H, J; Roosevelt 1980, 211, Fig. 65; Vargas 1981, 546, Lam. 54, D). The "coffee-beans" are made up of a pellet of clay applied to the face and then cut horizontally with an incised stroke. These eye types last into Camoruco 3 in small numbers. Camoruco 3 levels also have two other types of human lugs—those with plain slit eyes and small round or wedge-shaped heads (mode #12; Fig. 26, B, C; Howard 1943, Pl. 2, B, 6, F, D, 7, D, F; Roosevelt 1980, Fig. 65, 12-85) and those with flat heads and flattish coffee-bean eyes (mode #122; Fig. 26, D; Pl. 12, *bottom*, FF and 150-60; Roosevelt 1980, Fig. 65, 150-1 and 30-2). None of the stylistic variations of the lugs existed in large enough quantities to be tabulated and analyzed separately. The different contemporary renderings of the human image may have been features of micro-styles developed by different kinship or residence groups, and their spatial patterning has yet to be investigated. Because the variants of the human rim adornos are too rare to analyze separately, mode #136 represents all of the adornos plotted together.

The lugs themselves were usually not painted, though some Camoruco 3 examples bear splashes or, rarely, washes of the maroon paint (mode #14; Pl. 12, *bottom*, sherd 20-14) that covers some of the bowls that bear the adornos. The lugs often bear decoration of rectilinear incision and punctation (mode #19) occurring as hair, head ornaments, headbands, ear ornaments, and bracelets. This ornamentation is more common on Camoruco 3 lugs than on Camoruco 2 lugs. There are distinctive coiffures, the most common being one or two topknots crowned with a punctation or circle stamp. Many of the flat lugs have another hairdo—straight bangs on the forehead, indicated by multiple short parallel vertical lines. Sometimes the two styles are combined in flat topknots with vertical parallel incisions.

The human adornos face inward and upward on the rims of large, thickish open bowls, whose function for cooking is established by the thick soot often found on the outside of the bowls and on the backs of the lugs. The bowls on which the lugs occur are the primary Camoruco sponge-tempered ware, which is a variable gray-buff in color with a grayish core. The bowls have out-turned, curved sides and simple rims, which vary in form from rounded to slightly squared or tapered. It is probable that the bowls were for special, ceremonial cooking, rather than for daily cooking, for they are relatively scarce compared to the common, large, plain cooking bowls of the Camoruco phase. As a minor, decorated subset of cooking bowls, they may also have had a special function for cooking certain kinds of food for certain occasions.

The human lugs have been found at many sites in Parmana. Although no human bowl rim lugs exactly similar to those from Parmana have yet been found elsewhere, ones that are somewhat similar have been found in the area of Arauquin (Cruxent and Rouse 1958–59, Pl. 74,16) and in the Valencia phase of the Valencia Basin (Kidder 1944, Pl. 9,19). Those of the Mabaruma phase (Evans and Meggers 1960) are not particularly similar to the Arauquinoid ones in style and iconography. Human as well as animal adornos are an integral part of most styles of the Incised and Punctate Horizon of the Orinoco and Amazon, but few of the human lugs in other styles are very similar to those found in Parmana. It is difficult to envision an origin outside the Middle Orinoco for this particular type of decorative lug handle, because no other region yet known has anything really similar. The pattern of occurrence of the human lugs in the Parmana sequence, beginning first in Corozal 3 in small numbers and then slowly increasing to a peak at the end of Camoruco, is consonant with a local origin. Like other types of Camoruco ceramic art, however, the human lugs become "Arauquinized" during the Camoruco 3 phase—the style of physical representation changes somewhat, and rectilinear incision and maroon paint are added as decoration. As discussed in the conclusions, we know too little about the context and chronology of ceramic art in the Orinoco to know from where and why that stylistic influence spread.

4. Nondecorative Modes of Shape

DIAGNOSTIC RIM AND BASE, MODES #212–215 (Tables 79–90). One premise of the seriation was that decorated pottery would be more useful than plain for subdividing the sequence chronologically, because it would be more distinctive and variable through time. This turned out to be true in most cases. As explained in the section on paste and temper characteristics, the major temper categories were not useful for seriation because they did not have clear-cut, directional, short-term variation. It was expected that basic, functional aspects of pottery, which seem to influence nondecorative vessel-shape characteristics, would also remain more stable than decoration and be less useful for subdividing the sequence. This did turn out to be the case in general, but there were a few "diagnostic" (our term for seriatable, nondecorative pottery characteristics) modes of vessel shape whose stratigraphic distributions helped set phases or subphases off from one another. The vessel shapes less useful for seriation were those common in most phases or with bimodal or fluctuating distributions in the stratigraphy. The bimodal distributions generally reflected the fact that two distinct chronological modes had been inadvertently combined because they did not differ enough from one another in appearance to be classified separately. The fluctuating distributions were in some cases apparently produced by chance variation and in other cases by functional variation through time in the use of the area of the excavations. In any case, such distributions were not useful for seriating the pottery. There were, in addition, in Corozal tradition levels, numerous different shapes of complex and unusual rims, which were very rare and thus not useful for seriation purposes.

Certain vessel shapes were common in the Camoruco phase and rare in the Corozal phase. These included open bowls with beveled rims and open bowls with everted and/or beveled rims, which appear, on the evidence of soot on the outside walls, to be common cooking bowls. These bowl rim shapes were separately tabulated at first and then tabulated together as mode #212 (Tables 79–82) because they turned out to have identical stratigraphic distributions and intergrading shapes. The existence of numerous examples that were very difficult to classify as one mode or the other made it convenient to classify them together. For example, among the rims, the bevel facet ranges from sharp and well defined to vague or absent, and the eversion ranges from sharp to imperceptible. This variation even turned up sometimes on the same rim. I felt that this pattern of shape intergradation was evidence that the differences among the rims were produced by factors such as chance and motor habits that were not chronological in nature. The separate tabulations confirmed this by revealing an almost identical level distribution for the range of shapes. Also, when classified together, the everted and/or beveled rims made up a sufficient number for statistical analysis, whereas in the separate tabulations the numbers in some levels were insufficient. The combined type of bowl rims first appears in late Corozal 1 times in relatively low percentages (about .1 to .5%), becomes much more common (about 1 to 2%) in Camoruco 1 and 2, and then peaks (about 3 to 4%) during Camoruco 3. The distribution of the everted and/or beveled rims was significantly different between Corozal 3 and Camoruco 1 and between early and late Camoruco levels. Everted-rim jars, sometimes with beveled rims, also were common in Camoruco and rare in Corozal levels, but these were too rare overall to analyze fruitfully and are not tabulated here.

An example of a common rim mode with bimodal distribution is the simple rounded rim on open bowls, of which there were several hundred examples. Peaks in frequency occurred in Corozal 2 and 3 and Camoruco 2 and 3. Upon close examination, it was possible to see that the examples in Camoruco levels had a slightly different color, texture, and shape from those in the Corozal levels. Nevertheless, these differences were so subtle that it was not possible to separate the rims reliably for seriation, and so the rims are not separately tabulated or analyzed here.

Among the bases, the best mode for seriation was the flat, thickened base with a sharp angle at the juncture of the base and the vessel wall (mode #213). Several of the base sherds with this shape were large enough to include parts of the vessel rim, and it was possible to see that these bases are from both plain and decorated cooking bowls. (An example from an animal-effigy bowl from the burial of Skeleton 2, Excavation 3, is illustrated in Fig. 21, A.) This type of base is present from Corozal 1 through Camoruco 2 and is absent afterwards (Tables 83–86). The bases peak significantly (about 1% of all sherds) during Corozal 3. Flat, thickened bases with rounded junctures were abundant from late Camoruco 2 through Camoruco 3 and rare or absent before, a pattern that suggests that this shape of base replaced the one with a sharp angle. However, the bases with rounded juncture were too rare to analyze statistically and are not tabulated here. Round bowl bases (mode #214) were distributed in irregularly fluctuating percentages from late Corozal 1 through Camoruco 3 (Tables 87–90). Although the total number of round bases is sufficient for seriation, the base sherds are distributed through the levels of the subphases in relatively low frequencies. The bases' overall pattern of distribution, therefore, was not distinctive enough for very effective seriation.

The results of the study of plain shapes, then, produced a few useful chronological modes. In comparison with the study of the numerous styles, types, and attributes of pottery decoration, however, this aspect of the classification was much less useful for sequence information.

D. Distribution of Modes in the Traditions and Phases

Having described in detail the important modes used in the chronological seriation of the pottery from the Corozal site and related them to the tables and the illustrations, I will now summarize the distribution of modes in each of the traditions and phases to characterize the sequence of phases in terms of relative ceramic chronology. The significant patterning of distributions of the twenty major ceramic modes among the approximately thirty thousand sherds from the layers of the excavations is the primary evidence for the Corozal sequence, the first sequence of its kind for the Orinoco. This detailed sequence was based on study of a large number of modes from a large number of sherds, whose frequency and percentage distributions in the stratigraphic column were checked by statistical tests of significance. In addition to having a substantial empirical base, the sequence at Corozal has been confirmed by the results of excavation at other sites of the Parmana region. The illustrations of the excavations and pottery by photographs, drawings, and tables are intended to make the sequence intelligible to archaeologists interested in comparing it with prehistoric sequences in other areas. The relative placement of the Parmana sequence in the prehistoric era is based on its consistent stratigraphic occurrence underneath layers of historic material.

1. The Camoruco Tradition

The three Camoruco phases share the common general Camoruco modes of mauve paint (#152) and circle stamps (#160), which first appear in the sequence during the late Corozal and proliferate during the Camoruco tradition. They also share large human-effigy vessels (#40), modeled limbs (#57), and everted/beveled rims (#214), which first appear during the Corozal tradition.
CAMORUCO 3 PHASE. Camoruco 3 shares with Camoruco 2 the Camoruco human bowl rim lugs (#136), maroon paint (#14), and rectilinear incision (#19), but the two phases can be easily distinguished from each other by statistically significant differences in frequencies and percentages of these modes. The paint and incision are both extremely abundant in Camoruco 3 and very rare or absent from Camoruco 2 levels. Modeled limbs also are moderately abundant in Camoruco 3 and much rarer in Camoruco 2. Several rare modes also fall mainly in Camoruco 3, including Arauquinoid small human effigies (#32) and Camoruco human rim lugs. Animal-effigy bowls (#209), a commonly occurring special culinary bowl type in Camoruco 1 and 2, are almost

totally absent in Camoruco 3, as are the flat bases with angled junctures (#213) that these bowls have. Arauquinoid large human effigies are also significantly less abundant in Camoruco 3 than in Camoruco 2.

There are several mode changes within Camoruco 3 that may help to subdivide the phase. There are significant peaks in the percentages of rectilinear incision and maroon-painted sherds in the middle of the phase, and the large Arauquinoid human effigies undergo a significant decline during the second half of the phase. Thus the phase can be considered to be divided into early, middle, and late parts of about eighty years each, according to the absolute chronology.

CAMORUCO 2 PHASE. Camoruco 2 is defined by the presence of the general Camoruco modes mentioned above, by the presence of modes not present in Camoruco 3, and by the absence or extremely low frequency of the Arauquinoid modes—rectilinear incision, maroon paint, small human effigies, and human bowl rim lugs. Although in its latest levels it shares with Camoruco 3 the human rim lugs and the large human-effigy jars, the frequencies and percentages of the two phases are statistically significantly different. Camoruco 2 has appreciable percentages of the flat bases with angled junctures, which drop out completely in Camoruco 3. The Arauquinoid maroon paint and rectilinear incision very common in Camoruco 3 start their increases only at the end of the phase. The phase shares with Camoruco 1 and Corozal 3 the abundant sponge-tempered animal-effigy bowls. In Camoruco 2, the animal-effigy bowls occur less than one-third as frequently as in Camoruco 1 and Corozal 3 and seem to be being replaced functionally by the human adorno bowls that come in at this time and proliferate in late Camoruco 2. Camoruco 2 shares with Camoruco 1 a similarly low frequency of modeled limbs in comparison with Camoruco 3. Camoruco 2 is also similar to Camoruco 1 in the presence of certain Corozal modes in very small quantities, such as Saladoid-Barrancoid decoration (#204) and Corozal gritware (#140).

Within Camoruco 2 there are significant changes that may help to subdivide the phase. For example, the modeled limbs and human rim lugs increase significantly in numbers toward the end of the phase. The animal-effigy bowls undergo a statistically significant decline during the phase, and the large human-effigy jars also taper off in percentage in the second half of Camoruco 2. The phase therefore can be considered to be potentially divisible in two parts, early and late. According to the absolute chronology, these subdivisions of Camoruco 2 would represent about 150 years each.

CAMORUCO 1 PHASE. Camoruco 1 has the general Camoruco modes—modeled limbs, mauve paint, circle stamps, thick human effigies, and so forth. Unlike

Camoruco 2, it essentially lacks the common Camoruco 3 modes, such as Arauquinoid maroon paint and rectilinear incision, and has very few of some of the less abundant Camoruco 3 modes—Arauquinoid small effigy jars and Camoruco human lugs.

Camoruco 1 shares with Corozal 3 and Camoruco 2 the animal-effigy bowls, and it shares with Camoruco 2 and 3 and Corozal 3 the circle-stamp motif. Camoruco 1 is different from Camoruco 2 in having a greater frequency of the animal-effigy bowls. Camoruco 1 is also distinguished by the abundance of certain modes that are extremely rare in or absent from Corozal 3 levels. For example, large human effigies, circle stamps, and mauve paint are much more abundant in Camoruco 1 than in Corozal 3. Beveled-rim bowls are very common in Camoruco 1 and significantly rarer before. Except for a couple of sherds from disturbances, Camoruco 1 lacks certain common Corozal phase diagnostics, such as the red-and-white banded paint, the Corozal rectilinear incision, the shallow curvilinear incision, sherd-tempered wares, and the vertical rim strap handles. However, it has large numbers of some common modes that start in the Corozal phase in low frequencies and begin to increase in Corozal 3—such as the animal-effigy bowls, circle stamps, and large human-effigy jars. The phase also shares with Corozal phases the Saladoid-Barrancoid decoration and Corozal grit-tempered ware (#140), although in very low frequencies.

During Camoruco 1 there are mode changes that may allow the phase to be subdivided. For example, the percentage of mauve-painted sherds increases in each level from the beginning to the end of the phase, and early Camoruco 1 has significantly fewer mauve sherds than the late Camoruco 1 levels. According to these changes, the phase thus can be divided into an early and a late part. In the absolute chronology, these subdivisions would amount to about one hundred years each.

2. The Corozal Tradition

The Corozal tradition is characterized by the presence of certain common modes not characteristic of Camoruco levels—Corozal shallow curvilinear incision (#134), Corozal red-and-white paint in bands (#18), and Corozal rectilinear incision (#132). For the most part these are quite rare in the early part of Corozal 1. The Corozal tradition is also characterized by a mode—Corozal Saladoid-Barrancoid decoration (#204)—that is very common during the tradition and continues in very low quantities into Camoruco 1 and 2 phases. The early part of the tradition is characterized by numerous examples of Corozal sherdware (#135) and Corozal gritware (#140), which have become extremely rare by the end of the tradition.

COROZAL 3 PHASE. Corozal 3 is characterized by very rare examples of a number of modes that begin in that phase and continue into the Camoruco tradition—mauve paint, circle stamps, and modeled limbs. The animal-effigy vessels, which appear first in Corozal 2 phase, become abundant for the first time during Corozal 3. The modeled limbs and circle stamps are exceedingly rare in Corozal 3, though abundant in Camoruco 1 and 2. The animal-effigy bowls are, overall, more abundant in Corozal 3 than in Camoruco 1 and 2, though they fluctuate in quantity to some degree. Corozal 3 shares with Corozal 1 and 2 the red-and-white paint in bands, rectilinear incision, and curvilinear incision, but these are rare to very rare and fade out during the phase. Corozal 3 thus contrasts with Corozal 2 and Corozal 1 in having certain modes in much lower frequencies. It also shares with Corozal 1 and 2 the Saladoid-Barrancoid decoration, though in significantly lower percentages. Corozal 3 conspicuously lacks Corozal sherdware (except for one probably intrusive sherd) and has only a few sherds of Corozal grit-tempered ware and the rare mode of pigment rubbed into incisions (not tabulated).

During Corozal 3 there are changes that may help to subdivide the phase. The animal-effigy bowls increase rapidly in percentage from the beginning to the end of the phase, and the curvilinear incision tapers off rapidly during the phase. Thus, the phase can be divided into two parts, early and late, each about fifty years long.

COROZAL 2 PHASE. Corozal 2 is distinguished by a significant abundance of examples of Corozal red-and-white paint in bands, in comparison with other phases. Like late Corozal 1, it has an abundance of curvilinear incision and rectilinear incision. It has only extremely low frequencies of the Saladoid-style paint (#5), which tapers off during the phase. Corozal 2 has an abundance of vertical rim strap handles (#126), which come in during very late Corozal 1 times. It also has Saladoid-Barrancoid decoration and Corozal grit-tempered ware, but in lesser abundance than does Corozal 1. The rare mode of pigment rubbed into incisions is relatively abundant in Corozal 2. The Corozal sherd-tempered ware so abundant in Corozal 1 becomes very rare by Corozal 2.

Corozal 2 is set off from Corozal 3 by the deficiency of a number of modes that begin in Corozal 3 and develop to abundance in the Camoruco phase, such as circle stamps, mauve paint, and modeled limbs. Animal-effigy bowls and large human effigies seem to be present in very low percentages in Corozal 2 but are extremely rare until Corozal 3. There is a statistically significant drop in the frequency of Corozal red-and-white paint in the transition from Corozal 2 to Corozal 3, and a significant increase in Corozal rim strap handles from Corozal 1 to 2.

During Corozal 2 certain changes take place in the distribution of modes that may help to subdivide the phase. Corozal rectilinear incision and red-and-white paint in bands taper off rapidly from the early to late half of the phase. The sherdware is present in the first half of the phase and drops out entirely by the second half. Grit-tempered pottery drops significantly in percentage in the transition from the early part of the phase to the later part. Thus Corozal 2 can be divided into early and late parts, each of about one hundred years.

COROZAL 1 PHASE. Corozal 1 is characterized by the abundance of certain modes not abundant in any other phase. Only in Corozal 1 are Saladoid-Barrancoid decoration, Corozal grit tempering, and Parmana sherdwares very abundant. Certain modes are present in only very small quantities in Corozal 1 levels until late in the phase, and most of these increase further in abundance in Corozal 2. They include the important Corozal modes: shallow curvilinear incision, red-and-white paint in bands, and rectilinear incision. Pigment rubbed in incisions is present in most levels but in small numbers. All but the final Corozal 1 levels lack the rim strap handle bowls, which expand greatly in numbers in Corozal 2. Like Corozal 2, Corozal 1 lacks most of the modes that start in Corozal 3 and develop in the Camoruco tradition, such as circle stamps, large effigies, and modeled limbs. In addition, it has insignificant numbers of the animal-effigy bowls. Corozal 1 is different from all other time periods at the site in having a significantly smaller quantity of pottery in the levels, overall. Nonetheless, pottery is present in more than sufficient quantities for statistical analysis in all Corozal 1 levels but the base levels, which are 19 and 20 in Excavation 2 and 26 in Excavation 3.

During Corozal 1 there are significant changes in mode distribution that help to subdivide the phase further. Curvilinear and rectilinear incision and red-and-white paint in bands are rare or absent until the late part of the subphase, and vertical rim strap handles come in only during the last part of the phase. Sherd-tempered ware goes suddenly from large percentages in the earliest part of the phase, to more modest percentages in the middle of the phase, to low percentages during late Corozal. The average percentages of grit-tempered wares are much higher in the early part of the phase than in the later part. Saladoid-Barrancoid decoration is very abundant in early Corozal 1 times and only about half as abundant in the middle and late parts of the phase. Beveled/everted rims and round bases appear for the first time in late Corozal 1. Pottery in general is of relatively low frequency in all but the final levels of the phase. Thus Corozal 1 as represented at the Corozal site can be divided in three parts, early, middle, and late. Because the exact beginning date of the occupation at Corozal is unknown, the time span of the parts of the Corozal 1 phase is uncertain.

LA GRUTA TRADITION PHASES. A number of modes found in the Corozal phase are represented in related but distinct forms in the preceding La Gruta tradition phases—La Gruta, Ronquin, and Ronquin Sombra—and the differences in character and frequency between Corozal and the earlier phases give evidence supporting the placement of Corozal right after them. The modes are Corozal sherdware, Corozal gritware, Corozal Saladoid-Barrancoid decoration, and Saladoid red-and-white paint. The differences between the patterns of occurrence of these modes in Corozal and the La Gruta tradition phases are as follows.

In the La Gruta phases, gritware is the predominant ware (about 90% of all pottery), and spongeware is absent, as far as we know; in Corozal, the predominant ware is sponge tempered, and Corozal gritware never rises above about 17%. In the La Gruta phases, sherdware is much rarer than the gritware (about 10% or less); in Corozal, it is more abundant than gritware, peaking at about 40% in the earliest full levels of Corozal 1. This pattern fits with the placement of the Corozal phase immediately after Ronquin Sombra, the final La Gruta tradition phase, because the sherdware begins to increase in frequency in Ronquin Sombra but is still subordinate quantitatively to the majority gritware.

In La Gruta tradition phases, careful modeling, broad-line incision, and Saladoid paint are by far the predominant decoration. In Corozal, such decoration is very rare. For example, in La Gruta tradition phases, gritware zoomorphic adornos executed in this style are very common (many hundreds of examples); in Corozal, they are extremely rare (five examples). The same pattern of contrasting frequencies is true for Saladoid paint, which is very abundant during the earlier phases (many hundreds of examples) and very rare during Corozal (thirty-three examples).

These ceramic contrasts and continuities between the Corozal phase and the earlier phases, in conjunction with its stratigraphic location below Camoruco layers at the site of Corozal, establish the relative placement of the tradition in the Parmana sequence following Ronquin Sombra and preceding Camoruco.

4. Conclusions

A. Interpretation of the Parmana Sequence

During the prehistoric occupation of Parmana, there were many changes, in ceramics as well as in other aspects of lifeways, and the variation in these factors was greater during the later part of the sequence during in the earlier part. In this monograph, changes in ceramics during the middle and later parts of the sequence are traced in detail in order to provide a background for studies of specific changes in subsistence and settlement. The ceramics change in technology (evidenced by temper, color of paste, and tool marks), in style of decoration, in subject matter, and in vessel shape. The seriation of the pottery from the stratigraphic excavations at Corozal and other sites revealed that these patterns of change were multifarious and statistically significant. As such they provide an excellent chronological tapestry as backdrop for the prehistoric developmental sequence. Although the purpose of the ceramic analysis was primarily the prosaic, traditional archaeological one of creating a relative chronology, the ceramic changes are also more broadly interpretable both in and of themselves and in light of the other changes that were going on in the region at the same time.

The patterns of stylistic, functional, and technological change among the ceramic phases of the Parmana sequence are complex. As in other aspects of life, the rate of change and degree of diversity of ceramics are not constant. At some times, such as during the La Gruta and Camoruco traditions, one major ware with characteristic decoration predominates, accompanied by one or more lesser wares. In contrast, at certain junctures many decorative styles and motifs make their appearance for the first time, as during Corozal 1 and Camoruco 3. Sometimes, there is substantial complexity in wares and styles, as during the Corozal tradition, and there are substantial shifts in ware characteristics, as in the transitions between Corozal 1 and 2 and Corozal 3 and Camoruco 1. Sometimes, the shapes of common utilitarian vessels shift, as in late Corozal 1 and at the beginning of Camoruco 3.

In the next sections, I will summarize the nature of ceramic changes from one period to another and try to interpret them in the context of changes in other aspects of ancient lifeways.

1. The Stability of the La Gruta Tradition

The La Gruta tradition phases show the greatest stylistic and technological continuity in pottery and other aspects of ancient life. Essentially, throughout the period there are only two major wares, the abundant gritware and the rare sherdware, and two iconographies and styles, zoomorphic-geometric and geometric. The significance of the dichotomous pottery complex is obscure, but one possibility is that it may represent functional differences between wares, because, cross-culturally, ceramic form and tempering are often closely tied to vessel function (Rice 1987). As mentioned in the discussion below on iconography (Sec. A, 5), the difference in subject matter between the wares may also reflect different utilitarian roles. The grit-tempered, zoomorphic-geometric pottery of the Saladoid-Barrancoid series is the predominant La Gruta tradition ware by far, and the relative rarity and contrasting temper of the simply decorated Parmana sherdware could mean that it was a trade ware during that time. Whether it was traded in or not is not possible to determine without trace-element provenience studies and more information about pottery sequences in the surrounding region. The majority-minority ratio of the two wares continues until the late La Gruta tradition, and the two wares retain their respective technological, stylistic, and iconographic characters. In the Ronquin Sombra phase, the Parmana ware becomes more common, but it remains a numerically minor ware. Ceramic changes during that time are limited to minor fluctuations in details of paste, shape, and decoration. Parallel with the stability and continuity of the La Gruta tradition pottery complex, population size, as judged from numbers and sizes of surviving sites, seems quite stable. After the La Gruta phase, the location of the major habitation site in the region shifts from La Gruta to Ronquin, but the sites are similar in size and composition. The subsistence complex of all the La Gruta tradition phases is characterized by zoomorphic cooking bowls, ceraic griddles, microliths, faunal remains, and a scarcity of edible seeds, which suggests that a manioc-fish-game subsistence technology continues throughout the period.

2. Complexity and Change in the Corozal Tradition

An important characteristic of the succeeding Corozal tradition is that it has pottery from several different ceramic styles at the same time, where previously there had been only two major decorative ware groups, the gritwares and the sherdwares. These two earlier wares continue to be important in the early part of the Corozal tradition, but the increased ceramic complexity and rapid rate of change of early Corozal mark a major transition between the La Gruta and Corozal traditions. The traditional gritwares (mode #140) and sherdwares (mode #135) continue to be used during the early and middle Corozal tradition, although the most abundant ware becomes sponge-tempered shortly after the beginning of the tradition. At the beginning of Corozal 1, the two older wares together make up the majority—over 60%—of sherds in the levels, though gritware has dropped to about half the frequency of the sherdware. Many decorated types characteristic of the La Gruta tradition phases continue to be used in the Corozal tradition, though gritware decoration has become rare, impoverished, and crude compared to earlier gritware. The sherdware and the gritware drop to minor percentages by the end of Corozal 1, and by the end of the Corozal phase, these earlier wares have been nearly phased out in favor of the new sponge-tempered tradition.

The new spongewares continue many vessel shapes borrowed from the gritwares, but many vessel shapes new to the region appear in spongewares during late Corozal 1 and continue in use until the final prehistoric tradition, Camoruco. These new shapes include hemispherical serving or eating bowls with rounded or tapered, inturned rims, and cooking bowls with beveled and/or everted rims and slightly pedestaled flat bases.

Decorated spongewares appear first during the middle of Corozal 1 and expand rapidly in frequency. Within the new sponge-tempered Corozal tradition pottery complex, there are so many distinct stylistic types that it may be misleading to call it an integral stylistic tradition. Some decorated types of the new spongeware seem more or less distantly related to earlier complexes. One Corozal sponge-tempered style (mode #134) has shallow curvilinear incision and modeling that hark back in method of execution and iconography to Barrancoid types of the La Gruta tradition. Barrancoid elements of this curvilinear style include broad-line incision, rare modeled-incised animal heads, hemispherical incised nubbins on rims and carinas, and triangular and flanged incised rims. Another sponge-tempered style (#132) has simple rectilinear-incised decoration that seems to have its origins in the decorated Parmana sherdwares of the La Gruta tradition. Its shapes, however, are new and different. In a third sponge-tempered style (#126), there are bowls with vertical rim strap handles sometimes decorated with one or two simple nubbins or a crude animal head. The handles are similar in placement to La Gruta tradition gritware rim lug handles, and possibly the simple adornos have devolved from the exquisite modeled-carved animal ornaments of those earlier handles. The paste characteristics, vessel shapes, and crude style of modeling and incision, however, are entirely new. The decorative style of execution is related to the subsequent Camoruco tradition, which therefore could be said to build stylistically from such new sponge-tempered styles that develop in the later part of the Corozal tradition. Thus, some structural and iconographic aspects of the pottery decoration of Corozal spongewares seem directly related to earlier complexes, while the manner of execution seems quite new in the Parmana region.

The pottery of the Corozal tradition is so varied that it might be supposed that there has been mechanical mixture of sherds from chronologically distinct layers. It seems clear, however, that the different decorative and tempering entities associated with each other in the Corozal layers of sites were indeed made at the same time, and not just combined mechanically. The distribution of most Corozal wares, styles, and types in the deposit is coherent and quite restricted stratigraphically. If these materials had been combined by mechanical mixture, then one would expect more spread of material in the layers, as is found at sites such as Ronquin, where there is known to have been disturbance. Therefore, it seems a reasonable conclusion that the complexity of Corozal pottery is real and represents a distinctive pattern of human interaction. In fact, distinct pottery entities that occur in the same levels seem to interact with one another in certain ways. Not only does the La Gruta tradition influence the new Corozal tradition and vice versa, but it is not uncommon for bits of pottery of one tradition's wares to get into pottery of another, as accidental inclusions. For example, a few Corozal gritware sherds have sponge-tempered sherd bits embedded in the paste. Also, there are rare sherds that belong stylistically to one tradition but have the paste characteristics usual for another. For example, there are rare Corozal sherd-tempered sherds with the Parmanoid style of incised decoration that also contain traces of sponge or grit temper, and there are several grit-tempered sherds that bear Corozal rectilinear decoration usually found on sponge ware. There are also a few Corozal sponge-tempered sherds that have the shapes or bear motifs in Saladoid painting usually found on gritware. The decorative influence of the earlier styles on the new paste tradition seems to have been stronger than the reverse, and the older wares only uncommonly appear decorated in the new styles.

3. Corozal Tradition as a Transition

The traditional archaeological explanation for historical shifts in tropical lowland culture is that migration and population replacement has occurred (e.g., Meggers and Evans 1961; Meggers and Evans 1957; Sanoja and Vargas 1978; summaries of the subject in Oliver 1989 and Rouse 1986). But it seems likely that the Corozal phase ceramic changes represent more than an invasion of Corozal-culture foreigners that snuffed out the people of the La Gruta tradition culture. During Corozal, both old and new technologies, styles, and iconography coexist for from several hundred to more than a thousand years, depending on the chronology one uses. For example, the grit-tempering technology of the La Gruta tradition is very important during the early Corozal tradition and appears to continue into Camoruco times in low frequencies, eventually changing over to or being replaced by an Arauquinoid decorative gritware style. La Gruta decorated styles are important throughout Corozal both in the older gritwares and in the sponge-tempered wares new to the region. In addition, the sherdware pottery, present from the earliest known occupation in the Parmana region, has a florescence early in the Corozal tradition, although it drops out by its end. The Parmana sherdware decorated style of the La Gruta tradition seems also to be the progenitor of the Corozal style of rectilinear incision on sponge-tempered pottery. Thus, both ancient traditions of pottery decoration were incorporated in some way into the new tradition of sponge-tempered decorated pottery. This complex pattern of change and long-term interaction between traditions is not to be expected in a simple situation of population replacement. It makes sense to suppose that the older technologies and art styles continued to be important because some people committed to the earlier ways of the region were still around.

The sponge-tempered ceramic complex introduced in the Corozal phase is new to the region, and its origins are not easy to unravel, although the Parmana sequence and its relationships abroad give certain indications. The Corozal phase, with its beginning date of about 1000 B.C. in the long chronology, is one of the earliest lowland complexes to have sponge-tempered pottery. The La Gruta and Ronquin phases lack sponge-tempered wares, except for a unique clay zoomorphic figurine of nonlocal style found at La Gruta. Whether the Ronquin Sombra phase, immediately preceding the Corozal tradition, has any sponge-tempered pottery is difficult to tell for certain, because the only extensive known deposit of that phase is at the multicomponent site of Ronquin, where disturbance has mixed together sherds of all the different traditions. The stratigraphic distribution of sherds of different styles at the site suggests that the Ronquin Sombra phase was different from Ronquin and La Gruta only in details, except for an increasing proportion of the still-minority sherdware. The lower levels of my excavations in the Ronquin Sombra component at the site lack Corozal-like pottery, which is present only in the upper levels, and the small single-component Ronquin Sombra site at Los Merecurotes in the Parmana region also entirely lacks sponge-tempered pottery. The earliest sponge wares at Ronquin are exactly like those of the lower levels of Corozal site and of other sites, such as Parmana—Los Mangos. At none of these other sites is the Corozal phase pottery accompanied by pottery like the elaborately decorated gritware of Ronquin Sombra. As mentioned, the Corozal gritwares, although apparently derived from the La Gruta tradition, are perceptibly different from those of the La Gruta tradition phases.

In the Middle Orinoco, another early pottery complex with sponge tempering is Aguerito (Zucchi, Tarble, and Vaz 1984), and its chronology is comparable to that of Corozal. Although this and many northern lowland localities have roughly similar sequences, too few local sequences have been worked out, so the history of sponge tempering and other ceramic traits in the lowlands is not well understood. However, this pottery-tempering technology is clearly a trait of the humid tropical lowlands, because the species of freshwater sponges used for the pottery do not exist in temperate or desert regions of South America. Therefore, its spread cannot logically be attributed to influence from highland regions. Throughout the lowlands of South America, there is a trend toward the use of sponge tempering in later prehistory, and it is the major tempering substance of the pottery styles of the late prehistoric Incised and Punctate Horizon to which the Arauquinoid series belongs. Why this trend in tempering took place is not known. The needle like sponge-spicules are an efficient temper for maintaining tensile strength of wares, but their effect on the thermal and hygroscopic characteristics of the pottery is not known.

Despite their iconographic connections with styles of La Gruta tradition Saladoid-Barrancoid gritware and Parmana sherdware styles, it does not seem that the development of the new sponge-tempered styles from the earlier styles took place in the Parmana region. The Corozal sponge-tempered pottery is very different from the earlier gritware and sherdware, and there is no smooth transition through time from one to the other. In effect, the Corozal styles seem to come suddenly into the Parmana sequence already formed. It seems likely, therefore, that the original development of the new styles out of earlier styles may have taken place somewhere else nearby. The patterns of ceramic change for Corozal suggest that there may have been an influx of new ideas and possibly people from elsewhere at the start of the phase. The fact that a new staple crop, maize, comes into the sequence for the first time in early Corozal is a parallel pattern of introduction from the outside. Like the new pottery complex, the new crop complex seems to have been incorporated into the existing regional subsistence system, rather than replacing it immediately. There are other parallels between the ceramic changes and other changes. For example, the high rate of ceramic change in early Corozal is comparable to the rapid rate of increase in the region's population at the time, inferred from the changes in size and number of sites revealed by the site survey. Also, just as the new economy expands and gains dominance in the subsistence system by the end of Corozal, so too does the new ceramic tempering system become the predominant one at this time. Changes in the morphology of basic culinary and service-bowl types in the spongeware are likely to be related to the development of a new food complex. Perhaps the people who knew how to grow and process corn were the same who knew how to make the sponge-tempered pottery. Thus, early Corozal seems a period of rapid, extensive, and parallel change in several aspects of ancient lifeways.

The great distance between the new Corozal pottery wares, shapes, and decoration and the older Saladoid-Barrancoid pottery on the one hand, and the evidence for interaction between pottery of the different traditions on the other, suggest that people of different geographic origins may have come together in the same community (Roosevelt 1980; Zucchi, Tarble, and Vaz 1984). Since this period is a time of rapid change in subsistence technology and population growth, it may be that people using corn and sponge tempering migrated to regions where the subsistence economy could expand rapidly. A possible model for this process could be one derived from the pattern of rural migration in lowland South America today. There, people from communities with stagnant or shrinking economies migrate to areas where the economies can expand. Often land is scarce and expensive in their community of origin because existing land-holding systems are inflexible or because of population pressure, and families crowd together in inadequate housing, subsisting on uncertain wages. People are sensible of better opportunities for homesteading in less populated areas and are glad to move if that means an opportunity to establish a household of their own on unclaimed land. A trickle of migration can rapidly become a stream, for people can join relatives already in a place. If people of a different culture are already there, the immigrants may eventually end up working with them or for them and may marry into their families.

A situation of economic stagnation may have existed in Parmana during the earlier part of the prehistoric sequence. Before the Corozal tradition, subsistence economy and population size seem to have been relatively stable for more than one thousand years. If, as I have hypothesized (Roosevelt 1980), an older economy based on manioc, fish, and game did not provide much room for expansion, then the introduction of maize would have constituted an opportunity for families to raise their standard of living, expand in population, and as a result form more and larger communities. Indeed, changes in settlement in the

Parmana region indicate an increase in both the size and number of archaeological sites occupied at this time (Roosevelt 1980). Perhaps as maize was taken into more intensive cultivation in the Orinoco, some people migrated to areas with large expanses of land not intensively exploitable by earlier subsistence technologies. Parmana would have been an area wide open for utilization by maize cultivators, for its the seasonally flooded river bottoms are a rich agricultural resource not as appropriate for cultivation of long-maturing, flood-sensitive manioc but very good for short-term annual seed crops.

This tentative interpretation of Corozal as a transitional time period links the changes that took place in ceramic traditions with an economic shift and the accompanying demographic changes in a complex process of cultural transformation. It is suggested that the ceramic changes might be related to factors such as changing patterns of ethnicity or cultural identity as well as to changing demography and new subsistence adaptations. Evaluation of these possibilities and the development of stronger explanations for cultural change will require more comprehensive information about the occurrence of ceramics and other materials within activity areas in archaeological sites and between sites.

4. The Development of the Camoruco Tradition

Camoruco, the ceramic phase with which the Parmana sequence culminates, has both similarities to and differences from Corozal and the earlier phases. Although very different in particulars from the phases of the La Gruta tradition, Camoruco, like Corozal, has a basic resemblance to these earlier phases. All of the Parmana region traditions have an abundance of bowls with modeled-incised rim adornos and/or incised rims, although the style of execution varies. Representational art is important in all the phases, although the subject varies. All have a preponderance of the bowl form, and all have griddles. All the phases have numerous decorated cooking bowls (although undecorated bowls become the most common cooking vessel by far during Camoruco times). These similarities in ceramics among the phases all involve traits characteristic of the entire lowland region of South America, reinforcing the conclusion that the major stimulus for ceramic change during these periods was coming from within the lowlands. The particular Arauquinoid ceramic developments that influence the Camoruco tradition seem to be intensifications of characteristics that appear first in Corozal. Since the Incised and Punctate Horizon that the Arauquinoid series belongs to has far-flung influence reaching well into the northern Andean uplands (Labbe 1986), this would appear to be an instance of lowland ceramic traditions affecting highland ones.

CONCLUSIONS

The Camoruco and Corozal traditions resemble each other in certain pottery characteristics that contrast with the earlier La Gruta tradition pottery corpus. Both Camoruco and Corozal potteries are either grayish or buff in color, in contrast to the reddish brown or orange-brown pottery that predominates in the La Gruta tradition phases. Both Corozal and Camoruco have sponge spicules as the most important tempering material overall. Both have modeling and incision that are crude in comparison to that of the La Gruta tradition phases, and in both traditions plain pottery is more abundant than decorated pottery. Both have painted styles not found in La Gruta tradition phases. Both have human images rare in or absent from the earlier iconography.

The pattern of ceramic change from Corozal to Camoruco is different from the changes from the La Gruta to Corozal traditions and seems to have been more of an in-place evolution. The beginning of the Camoruco tradition sees the phasing out of earlier La Gruta tradition pottery styles and of Corozal sponge-tempered styles that were closely related to La Gruta tradition styles. The plastic-decorated pottery style of the Camoruco complex seems to develop out of the crude, sponge-tempered, plastic-decorated pottery style that comes in during Corozal. "Naturalistic" human representations first appear in Corozal and proliferate greatly during Camoruco. Mauve paint, absent from the La Gruta tradition and present in rare examples during Corozal, becomes a common decorative paint during the Camoruco tradition. During the transition to the Camoruco tradition, there is gradual change in ceramic paste characteristics, with sponge spicules increasing in abundance in the pottery and clay-bit temper becoming more common than crushed-sherd temper. This slow change in emphasis would appear to be a local evolution, unlike the rapid and radical changes in paste characteristics that occur during the Corozal tradition. In many ways, therefore, Corozal is a precursor of Camoruco, and many pottery traits that first appear in Corozal develop further and expand in use during Camoruco.

In contrast to other ceramic developments during the Camoruco tradition, many of the specific traits that link Camoruco to the Arauquinoid series seem to come into use quite suddenly. These traits include maroon paint, complex rectilinear incision, and highly decorated human adornos and effigies. This pattern of change raises the possibility that this particular pottery complex developed elsewhere and then came to influence Parmana region potters. Nevertheless, these new traits seem to come from a complex similar to the early pottery of the Camoruco tradition, rather than from a totally distinct cultural area. They seem, actually, to be a rapid reorientation and intensification of traits present in early Camoruco.

The nature of pottery change during the Camoruco tradition is thus quite different from that of the Corozal tradition and suggests some kind of local development under outside cultural influence rather than the multiethnic influx, settlement, and interaction that Corozal seems to exemplify. For example, ceramics are much more diverse during Corozal times than during Camoruco, with several distinct wares and contrasting decorative styles. Crude plastic-decorative styles, such as that on the Corozal rim strap handles, coexist with very fine ones, such as Corozal curvilinear incision. At the time, fine and crude decorated potteries occur in approximately equal amounts. During Camoruco, style is much more uniform. There are one major plastic decoration style and two major painted styles. Other decorative types are very rare. Much of Camoruco pottery seems mass-produced in comparison with earlier pottery. Plastic decoration is sloppy, surfaces are finished carelessly, and vessel contours are not uniform. Only some examples of the rare decorated service wares are finely made. (During the earlier La Gruta tradition phases, in contrast, most pottery was finely finished and very uniform morphologically.) In addition, the ratio of decorated to undecorated pottery changes between Corozal and Camoruco, with an increase through time in the proportions of undecorated. During Corozal and the earlier La Gruta tradition, the majority of cooking vessels appear to have had some decoration. During Camoruco, the majority of cooking vessels seem to have been plain.

This complex patterning of change and variation is difficult to interpret without information about changes in within-settlement patterning, but it seems likely to have been related to changes in the organization of craft production and consumption and in the organization of the economy in general. Perhaps the decreased ratio of decorated to undecorated pottery, the deterioration of decorative quality, and the development of rare fine decorated wares reflect increasing social differentiation or stratification and accompanying sumptuary distinctions. The Camoruco ceramic developments indeed are paralleled to some degree in other aspects of life. Many elements of lifeways that began in Corozal are further developed or intensified in Camoruco. For example, maize first appears in the early part of the Corozal tradition and has become the primary staple food by Camoruco times. The history of population change also resembles the patterns of change in other aspects, in that population growth begins in Corozal after a long period of apparent stagnation and then continues to a maximum during Camoruco. The pattern of site spacing along the Orinoco banks in Parmana is set also in early Corozal times and continues in Camoruco, although maximum site size becomes much larger in Camoruco. This shared settlement pattern is characterized by relatively even spacing of sites of similar size. Only in late Camoruco times does the pattern change, and one site, Corozal, becomes many times larger than any other known in the region. This development of a possible primary center at a time when the region becomes part of a supraregional horizon style may reflect the development of forms of paramount leadership that fit into a system of interregional war and alliance. Development of a broader data base—including changes in community organization and in human physiology, health, demography and stature—would provide information needed to test such interpretations about social, economic, and political organization. How ceramic hange and change in other aspects of prehistoric lifeways in Parmana were related to each other in the trajectory of cultural evolution seems worthy of special focus in future research.

To summarize, the ceramic complexes of the Corozal and Camoruco phases seem to have their distant stylistic origins in the Saladoid and Barrancoid series and have some functional and iconographic continuities with them, but their pottery has diverged significantly from the earlier traditions in certain aspects of technology, function, and decoration. Based on the nature and rate of changes in pottery, the Corozal tradition seems to represent an intrusion into the Parmana region and a major cultural-ecological transition. The Camoruco tradition could well have developed locally out of Corozal in Parmana, but the specific Arauquinoid ceramic complex that takes form in late Camoruco times indicates a sudden intensification of outside contacts as well as a rapid in-place crystallization of new economic, social, political, and religious forms.

5. Interpretation of Iconographic Change

Although archaeologists customarily study prehistoric pottery for basic information about culture-history sequences, the pottery is actually a form of art with symbolic content that may, under analysis, yield important information about prehistoric ideology and religion. The iconography of the prehistoric ceramic art of Parmana changes through time in significant ways that may mark conceptual and ritual changes during times of economic and sociopolitical change. The sequence of iconography that is found in Parmana also is found over a wide area of Greater Amazonia. Therefore, it potentially has more than regional interest for anthropologists. Because we are beginning to learn something about parallel changes in subsistence and settlement, it is possible to offer some preliminary interpretations of the ideological significance of the iconography and its history.

During the La Gruta tradition of Parmana, plastic ceramic iconography emphasizes animal representations and "geometric" motifs. The Corozal phase grit-tempered decorative types (Pl. 7, *bottom*), which are directly derived from the La Gruta tradition decorative types, share their zoomorphic-geometric iconography, as does the related Corozal phase type of sponge-tempered curvilinear incision (Pl. 8, *top*; Roosevelt 1980, Fig. 62, 8-9, 8-28). However, since the Corozal versions are rather crude, rare holdovers of the style, the abundant and elaborately decorated pottery from the La Gruta, Ronquin, and Ronquin Sombra phases has the best and most numerous examples of the iconography for study. The most common animals in the La Gruta tradition art are higher terrestrial mammals with upstanding ears, somewhat pointed muzzles, and short, rabbitlike tails. A few other animals have flat, round faces and small rounded ears, and may be sloths or kinkajous, and peccaries are represented. There also are what appear to be rare insects, fish, turtles, and aquatic mammals. Without intensive comparisons with the actual living species, few can at present be identified, and perhaps most will always be obscure because of the strong stylization of their features. Only a few distinctive animals can be identified as a specific type of mammal, such as the dolphin (Roosevelt 1980, Fig. 54, 242-7). Although obvious human representations are difficult to find in the art, some of the creatures with the upstanding ears and elongated muzzles of animals appear also to have been given anthropomorphic qualities, such as bipedal stance. These few anthropomorphic representations have non-human features such as zoomorphic noses (Vargas 1981, Lam. 24, 25), or paws instead of hands.

In the La Gruta tradition pottery, there are also "geometric" images, such as arcs, "rainbows," dots, nubbins with dots, or mounds with dots and circles (Roosevelt 1980, Fig. 50). Many of these may represent disembodied animal features. In the integral animal figures, the geometrics are used as the ears, eyes, or eyebrows. The nubbins with dots (Roosevelt 1980, Fig. 50, #119-1bb-2) are animal ears (Roosevelt 1980, Fig. 52, 53), the mounds with dots (Roosevelt 1980, Fig. 50, 123-117) are eyes or noses (Roosevelt 1980, 204, #137-177; Roosevelt 1978, Fig. 3, N), and the "rainbows" are brows depicted above animals' eyes (Roosevelt 1980, 198, #136-5; Roosevelt 1978, Fig. 3, N). Plain grooves are sometimes purely geometric and structural, as demarcation for decorative geometric panels, or they are used to outline an animal's face or eyes. Figurative painted decoration that has been damaged by long burial in the ground is not readily interpreted inconographically, but geometrics like zigzags and volutes can be discerned. The paint is sometimes used to adorn hollow zoomorphic images. Usually the animal's hide is painted white, and the eye mounds or nostrils are painted red (Roosevelt 1980, Fig. 55).

Animals continue as an important motif in the pottery of later traditions in Parmana. During middle Corozal times, animals, usually long-beaked birds, occasionally adorn the cooking bowls with vertical rim strap handles (Fig. 20). Perhaps these images indirectly reflect the primary importance of fish among faunal food, for the birds seem to be members of the heron family, many of which subsist on small fish as well as aquatic invertebrates. (Commonly in Amazonian Indians' cosmologies, the main predators on animal populations are considered their spiritual rulers or owners and are appealed to in curing rituals, as explained below.) During late Corozal and early Camoruco, the most common decorated cooking-bowl type in the sponge-tempered ware has animal-head and paw/wing lug handles on the rim. The depictions are cruder than the Saladoid-Barrancoid ones, being made by sloppy appliqué and coarse incision and punctation, and their identification remains obscure for the most part. Both birds and mammals such as bats are represented.

The importance of animal images in the early phases of Parmana fits with the evidence for the importance of faunal protein in the diet. In a system whose staple crop is a starchy plant such as manioc, faunal protein is the bulk limiting factor in subsistence. For this reason, the ritual and ideological system might be expected to reflect interest in controlling or influencing faunal resources. The earlier predominance of animal images thus may reflect the nutritional importance of hunting and fishing to supplement a manioc diet. The animal images might presumably be connected with ritual observances, myths, and prohibitions through which the animal world is ostensibly manipulated. Today in Amazonia, among peoples using the manioc-fish-game subsistence complex, art imagery focuses on animals, and shamanistic efforts are concentrated on dealing with certain ancestral spirits titled "Masters of the Animals," who, by their putative power over human disease, fertility, and game abundance, are thought to control the balance between humans and their environment (e.g., Reichel-Dolmatoff 1971; Roth 1915; C. Hugh-Jones 1979; S. Hugh-Jones 1979). Perhaps the animal iconography of the early prehistoric pottery complexes represents a similar ritual system. The rare anthropomorphized animal images, which are restricted to certain "special" vessel types such as effigy bottles, may represent a concept akin to the "Masters of the Animals," which are mythological animals who talk and act like humans. The combination of human and animal qualities in certain rare examples of the art could thus be interpreted as a kind of "alter ego" motif, representing the transformation achieved by shamans with the assistance of their animal helpers, for the purpose of communicating with the ancestral spirits. The archaeological bottles that bear these representations might have held drug potions or other stimulants used to reach the trances by which the transformations take place.

Identifiable nonzoomorphic human representations are very rare in Parmana ceramic art until the Camoruco phase. There are none yet known from the La Gruta, Ronquin, and Ronquin Sombra phases. Human effigies seem to come into the sequence first in the Corozal phase. They are quite rare until late Corozal and are very crude, variable, and unstandardized (Pl. 13, B; Roosevelt 1980, Fig. 60). In contrast, one of the outstanding iconographic features of Camoruco tradition pottery is the prominence of human representations. These images are modeled and decorated with incision and punctation (Pl. 12), as either bowl lugs or effigy jars. Interestingly, the human images change somewhat in their use and appearance during the Camoruco phase. Early in the phase, they appear almost exclusively as effigy jars. Later in the phase, the human-effigy jars continue, but humans also are commonly used as bowl lugs, almost replacing animals in this context. The vessel effigies change in character through time, with large unpainted jars being characteristic of early Camoruco, and small, maroon-painted effigy jars and cups being more common late in the phase. The human lugs also change through time and become less carefully made but more highly decorated, particularly on wrists and heads. The maximum frequency of the human representations comes in the last prehistoric phase in the region and coincides with the diminution of animal images to very small numbers. Thus, three-dimensional representational pottery art has moved from animals to humans for its major subjects by the final Camoruco phase. At the same time, the major incised style of the period, Arauquinoid rectilinear incision, has lost the zoomorphic iconography of the major incised style of the La Gruta tradition phases and become a purely geometric ornament on the human images.

The timing of the first appearance of nonzoomorphic human images may be significant, coinciding as it does with the establishment of intensive maize cultivation, the expansion of regional population density, and the possible formation of a chiefdom or ranked society. The increasing emphasis on human images in the ceramic sequence co-occurs exactly with the establishment of fully efficient agriculture, in which most of the calories and protein of subsistence are produced by cultivating agricultural crops, rather than by hunting and fishing. In Parmana, according to the chemistry of human bone collagen (van der Merwe, Roosevelt, and Vogel 1981), maize became a staple and its protein came to be the primary protein source, rather than faunal protein, although fish was still used to supplement the maize protein. Thus as animals became less important quantitatively in subsistence, they became less important than humans in art. It has been suggested that an emphasis on human images in preindustrial art may be related in part to the rise of ranking or social stratification, because of the practice of glorifying the ancestors of elite people with memorial images as justification of the elite peoples' status (Roosevelt 1987a, 1991a). Thus, some human images, such as the human effigies, might be interpreted as representations of chiefly ancestors. This explanation might fit the situation in Parmana, because the human images are most common in levels of Camoruco 3, which is the subphase that sees the spread of the Arauquinoid Horizon, often interpreted as the spread of a conquest chiefdom.

Many of the human images of Camoruco, however, are "fertility" figures representing pregnant or sexually displayed females. Such human images may relate to a "demographic" ideology favored during the development of chiefdom societies (Roosevelt 1987b, 1991a). That is, with an expanding economy and incipient stratification, there would be a premium on the availability of labor, for intensive cultivation of bottomlands or for the production of labor-intensive crafts for elite consumption and abundant utilitarian items for commoner consumption. With time, competition among societies for space and influence could lead to expanded warfare, which, like agricultural intensification, can be a stimulus to population increase for defensive purposes. Marriage and reproduction as sources of land and labor are commonly given ritual emphasis in chiefly societies. In this context, ideologies favoring natality might be emphasized and reflected in the iconography art used in initiation rites and marriage. Whether these connections among art, economy, and organization are generally true worldwide is not at all clear, but the hypotheses may be illuminating for the Middle Orinoco, where the rise of human iconography correlates with the establishment of a populous ranked society supported by a fully agricultural subsistence economy based mainly on seed-crop cultivation. A similar economic-iconographic sequence is found in the Amazon Basin proper, where the earlier phases of probable root-crop horticulturalists have primarily zoomorphic-geometric representational decoration, and many later phases of intensive agriculturalists are characterized by a reduction in the size and iconographic centrality of zoomorphic images and the increasing prominence and/or size of human-effigy vessels, statues on special seats, and female figurines (Roosevelt 1987b, 1991a).

The meaning of correlations among changes in settlement, subsistence, and ceramic art in Greater Amazonia can be investigated further in a number of ways. Knowing more about the archaeological context of the art will help us evaluate existing interpretations about its function, so more excavation aimed at recovering the stratigraphic and structural associations of art objects is needed. In addition, if more were known about changes in social and political organization, then more extensive interpretations would be possible, for the nature of art as a system of visual symbols and objects for ritual and political manipulation is closely tied to lifeways and the organization of human communities. Unsynthesized information about the function of ethnographic Amazonian art objects exists in the documentation of older systematic museum collections. By comparisons of the character and associations of ethnographic art with ancient art, we could learn more about the changing societal role of art. Cross-cultural comparisons of the social context and functions of modern native art worldwide could also be illuminating. Many images and objects similar to those in the archaeological Amazonian art corpus exist in African, Asian, and Oceanian art. By comparing the characteristics and contexts of this diverse art, we could learn enough about preindustrial art to use the ancient art objects and their archaeological contexts as information about the ideologies and rituals of ancient peoples. Further development of a general body of data about the role of art in ideology, ritual, social organization, and economy by systematic comparisons between ethnographic and prehistoric societies would allow archaeologists to construct better hypotheses about the meaning and uses of ancient art. So far, we have used archaeological art primarilyfor chronology, as in this monograph, but it could have interpretive scope far beyond this.

B. Long-Distance Relationships

The prehistoric pottery of the Parmana region is related to pottery styles over a wide area of South America. Interpretation of the significance of cross-regional relationships is an important problem for lowland archaeology. In the last two decades much progress has been made in expanding our knowledge of regional sequences, but still the majority of regions are unknown. With such incomplete knowledge, it is difficult to interpret the history and nature of cross-regional relationships of ceramic complexes because chronological relationships are impossible to establish. Nonetheless, existing knowledge does offer some grounds for the evaluation of earlier interpretations and for the development of hypotheses for investigation in the future.

Several authors have made exhaustive reviews of the ceramic relationships of lowland archaeological phases (Osgood and Howard 1943; Howard 1947; Cruxent and Rouse 1958–59; Rouse and Cruxent 1963; Brochado and Lathrap

MS; Foster and Lathrap 1973; Willey 1971; Meggers and Evans 1983). These studies form the basis for current interpretations of general ceramic affinities. In the discussion of the Corozal site seriation modes above (Chap. 3), I mention the specific relationships of Parmana pottery to other northern lowland complexes. My specific observations on wares, styles, types, and motifs, as mentioned above, are based on a review of the relevant pottery collections in museums and my excavations at Santarem and Marajo. Below, the broader cross-regional ceramic relationships will be characterized and interpreted. The focus of discussion will be the Saladoid and Barrancoid series and the Incised and Punctate Horizon, which are the major supraregional entities to which the Parmana ceramics are related.

1. The Saladoid and Barrancoid Series

Two major stylistic entities represented in the pottery of the Corozal site are the closely related Saladoid and Barrancoid series, whose styles are widespread in the Orinoco, Caribbean, and Amazon regions. The Corozal site ceramic modes related to these series are Corozal grit-tempered pottery (#140), Saladoid-Barrancoid decoration (#204), Saladoid red-and-white painting (#5), and Corozal curvilinear incision (#134). (The Parmana sherdware [#135] is associated with but not stylistically related to these series.) The Saladoid and Barrancoid series were first formally defined by Cruxent and Rouse (1958–59) from styles of the Lower Orinoco in Venezuela and have since been applied mainly to ceramic styles of northern South America and the Antilles. There are in the Amazon Basin proper, however, styles that may be distantly related to these series (Lathrap 1970; Palmatary 1960; Brochado and Lathrap MS; Hilbert 1955, 1959a, 1968; Hilbert and Hilbert 1980; Roosevelt 1986, 1991d), and a very closely related style has been discovered in the Guianas (Boomert 1983). Some of the Amazonian styles related to the series were originally placed in the Incised Rim Horizon (Meggers and Evans 1961). However, although virtually all Saladoid and Barrancoid styles in the lowlands have incised rims, many styles of the series are not related to the styles of the Incised Rim Horizon, and most styles of that horizon are not Saladoid or Barrancoid in character. Further study of the Amazonian styles will probably encourage the definition of new series and subseries related to the Orinoco series (I. Rouse, personal communication).

The earliest styles related to the Saladoid and Barrancoid series are highly decorated styles characterized by broad-line incision and modeling in zoomorphic and geometric motifs and elaborate red-and-white "negative" painting.

The plastic decoration is usually referred to as Barrancoid after the sites of Barrancas and Los Barrancos, and the painting is called Saladoid, after the site of Saladero, all in the Lower Orinoco (Cruxent and Rouse 1958–58; Rouse and Cruxent 1963). Because some scholars use the term Saladoid for complexes that have only the paint and not the plastic decoration, I use the term Saladoid-Barrancoid for styles that have both kinds of decoration, which is the case for all the Venezuelan styles of the series. In the Orinoco, the red-and-white painting drops out through time, and the incised and modeled decoration predominates. In the Caribbean islands, at first the red-and-white paint is emphasized over the plastic decoration, which becomes important later and ultimately replaces the red-and-white paint. The mainland pottery of the series tends to be well-made, reddish pottery, usually tempered with grit. The common vessel of the series is the bowl with zoomorphic adornos and/or incision on the rim. These bowls were used for cooking, and there are also numerous thick ceramic griddles and many other vessel shapes. (The Parmana styles of the series are described in detail in the summary of the Parmana sequence and in the descriptions of the modes in Chapter 3 *above*.)

The probable geographic origin of the Saladoid-Barrancoid series is disputed. At first, the origins were sought around 1000 B.C. in Saladoid styles of the Lower Orinoco, where the series was originally defined and where the earliest radiocarbon dates for the series had been assayed (Cruxent and Rouse 1958–59; Rouse and Cruxent 1963). Then, La Gruta was discovered in the Middle Orinoco and produced several dates between about 2100 and 1600 B.C. (Roosevelt 1978; Rouse 1978; Vargas 1981). However, now that a series of more or less closely related styles has been found in the Guianas and the Amazon, the question of origins has opened up again, and the Orinoco's claim to temporal priority in the series will have to be checked with dated sequences from the Amazon and the Guianas. In the Upper Amazon of Peru, Barrancoid pottery complexes such as Hupa-Iya have been identified (Lathrap 1970), but these are among the later examples of that series, and as yet no Saladoid styles have been found. Since a fair amount of culture-historical work has been done in the Peruvian Amazon, it is probable that the Saladoid and Barrancoid series did not originate there. The cultural history of the Bolivian Amazon is still poorly known, so its part in the spread of the ceramic series is uncertain. Possible Barrancoid pottery with red paint has been found in basal layers of earth mounds in the Bolivian Amazon, dated between 800 B.C. and the time of Christ (Dougherty and Calandra 1981-82; Smithsonian Anthropology Archives 1965-85). The Saladoid complexes of the Caribbean coast of Venezuela and the Antilles all postdate the early mainland complexes of the Lower and Middle Orinoco, and the earliest-known Saladoid complex near the Surinam coast is dated to about 50 B.C. Scholars who believe that lowland cultures were derived from Andean cultures have attributed the origin of early Saladoid and Barrancoid styles to influence from the Peruvian Andes (Meggers and Evans 1983; Sanoja ad Vargas 1978). However, no similar styles have ever been found there. Several Andean styles of the late first millennium B.C., such as Puerto Moorin and Moche, have complex red-and-white painted decoration, but the styles substantially postdate several of the lowland styles and do not resemble them in iconography, technology, or vessel shape. None of the Andean early incised styles even vaguely resemble the lowland styles. Another possible source could be Caribbean Colombia, where pottery styles with incised rim decoration and ornamental zoomorphic lugs occur very early in the fourth millennium B.C. (Reichel-Dolmatoff 1965a, 1965b, 1985) and continue in use until about 500 B.C. It may be that the style ancestral to the Saladoid-Barrancoid styles came into being through a fusion of early Colombian and Brazilian plastic-decorated styles with some as yet unidentified early styles of red-and-white painting, but red-and-white painting similar to the Saladoid painting has never been described among the early complexes of Colombia.

The Saladoid-Barrancoid styles have great integrity over time and space, but their development is not synchronized as in true horizon styles. Perhaps better termed sloping horizons, they have very slow diffusion rates and seem linked more by common origins than by contemporary communication. The styles are not, therefore, very useful for cross-dating, because sherds with identical motifs can be hundreds of years apart in age. The spread of the styles is widely thought to represent the spread of root-crop horticulturalists throughout the lowlands, and the finds from Parmana are consistent with this identification. The numerous ceramic griddles that many of the styles have and the zoomorphic iconography seem to exemplify evidence of the technology and ideology of a subsistence system based on calories from manioc and protein from fish and game. It is usually suggested that the styles of the series spread by the slow migration of Arawakan-speaking settlers moving out into new regions (Lathrap 1970). The spatial-temporal patterning of the series is consonant with such a slow migration, but the theory has weak empirical grounds, for Saladoid-Barrancoid styles had gone out of use by the time of the conquest, and no group documented as speaking an Arawakan language has ever been shown to be using a style of the series. Furthermore, in Amazonia today native populations do not segregate cross-regionally by distinctive ceramic styles, lifeways, or languages (Black et al. 1983; Thomas Myers, personal communication). In fact, the integral ceramic styles are used by peoples of many different language groups and subsistence adaptations. Such neat segregation of language, subsistence, and pottery style seems to occur only in the theories of archaeologists. The question of the languages of the bearers of Saladoid and Barrancoid styles will probably never be solved. Even if someone finds an ethnohistoric ceramic style of the series with linguistic documentation, the question would remain whether the style and the language grop were consistently associated. As to the possibility that the styles of the series were spread by a migration of a particular group of people, only biological distance studies of prehistoric skeletons from cultures using various styles could reveal whether there is greater genetic affinity among the makers of these Saladoid-Barrancoid styles than with people using other styles (Roosevelt 1987a, 1991a).

2. Incised and Punctate Horizon

Camoruco pottery and certain styles of Corozal sponge-tempered pottery belong to the Incised and Punctate Horizon, a late prehistoric supraregional ceramic series of the Amazon and Orinoco (Meggers and Evans 1961; Lathrap 1970; Willey 1971; Roosevelt 1980). The styles of this series share sharp-tooled incision and punctation in panels and crudely modeled representational lugs and appliqué ornaments. Most of the styles of the Incised and Punctate Horizon have abundant sponge-spicule tempering, rather than the grit of the earlier styles. The color of the fabric is buff to gray and variable in comparison with the earlier pottery's uniform red or orange color, and it is usually poorly surface finished. Both humans and animals are shown in this art, as well as geometric images recalling basketry and fabric designs. Many styles are also decorated with an overall dark red wash, usually fugitive, and some bear repetitive polychrome painting in simple geometric motifs. In general, the ceramics of this series give an impression of a craft deteriorating under the exigencies of mass production.

The Incised and Punctate Horizon extends over a large area of South America, including the Orinoco, the Caribbean and northern highland Colombia, the Amazon, and the Antilles. The Arauquinoid and Valencioid series are subseries of the horizon in the Orinoco and Caribbean coast range of Venezuela. Many of the incised and punctate styles of the Guianas and the Lower Amazon, such as Santarem, Arua, and Maraca, have not yet been assigned to subseries within the horizon. Because of a lack of stratigraphic and radiometric information, the chronological and historical relationships of the different styles of the series are not yet clear. It appears to have arisen from styles of the Saladoid-Barrancoid series, transformed by mass production, the implementation of sponge tempering, and the iconographic shift of emphasis from humans to animals. The use of ornamental lugs and the emphasis of incision in panels on rims could be derived from an ancestral Barrancoid style. The style of Los Barrancos, which has lost red-and-white painting and has incorporated sponge tempering, could be the intermediate style in the transition. The Corozal tradition is also a possible transition candidate. However, because so few regions' ceramic sequences are known, choosing specific ancestors for the horizon at this time seems premature.

The Incised and Punctate Horizon is thought to represent the spread of conquest chiefdoms through the tropical lowlands east of the Andes, from about A.D. 1000 to 1500. The chiefdoms of this horizon are not the earliest known chiefdoms of the lowlands, which are those of the Polychrome Horizon in the Amazon Basin (about A.D. 400–1300), a style series also derived from the Saladoid-Barrancoid series. This style has sinuous, intricate polychrome painting as well as abundant incision and excision and some modeling. The Polychrome Horizon's origin, once thought to be the Andes, now seems more likely to have been in the Lower Amazon, where the earliest style of the horizon, Marajoara, has been found. The polychrome styles of the Andes foothills are all late prehistoric in date. In addition, the Polychrome styles, with their abundance of adorno bowls and red-and-white painting, are clearly of lowland character rather than Andean or Mesoamerican. But despite its apparent lowland origin and association with the chiefdom lifeway, the Polychrome Horizon definitely does not seem ancestral to the styles of the Incised and Punctate Horizon. The change from polychrome to incised and punctate styles in the different Amazon regions known so far is abrupt and lacking in developmental continuities. This makes the Amazon a less likely homeland for the Incised and Punctate Horizon than the Orinoco, where there at least are earlier traditions, such as Corozal, with traits that appear to presage some of the diagnostic traits of incised and punctate styles. These findings notwithstanding, the question of the roles of the many other regions where we have no ceramic sequences is still unanswered.

The general geographic origin of the later Incised and Punctate Horizon is thus not clear at all. The predominant tempering technology of the horizon, sponge tempering, is indisputably lowland, for the freshwater sponges used for the temper exist primarily in the tropical lowland habitat. Nonetheless, the horizon is closely related stylistically to late prehistoric plastic-decorated styles of the northern Andes and Caribbean coast ranges in Colombia (Labbe 1986; Reichel-Dolmatoff 1965b, 1986). It is certainly possible that the original styles of the horizon were formed in the northern highlands and the tempering technology added only after they spread to lower altitudes. This would accord with the hypothesis that early lowland corn, the staple crop of some lowland phases of the horizon, was introduced from the northern Andes. But the hypothesis of a lowland origin for the horizon is equally likely in light of present evidence and is more economical, because it does not require separate origins for the decoration and tempering technology. Because of the question of the role of environment in preindustrial cultural development, it is important to find out eventually where this horizon began, whether in the tropical lowlands or in the northern Andes highlands. For this, it will be necessary to have detailed chronologies from both areas, and these are not yet available. Further, it will be important to know how the late prehistoric chiefdoms of the Incised and Punctate Horizon compare to the earlier polychrome chiefdoms, such as Marajoara, in settlement pattern, community composition and organization, subsistence, demography, and relationships with other regions. We already have some indications of significant differences, such as family organization, gender roles, division of labor, cosmology, and rulership, but for effective comparisons, we will need more specific information about both kinds of chiefdoms than exists today.

In the lowlands the various styles of the Incised and Punctate Horizon have the space-time characteristics of true horizons in that they spread very rapidly and far. Such space-time characteristics have traditionally been interpreted as the product of the political-military expansion of chiefdoms and states. In addition, in some areas there is evidence for the existence of paramount chiefship. For example, supraregional chiefs were observed in the Orinoco and Lower Amazon at the start of the European conquest, and in the latter area, there exist large terra cotta statues of men and women with emblems of office. It has been suggested that the regional styles of the Incised and Punctate Horizon represent the spread of Carib-speaking chiefdoms by conquest (Lathrap 1970), but as in the case of the Saladoid-Barrancoid series, there is no reason to suppose that people of only one language group were associated with pottery of the series. Possibly the close similarities between the regional styles of the series arose from intense contact among both allies and enemies, but at present it is difficult to evaluate explanations of the stylistic phenomena. Research to verify or falsify theories about the relationship of ceramic style to social and political organization will require study of the content and organization of the archaeological communities through survey and excavation within sites in a regional settlement system. As with the hypotheses about the ethnic-demographic significance of the Saladoid-Barrancoid series, it will also be important to compare skeletal biological distances within and between styles of the series and with other cultural entities, to evaluate the role of mass migration in the spread of the horizon.

The economic processes involved in the spread of the Incised and Punctate Horizon have also been little investigated. It has been proposed that the spread of the horizon was accompanied by a conversion to staple maize economies, and archaeobotanical and geochemical studies of the biological remains associated with two member styles in the Peruvian Amazon and Middle Orinoco have yielded corroborative evidence (Roosevelt 1980, 1987a, 1989; van der Merwe, Roosevelt, and Vogel 1981; Roosevelt, Krueger, and Sullivan MSa). A third style, Santarem of the Lower Amazon, is associated with staple maize cultivation on the strength of ethnohistoric accounts and archaeobotany (Roosevelt 1986, 1991d; Roosevelt et al. MS). Investigation of the possible role of this economic transition in the development of the horizon will require more comprehensive study of paleodiet among the related phases. Maize is usually considered to have diffused into the lowlands from the northwest (Roosevelt 1980), but no one has investigated the history of the crop there or in southern and eastern South America, where primitive maize cultivars have been recovered from several early rock shelters (e.g., Fernandez Distel 1988; Miller 1987). Trade in exotic materials, production of labor-intensive crafts for trade, and mass production of ordinary goods seem to characterize most of the phases of the horizon, but these aspects of economy have not yet been investigated with trace-element provenience studies or study of the characteristics of craft production in the complexes.

For all these interpretive questions and problems, the extensive sites of the horizon are a substantial archaeological resource for future work.

C. The Significance of Corozal for Future Research

The results of the work at Corozal shed light on the nature of the lowland archaeological record, the methods effective for work there, and the characteristics of the lowland sequence of cultural development. The general significance of the project's substantive findings about the lowland cultural sequence is discussed above, in the introduction and in the preceding sections of this chapter. In essence, those results document a dynamic cultural trajectory more independent of outside influence than was envisioned earlier. Perhaps of greater practical significance, given the limitations on the scope of any particular research project, the results of the Corozal excavations and ceramic seriation illustrate the hitherto underestimated potential of tropical lowland sites to yield information of archaeological interest. Although prominent publications about the lowlands suggest a paucity of archaeological materials and structures in lowland sites, the evidence recovered at Corozal was in contrast abundant and multifaceted, with much more complex archaeological patterning than is acknowledged in the literature. Numerous stratigraphic layers and features, ceramics, lithics, and biological remains were found in complex, patterned associations at the site. Other research in the general area shows that such materials are not unique to Parmana but potentially recoverable from the majority of lowland sites, and in the future they can be exploited for information useful for resolving theoretical issues in archaeology, social anthropology, and human ecology. Much can be learned if the chronological work at Corozal is followed by more comprehensive investigation in the future.

Specifically, the Corozal excavations and seriation have shown that excavating by stratigraphic layers yields abundant chronological information even in tropical lowland areas, where this manner of excavation usually has not been the custom. The excavations revealed microstratigraphic layering that tropical sites are not commonly thought to have, and the ceramic analysis showed that these layers have temporal, as well as possible functional, significance in terms of the activities that they represent. Rather than an undifferentiated mass of soil, we encountered deposits containing numerous observable stratigraphic layers, structural traces, and well-defined lenses and artifact features that we could for the most part follow during the process of excavation. Our pottery samples, collected according to this layering, manifested statistically significant changes through time in the representation of stylistic and technical attributes. This study thus demonstrates that excavation carried out by "natural," rather than purely "artificial," levels and seriation by a variety of time-sensitive modes, rather than only by wares or types, make an effective strategy for creating lowland archaeological sequences. Such methods make it possible to use stratigraphic layering for chronological purposes by revealing the distinctions in pottery characteristics through the column of layers. By means of stratigraphic excavation and ceramic attribute analysis at Corozal, the later part of the Parmana sequence was divisible into six phases, rather than the one late prehistoric phase that had been established previously by use of artificial levels and taxonomic type variety classification.

The division of the archaeological sequence into shorter chronological units was important for the goals of the Parmana project because it helped to highlight patterns of prehistoric developmental change in the region. During the timespan of the sequence, several significant changes in lifeways were taking place, including an unsuspected shift in subsistence, an increase in population, changes in community organization and outside relations, and changes in craft technology, art and style, and iconography. The existence of a detailed ceramic sequence permitted these changes to be observed and some of their temporal relationships with other factors to be explored. For example, the changes in corn races and corn abundance and shifts in human bone chemistry, which documented a major transition in the use of staple foods, occurred within a period of only a few hundred years, and their timing would not have been detectable in a less detailed sequence. The characteristics of the sigmoid population growth curve also could not have come to light had the settlement study been based on the earlier sequence. The earlier, single late prehistoric ceramic period for the region would have obscured such changes, all of which would have fallen into the one period.

Perhaps even more useful for future work than the phase divisions are the statistically significant changes in ceramic stratification that became apparent within the phases. Some of these smaller divisions represent relatively short time periods of 50 years or less. Such fine time units in terms of ceramics will be needed when archaeologists start to investigate sites more intensively and comprehensively to evaluate the nature and history of cultural phenomena like the Arauquinoid Horizon. For example, study of change through time in socioeconomic differentiation, based on burial furnishings and osteological evidence of physiological condition, requires that burials be datable by the styles of their ceramics, for radiocarbon dating is expensive and often has larger error ranges than the smaller time units. In the same way, analysis of within-site variation in craft production requires that contemporaneity in artifactual features be recognizable through the identification of microstylistic traits. The fruitful study of regional settlement patterns for socioeconomic and political information also requires refined chronologies to help establish the contemporaneity of site occupations. If the microperiodization of the Parmana sequence can be verified and refined, then there will be the type of regional chronology suitable for the investigation of economic, social, and political change in the prehistory of Parmana.

The site of Corozal also gives a concrete example of the fact that tropical lowland sites have excellent physical preservation of prehistoric objects: abundant identifiable carbonized plant remains, including wood, leaves, flowers, fruits, stems, roots, and seeds from both domestic and wild species, and large amounts of identifiable human and animal bone (Roosevelt 1980; Smith and Roosevelt MS;. Roosevelt 1984a, 1989, 1991d; Roosevelt et al. 1991, MS; Wing, Garson, and Simon MS; van der Merwe, Roosevelt, and Vogel 1981). Other types of objects recovered in large quantities with fine screening and water separation were stone tools and debitage, beads and other ornaments, lignite artifacts and debris, wattle and daub, burnt adobe from hearths, debris from ceramic manufacture, and bone tools and ornaments. Many diverse objects were also recovered in place in the project excavations as parts of stratigraphic units, and together these constitute potential evidence for a wide range of human activities. Not only were utilitarian food-processing objects recovered in place, but also a number of noteworthy art objects, such as human figurines. The archaeological features can therefore be evidence of a wide range of mundane and ritual activities. The many burials that evidently exist in the site are potential evidence for or against biological diversity during periods for which multiethnic communities are hypothesized and could also reveal changing patterns of biological distance and individuals' access to resources, both crucial evidence of family organization and status systems. The stratigraphy, the different styles and functional types of artifacts, and the nature and representation of ecofacts change substantially through time and thus are potential evidence of a considerable amount of cultural evolution and human-ecological change. Given awareness by archaeologists of this richness of evidence, future work should be able to achieve more and better information than we have achieved in the past.

To capture such information, however, future problem-oriented work will need to expand excavations horizontally across large sites such as Corozal. Because of the state of knowledge of Parmana at the time and the developmental focus of the Parmana project as a whole, the excavations at Corozal were vertical cuts aimed at gaining a time sequence and general information about subsistence change. For obvious reasons, columnar excavations are not appropriate for investigating the range of contemporary activities or the composition and function of the groups living in a settlement. Because such excavations cannot reveal artifactual and stratigraphic variation across the site at any one time, in our project we could not directly investigate the possibility of functional and microstylistic variation within the site. Accordingly, we still do not know very much about the nature of the site community and its similarities to and differences from those of other sites. Some of our questions about patterns of craft production and consumption in the prehistoric societies represented in the Parmana sequence could be investigated by study of within-site variation. For example, the functional significance of the existence of rare decorated cooking vessels as well as abundant plain cooking vessels might be clarified if the pattern of the vessels' horizontal distributions could be determined. Special feasting dishes might have a distribution that contrasted with utilitarian vessels, as is the case at a Marajoara site that we have studied in the

Lower Amazon (Roosevelt 1990b, 1991a), and the distribution might inform us about the participation of different groups in community rituals. Additionally, the social, economic, and genealogical correlates of the ceramic microstyles, such as the different punctation styles of the Camoruco tradition, might be better understood if the styles' spatial relationships to structures and activity areas within the site could be ascertained.

The columnar excavation strategy also prevents us from getting a sufficient sample from the mortuary population of any period to reveal the nature of variation within the population, because we could excavate only those few skeletons that happened to fall within the 16 square meters of the excavation column. By excavating stratigraphically and seriating the layers according to chronologically sensitive modes, we were able to differentiate skeletons of different phases and use them as evidence of quantitative temporal change in subsistence, through bone-chemistry tests (van der Merwe, Roosevelt, and Vogel 1981). However, the lack of an adequate number of contemporary skeletons prevents any inferences about the composition and organization of the population as a whole. Since prehistoric sociopolitical evolution worldwide is characterized by distinctive shifts in patterns of access to life-sustaining resources within populations (Roosevelt 1984b), the knowledge gained from population-based osteological study is crucial to an understanding of the changing organization of ancient societies. Interpreting the relationships of such factors as genetics and artifact styles, gender and occupations, demography and resource availability requires well-documented, statistically significant osteological data. Thus, progress in the study of prehistoric cultural development and assessment of the basic characteristics of the ancient societies will require knowledge of the patterning of both artifacts and biological remains in contemporary activity areas, facilities, and structures at sites, and that will require the excavation of broader areas in the future.

Although our Corozal excavations cannot yield this type of comprehensive information, designed as they were for quite a different purpose, they nonetheless reveal the existence of the kind of variability and patterning that could yield such information if broad-area excavation, geophysical mapping, and systematic sampling could be done at the site. Now that a detailed sequence has been established for the Parmana region, in the future it would be valuable to study the Corozal site as a whole and geophysically survey and systematically excavate in different areas of the site, as has been possible at the Marajoara sites of Aterro dos Bichos and Guajara (Roosevelt 1989, 1990b, 1991a). Of all the sites known to me in the Orinoco, Corozal seems one of the most promising for an intensive investigation of a site plan for community composition, because of its depth, large size, object richness, well-preserved biological remains, within-site stratigraphic variability, and temporal depth. The excavations at Corozal suggest that the site contains numerous features that are geophysically detectable, such as burials, hearths, earthen house floors, and refuse areas. Geophysical remote-sensing survey methods such as resistivity or conductivity could be used to map the extent of refuse and floor areas, and magnetic survey would be useful to locate clay hearths, whose presence at the site is documented by the numerous finds of burnt adobe fragments. Pits for burials and other intrusions can usually be detected by ground-probing radar, allowing cemeteries and disturbances to be mapped. Use of such survey methods permits large, complex archaeological sites such as Corozal to be mapped and excavated more effectively by establishing sampling strata through the geophysics and allowing unexcavated parts to be studied through their geophysical signatures after the relationship of geophysics and stratigraphy in the excavated part of the site has been established.

Because of the various projects carried out in the Middle Orinoco region in the 1970s, the region now has one of the most detailed ceramic sequences in the lowlands. The results of the Parmana project show that many sites in the region are rich in highly patterned archaeological remains, like Corozal. Accordingly, over and above within-site patterning, Parmana will be a good area in the future for intensive pattern survey of regional settlement. At present, the patterns of increase in occupied site areas through prehistory are known in some detail, but we have no systematic information about the different possible functions of specific sites. Because of the nature of the developmental sequence, which incorporates the apparent transformation of a village society into a chiefdom, intensive study of within-site patterning in different sites will be important, to understand the composition and functioning of different types of sites in the settlement system. To be effective for this purpose, our approach to regional settlement survey will need to be augmented. The distribution of surface sites throughout the landscape can be investigated through remote sensing calibrated to the geophysical signatures of known sites, and the occurrence of buried sites can be estimated through systematic subsurface sampling. Knowledge of within-site variability gleaned from the comprehensive studies of individual sites can then be used to assess the different possible functions of the sites and the range of activities that took place in them.

Through such research, we finally can move closer than we could in the past to reconstructing the integral societies and populations that once existed in the Middle Orinoco and can use archaeology to learn about the causes and characteristics of an ancient complex society in the tropical forest.

Tables

Table 1. Chronological chart for Parmana region phases

Camoruco 3 phase	A.D. 1300–1550
Camoruco 2 phase	A.D. 1000–1300
Camoruco 1 phase	A.D. 800–1000
Corozal 3 phase	A.D. 700–800
Corozal 2 phase	A.D. 500–700
Late Corozal 1 phase	?–A.D. 500
Early Corozal 1 phase	1000 B.C.–?
Ronquin Sombra phase	1300–1000 B.C.
Ronquin phase	1600–1300 B.C.
La Gruta phase	2500–1600 B.C.

Table 2. Phase and stratigraphic identifications and provenience numbers of the levels of Excavation 2

Level	Phase	Strata	Provenience No.
1	Camoruco 3 /Recent	W, V	49
2	Camoruco 3	V, U, T	32
3	Camoruco 3	S	34
4	Camoruco 3	R	80
5–6	Camoruco 3/2	Q, P, O	12, 60, 393, 490, 547
7	Camoruco 2	N, M	48
8	Camoruco 2	L, K, J	4, 28, 380
9	Camoruco 1	K, J, I	43
10	Camoruco 1	I	35
11	Camoruco 1 /Corozal 3	H and feature	47
12	Corozal 3	G	10, 36
13	Corozal 2	F	3, 26
14	Corozal 2	E	2
15	Corozal 1	D	7, 29
16–16w	Corozal 1	D, C, and feature	37, 62
16e	Corozal 1	C	42
17	Corozal 1	C	45
18	Corozal 1	B	27
19	Corozal 1	A	54
20	Corozal 1	A	40
16	West-wall burial	D, C	542
16	Center burial	D, C	293
16	North-wall burial	D, C	644
18	Child's burial	C, B, A	545

Table 3. Phase and stratigraphic identification and provenience numbers of the levels of Excavation 3

Level	Phase	Strata	Provenience No.
1	Recent	W	385
2	Camoruco 3	V	30
3	Camoruco 3	U	150
4	Camoruco 3	T	1
5	Camoruco 3	S, Q, P	20, 63 (feature)
6	Camoruco 3	R, Q, P	25, 394, 539, 546
7	Camoruco 3/2	P, Q	11
8	Camoruco 2	O	58
9	Camoruco 2	N	33
10	Camoruco 2	M	53, 57, 59, 72, 76, 77, 78, 79, 629, 646
11–12A	Camoruco 2	Lenses	38, 74
11–12B	Corozal 2/1	L, K	39, 44
13	Corozal 1	K, J, I	55
14	Corozal 1	I	23
15	Corozal 1/Corozal 3	H and feature	19
16	Corozal 3	feature	41
17	Corozal 3	G and feature	22
21	Corozal 3/2	F and feature	152
22	Corozal 2	E	24
23	Corozal 2	E	31
24	Corozal 1	D	21
25	Corozal 1	D, C, and feature	8
26	Corozal 1	B	46
16–17	Skeleton 1	G, F	61
18	Skeleton 2	G, F	56
18–19	Skeleton 3	G, F	6, 147, 149, 203
18–22	Skeleton 4	F, E	50
25	Feature	D, C	51
25	Skeleton 2	D, C	46a
25	Skeleton 3	D, C	148

Table 4. Areal extent and approximate depths of the levels of Excavation 2

Level	Extent	From	Location	To	Location
1	overall	surface		25 cm	
2	overall	25 cm		45 cm	
3	overall	45 cm		60–65 cm	
4	overall	60–65 cm		77 cm	east
		60–65 cm		80 cm	west
5	overall	77 cm	east	90 cm	northeast
		80 cm	west	95 cm	east, center
6	overall	90 cm	northeast	117 cm	west
		95 cm	east, center	112 cm	east, center
7	overall	117 cm	east	138 cm	
		112 cm	west and center		
8	overall	138 cm		153 cm	
9	overall	153 cm		165 cm	west
				168 cm	east
10	overall	165 cm	west	185 cm	
		168 cm	east		
11	overall	185 cm		210 cm	
12	overall	210 cm		230 cm	
13	overall	230 cm		250 cm	
14	overall	250 cm		272 cm	
15	overall	272 cm		290–295 cm	
16	divided in half east to west	290 cm		300 cm	
		295 cm		300 cm	
17	overall excepting burials	300 cm		305–310 cm	
18	overall	305–310 cm		320 cm	
19	overall	320 cm		340 cm	
20	overall	340 cm		350 cm	
21	only at center of excavation	350 cm		370–375 cm	

N.B. All levels are approximate within a few centimeters deviation.

Table 5. Location and approximate depths of the features of Excavation 2

Level	Feature	Location	Depth
13 and 14	Charcoal and clay lenses	Southeast corner of the excavation	about 250 cm
16	West-wall burial	Center of west sidewall, partically embedded	from 290 cm to 300 cm
16	Center burial	Center southwest of excavation	from 280 cm to about 310 cm
16	North-wall burial	East of center of north sidewall	285–290 cm to about 305 cm
18 and 19	Child burial	Along east sidewall 110 cm to 140 cm north of south sidewall	310 cm to 340 cm

Table 6. Areal extent and approximate depths of the levels of Excavation 3

LEVEL	EXTENT	FROM	LOCATION	TO	LOCATION
1	overall	surface		20 cm	
2	overall	20 cm		30 cm	
3	overall	30 cm		40 cm	
4	overall	40 cm		52 cm	east
				54 cm	west
5	overall	52 cm	east		
	except for	54 cm	west	65–70 cm	
	southeast corner				
	at hearth feature				
6	overall	65–70 cm		90 cm	
	except for southeast corner				
7	overall	90 cm		102 cm	east
				103 cm	center
				101 cm	west
8	overall	102 cm	east	120 cm	east
		103 cm	center	116 cm	center
		101 cm	west	114 cm	west
9	overall	120 cm	east	125 cm	west
		116 cm	center	130 cm	elsewhere
		114 cm	west		

TABLE 6 • CONT'D

LEVEL	EXTENT	FROM	LOCATION	TO	LOCATION
10	overall	125 cm	west	145 cm	northeast
		130 cm	elsewhere	145 cm	southeast
				143 cm	center
				140 cm	south
				137 cm	southwest
				133 cm	northwest
11A	center and southeast	140 cm	south	150 cm	center
		143 cm	center	157 cm	east
		145 cm	east		
12A	center, southeast and southwest	140 cm	west	170 cm	east
		150 cm	center	140 cm	west
		157 cm	east	150 cm	center
11B	west and north	133 cm	northwest	160 cm	west
		137 cm	southwest	160 cm	center
12B	northwest third	140 cm	west	170 cm	east
		150 cm	center		
		157 cm	east		

TABLE 6 • CONT'D

LEVEL	EXTENT	FROM	LOCATION	TO	LOCATION
13	overall	160 cm	west	175 cm	southwest
		170 cm	east	170 cm	northwest
				185 cm	northeast
				181 cm	southeast
				180 cm	north center
				176 cm	south center
14	overall	175 cm	west	198 cm	northwest
		176 cm	center	200 cm	center
		181 cm	east	200 cm	east
15	overall	195 cm	southwest	195 cm	southwest
		198 cm	northwest	212 cm	southwest
		200 cm	east	209 cm	northwest
				215 cm	east
				215 cm	center
16	semicircle along center of north side	215 cm	north center	220 cm	north center

TABLE 6 • CONT'D

LEVEL	EXTENT	FROM	LOCATION	TO	LOCATION
17	overall except	211 cm	west		
	for skeletons	212 cm	northwest	225 cm	northwest
		220 cm	center	230 cm	center and east
		220 cm	east		

Levels 18, 19, and 20 include only Skeletons 2, 3, and 4–5; see Table 7.

21	overall	225 cm	west		
		230 cm	elsewhere	250 cm	elsewhere
				253 cm	northwest
22	overall	250 cm	elsewhere		
		253 cm	northwest	262 cm	
23	overall	262 cm		275 cm	
24	overall	275 cm		285 cm	
	except for Skeleton 1				

TABLE 6 • CONT'D

LEVEL	EXTENT	FROM	LOCATION	TO	LOCATION
25	overall except for burial pits	285 cm		300 cm	
26	overall except for burial pits	300 cm		315–320 cm	

N.B. All levels are approximate within a few centimeters deviation.

Table 7. Location and approximate depths of the features of Excavation 3

Level	Feature	From	To	Orientation
5	Hearth	54 cm	70 cm	—
16–17	Skeleton 1	212 cm	215 cm	southeast corner
18	Skeleton 2	225 cm	250 cm	center west and northeast
18–19	Skeleton 3	240 cm	252 cm	center and north
18–22	Skeleton 4–5	235 cm	255 cm	
24–25	Skeleton 1	285 cm	295 cm	
25–26	Skeletons 2 and 3	295 cm	300 cm	

Table 8. Radiocarbon dates from the Middle Orinoco (1)

Sample No.	Material	Excavation Level	δ¹³C	Date B.P	Date A.D./B.C. (2)
La Gruta site		**La Gruta Phase**			
Rouse					
I-8937	charcoal fragments	1A2 75–100 cm	—	935 ± 80	A.D. 1015*
QC-444A	charcoal fragments	3A2 75–100 cm	—	380 ± 100	A.D. 1570**
I-8548	charcoal fragments	3A3 50–100 cm	—	4065 ± 85	2115 B.C.
I-8546	charcoal fragments	3A2 50–75 cm	—	3710 ± 85	1760 B.C.
Roosevelt					
OxA-2532	charcoal fragment	5 Level 15 ca. 170–205 cm	27.4‰	4790 ± 90	2840 B.C.
I-8970	charcoal fragments	5 Level 13 ca. 165–190 cm	—	4090 ± 105	2140 B.C.
QC-444B	charcoal fragments1	5 Level 13 ca. 165–190 cm	—	1230 ± 130	A.D. 720*
OxA-2530	Cordia seed	5 Level 13 ca. 165–190 cm	26.1‰	290 ± 80	A.D. 1660**

TABLE 8 • CONT'D

Sample No.	Material	Excavation Level	δ¹³C	Date B.P	Date A.D./B.C. (2)
I-9232	charcoal fragments	5 Level 16 ca. 185–205 cm	—	3665 ± 85	*1585 B.C.*
OxA-2531	Sterculia seed	5 Level 16 ca. 185–205 cm	27.2‰	230 ± 80	A.D. 1720**
Y-?	charcoal fragments	5 Level 8 ca. 95–107 cm	—	1150 ± ?	A.D. 800*
I-8969	charcoal fragments	3 Level 7 ca. 125–140 cm	—	1765 ± 80	A.D. 185*
I-8968	charcoal fragments	3 Level 6 ca. 105–125 cm	—	1645 ± 80	A.D. 305*
Vargas and Sanoja					
I-10742	material unknown	3–7 120–140 cm	—	3320 ± 100	*1370 B.C.*
I-10747	material unknown	3–7 120–140 cm	—	1230 ± 130	A.D. 720*
I-10740	material unknown	4–9 80–90 cm	—	8210 ± 190	6260 B.C.*

TABLE 8 • CONT'D

SAMPLE NO.	MATERIAL	EXCAVATION LEVEL	δ¹³C	DATE B.P	DATE A.D./B.C. (2)
I-9519	material unknown	1–6? 60–80 cm	—	2605 ± 85	655 B.C.*
I-9520	material unknown	1–8 60–80 cm	—	725 ± 150	A.D. 1224*
RONQUIN SITE					
		Ronquin Phase			
Rouse					
I-8542	charcoal fragments	1F0 175–200 cm	—	1240 ± 105	A.D. 710*
I-8541	charcoal fragments	1G3 150–175 cm	—	less than 200 years B.P.	A.D. 1750**
I-8547	charcoal fragments	1F0 125–150 cm	—	1220 ± 80	A.D. 730*
Roosevent					
QC-328	charcoal fragments	9 Level 10 ca. 147–160 cm	—	(sample too small)	—
QC-444E	charcoal fragments	9 Level 10 ca. 147–160 cm	—	1900 ± 220	50 B.C.*
QC-327	charcoal fragments	9 Level 9 ca. 137–147 cm	—	1295 ± 90 (sample too small)	(A.D. 655)

TABLE 8 • CONT'D

SAMPLE NO.	MATERIAL	EXCAVATION LEVEL	$\delta^{13}C$	DATE B.P.	DATE A.D./B.C. (2)
		Ronquin Sombra Phase			
Rouse					
I-8545	charcoal fragments	1A1 175–200 cm	—	1560 ± 80	A.D. 390*
I-8544	charcoal fragments	1A1 150–175 cm	—	1515 ± 80	A.D. 435*
QC-444D	charcoal fragments	1A1 ——	—	1360 ± 140	A.D. 590*
Roosevelt					
I-9233	charcoal fragments	8 Level 9 ca. 125–135 cm	—	1720 ± 80	A.D. 230*
Qc-311B	charcoal fragments	8 Level 8 ca. 110–125 cm	—	1450 ± 75	A.D. 500*
Qc-311A	charcoal fragments	8 Level 7 ca. 95–110 cm	—	1170 ± 95	A.D. 780*
Vargas and Sanoja					
SI-1371	material unknown	2–6 100–120 cm	—	1615 ± 50	A.D. 355*

TABLE 8 • CONT'D

Sample No.	Material	Excavation Level	$\delta^{13}C$	Date B.P	Date A.D./B.C. (2)
Rouse		**Camoruco Phase**			
I-8543	charcoal fragments	1A2 50–66 cm	—	750 ± 80	A.D. 1200
Cruxent					
I-8540	charcoal fragments	A 50–65 cm	—	less than 180 years B.P.	A.D. 1770**
SI-1369	material unknown	1–3 40–60 cm	—	850 ± 130	A.D. 1100
SI-1368	material unknown	1–2 20–40 cm	—	545 ± 60	A.D. 1400
SI-1370	material unknown	2–4 60–80 cm	—	490 ± 45	A.D. 1460
Los Merecurotes Site		**Ronquin Sombra Phase**			
Roosevelt					
I-8971	charcoal fragments	1 Level 5 85–110 cm	—	2970 ± 85	1020 B.C.

TABLE 8 • CONT'D

SAMPLE NO.	MATERIAL	EXCAVATION LEVEL	$\delta^{13}C$	DATE B.P	DATE A.D./B.C. (2)
PARMANA 1 SITE		**Early Corozal 1 Phase**			
Roosevelt					
OxA-2534	charcoal fragments	1 Level 9 ca. 190–210 cm	27.1‰	3000 ± 85	*1050 B.C.*
OxA-2535	charcoal fragments	1 Level 9 ca. 190–210 cm	27.2‰	2990 ± 85	*1040 B.C.*
QC-217B	charcoal fragments	1 Level 7 ca. 125–150 cm	—	2805 ± 130	*855 B.C.*
QC-271A	charcoal fragments	1 Level 7 ca. 125–150 cm	—	2650 ± 80	*700 B.C.*
COROZAL SITE		**Late Corozal 1 Phase**			
Roosevelt					
OxA-2503	palm seed	2 Level 9 ca. 320–340 cm	24.5‰	340 ± 70	A.D. 1610**
OxA-2498	2 maize kernel fragments	2 Level 18 ca. 310–320 cm	10.1‰	685 ± 65	A.D. 1265*

TABLE 8 • CONT'D

Sample No.	Material	Excavation Level	$\delta^{13}C$	Date B.P	Date A.D./B.C. (2)
OxA-2529	charcoal fragments	2 Level 18 ca. 310–320 cm	26.6‰	1380 ± 80	A.D. 570
OxA-2528	charcoal fragments	2 Level 17 ca. 300–310 cm	25.6‰	1450 ± 80	A.D. 500
OxA-2527	charcoal fragments	2 Level 16W ca. 290–300 cm	27.7‰	1370 ± 80	A.D. 580
OxA-2494	carbon in sherd 29–156	2 Level 15 ca. 272–295 cm	16.5‰	1320 ± 80	A.D. 630
OxA-2494	carbon on sherd 29–156	2 Level 15 ca. 272–295 cm	12.8‰	1250 ± 70	A.D. 700
I-9231	charcoal fragments	2 Level 15 ca. 272–295 cm	—	955 ± 80	A.D. 995
		Corozal 2 Phase			
QC-323	charcoal fragments	2 Level 14 ca. 250–272 cm	—	1740 ± 100	A.D. 210*

TABLE 8 • CONT'D

Sample No.	Material	Excavation Level	$\delta^{13}C$	Date B.P	Date A.D./B.C. (2)
OxA-5202	small palm-seed fragments	2 Level 14 ca. 250–272 cm	24.4‰	1040 ± 70	A.D. 910
OxA-2501	Malpighiaceae berry	2 Level 13 ca. 230–250 cm	26.3‰	152.3 ± 1.6%	modern**
Corozal 3 Phase					
QC-322	charcoal fragments	2 Level 12 ca. 210–230 cm	—	820 ± 85	A.D. 1130
OxA-2497	small maize-kernel fragments	2 Level 12 ca. 210–230 cm	10.2‰	610 ± 70	A.D. 1340*
Camoruco 1 Phase					
QC-326	charcoal fragments	3 Level 5 ca. 198–215 cm	—	1200 ± 85	A.D. 750
OxA-2500	maize-kernel fragment	3 Level 14 ca. 175–200 cm	10.6‰	865 ± 70	A.D. 1085
OxA-2492	carbon in sherd	2 Level 9 ca. 153–168 cm	19.4‰	915 ± 70	A.D. 1035
OxA-2491	carbon on sherd	2 Level 9 ca. 153–168 cm	15.4‰	695 ± 70	A.D. 1255

TABLE 8 • CONT'D

SAMPLE NO.	MATERIAL	EXCAVATION LEVEL	$\delta^{13}C$	DATE B.P	DATE A.D./B.C. (2)
QC-321	charcoal fragments	2 Level 9 ca. 153–168 cm	—	410 ± 85	A.D. 1540**
QC-325	charcoal fragments	3 Level 12A ca. 150–170 cm	—	830 ± 85	*A.D. 1120*
Camoruco 2 Phase					
QC-324A	charcoal fragments	3 Level 11A ca. 140–157 cm	—	460 ± 80	*A.D. 1490*
OxA-2496	Maize-kernel fragment	2 Level 8 ca. 138–153 cm	10.4‰	820 ± 70	*A.D. 1130*
QC-320	charcoal fragment	2 Level 8 ca. 138–153 cm	—	260 ± 80	A.D. 1690**
QC-310A	charcoal fragments	3 Level 10 ca. 125–145 cm	—	510 ± 70	*A.D. 1440*
QC-310B	charcoal fragments	3 Level 10 ca. 125–145 cm	—	410 ± 80	*A.D. 1540*

TABLE 8 • CONT'D

SAMPLE NO.	MATERIAL	EXCAVATION LEVEL	$\delta^{13}C$	DATE B.P	DATE A.D./B.C. (2)
OxA-2490	carbon in sherd 48-119	2 Level 7 ca. 117–138 cm	11.8‰	1020 ± 70	A.D. 930
QC-319	charcoal fragments	2 Level 7 ca. 117–138 cm	—	715 ± 75	A.D. 1235
OxA-2489	carbon on sherd 48-119	2 Level 7 ca. 117–138 cm	12.9‰	550 ± 70	A.D. 1400
		Camoruco 3 Phase			
OxA-2495	maize-kernel fragment	2 Level 4 ca. 60–80 cm	9.4‰	610 ± 65	A.D. 1530
QC-309	charcoal fragments	3 Level 4 ca. 40–54 cm	—	860 ± 70	A.D. 1090
OxA-2499	maize kernel	3 Level 4 ca. 40–54 cm	9.0‰	420 ± 65	A.D. 1530
OxA-2488	carbon in sherd 32-355	2 Level 2 ca. 25–45 cm	23.2‰	475 ± 70	A.D. 1475

TABLE 8 • CONT'D

SAMPLE NO.	MATERIAL	EXCAVATION LEVEL	δ¹³C	DATE B.P	DATE A.D./B.C. (2)
OxA-2487	carbon on sherd 32-355	2 Level 2 ca. 25–45 cm	21.3‰	390 ± 70	*A.D. 1560*
LOS MANGOS SITE		**Corozal Phase**			
QC-313A	charcoal fragments	1 Level 18	——	1170 ± 90	*A.D. 780*
QC-313C	charcoal fragments	1 Level 18	——	760 ± 100	A.D. 1190*
QC-312A	charcoal fragments	1 Level 17	——	340 ± 80	A.D. 1610**
QC-312B	charcoal fragments (very small sample, diluted)	1 Level 17	——	900 ± 90	(A.D. 1050)
LOS ALGARROBOTES SITE		**Camoruco 3 Phase**			
OxA-2533	palm-wood and -kernel fragment	1 Level 10 133–145 cm	25.4‰	510 ± 80	*A.D. 1440*

TABLE 8 • CONT'D

SAMPLE NO.	MATERIAL	EXCAVATION LEVEL	$\delta^{13}C$	DATE B.P	DATE A.D./B.C. (2)
CAMORUCO SITE					
		Camoruco 3 Phase			
Zucchi					
I-8626	charcoal fragments	A2 250–275 cm	—	670 ± 80	A.D. 1280
I-8625	charcoal framents	A2 225–250 cm	—	625 ± 80	A.D. 1325
I-8624	charcoal fragments	A2 150–175 cm	—	550 ± 80	A.D. 1400
I-8624	charcoal fragments	A1 150–175 cm	—	550 ± 80	A.D. 1400
I-8623	charcoal fragments	A1 100–125 cm	—	470 ± 80	A.D. 1480
I-8622	charcoal fragments	A1 50–75 cm	—	455 ± 85	A.D. 1495
AGUERITO SITE					
		Phases Related to La Gruta Tradition			
Zucchi					
I-10009	charcoal fragments	5 100–125 cm	—	5680 ± 165	3730 B.C.
Gx-5181	charcoal fragments	2 100–125 cm	—	5425 ± 195	3475 B.C.

TABLE 8 • CONT'D

Sample No.	Material	Excavation Level	δ¹³C	Date b.p	Date a.d./b.c. (2)
		Phases Related to Corozal Tradition			
Gx-5180	charcoal fragments	4 100–125 cm	—	3980 ± 150	2030 b.c.
G-6269	charcoal fragments	3 100–125 cm	—	2890 ± 145	940 b.c.
I-9450	charcoal fragments	1 100–125 cm	—	2760 ± 90	810 b.c.
I-10008	charcoal fragments	1 75–100 cm	—	1490 ± 105	a.d. 460
Gx-6264	charcoal fragments	1 75–100 cm	—	1550 ± 170	a.d. 400
Gx-5181	charcoal fragments	2 75–100 cm	—	830 ± 125	a.d. 1120
Gx-6267	charcoal fragments	2 75–100 cm	—	665 ± 120	a.d. 1285*
Gx-5179	charcoal fragments	3 75–100 cm	—	1235 ± 135	a.d. 715
		Phases Related to Camoruco Tradition			
I-10007	charcoal fragments	5 50–70 cm	—	995 ± 115	a.d. 955
I-10006	charcoal fragments	5 25–50 cm	—	885 ± 110	a.d. 1065

TABLE 8 • CONT'D

Sample No.	Material	Excavation Level	$\delta^{13}C$	Date B.P	Date A.D./B.C. (2)
Gx-6266	charcoal fragments	2 50–75 cm	—	840 ± 120	*A.D. 1110*
Gx-6265	charcoal fragments	2 25–50 cm	—	485 ± 120	*A.D. 1465*
Gx-6263	charcoal fragments	2 25–50 cm	—	less than 200 years old**	
Gx-6262	charcoal fragments	1 0–25 cm	—	245 ± 130	A.D. 1705**
Gx-6268	charcoal fragments	3 50–75 cm	—	less than 200 years old**	

TUCURAGUA SITE

Camoruco 3 Phase

Zucchi

| I-8627 | charcoal fragments | A4 50–75 cm | — | 565 ± 80 | *A.D. 1385* |

* Dates substantially out of stratigraphic order, indicating presence of anachronous carbon.
** Dates of historic or modern age from prehistoric strata, indicating intrusion of recent charcoal.
(1) All Oxford dates are by accelerator mss spectrometry. All others are conventional radiocarbon dates. The Libby half-life of 5568 years has been used to calculate all the dates in the table.
(2) Italicized dates are those whose 2-sigma ranges fall in roughly stratigraphic order.

Table 9. Sherd totals per level, Excavation 2

Level	Phase	Number of Examples (X = 100)	Total: 15,664
1	Recent		81
2	Camoruco 3	XXXXXXXXXX X	1147
3		XXXXXXXXX	936
4		XXXXXXXX	817
5–6		XXXXXXXXXX XXXXX	1477
7	Camoruco 2	XXXXXXXXXX XXXXXX	1566
8		XXXXXXXXXX X	1070
9	Camoruco 1	XXXXXX	607
10		XXXXXXXXXX XXXXXX	1581
11		XXXXXXX	709
12	Corozal 3	XXXXXXXXXX XXX	1255
13	Corozal 2	XXXXXXXXXX X	1149
14		XXXXXXXXXX XXXXXXX	1705
15	Corozal 1	XXXXXXXX	767
16–16W		XXX	333
16E		XX	160
17		X	115
18		X	128
19		—	43
20		—	15
16	West Burial	—	0
16	Central Burial	—	1
16	North Burial	—	2
18	Child Burial	—	0

Table 10. Sherd totals per level, Excavation 3

Level	Phase	Number of Examples (X = 100)	Total: 14,121
—— 1 — Recent ——			18
2	Camoruco 3	XXXXX	456
3		XXXX	361
4		XXXXXXXX	788
5		XXXXXXX	748
6		XXXXX	539
—— 7 ——————		XXXXXX	594
8	Camoruco 2	XXXXX	497
9		XXXX	411
10		XXXXXXXX	897
11–12A		XXXX	424
11–12B ————		XXXX	356
13	Camoruco 1	XXXXXXXXXX XXX	1255
14		XXXXXXXXXX XXXX	1437
—— 15 ——————		XXXXXXXXXX XX	1155
16	Corozal 3	XX	184
17		XXXXXX	556
—— 21 ——————		XXX	341
22	Corozal 2	XXXXXXX	663
—— 23		XXXXXXXXXX	1039
24	Corozal 1	XXXXXX	637
25		XXXX	421
26			46
16–17	Skeleton 1	X	56
18	Skeleton 2		44
18–19	Skeleton 3	X	57
18–22	Skeleton 4		39
25	Feature		29
25	Skeleton 2	X	61
25	Skeleton 3		12

Table 11. Frequency of mode #135, Corozal sherdware, Excavation 2

Level	Phase	Number of Examples (X = 1)	Total: 181
1	Recent	—	0
2	Camoruco 3	—	0
3		—	0
4		—	0
5–6		—	0
7	Camoruco 2	X	1
8		—	0
9	Camoruco 1	—	0
10		—	0
11		X	1
12	Corozal 3	X	1
13	Corozal 2	—	0
14		XXXXXXXXX	9
15	Corozal 1	XXXXXXXXXX XXXXXXXXXX XXXXX	25
16–16W		XXXXXXXXXX XXXX	14
16E		XXXXXXXXXX XXXXXXXXXX XXXXXXX X	31
17		XXXXXXXXXX XXXXXXXXXX XXXXX	25
18		XXXXXXXXXX XXXXXXXXXX XXXXXXXXXX XXXXXXXXXX XXXXXXXXXX XXX	53
19		XXXXXXXXXX XXX	13
20		XXXXXX	6

TABLE 11 • CONT'D

LEVEL	PHASE	NUMBER OF EXAMPLES (X = 1)	TOTAL: 181
16	West burial	—	0
16	Central burial	X	1
16	North burial	X	1
18	Child burial	—	0

STATISTICAL SIGNIFICANCE OF FREQUENCY DISTRIBUTION BY PHASE

$$\text{Excavation } X^2 = 1402.77$$
$$\text{Corozal 3/Corozal 2 } X^2 = 1.93$$
$$\text{Corozal 2/Corozal 1 } X^2 = 281.51$$

Table 12. Percentages of mode #135, Corozal sherdware, Excavation 2

LEVEL	PHASE	PERCENT OF TOTAL SHERDS IN LEVEL (X = .1%)
1	Recent	(00.00)
2	Camoruco 3	00.00 —
3		00.00 —
4		00.00 —
5-6		00.00 —
7	Camoruco 2	00.06 X
8		00.00 —
9	Camoruco 1	00.00 —
10		00.00 —
11		00.14 X
12	Corozal 3	00.08 X
13	Corozal 2	00.00 —
14		00.53 XXXXX
15	Corozal 1	03.26 XXXXXXXXXX XXXXXXXXXX XXXXXXXXXX XXX
16–16W		04.20 XXXXXXXXXX XXXXXXXXXX XXXXXXXXXX XXXXXXXXXX XX
16E		19.38 XXXXXXXXXX XXXXXXXXXX XXXXXXXXXX XXXXXXXXXX XXXXXXXXXX X+
17		21.74 XXXXXXXXXX XXXXXXXXXX XXXXXXXXXX XXXXXXXXXX XXXXXXXXXX X+
18		41.41 XXXXXXXXXX XXXXXXXXXX XXXXXXXXXX XXXXXXXXXX XXXXXXXXXX X+
19		(30.23)
20		(40.00)

TABLE 12 • CONT'D

LEVEL	PHASE	PERCENT OF TOTAL SHERDS IN LEVEL ($X = .1\%$)
16	West burial	(00.00)
16	Central burial	(100.00)
16	North burial	(50.00)
18	Child burial	(00.00)

STATISTICAL SIGNIFICANCE OF PERCENT DIFFERENCES BY LEVEL

Levels 12/14: 2.08   Levels 13/14: 2.47   Levels 13/15: 6.16
Levels 14/15: 5.39   Levels 14/16–16W: 5.81   Levels 15/16–16W: 0.78
Levels 15/16E: 7.78   Levels 16–16W/16E: 5.48   Levels 16–16W/17: 5.75
Levels 16E/17: 0.48   Levels 17/18: 3.28

Table 13. Frequency of mode #135, Corozal sherdware, Excavation 3

Level	Phase	Number of Examples (X = 1)	Total: 45
1	Recent	—	0
2	Camoruco 3	—	0
3		—	0
4		—	0
5		—	0
6		—	0
7		—	0
8	Camoruco 2	X	1
9		—	0
10		X	1
11–12A		—	0
11–12B		—	0
13	Camoruco 1	—	0
14		—	0
15		XX	2
16	Corozal 3	—	0
17		X	1
21		—	0
22	Corozal 2	—	0
23		XX	2
24	Corozal 1	XXX	3
25		XXXXXXXXXX XXXXXX	16
26		XXXXXXXXXX XXX	13
16–17	Skeleton 1	X	1
18	Skeleton 2	—	0
18–19	Skeleton 3	—	0
18–22	Skeleton 4	—	0
25	Feature	—	0
25	Skeleton 2	XXXXX	5
25	Skeleton 3	—	0

Statistical significance of frequency distribution by phase

Excavation $X^2 = 305.52$
Corozal 2/Corozal 1 $X^2 = 45.48$

Table 14. Percentages of mode #135, Corozal sherdware, Excavation 3

LEVEL	PHASE	PERCENT OF TOTAL SHERDS IN LEVEL (X = .1%)
1	Recent	(00.00)
2	Camoruco 3	00.00 —
3		00.00 —
4		00.00 —
5		00.00 —
6		00.00 —
7		00.00 —
8	Camoruco 2	00.20 XX
9		00.00 —
10		00.11 X
11–12A		00.00 —
11–12B		00.00 —
13	Camoruco 1	00.00 —
14		00.00 —
15		00.17 XX
16	Corozal 3	00.00 —
17		00.18 XX
21		00.00 —
22	Corozal 2	00.00 —
23		00.19 XX
24	Corozal 1	00.47 XXXXX
25		03.80 XXXXXXXXXX XXXXXXXXXX XXXXXXXXXX XXXXXXXX
26		(28.26)

TABLE 14 • CONT'D

LEVEL	PHASE	PERCENT OF TOTAL SHERDS IN LEVEL ($X = .1\%$)
16–17	Skeleton 1	(01.79)
18	Skeleton 2	(00.00)
18–19	Skeleton 3	(00.00)
18–22	Skeleton 4	(00.00)
25	Feature	(00.00)
25	Skeleton 2	(08.20)
25	Skeleton 3	(00.00)

STATISTICAL SIGNIFICANCE OF PERCENT DIFFERENCES BY LEVEL

Levels 13/17: 1.50	Levels 15/17: 0.03
Levels 16/17: 0.58	Levels 17/21: 0.78
Levels 17/22: 1.09	Levels 17/23: 0.06
Levels 21/23: 0.81	Levels 22/23: 1.13
Levels 22/24: 1.77	Levels 23/24: 1.01
Levels 24/25: 3.99	

Table 15. Frequency of mode #140, Corozal gritware, Excavation 2

Level	Phase	Number of Examples (X = 1)	Total: 175
1	Recent	X	1
2	Camoruco 3	X	1
3		X	1
4		—	0
5-6		XXX	3
7	Camoruco 2	XXXX	4
8		XX	2
9	Camoruco 1	X	1
10		XXX	3
11		—	0
12	Corozal 3	XXXX	4
13	Corozal 2	XXXXX	5
14		XXXXXXXXXXXX XXX	13
15	Corozal 1	XXXXXXXXXXXX XXXXXXXXXX XXXXXXXX	30
16-16W		XXXXXXXXXX XXXXXXXXXX XXXXXXXXXX XXXXXX	36
16E		XXXXXXXXX XXXXXXXXXX XXXXXXX	26
17		XXXXXXXXX XXXXXXXX	17
18		XXXXXXXXXX XXXXXXXXXX XX	22
19		X	1
20		XXXXXX	5

TABLE 15 • CONT'D

LEVEL	PHASE	NUMBER OF EXAMPLES (X = 1)	TOTAL: 175
16	West burial	—	0
16	Central burial	—	0
16	North burial	—	0
18	Child burial	—	0

STATISTICAL SIGNIFICANCE OF FREQUENCY DISTRIBUTION BY PHASE

$$\begin{aligned}
\text{Excavation } X^2 &= 924.87 \\
\text{Camoruco 3/Camoruco 2 } X^2 &= 0.21 \\
\text{Camoruco 2/Camoruco 1 } X^2 &= 0.02 \\
\text{Corozal 3/Corozal 2 } X^2 &= 2.33 \\
\text{Corozal 2/Corozal 1 } X^2 &= 195.26
\end{aligned}$$

Table 16. Percentages of mode #140, Corozal gritware, Excavation 2

Level	Phase	Percent of Total Sherds in Level (X = .1%)	
1	— Recent —	(01.23)	
2	Camoruco 3	00.09	X
3		00.11	X
4		00.00	—
5–6		00.20	XX
7	Camoruco 2	00.26	XXX
8		00.19	XX
9	Camoruco 1	00.16	XX
10		00.19	XX
11		00.00	—
12	Corozal 3	00.32	XXX
13	Corozal 2	00.44	XXXX
14		00.76	XXXXXXXX
15	Corozal 1	03.91	XXXXXXXXXXXXXXXXXXXXXXXXXXXXXXXXXXXXXXXX
16–16W		10.81	XXXXXXXXXXXXXXXXXXXXXXXXXXXXXXXXXXXXXXXXXXXXXXXXXXXXXXXXXXXXXXXXXXXXXXXXXXXXXXXXXXXXXXXXXXXXXXXXXXXX+
16E		16.25	XXXXXXXXXXXXXXXXXXXXXXXXXXXXXXXXXXXXXXXXXXXXXXXXXXXXXXXXXXXXXXXXXXXXXXXXXXXXXXXXXXXXXXXXXXXXXXXXXXXX+
17		14.78	XXXXXXXXXXXXXXXXXXXXXXXXXXXXXXXXXXXXXXXXXXXXXXXXXXXXXXXXXXXXXXXXXXXXXXXXXXXXXXXXXXXXXXXXXXXXXXXXXXXX+
18		17.19	XXXXXXXXXXXXXXXXXXXXXXXXXXXXXXXXXXXXXXXXXXXXXXXXXXXXXXXXXXXXXXXXXXXXXXXXXXXXXXXXXXXXXXXXXXXXXXXXXXXX+
19		(02.33)	
20		(33.33)	

TABLE 16 • CONT'D

LEVEL	PHASE	PERCENT OF TOTAL SHERDS IN LEVEL ($X = .1\%$)
16	West burial	(00.00)
16	Central burial	(00.00)
16	North burial	(00.00)
18	Child burial	(00.00)

STATISTICAL SIGNIFICANCE OF PERCENT DIFFERENCES BY LEVEL

Levels 3/5–6: 0.57   Levels 5–6/7: 0.30   Levels 5–6/9: 0.18
Levels 10/12: 0.69   Levels 12/13: 0.47   Levels 13/14: 1.08
Levels 14/15: 5.54   Levels 15/16–16W: 4.43   Levels 16–16W/17: 1.14
Levels 16E/18: 0.21   Levels 17/18: 0.51

Table 17. Frequency of mode #140, Corozal gritware, Excavation 3

Level	Phase	Number of Examples (X = 1)	Total: 91
1	Recent	—	0
2	Camoruco 3	xxx	3
3		—	0
4		—	0
5		—	0
6		xx	2
7		—	0
8	Camoruco 2	xx	2
9		—	0
10		x	1
11–12A		x	1
11–12B		—	0
13	Camoruco 1	xxx	3
14		xxxx	4
15		xx	2
16	Corozal 3	—	0
17		xxx	3
21	Corozal 2	xx	2
22		xx	2
23		xxxxxxxxx xxxxxxx	17
24	Corozal 1	xxxxxxxxxx x	11
25		xxxxxxxxx xxxxxxxxx	18
26		xx	2

TABLE 17 • CONT'D

LEVEL	PHASE	NUMBER OF EXAMPLES (X = 1)	TOTAL: 91
16–17	Skeleton 1	—	0
18	Skeleton 2	XX	2
18–19	Skeleton 3	—	0
18–22	Skeleton 4	XXX	3
25	Feature	X	1
25	Skeleton 2	XXXXXXX	7
25	Skeleton 3	XXXXXX	5

STATISTICAL SIGNIFICANCE OF FREQUENCY DISTRIBUTION BY PHASE

$$\begin{aligned}
\text{Excavation } X^2 &= 142.33 \\
\text{Camoruco 2/Camoruco 1 } X^2 &= 0.20 \\
\text{Camoruco 1/Corozal 3 } X^2 &= 0.12 \\
\text{Corozal 3/Corozal 2 } X^2 &= 5.07 \\
\text{Corozal 2/Corozal 1 } X^2 &= 11.47
\end{aligned}$$

Table 18. Percentages of mode #140, Corozal gritware, Excavation 3

Level	Phase	Percent of Total Sherds in Level (X = .1%)	
1	Recent	(00.00)	
2	Camoruco 3	00.66	XXXXXXX
3		00.00	—
4		00.00	—
5		00.00	—
6		00.37	XXXX
7		00.00	—
8	Camoruco 2	00.40	XXXX
9		00.00	—
10		00.11	X
11–12A		00.24	XX
11–12B		00.00	—
13	Camoruco 1	00.24	XX
14		00.28	XXX
15		00.17	XX
16	Corozal 3	00.00	—
17		00.54	XXXXX
21		00.59	XXXXXX
22	Corozal 2	00.30	XXX
23		01.64	XXXXXXXXXX XXXXXX
24	Corozal 1	01.73	XXXXXXXXXX XXXXXXX
25		04.28	XXXXXXXXXX XXXXXXXXXX XXXXXXXXXX XXXXXXXXXX XXX
26		(04.35)	

TABLE 18 • CONT'D

LEVEL	PHASE	PERCENT OF TOTAL SHERDS IN LEVEL ($X = .1\%$)
16–17	Skeleton 1	(00.00)
18	Skeleton 2	(04.55)
18–19	Skeleton 3	(00.00)
18–22	Skeleton 4	(07.69)
25	Feature	(03.45)
25	Skeleton 2	(11.48)
25	Skeleton 3	(41.67)

STATISTICAL SIGNIFICANCE OF PERCENT DIFFERENCES BY LEVEL

Levels 2/3: 1.54
Levels 10/11–12A: 0.54
Levels 11–12A/13: 0.01
Levels 14/17: 0.88
Levels 17/22: 0.65
Levels 23/24: 0.14

Levels 5/6: 1.67
Levels 11–12A/11–12B: 0.92
Levels 14/15: 0.55
Levels 17/21: 0.09
Levels 22/23: 2.56
Levels 24/25: 2.49

Table 19. Frequency of mode #204, Corozal Saladoid-Barrancoid decoration, Excavation 2

LEVEL	PHASE	NUMBER OF EXAMPLES (X = 1)	TOTAL: 129
1	Recent	—	0
2	Camoruco 3	—	0
3		—	0
4		—	0
5–6			0
7	Camoruco 2	X	1
8		X	1
9	Camoruco 1	—	0
10		XX	2
11		XXX	3
12	Corozal 3	XXXXXX	6
13	Corozal 2	XXXXXXXXXX XXXX	14
14		XXXXXXXXXX XXXXXXXXXX XXXXXXXXX	29
15	Corozal 1	XXXXXXXXXX XXXXXXXXXX XXXXX	25
16–16W		XXXXXXXXXX XXXXXXX	17
16E		XXXXXXX	7
17		XXXXX	5
18		XXXXXXXXXX XXXX	14
19		XX	2
20		XXX	3

TABLE 19 • CONT'D

LEVEL	PHASE	NUMBER OF EXAMPLES (X = 1)	TOTAL: 129
16	West burial	—	0
16	Central burial	—	0
16	North burial	—	0
18	Child burial	—	0

STATISTICAL SIGNIFICANCE OF FREQUENCY DISTRIBUTION BY PHASE

Excavation X^2 = 371.77
Camoruco 1/Corozal 3 X^2 = 1.92
Corozal 3/Corozal 2 X^2 = 9.72
Corozal 2/Corozal 1 X^2 = 38.40

Table 20. Percentages of mode #204, Corozal Saladoid-Barrancoid decoration, Excavation 2

Level	Phase	Percent of Total Sherds in Level (X = .1%)	
1	Recent	(00.00)	
2	Camoruco 3	00.00	—
3		00.00	—
4		00.00	—
5–6		00.00	—
7	Camoruco 2	00.06	X
8		00.09	X
9	Camoruco 1	00.00	—
10		00.13	X
11		00.42	XXXX
12	Corozal 3	00.48	XXXXX
13	Corozal 2	01.22	XXXXXXXXXXXX XX
14		01.70	XXXXXXXXXXXX XXXXXXX
15	Corozal 1	03.26	XXXXXXXXXX XXXXXXXXXX XXXXXXXXXX XXX
16–16W		05.11	XXXXXXXXXX XXXXXXXXXX XXXXXXXXXX XXXXXXXXXX XXXXXXXXXX X
16E		04.38	XXXXXXXXXX XXXXXXXXXX XXXXXXXXXX XXXXXXXXXX XXXX
17		04.35	XXXXXXXXXX XXXXXXXXXX XXXXXXXXXX XXXXXXXXXX XXXX
18		10.94	XXXXXXXXXX XXXXXXXXXX XXXXXXXXXX XXXXXXXXXX XXXXXXXXXX X+
19		(04.65)	
20		(20.00)	

TABLE 20 • CONT'D

LEVEL	PHASE	PERCENT OF TOTAL SHERDS IN LEVEL ($X = .1\%$)
16	West burial	(00.00)
16	Central burial	(00.00)
16	North burial	(00.00)
18	Child burial	(00.00)

STATISTICAL SIGNIFICANCE OF PERCENT DIFFERENCES BY LEVEL

Levels 7/8: 0.27
Levels 10/11: 1.41
Levels 13/14: 1.04
Levels 16–16W/16E: 0.35

Levels 8/9: 0.75
Levels 11/12: 0.17
Levels 14/15: 2.45
Levels 16E/17: 0.01

Levels 9/10: 0.88
Levels 12/13: 2.00
Levels 15/16–16W: 1.47
Levels 16E/18: 2.13

Table 21. Frequency of mode #204, Corozal Saladoid-Barrancoid decoration, Excavation 3

Level	Phase	Number of Examples (X = 1)	Total: 67
1	Recent	—	0
2	Camoruco 3	—	0
3		—	0
4		—	0
5		—	0
6		—	0
7		—	0
8	Camoruco 2	—	0
9		—	0
10		—	0
11–12A		—	0
11–12B		—	0
13	Camoruco 1	X	1
14		XX	2
15		XXX	3
16	Corozal 3	—	0
17		X	1
21		XX	2
22	Corozal 2	XXXXXXXXX	9
23		XXXXXXXXXX X	11
24	Corozal 1	XXXXXXXXXX XXXXXXX	17
25		XXXXXXXXXX X	11
26		XXX	3
16–17	Skeleton 1	X	1
18	Skeleton 2	—	0
18–19	Skeleton 3	—	0
18–22	Skeleton 4	—	0
25	Feature	XXXX	4
25	Skeleton 2	XX	2
25	Skeleton 3	—	0

Statistical Significance of Frequency Distribution by Phase

Excavation X = 198.74
Camoruco 1/Corozal 3 X = 0.00
Corozal 3/Corozal 2 X = 8.64
Corozal 2/Corozal 1 X^2 = 10.54

Table 22. Percentages of mode #204, Corozal Saladoid-Barrancoid decoration, Excavation 3

LEVEL	PHASE	PERCENT OF TOTAL SHERDS IN LEVEL (X = .1%)	
1	— Recent —	(00.00)	
2	Camoruco 3	00.00	—
3		00.00	—
4		00.00	—
5		00.00	—
6		00.00	—
7		00.00	—
8	Camoruco 2	00.00	—
9		00.00	—
10		00.00	—
11–12A		00.00	—
11–12B		00.00	—
13	Camoruco 1	00.08	X
14		00.14	X
15		00.26	XXX
16	Corozal 3	00.00	—
17		00.18	XX
21		00.59	XXXXXX
22	Corozal 2	01.36	XXXXXXXXXXXX XXXX
23		01.06	XXXXXXXXXX X
24	Corozal 1	02.67	XXXXXXXXXX XXXXXXXXXX XXXXXXX
25		02.61	XXXXXXXXXX XXXXXXXXXX XXXXXX
26		(06.52)	

TABLE 22 • CONT'D

LEVEL	PHASE	PERCENT OF TOTAL SHERDS IN LEVEL ($X = .1\%$)
16–17	Skeleton 1	(01.79)
18	Skeleton 2	(00.00)
18–19	Skeleton 3	(00.00)
18–22	Skeleton 4	(00.00)
25	Feature	(13.79)
25	Skeleton 2	(03.28)
25	Skeleton 3	(00.00)

STATISTICAL SIGNIFICANCE OF PERCENT DIFFERENCES BY LEVEL

Levels 11–12A/13: 0.58   Levels 11–12B/13: 0.53
Levels 13/14: 0.46   Levels 14/15: 0.70
Levels 14/16: 0.51   Levels 14/13: 0.46
Levels 15/17: 0.32   Levels 16/17: 0.58
Levels 16/25: 2.21   Levels 21/22: 1.11
Levels 21/23: 0.78   Levels 22/23: 0.56
Levels 23/24: 2.50   Levels 24/25: 0.06

Table 23. Frequency of mode #5, Saladoid paint, Excavation 2

Level	Phase	Number of Examples (X = 1)	Total: 24
1	Recent	—	0
2	Camoruco 3	—	0
3		—	0
4		—	0
5–6		—	0
7	Camoruco 2	—	0
8		—	0
9	Camoruco 1	—	0
10		X	1
11		—	0
12	Corozal 3	—	0
13	Corozal 2	—	0
14		—	0
15	Corozal 1	XXXXXX	6
16–16W		XXXXX	5
16E		XXXXXXX	7
17		—	0
18		XXXX	4
19		X	1
20		—	0
16	West burial	—	0
16	Central burial	—	0
16	North burial	—	0
18	Child burial	—	0

Statistical significance of frequency distribution by phase

Corozal 2/Corozal 1 $X^2 = 39.48$

Table 24. Percentages of mode #5, Saladoid paint, Excavation 2

Level	Phase	Percent of Total Sherds in Level (X = .1%)	
1	Recent	(00.00)	
2	Camoruco 3	00.00	—
3		00.00	—
4		00.00	—
5–6		00.00	—
7	Camoruco 2	00.00	—
8		00.00	—
9	Camoruco 1	00.00	—
10		00.06	x
11		00.00	—
12	Corozal 3	00.00	—
13	Corozal 2	00.00	—
14		00.00	—
15	Corozal 1	00.78	xxxxxxxx
16–16W		01.50	xxxxxxxxxx xxxxx
16E		04.38	xxxxxxxxxx xxxxxxxxxx xxxxxxxxxx xxxxxxxxxx xxxx
17		00.00	—
18		03.13	xxxxxxxxxx xxxxxxxxxx xxxxxxxxxx x
19		(02.33)	
20		(00.00)	

TABLE 24 • CONT'D

LEVEL	PHASE	PERCENT OF TOTAL SHERDS IN LEVEL ($X = .1\%$)
16	West burial	(00.00)
16	Central burial	(00.00)
16	North burial	(00.00)
18	Child burial	(00.00)

STATISTICAL SIGNIFICANCE OF PERCENT DIFFERENCES BY LEVEL

Levels 9/10: 0.62
Levels 10/11: 0.67
Levels 13/15: 3.00
Levels 13/16–16W: 4.16
Levels 14/15: 3.66
Levels 14/16–16W: 5.07
Levels 14/16E: 8.65
Levels 15/16–16W: 1.10
Levels 15/16E: 3.52
Levels 16–16W/16E: 1.94
Levels 16–16W/17: 1.32
Levels 16E/18: 0.55
Levels 16E/17: 2.27
Levels 17/18: 1.91

Table 25. Frequency of mode #5, Saladoid paint, Excavation 3

Level	Phase	Number of Examples (X = 1)	Total: 9
1	Recent	—	0
2	Camoruco 3	—	0
3		—	0
4		—	0
5		—	0
6		—	0
7		—	0
8	Camoruco 2	—	0
9		—	0
10		—	0
11–12A		—	0
11–12B		—	0
13	Camoruco 1	—	0
14		—	0
15		X	1
16	Corozal 3	—	0
17		—	0
21		—	0
22	Corozal 2	XX	2
23		—	0
24	Corozal 1	XXX	3
25		X	1
26		—	0
16–17	Skeleton 1	—	0
18	Skeleton 2	—	0
18–19	Skeleton 3	—	0
18–22	Skeleton 4	—	0
25	Feature	X	1
25	Skeleton 2	X	1
25	Skeleton 3	—	0

Table 26. Percentages of mode #5, Saladoid paint, Excavation 3

Level	Phase	Percent of Total Sherds in Level (X = .1%)	
1	Recent	(00.00)	
2	Camoruco 3	00.00	—
3		00.00	—
4		00.00	—
5		00.00	—
6		00.00	—
7		00.00	—
8	Camoruco 2	00.00	—
9		00.00	—
10		00.00	—
11–12A		00.00	—
11–12B		00.00	—
13	Camoruco 1	00.00	—
14		00.00	—
15		00.09	X
16	Corozal 3	00.00	—
17		00.00	—
21		00.00	—
22	Corozal 2	00.30	XXX
23		00.00	—
24	Corozal 1	00.47	XXXXX
25		00.24	XX
26		(00.00)	

TABLE 26 • CONT'D

LEVEL	PHASE	PERCENT OF TOTAL SHERDS IN LEVEL ($X = .1\%$)
16–17	Skeleton 1	(00.00)
18	Skeleton 2	(00.00)
18–19	Skeleton 3	(00.00)
18–22	Skeleton 4	(00.00)
25	Feature	(03.45)
25	Skeleton 2	(01.64)
25	Skeleton 3	(00.00)

STATISTICAL SIGNIFICANCE OF PERCENT DIFFERENCES BY LEVEL

Levels 14/15: 1.12 Levels 15/16: 0.40
Levels 15/22: 1.09 Levels 15/24: 1.65
Levels 17/22: 1.30 Levels 21/22: 1.02
Levels 22/23: 1.77 Levels 22/24: 0.49
Levels 22/25: 0.20 Levels 23/24: 2.21
Levels 23/25: 1.57

Table 27. Frequency of mode #134, Corozal curvilinear incision, Excavation 2

LEVEL	PHASE	NUMBER OF EXAMPLES (X = 1)	TOTAL: 75
1	Recent	—	0
2	Camoruco 3	—	0
3		—	0
4		—	0
5–6		—	0
7	Camoruco 2	—	0
8		—	0
9	Camoruco 1	—	0
10		—	0
11		XX	2
12	Corozal 3	XXXXXX	6
13	Corozal 2	XXXXXXXXXX XXXX	14
14		XXXXXXXXXX XXXXXXXXXX XXXXXXXXXX	30
15	Corozal 1	XXXXXXXXXX XXX	13
16–16W		XXXXXXXX	7
16E		—	0
17		XX	2
18		X	1
19		—	0
20		—	0

TABLE 27 • CONT'D

LEVEL	PHASE	NUMBER OF EXAMPLES (X = 1)	TOTAL: 75
16	West burial	—	0
16	Central burial	—	0
16	North burial	—	0
18	Child burial	—	0

STATISTICAL SIGNIFICANCE OF FREQUENCY DISTRIBUTION BY PHASE

Excavation X^2 = 144.54
Corozal 3/Corozal 2 X^2 = 10.20
Corozal 2/Corozal 1 X^2 = 0.00

Table 28. Percentages of mode #134, Corozal curvilinear incision, Excavation 2

LEVEL	PHASE	PERCENT OF TOTAL SHERDS IN LEVEL (X = .1%)
1	Recent	(00.00)
2	Camoruco 3	00.00 —
3		00.00 —
4		00.00 —
5–6		00.00 —
7	Camoruco 2	00.00 —
8		00.00 —
9	Camoruco 1	00.00 —
10		00.00 —
11		00.28 XXX
12	Corozal 3	00.48 XXXXX
13	Corozal 2	01.22 XXXXXXXXXXXX XX
14		01.76 XXXXXXXXXXX XXXXXXXX
15	Corozal 1	01.69 XXXXXXXXXXX XXXXXXX
16–16W		02.10 XXXXXXXXXX XXXXXXXXXX X
16E		00.00 —
17		01.74 XXXXXXXXXXX XXXXXXX
18		00.78 XXXXXXXX
19		(00.00)
20		(00.00)

TABLE 28 • CONT'D

LEVEL	PHASE	PERCENT OF TOTAL SHERDS IN LEVEL ($X = .1\%$)
16	West burial	(00.00)
16	Central burial	(00.00)
16	North burial	(00.00)
18	Child burial	(00.00)

STATISTICAL SIGNIFICANCE OF PERCENT DIFFERENCES BY LEVEL

Levels 10/12: 2.75	Levels 11/12: 0.66	Levels 12/13: 2.00
Levels 13/14: 1.15	Levels 14/15: 0.11	Levels 14/16E: 1.69
Levels 15/16–16W: 0.46	Levels 15/16E: 1.66	Levels 15/17: 0.03
Levels 16–16W/16E: 1.85	Levels 16–16W/17: 0.24	Levels 16–16W/18: 0.97
Levels 16E/18: 1.12	Levels 17/18: 0.68	

Table 29. Frequency of mode #134, Corozal curvilinear incision, Excavation 3

LEVEL	PHASE	NUMBER OF EXAMPLES (X = 1)	TOTAL: 50
—— 1 — Recent ——		—	0
2	Camoruco 3	—	0
3		—	0
4		—	0
5		—	0
6		—	0
—— 7 ——————		—	0
8	Camoruco 2	—	0
9		—	0
10		—	0
11–12A		—	0
11–12B ——————		—	0
13	Camoruco 1	—	0
14		X	1
—— 15 ——————		X	1
16	Corozal 3	—	0
17		X	1
—— 21 ——————		XXXX	4
22	Corozal 2	XXXXXXXXXX	10
23		XXXXXXXXXX XXXX	14
24	Corozal 1	XXXXXXXXXX XXXX	14
25		XXX	3
26		—	0
16–17	Skeleton 1	—	0
18	Skeleton 2	—	0
18–19	Skeleton 3	—	0
18–22	Skeleton 4	—	0
25	Feature	X	1
25	Skeleton 2	X	1
25	Skeleton 3	—	0

STATISTICAL SIGNIFICANCE OF FREQUENCY DISTRIBUTION BY PHASE

Excavation X^2 = 133.92
Corozal 3/Corozal 2 X^2 = 12.31
Corozal 2/Corozal 1 X^2 = 0.03

Table 30. Percentages of mode #134, Corozal curvilinear incision, Excavation 3

Level	Phase	Percent of Total Sherds in Level (X = .1%)	
1	Recent	(00.00)	
2	Camoruco 3	00.00	—
3		00.00	—
4		00.00	—
5		00.00	—
6		00.00	—
7		00.00	—
8	Camoruco 2	00.00	—
9		00.00	—
10		00.00	—
11–12A		00.00	—
11–12B		00.00	—
13	Camoruco 1	00.00	—
14		00.07	X
15		00.09	X
16	Corozal 3	00.00	—
17		00.18	XX
21		01.17	XXXXXXXXXXX XX
22	Corozal 2	01.51	XXXXXXXXXXX XXXXX
23		01.35	XXXXXXXXXXX XXXX
24	Corozal 1	02.20	XXXXXXXXXXX XXXXXXXXXXX XX
25		00.71	XXXXXXXX
26		(00.00)	

TABLE 30 • CONT'D

LEVEL	PHASE	PERCENT OF TOTAL SHERDS IN LEVEL (X = .1%)
16–17	Skeleton 1	(00.00)
18	Skeleton 2	(00.00)
18–19	Skeleton 3	(00.00)
18–22	Skeleton 4	(00.00)
25	Feature	(03.45)
25	Skeleton 2	(01.64)
25	Skeleton 3	(00.00)

STATISTICAL SIGNIFICANCE OF PERCENT DIFFERENCES BY LEVEL

Levels 14/15: 0.15	Levels 14/17: 0.70
Levels 15/16: 0.40	Levels 15/17: 0.53
Levels 16/17: 0.58	Levels 16/22: 1.68
Levels 16/23: 1.58	Levels 17/21: 1.94
Levels 17/22: 2.44	Levels 17/23: 2.30
Levels 21/22: 0.43	Levels 22/23: 0.27
Levels 23/24: 1.32	Levels 24/25: 1.88
Levels 24/26: 1.02	Levels 25/26: 0.57

Table 31. Frequency of mode #132, Corozal rectilinear incision, Excavation 2

Level	Phase	Number of Examples (X = 1)	Total: 40
——— 1	— Recent ———	—	0
2	Camoruco 3	—	0
3		—	0
4		—	0
——— 5–6 ———————————		—	0
7	Camoruco 2	—	0
———— 8 ———————————		—	0
9	Camoruco 1	—	0
10		—	0
——— 11 ———————————		—	0
———— 12 __ Corozal 3 ____		X	1
13	Corozal 2	X	1
———— 14 ———————————		XXXXXXXXXX XXXXXXXXX	19
15	Corozal 1	XXXXXXXXXX X	11
16–16W		XXXXX	5
16E		XX	2
17		—	0
18		—	0
19		X	1
20		—	0
16	West burial	—	0
16	Central burial	—	0
16	North burial	—	0
18	Child burial	—	0

Statistical significance of frequency distribution by phase

Excavation X^2 = 105.90
Corozal 3/Corozal 2 X^2 = 7.65
Corozal 2/Corozal 1 X^2 = 2.51
Level 13/14 X^2 = 8.99
Level 14/15 X^2 = 0.22

Table 32. Percentages of mode #132, Corozal rectilinear incision, Excavation 2

Level	Phase	Percent of Total Sherds in Level ($X = .1\%$)	
1	— Recent —	(00.00)	
2	Camoruco 3	00.00	—
3		00.00	—
4		00.00	—
5–6		00.00	—
7	Camoruco 2	00.00	—
8		00.00	—
9	Camoruco 1	00.00	—
10		00.00	—
11		00.00	—
12	Corozal 3	00.08	X
13	Corozal 2	00.09	X
14		01.11	XXXXXXXXXX X
15	Corozal 1	01.43	XXXXXXXXXX XXXX
16–16W		01.50	XXXXXXXXXX XXXXX
16E		01.25	XXXXXXXXXX XXX
17		00.00	—
18		00.00	—
19		(02.33)	
20		(00.00)	

TABLE 32 • CONT'D

LEVEL	PHASE	PERCENT OF TOTAL SHERDS IN LEVEL ($X = .1\%$)
16	West burial	(00.00)
16	Central burial	(00.00)
16	North burial	(00.00)
18	Child burial	(00.00)

STATISTICAL SIGNIFICANCE OF PERCENT DIFFERENCES BY LEVEL

Levels 12/13: 0.06	Levels 12/14: 3.40	Levels 13/15: 3.66
Levels 14/15: 0.67	Levels 14/16–16W: 0.60	Levels 14/16E: 0.16
Levels 14/17: 1.14	Levels 16–16W/16E: 0.22	Levels 16–16W/17: 1.32
Levels 16E/17: 1.20	Levels 16E/18: 1.27	Levels 13/14: 3.23

Table 33. Frequency of mode #132, Corozal rectilinear incision, Excavation 3

Level	Phase	Number of Examples (X = 1)	Total: 39
1	Recent	—	0
2	Camoruco 3	—	0
3		—	0
4		—	0
5		—	0
6		—	0
7		—	0
8	Camoruco 2	—	0
9		—	0
10		—	0
11–12A		—	0
11–12B		—	0
13	Camoruco 1	—	0
14		—	0
15		—	0
16	Corozal 3	—	0
17		—	0
21		—	0
22	Corozal 2	X	1
23		XXXXXXXXXX X	11
24	Corozal 1	XXXXXXXXXX X	11
25		XXXXXXXXXX XXXX	14
26		—	0
16–17	Skeleton 1	—	0
18	Skeleton 2	—	0
18–19	Skeleton 3	—	0
18–22	Skeleton 4	—	0
25	Feature	X	1
25	Skeleton 2	X	1
25	Skeleton 3	—	0

Statistical significance of frequency distribution by phase

Excavation X^2 = 203.78
Corozal 3/Corozal 2 X^2 = 7.86
Corozal 2/Corozal 1 X^2 = 13.61

Table 34. Percentages of mode #132, Corozal rectilinear incision, Excavation 3

Level	Phase	Percent of Total Sherds in Level (X = .1%)	
— 1 —	Recent	(00.00)	
2	Camoruco 3	00.00	—
3		00.00	—
4		00.00	—
5		00.00	—
6		00.00	—
— 7 —		00.00	—
8	Camoruco 2	00.00	—
9		00.00	—
10		00.00	—
11–12A		00.00	—
11–12B		00.00	—
13	Camoruco 1	00.00	—
14		00.00	—
— 15 —		00.00	—
16	Corozal 3	00.00	—
17		00.00	—
— 21 —		00.00	—
22	Corozal 2	00.15	XX
23		01.06	XXXXXXXXXX X
24	Corozal 1	01.73	XXXXXXXXXX XXXXXXX
25		03.33	XXXXXXXXXX XXXXXXXXXX XXXXXXXXXX XXX
26		(00.00)	

TABLE 34 • CONT'D

LEVEL	PHASE	PERCENT OF TOTAL SHERDS IN LEVEL ($X = .1\%$)
16–17	Skeleton 1	(00.00)
18	Skeleton 2	(00.00)
18–19	Skeleton 3	(00.00)
18–22	Skeleton 4	(00.00)
25	Feature	(03.45)
25	Skeleton 2	(01.64)
25	Skeleton 3	(00.00)

STATISTICAL SIGNIFICANCE OF PERCENT DIFFERENCES BY LEVEL

Levels 16/22: 0.53   Levels 15/23: 3.51
Levels 16/24: 1.79   Levels 16/25: 2.50
Levels 17/22: 0.92   Levels 21/22: 0.72
Levels 22/23: 2.18   Levels 22/24: 2.97
Levels 22/25: 4.36   Levels 23/24: 1.17
Levels 23/25: 3.02   Levels 24/25: 1.68

Table 35. Frequency of mode #18, Corozal red-and-white paint, Excavation 2

Level	Phase	Number of Examples (X = 1)	Total: 77
1	Recent	—	0
2	Camoruco 3	—	0
3		—	0
4		—	0
5–6		—	0
7	Camoruco 2	—	0
8		—	0
9	Camoruco 1	—	0
10		—	0
11		—	0
12	Corozal 3	XXXXXXX	7
13	Corozal 2	XXXXX	5
14		XXXXXXXXXX XXXXXXXXXX XXXXXXXXXX XX	42
15	Corozal 1	XXXXXXXXXX XXXXX	15
16–16W		XXXX	4
16E		X	1
17		—	0
18		XX	2
19		X	1
20		—	0

TABLE 35 • CONT'D

LEVEL	PHASE	NUMBER OF EXAMPLES ($X = 1$)	TOTAL: 77
16	West burial	—	0
16	Central burial	—	0
16	North burial	—	0
18	Child burial	—	0

STATISTICAL SIGNIFICANCE OF FREQUENCY DISTRIBUTION BY PHASE

$$\text{Excavation } X^2 = 156.31$$
$$\text{Corozal 3/Corozal 2 } X^2 = 11.65$$
$$\text{Corozal 2/Corozal 1 } X^2 = 0.10$$

Table 36. Percentages of mode #18, Corozal red-and-white paint, Excavation 2

Level	Phase	Percent of Total Sherds in Level (X = .1%)	
1	— Recent —	(00.00)	
2	Camoruco 3	00.00	—
3		00.00	—
4		00.00	—
5–6		00.00	—
7	Camoruco 2	00.00	—
8		00.00	—
9	Camoruco 1	00.00	—
10		00.00	—
11		00.00	—
12	Corozal 3	00.56	XXXXXXX
13	Corozal 2	00.44	XXXX
14		02.46	XXXXXXXXXX XXXXXXXXX XXXXX
15	Corozal 1	01.96	XXXXXXXXXX XXXXXXXXX
16–16W		01.20	XXXXXXXXXX XX
16E		00.63	XXXXXXX
17		00.00	—
18		01.56	XXXXXXXXX XXXXXX
19		(02.33)	
20		(00.00)	

TABLE 36 • CONT'D

LEVEL	PHASE	PERCENT OF TOTAL SHERDS IN LEVEL ($X = .1\%$)
16	West burial	(00.00)
16	Central burial	(00.00)
16	North burial	(00.00)
18	Child burial	(00.00)

STATISTICAL SIGNIFICANCE OF PERCENT DIFFERENCES BY LEVEL

Levels 9/12: 1.84   Levels 9/13: 1.63   Levels 10/13: 2.63
Levels 11/12: 1.99   Levels 11/13: 1.76   Levels 12/13: 0.43
Levels 13/14: 4.18   Levels 14/15: 0.78   Levels 15/16–16W: 0.88
Levels 15/16E: 1.18   Levels 16–16W/16E: 0.60 Levels 16E/17: 0.85
Levels 17/18: 1.35

Table 37. Frequency of mode #18, Corozal red-and-white paint, Excavation 3

Level	Phase	Number of Examples (X = 1)	Total: 74
—— 1 —	Recent ——	—	0
2	Camoruco 3	—	0
3		—	0
4		—	0
5		—	0
6		—	0
—— 7 ——————————		—	0
8	Camoruco 2	—	0
9		—	0
10		—	0
11–12A		—	0
11–12B ——————————		—	0
13	Camoruco 1	—	0
14		—	0
—— 15 ——————————		—	0
16	Corozal 3	—	0
17		—	0
—— 21 ——————————		—	0
22	Corozal 2	XXXXXXXXXX XXXXXXXXXX	20
—— 23 ——————————		XXXXXXXXXX XXXXXXXXXX XXXXXXX	27
24	Corozal 1	XXXXXXXXXX XXX	13
25		XXXXXXXXXX XX	12
26		X	1
16–17	Skeleton 1	—	0
18	Skeleton 2	—	0
18–19	Skeleton 3	—	0
18–22	Skeleton 4	—	0
25	Feature	—	0
25	Skeleton 2	X	1
25	Skeleton 3	—	0

Statistical significance of frequency distribution by phase

Excavation X^2 = 267.80
Corozal 3/Corozal 2 X^2 = 36.09
Corozal 2/Corozal 1 X^2 = 0.02

Table 38. Percentages of mode #18, Corozal red-and-white paint, Excavation 3

Level	Phase	Percent of Total Sherds in Level (X = .1%)	
1	— Recent —	(00.00)	
2	Camoruco 3	00.00	—
3		00.00	—
4		00.00	—
5		00.00	—
6		00.00	—
7		00.00	—
8	Camoruco 2	00.00	—
9		00.00	—
10		00.00	—
11–12A		00.00	—
11–12B		00.00	—
13	Camoruco 1	00.00	—
14		00.00	—
15		00.00	—
16	Corozal 3	00.00	—
17		00.00	—
21		00.00	—
22	Corozal 2	03.02	XXXXXXXXXX XXXXXXXXXX XXXXXXXXXX
23		02.60	XXXXXXXXXX XXXXXXXXXX XXXXXX
24	Corozal 1	02.04	XXXXXXXXXX XXXXXXXXXX
25		02.85	XXXXXXXXXX XXXXXXXXXX XXXXXXXXX
26		(02.17)	

TABLE 38 • CONT'D

LEVEL	PHASE	PERCENT OF TOTAL SHERDS IN LEVEL ($X = .1\%$)
16–17	Skeleton 1	(00.00)
18	Skeleton 2	(00.00)
18–19	Skeleton 3	(00.00)
18–22	Skeleton 4	(00.00)
25	Feature	(00.00)
25	Skeleton 2	(01.64)
25	Skeleton 3	(00.00)

STATISTICAL SIGNIFICANCE OF PERCENT DIFFERENCES BY LEVEL

Levels 16/22: 2.38   Levels 16/23: 2.21
Levels 16/24: 1.95   Levels 17/22: 4.13
Levels 17/23: 3.83   Levels 17/24: 3.39
Levels 21/22: 3.24   Levels 22/23: 0.51
Levels 22/24: 1.12   Levels 23/24: 0.73
Levels 23/25: 0.27   Levels 24/25: 0.85

Table 39. Frequency of mode #126, Corozal bowl rim strap handles, Excavation 2

Level	Phase	Number of Examples (X = 1)	Total: 53
1	Recent	—	0
2	Camoruco 3	—	0
3		—	0
4		XX	2
5–6		XX	2
7	Camoruco 2	—	0
8		—	0
9	Camoruco 1	—	0
10		—	0
11		XXX	3
12	Corozal 3	XXXXXXXXXX XXXX	14
13	Corozal 2	XXXXXXXXXX X	11
14		XXXXXXXXXX XXXXX	15
15	Corozal 1	XXXX	4
16–16W		X	1
16E		X	1
17		—	0
18		—	0
19		—	0
20		—	0
16	West burial	—	0
16	Central burial	—	0
16	North burial	—	0
18	Child burial	—	0

Statistical Significance of Frequency Distribution by Phase

Excavation X^2 = 66.62
Camoruco 1/Corozal 3 X^2 = 15.58
Corozal 3/Corozal 2 X^2 = 0.01
Corozal 2/Corozal 1 X^2 = 3.19

Table 40. Percentages of mode #126, Corozal bowl rim strap handles, Excavation 2

LEVEL	PHASE	PERCENT OF TOTAL SHERDS IN LEVEL (X = .1%)	
1	Recent	(00.00)	
2	Camoruco 3	00.00	—
3		00.00	—
4		00.24	XX
5–6		00.14	X
7	Camoruco 2	00.00	—
8		00.00	—
9	Camoruco 1	00.00	—
10		00.00	—
11		00.42	XXXX
12	Corozal 3	01.12	XXXXXXXXXXX X
13	Corozal 2	00.96	XXXXXXXXXX
14		00.88	XXXXXXXXX
15	Corozal 1	00.52	XXXXX
16–16W		00.30	XXX
16E		00.63	XXXXXXX
17		00.00	—
18		00.00	—
19		(00.00)	
20		(00.00)	

TABLE 40 • CONT'D

LEVEL	PHASE	PERCENT OF TOTAL SHERDS IN LEVEL ($X = .1\%$)
16	West burial	(00.00)
16	Central burial	(00.00)
16	North burial	(00.00)
18	Child burial	(00.00)

STATISTICAL SIGNIFICANCE OF PERCENT DIFFERENCES BY LEVEL

Levels 3/4: 1.51   Levels 4/5-6: 0.60   Levels 10/11: 2.59
Levels 11/12: 1.59   Levels 11/13: 1.29   Levels 11/14: 1.19
Levels 12/13: 0.38   Levels 13/14: 0.21   Levels 14/15: 0.94
Levels 15/16-16W: 0.50   Levels 16-16W/16E: 0.53   Levels 16-16W/17: 0.59
Levels 16-16W/18: 0.62   Levels 16E/17: 0.85   Levels 16E/18: 0.90

Table 41. Frequency of mode #126, Corozal bowl rim strap handles, Excavation 3

Level	Phase	Number of Examples (X = 1)	Total: 45
1	Recent	—	0
2	Camoruco 3	—	0
3		—	0
4		X	1
5		—	0
6		—	0
7		—	0
8	Camoruco 2	—	0
9		—	0
10		—	0
11–12A		X	1
11–12B		X	1
13	Camoruco 1	XX	2
14		—	0
15		—	0
16	Corozal 3	X	1
17		XXX	3
21		X	1
22	Corozal 2	XXXXXXXX	8
23		XXXXXXXXXX XXX	13
24	Corozal 1	XXXXXXXXXX X	11
25		X	1
26		—	0
16–17	Skeleton 1	—	0
18	Skeleton 2	XX	2
18–19	Skeleton 3	—	0
18–22	Skeleton 4	—	0
25	Feature	—	0
25	Skeleton 2	—	0
25	Skeleton 3	—	0

Statistical significance of frequency distribution by phase

Excavation X^2 = 81.26
Corozal 3/Corozal 2 X^2 = 5.68
Corozal 2/Corozal 1 X^2 = 0.01

Table 42. Percentages of mode #126, Corozal bowl rim strap handles, Excavation 3

LEVEL	PHASE	PERCENT OF TOTAL SHERDS IN LEVEL (X = .1%)	
1	— Recent —	(00.00)	
2	Camoruco 3	00.00	—
3		00.00	—
4		00.13	X
5		00.00	—
6		00.00	—
7		00.00	—
8	Camoruco 2	00.00	—
9		00.00	—
10		00.00	—
11–12A		00.24	XX
11–12B		00.28	XXX
13	Camoruco 1	00.16	XX
14		00.00	—
15		00.00	—
16	Corozal 3	00.54	XXXXXX
17		00.54	XXXXXX
21		00.29	XXX
22	Corozal 2	01.21	XXXXXXXXXXXX XX
23		01.25	XXXXXXXXXXXX XXX
24	Corozal 1	01.73	XXXXXXXXXXXX XXXXXXXX
25		00.24	XX
26		(00.00)	

TABLE 42 • CONT'D

LEVEL	PHASE	PERCENT OF TOTAL SHERDS IN LEVEL ($X = .1\%$)
16–17	Skeleton 1	(00.00)
18	Skeleton 2	(04.55)
18–19	Skeleton 3	(00.00)
18–22	Skeleton 4	(00.00)
25	Feature	(00.00)
25	Skeleton 2	(00.00)
25	Skeleton 3	(00.00)

STATISTICAL SIGNIFICANCE OF PERCENT DIFFERENCES BY LEVEL

Levels 3/4: 0.68	Levels 4/5: 0.97	Levels 4/16: 1.12
Levels 4/15: 1.21	Levels 4/17: 1.37	Levels 4/21: 0.61
Levels 10/11–12A: 1.46	Levels 11–12A/11–12B: 0.12	Levels 14/16: 2.80
Levels 14/17: 2.79	Levels 15/16: 2.51	Levels 16/17: 0.01
Levels 16/21: 0.44	Levels 16/22: 0.78	Levels 16/23: 0.83
Levels 16/24: 1.18	Levels 17/14: 2.79	Levels 17/21: 0.54
Levels 17/22: 1.23	Levels 17/23: 1.36	Levels 21/22: 1.45
Levels 22/23: 0.08	Levels 22/24: 0.78	Levels 23/24: 0.80
Levels 23/25: 1.80		

Table 43. Frequency of mode #209, spongeware animal-effigy bowls, Excavation 2

Level	Phase	Number of Examples (X = 1)	Total: 73
1	Recent	—	0
2	Camoruco 3	—	0
3		X	1
4		—	0
5–6		XXXX	4
7	Camoruco 2	XXXX	4
8		XXXXXXX	7
9	Camoruco 1	XXXXXXXX	8
10		XXXXXXXXXX XXXXXX	16
11		XXXXXXXXXX XXXX	14
12	Corozal 3	XXXXXXXXXX XXX	13
13	Corozal 2	XX	2
14		XX	2
15	Corozal 1	XX	2
16–16W		—	0
16E		—	0
17		—	0
18		—	0
19		—	0
20		—	0
16	West burial	—	0
16	Central burial	—	0
16	North burial	—	0
18	Child burial	—	0

Statistical significance of frequency distribution by phase

Excavation X^2 = 74.77
Camoruco 3/Camoruco 2 X^2 = 6.00
Camoruco 2/Camoruco 1 X^2 = 12.55
Camoruco 1/Corozal 3 X^2 = 0.01
Corozal 3/Corozal 2 X^2 = 21.38

Table 44. Percentages of mode #209, spongeware animal-effigy bowls, Excavation 2

LEVEL	PHASE	PERCENT OF TOTAL SHERDS IN LEVEL (X = .1%)
1	Recent	(00.00)
2	Camoruco 3	00.00 —
3		00.11 X
4		00.00 —
5–6		00.27 XXX
7	Camoruco 2	00.26 XXX
8		00.65 XXXXXXX
9	Camoruco 1	01.32 XXXXXXXXXXX XXX
10		01.01 XXXXXXXXXX
11		01.97 XXXXXXXXXX XXXXXXXXXX
12	Corozal 3	01.04 XXXXXXXXXX
13	Corozal 2	00.17 XX
14		00.12 X
15	Corozal 1	00.26 XXX
16–16W		00.00 —
16E		00.00 —
17		00.00 —
18		00.00 —
19		(00.00)
20		(00.00)

TABLE 44 • CONT'D

LEVEL	PHASE	PERCENT OF TOTAL SHERDS IN LEVEL ($X = .1\%$)
16	West burial	(00.00)
16	Central burial	(00.00)
16	North burial	(00.00)
18	Child burial	(00.00)

STATISTICAL SIGNIFICANCE OF PERCENT DIFFERENCES BY LEVEL

Levels 5–6/7: 0.08	Levels 5–6/8: 1.46	Levels 7/8: 1.56
Levels 8/9: 1.39	Levels 9/10: 0.62	Levels 9/11: 0.93
Levels 11/12: 1.72	Levels 12/13: 2.68	Levels 13/14: 0.40
Levels 14/15: 0.82	Levels 15/16–16W: 0.93	

Table 45. Frequency of mode #209, spongeware animal-effigy bowls, Excavation 3

Level	Phase	Number of Examples (X = 1)	Total: 72
1	Recent	—	0
2	Camoruco 3	—	0
3		—	0
4		—	0
5		x	1
6		—	0
7		x	1
8	Camoruco 2	xxxx	4
9		—	0
10		—	0
11–12A		xxxx	4
11–12B		xxxx	4
13	Camoruco 1	xxxxxxx	7
14		xxxxxxxxxx xxxxxxxxxx	20
15		xxxxxxxxxx xxx	13
16	Corozal 3	xxxx	4
17		xxxxxx	6
21		x	1
22	Corozal 2	—	0
23		—	0
24	Corozal 1	—	0
25		x	1
26		—	0

TABLE 45 • CONT'D

LEVEL	PHASE	NUMBER OF EXAMPLES (X = 1)	TOTAL: 72
16–17	Skeleton 1	—	0
18	Skeleton 2	XXXXXX	6
18–19	Skeleton 3	—	0
18–22	Skeleton 4	—	0
25	Feature	—	0
25	Skeleton 2	—	0
25	Skeleton 3	—	0

STATISTICAL SIGNIFICANCE OF FREQUENCY DISTRIBUTION BY PHASE

$$\text{Excavation } X^2 = 61.89$$
$$\text{Camoruco 3/Camoruco 2 } X^2 = 5.42$$
$$\text{Camoruco 2/Camoruco 1 } X^2 = 8.39$$
$$\text{Camoruco 1/Corozal 3 } X^2 = 0.02$$
$$\text{Corozal 3/Corozal 2 } X^2 = 19.29$$

Table 46. Percentages of mode #209, spongeware animal-effigy bowls, Excavation 3

Level	Phase	Percent of Total Sherds in Level (X = .1%)	
1	Recent	(00.00)	
2	Camoruco 3	00.00	—
3		00.00	—
4		00.00	—
5		00.13	X
6		00.00	—
7		00.17	XX
8	Camoruco 2	00.80	XXXXXXXX
9		00.00	—
10		00.00	—
11–12A		00.94	XXXXXXXXX
11–12B		01.12	XXXXXXXXXX x
13	Camoruco 1	00.56	XXXXXX
14		01.39	XXXXXXXXXX XXXX
15		01.13	XXXXXXXXXXX x
16	Corozal 3	02.17	XXXXXXXXXX XXXXXXXXXX XX
17		01.08	XXXXXXXXXX x
21		00.29	XXX
22	Corozal 2	00.00	—
23		00.00	—
24	Corozal 1	00.00	—
25		00.24	XX
26		(00.00)	

TABLE 46 • CONT'D

LEVEL	PHASE	PERCENT OF TOTAL SHERDS IN LEVEL (X = .1%)
16–17	Skeleton 1	(00.00)
18	Skeleton 2	(13.64)
18–19	Skeleton 3	(00.00)
18–22	Skeleton 4	(00.00)
25	Feature	(00.00)
25	Skeleton 2	(00.00)
25	Skeleton 3	(00.00)

STATISTICAL SIGNIFICANCE OF PERCENT DIFFERENCES BY LEVEL

Levels 3/8: 1.71	Levels 5/6: 0.85
Levels 5/7: 0.16	Levels 5/8: 1.83
Levels 6/7: 0.95	Levels 6/8: 2.09
Levels 7/8: 1.55	Levels 8/9: 1.82
Levels 11–12A/11–12B: 0.25	Levels 13/14: 2.17
Levels 14/15: 0.60	Levels 15/16: 1.18
Levels 16/17: 1.11	Levels 17/21: 1.30
Levels 21/22: 1.40	Levels 21/25: 0.15
Levels 24/25: 1.23	

Table 47. Frequency of mode #152, Camoruco mauve paint, Excavation 2

Level	Phase	Number of Examples (X = 1)	Total: 235
1	— Recent —	XXXXXXXX	8
2	Camoruco 3	XXXXX	5
3		XXXXXXXXXX XXXXXXXXX	19
4		XXXXXXXXXX XXXXXXXXXX XXXXXXXXXX XXXXXXXXXX XX	42
— 5–6 —		XXXXXXXXXX XXXXXXXXXX XXXXXXXXX	39
7	Camoruco 2	XXXXXXXXXX XXXXXXXXXX XXXXXXXXXX XXXXX	35
8		XXXXXXXXXX XXXXXXXXXX XXXXXXXXXX XXXXXXXXXX XXXXX	45
9	Camoruco 1	XXXXXXXXXX X	11
10		XXXXXXXXXX XXXXXXXXXX X	21
— 11 —		XXXXXXXXX	9
— 12 —	— Corozal 3 —	X	1
13	Corozal 2	—	0
— 14 —		—	0
15	Corozal 1	—	0
16–16W		—	0
16E		—	0
17		—	0
18		—	0
19		—	0
20		—	0

TABLE 47 • CONT'D

LEVEL	PHASE	NUMBER OF EXAMPLES (X = 1)	TOTAL: 235
16	West burial	—	0
16	Central burial	—	0
16	North burial	—	0
18	Child burial	—	0

STATISTICAL SIGNIFICANCE OF FREQUENCY DISTRIBUTION BY PHASE

$$\text{Excavation } X^2 = 156.14$$
$$\text{Camoruco 3/Camoruco 2 } X^2 = 0.96$$
$$\text{Camoruco 2/Camoruco 1 } X^2 = 13.48$$
$$\text{Camoruco 1/Corozal 3 } X^2 = 11.77$$

Table 48. Percentages of mode #152, Camoruco mauve paint, Excavation 2

Level	Phase	Percent of Total Sherds in Level (X = .1%)	
1	Recent	(09.88)	
2	Camoruco 3	00.44	XXXX
3		02.03	XXXXXXXXXX XXXXXXXXX
4		05.14	XXXXXXXXXX XXXXXXXXXX XXXXXXXXXX XXXXXXXXXX XXXXXXXXXX X
5–6		02.64	XXXXXXXXXX XXXXXXXXXX XXXXXX
7	Camoruco 2	02.23	XXXXXXXXXX XXXXXXXXXX XX
8		04.21	XXXXXXXXXX XXXXXXXXXX XXXXXXXXXX XXXXXXXXXX XX
9	Camoruco 1	01.81	XXXXXXXXXX XXXXXXXX
10		01.33	XXXXXXXXXX XXX
11		01.27	XXXXXXXXXX XXX
12	Corozal 3	00.08	X
13	Corozal 2	00.00	—
14		00.00	—
15	Corozal 1	00.00	—
16–16W		00.00	—
16E		00.00	—
17		00.00	—
18		00.00	—
19		(00.00)	
20		(00.00)	

TABLE 48 • CONT'D

LEVEL	PHASE	PERCENT OF TOTAL SHERDS IN LEVEL (X = .1%)
16	West burial	(00.00)
16	Central burial	(00.00)
16	North burial	(00.00)
18	Child burial	(00.00)

STATISTICAL SIGNIFICANCE OF PERCENT DIFFERENCES BY LEVEL

Levels 2/3: 3.39	Levels 3/4: 3.55	Levels 3/7: 0.34
Levels 3/8: 2.77	Levels 4/5–6: 3.11	Levels 4/7: 3.81
Levels 4/8: 0.96	Levels 5–6/7: 0.73	Levels 7/8: 2.90
Levels 7/9: 0.61	Levels 7/10: 1.92	Levels 8/9: 2.62
Levels 8/10: 4.66	Levels 8/11: 3.53	Levels 9/10: 0.84
Levels 9/12: 4.38	Levels 10/11: 0.11	Levels 10/12: 3.76
Levels 11/12: 3.56	Levels 12/13: 0.96	Levels 12/14: 1.17

Table 49. Frequency of mode #152, Camoruco mauve paint, Excavation 3

Level	Phase	Number of Examples (X = 1)	Total: 196
1	Recent	xxx	3
2	Camoruco 3	xxxxxxxxxx xxxxxxxxxx xxxxx	25
3		x	1
4		xxxxxxx	7
5		xxxxxxxxxx xxxxxxx	17
6		xxxxxxxxxx	10
7		xxxxxxxxxx xxxx	14
8	Camoruco 2	xxxxxxxxxx xxxx	14
9		xxxxxx	6
10		xxxxxxxxxx xxxxxx	16
11–12A		xxxxxxxxxx	10
11–12B		xxxx	4
13	Camoruco 1	xxxxxxxxxx xxxxxxxxxx xxxxxx	36
14		xxxxxxxxxx xxxxxxxxxx xxxxxxxx	28
15		xxxx	4
16	Corozal 3	—	0
17		x	1
21		—	0
22	Corozal 2	—	0
23		—	0
24	Corozal 1	—	0
25		—	0
26		—	0

TABLE 49 • CONT'D

LEVEL	PHASE	NUMBER OF EXAMPLES (X = 1)	TOTAL: 196
16–17	Skeleton 1	—	0
18	Skeleton 2	xxxxxx	6
18–19	Skeleton 3	—	0
18–22	Skeleton 4	—	0
25	Feature	—	0
25	Skeleton 2	—	0
25	Skeleton 3	—	0

STATISTICAL SIGNIFICANCE OF FREQUENCY DISTRIBUTION BY PHASE

Excavation X^2 = 86.89
Camoruco 3/Camoruco 2 X^2 = 0.09
Camoruco 2/Camoruco 1 X^2 = 0.01
Camoruco 1/Corozal 3 X^2 = 21.75

Table 50. Percentages of mode #152, Camoruco mauve paint, Excavation 3

Level	Phase	Percent of Total Sherds in Level (X = .1%)	
1	— Recent —	(16.67)	
2	Camoruco 3	05.48	xxxxxxxxxx xxxxxxxxxx xxxxxxxxxx xxxxxxxxxx xxxxxxxxxx xx
3		00.28	xxx
4		00.89	xxxxxxxxx
5		02.27	xxxxxxxxxx xxxxxxxxxx xxx
6		01.86	xxxxxxxxxx xxxxxxxxx
7		02.36	xxxxxxxxxx xxxxxxxxxx xxxx
8	Camoruco 2	02.82	xxxxxxxxxx xxxxxxxxxx xxxxxxxxx
9		01.46	xxxxxxxxxx xxxxx
10		01.78	xxxxxxxxxx xxxxxxxx
11–12A		02.36	xxxxxxxxxx xxxxxxxxxx xxxx
11–12B		01.12	xxxxxxxxxx x
13	Camoruco 1	02.87	xxxxxxxxxx xxxxxxxxxx xxxxxxxxx
14		01.95	xxxxxxxxxx xxxxxxxxx
15		00.35	xxxx
16	Corozal 3	00.00	—
17		00.18	xx
21		00.00	—
22	Corozal 2	00.00	—
23		00.00	—
24	Corozal 1	00.00	—
25		00.00	—
26		(00.00)	

TABLE 50 • CONT'D

LEVEL	PHASE	PERCENT OF TOTAL SHERDS IN LEVEL ($X = .1\%$)
16–17	Skeleton 1	(00.00)
18	Skeleton 2	(00.00)
18–19	Skeleton 3	(00.00)
18–22	Skeleton 4	(00.00)
25	Feature	(00.00)
25	Skeleton 2	(00.00)
25	Skeleton 3	(00.00)

STATISTICAL SIGNIFICANCE OF PERCENT DIFFERENCES BY LEVEL

Levels 3/4: 1.16   Levels 4/5: 2.19
Levels 4/6: 1.54   Levels 5/6: 0.52
Levels 5/8: 0.60   Levels 6/7: 0.59
Levels 6/8: 1.03   Levels 6/9: 0.47
Levels 5/10: 0.70   Levels 9/13: 1.58
Levels 9/14: 0.65   Levels 10/13: 1.62
Levels 13/14: 1.56 Levels 14/15: 3.67
Levels 15/16: 0.80 Levels 15/17: 0.60
Levels 16/17: 0.58 Levels 17/21: 0.78
Levels 17/22: 1.09

Table 51. Frequency of mode #14, Arauquinoid maroon paint, Excavation 2

Level	Phase	Number of Examples (X = 1)	Total: 260
1	Recent	XXX	3
2	Camoruco 3	XXXXXXXXXX XXXXXXXXXX XXXXXXXXXX XXXXXXXXXX XXXXXXXXXX XXXXXXXXXX XXXXXXXXXX XXXXXXXXXX XXXXXXXXXX XXXXXXXXXX XX+	105
3		XXXXXXXXXX XXXXXXXXXX XXXXXXXXXX XXXXXXXXXX XXXXXXXXXX XXXXXXXXXX XXXXXXXXXX XXXXXXXXXX XX+	90
4		XXXXXXXXXX XXXXXXXXXX XXXXXXXXXX XXXXXXXXXX	40
5–6		XXXXXXXXXX XXXXXXXX	18
7	Camoruco 2	XX	2
8		X	1
9	Camoruco 1	—	0
10		X	1
11		—	0
12	Corozal 3	—	0
13	Corozal 2	—	0
14		—	0
15	Corozal 1	—	0
16–16W		—	0
16E		—	0
17		—	0
18		—	0
19		—	0
20		—	0

TABLE 51 • CONT'D

LEVEL	PHASE	NUMBER OF EXAMPLES (X = 1)	TOTAL: 260
16	West burial	—	0
16	Central burial	—	0
16	North burial	—	0
18	Child burial	—	0

STATISTICAL SIGNIFICANCE OF FREQUENCY DISTRIBUTION BY PHASE

Excavation X^2 = 742.92
Camoruco 3/Camoruco 2 X^2 = 196.90
Camoruco 2/Camoruco 1 X^2 = 5.25

Table 52. Percentages of mode #14, Arauquinoid marooon paint, Excavation 2

Level	Phase	Percent of Total Sherds in Level (X = .1%)
1	Recent	(03.70)
2	Camoruco 3	09.15 XXXXXXXXXX XXXXXXXXXX XXXXXXXXXX XXXXXXXXX+
3		09.62 XXXXXXXXXX XXXXXXXXX XXXXXXXXXX XXXXXXXXX+
4		04.90 XXXXXXXXXX XXXXXXXXXX XXXXXXXXXX XXXXXXXXX
5–6		01.22 XXXXXXXXXXX XX
7	Camoruco 2	00.13 X
8		00.09 X
9	Camoruco 1	00.00 —
10		00.06 X
11		00.00 —
12	Corozal 3	00.00 —
13	Corozal 2	00.00 —
14		00.00 —
15	Corozal 1	00.00 —
16–16W		00.00 —
16E		00.00 —
17		00.00 —
18		00.00 —
19		(00.00)
20		(00.00)

TABLE 52 • CONT'D

LEVEL	PHASE	PERCENT OF TOTAL SHERDS IN LEVEL (X = .1%)
16	West burial	(00.00)
16	Central burial	(00.00)
16	North burial	(00.00)
18	Child burial	(00.00)

STATISTICAL SIGNIFICANCE OF PERCENT DIFFERENCES BY LEVEL

Levels 1/2: 1.67 Levels 2/3: 0.36 Levels 2/7: 11.93
Levels 3/4: 3.76 Levels 3/7: 12.20 Levels 4/5–6: 5.37
Levels 4/7: 8.40 Levels 4/8: 7.09 Levels 5–6/7: 3.72
Levels 7/8: 0.26 Levels 7/9: 0.88 Levels 7/10: 0.59

Table 53. Frequency of mode #14, Arauquinoid maroon paint, Excavation 3

Level	Phase	Number of Examples (X = 1)	Total: 326
1	Recent	—	0
2	Camoruco 3	XXXXXXXXXX XXXXXXXXXX XXXXXXXXXX XXXXXXXXXX XXXX	44
3		XXXXXXXXXX XXXXXXXXXX XXXXXXXXXX XXXXXXXXXX XXXXX	45
4		XXXXXXXXXX XXXXXXXXXX XXXXXXXXXX XXXXXXXXXX XXXXXXXXXX XX+	110
5		XXXXXXXXXX XXXXXXXXXX XXXXXXXXXX XXXXXXXXXX XXXXXXXXXX XX+	90
6		XXXXXXXXXX XXXXXXXXXX XXX	23
7		XXXXXXXXXX	10
8	Camoruco 2	X	1
9		—	0
10		X	1
11–12A		—	0
11–12B		—	0
13	Camoruco 1	X	1
14		X	1
15		—	0
16	Corozal 3	—	0
17		—	0
21		—	0
22	Corozal 2	—	0
23		—	0
24	Corozal 1	—	0
25		—	0
26		—	0

TABLE 53 • CONT'D

LEVEL	PHASE	NUMBER OF EXAMPLES (X = 1)	TOTAL: 326
16–17	Skeleton 1	—	0
18	Skeleton 2	—	0
18–19	Skeleton 3	—	0
18–22	Skeleton 4	—	0
25	Feature	—	0
25	Skeleton 2	—	0
25	Skeleton 3	—	0

STATISTICAL SIGNIFICANCE OF FREQUENCY DISTRIBUTION BY PHASE

Excavation X^2 = 1027.69
Camoruco 3/Camoruco 2 X^2 = 260.51
Camoruco 2/Camoruco 1 X^2 = 2.92

Table 54. Percentages of mode #14, Arauquinoid maroon paint, Excavation 3

Level	Phase	Percent of Total Sherds in Level (X = .1%)	
1	— Recent —	(00.00)	
2	Camoruco 3	09.65	XXXXXXXXXX XXXXXXXXXX XXXXXXXXXX XXXXXXXXXX X+
3		12.47	XXXXXXXXXX XXXXXXXXXX XXXXXXXXXX XXXXXXXXXX X+
4		13.96	XXXXXXXXXX XXXXXXXXXX XXXXXXXXXX XXXXXXXXXX X+
5		12.03	XXXXXXXXXX XXXXXXXXXX XXXXXXXXXX XXXXXXXXXX X+
6		04.27	XXXXXXXXXX XXXXXXXXXX XXXXXXXXXX XXX
7		01.68	XXXXXXXXXX XXXXXXX
8	Camoruco 2	00.20	XX
9		00.00	—
10		00.11	X
11–12A		00.00	—
11–12B		00.00	—
13	Camoruco 1	00.08	X
14		00.07	X
15		00.00	—
16	Corozal 3	00.00	—
17		00.00	—
21		00.00	—
22	Corozal 2	00.00	—
23		00.00	—
24	Corozal 1	00.00	—
25		00.00	—
26		(00.00)	

TABLE 54 • CONT'D

LEVEL	PHASE	PERCENT OF TOTAL SHERDS IN LEVEL ($X = .1\%$)
16–17	Skeleton 1	(00.00)
18	Skeleton 2	(00.00)
18–19	Skeleton 3	(00.00)
18–22	Skeleton 4	(00.00)
25	Feature	(00.00)
25	Skeleton 2	(00.00)
25	Skeleton 3	(00.00)

STATISTICAL SIGNIFICANCE OF PERCENT DIFFERENCES BY LEVEL

Levels 2/3: 1.28	Levels 3/4: 0.69
Levels 4/5: 1.12	Levels 4/6: 5.77
Levels 5/6: 4.86	Levels 6/7: 2.58
Levels 6/8: 4.35	Levels 7/8: 2.44
Levels 7/9: 2.64	Levels 8/9: 0.91
Levels 8/10: 0.42	Levels 9/10: 0.68
Levels 8/13: 0.68	Levels 8/14: 0.79
Levels 13/14: 0.10	Levels 11–12B/13: 0.53
Levels 10/11–12A: 0.69	Levels 10/11–12B: 0.63

Table 55. Frequency of mode #19, Arauquinoid rectilinear incision, Excavation 2

Level	Phase	Number of Examples (X = 1)	Total: 66
1	Recent	—	0
2	Camoruco 3	xxxxxxx	7
3		xxxxxxxxxx xxxxxxxxxx xxxxxxxxxx	30
4		xxxxxxxxxx	10
5–6		xxxxxxxxxx xxxxxx	16
7	Camoruco 2	—	0
8		xxx	3
9	Camoruco 1	—	0
10		—	0
11		—	0
12	Corozal 3	—	0
13	Corozal 2	—	0
14		—	0
15	Corozal 1	—	0
16–16W		—	0
16E		—	0
17		—	0
18		—	0
19		—	0
20		—	0

TABLE 55 • CONT'D

LEVEL	PHASE	NUMBER OF EXAMPLES ($X = 1$)	TOTAL: 66
16	West burial	—	0
16	Central burial	—	0
16	North burial	—	0
18	Child burial	—	0

STATISTICAL SIGNIFICANCE OF FREQUENCY DISTRIBUTION BY PHASE

Excavation X^2 = 136.06
Camoruco 3/Camoruco 2 X^2 = 24.27
Camoruco 2/Camoruco 1 X^2 = 6.64

Table 56. Percentages of mode #19, Arauquinoid rectilinear incision, Excavation 2

Level	Phase	Percent of Total Sherds in Level (X = .1%)
1	Recent	(00.00)
2	Camoruco 3	00.61 XXXXXX
3		03.21 XXXXXXXXXX XXXXXXXXXX XXXXXXXXXX XX
4		01.22 XXXXXXXXXX XX
5–6		01.08 XXXXXXXXXX X
7	Camoruco 2	00.00 —
8		00.28 XXX
9	Camoruco 1	00.00 —
10		00.00 —
11		00.00 —
12	Corozal 3	00.00 —
13	Corozal 2	00.00 —
14		00.00 —
15	Corozal 1	00.00 —
16–16W		00.00 —
16E		00.00 —
17		00.00 —
18		00.00 —
19		(00.00)
20		(00.00)

TABLE 56 • CONT'D

LEVEL	PHASE	PERCENT OF TOTAL SHERDS IN LEVEL ($X = .1\%$)
16	West burial	(00.00)
16	Central burial	(00.00)
16	North burial	(00.00)
18	Child burial	(00.00)

STATISTICAL SIGNIFICANCE OF PERCENT DIFFERENCES BY LEVEL

Levels 2/3: 4.46	Levels 3/4: 2.77	Levels 4/5-6: 0.30
Levels 4/8: 2.46	Levels 5-6/7: 4.13	Levels 5-6/8: 2.32
Levels 7/8: 2.10	Levels 8/9: 1.31	Levels 8/10: 2.11

Table 57. Frequency of mode #19, Arauquinoid rectilinear incision, Excavation 3

LEVEL	PHASE	NUMBER OF EXAMPLES (X = 1)	TOTAL: 52
1	Recent	—	0
2	Camoruco 3	XXXXXXXX	8
3		XXXXXXXX	8
4		XXXXXXXXXX XXXX	14
5		XXXXXXXXXX XXX	13
6		XXXX	4
7		XXX	3
8	Camoruco 2	X	1
9		—	0
10		—	0
11–12A		X	1
11–12B		—	0
13	Camoruco 1	—	0
14		—	0
15		—	0
16	Corozal 3	—	0
17		—	0
21		—	0
22	Corozal 2	—	0
23		—	0
24	Corozal 1	—	0
25		—	0
26		—	0
16–17	Skeleton 1	—	0
18	Skeleton 2	—	0
18–19	Skeleton 3	—	0
18–22	Skeleton 4	—	0
25	Feature	—	0
25	Skeleton 2	—	0
25	Skeleton 3	—	0

STATISTICAL SIGNIFICANCE OF FREQUENCY DISTRIBUTION BY PHASE

Excavation X^2 = 148.40
Camoruco 3/Camoruco 2 X^2 = 32.15

Table 58. Percentages of mode #19, Arauquinoid rectilinear incision, Excavation 3

Level	Phase	Percent of Total Sherds in Level	(X = .1%)
1	Recent	(00.00)	
2	Camoruco 3	01.75	xxxxxxxxxxxxxxxxx
3		02.22	xxxxxxxxxxxxx xxxxxxxxxxxx xx
4		01.78	xxxxxxxxxxxx xxxxxxxx
5		01.74	xxxxxxxxxxxx xxxxxxxx
6		00.74	xxxxxxxx
7		00.51	xxxxxx
8	Camoruco 2	00.20	xx
9		00.00	—
10		00.00	—
11–12A		00.24	xx
11–12B		00.00	—
13	Camoruco 1	00.00	—
14		00.00	—
15		00.00	—
16	Corozal 3	00.00	—
17		00.00	—
21		00.00	—
22	Corozal 2	00.00	—
23		00.00	—
24	Corozal 1	00.00	—
25		00.00	—
26		(00.00)	

TABLE 58 • CONT'D

LEVEL	PHASE	PERCENT OF TOTAL SHERDS IN LEVEL ($X = .1\%$)
16–17	Skeleton 1	(00.00)
18	Skeleton 2	(00.00)
18–19	Skeleton 3	(00.00)
18–22	Skeleton 4	(00.00)
25	Feature	(00.00)
25	Skeleton 2	(00.00)
25	Skeleton 3	(00.00)

STATISTICAL SIGNIFICANCE OF PERCENT DIFFERENCES BY LEVEL

Levels 2/3: 0.47   Levels 3/4: 0.50
Levels 4/5: 0.06   Levels 5/6: 1.54
Levels 5/13: 4.69   Levels 6/7: 0.51
Levels 6/8: 1.26   Levels 7/8: 0.83
Levels 8/9: 0.91   Levels 8/10: 1.34
Levels 8/11–12A: 0.11   Levels 8/11–12B: 0.85
Levels 11–12A/13: 1.72

Table 59. Frequency of mode #160, circle-stamp motif, Excavation 2

LEVEL	PHASE	NUMBER OF EXAMPLES (X = 1)	TOTAL: 92
1	Recent	—	0
2	Camoruco 3	XXXXXXXXX	9
3		XXXXXXXXXX XXX	13
4		XXXXXX	6
5–6		XXXXXXXXXX XXXXXXXXXX	20
7	Camoruco 2	XXXXXXXXXX X	11
8		XXXXXXXX	8
9	Camoruco 1	XX	2
10		XXXXXXXXXX	10
11		XXXXXXXXXX X	11
12	Corozal 3	XX	2
13	Corozal 2	—	0
14		—	0
15	Corozal 1	—	0
16–16W		—	0
16E		—	0
17		—	0
18		—	0
19		—	0
20		—	0
16	West burial	—	0
16	Central burial	—	0
16	North burial	—	0
18	Child burial	—	0

STATISTICAL SIGNIFICANCE OF FREQUENCY DISTRIBUTION BY PHASE

Excavation X^2 = 43.64
Camoruco 3/Camoruco 2 X^2 = 0.34
Camoruco 2/Camoruco 1 X^2 = 0.25
Camoruco 1/Corozal 3 X^2 = 0.81

Table 60. Percentages of mode #160, circle-stamp motif, Excavation 2

Level	Phase	Percent of Total Sherds in Level (X = .1%)
1	Recent	(00.00)
2	Camoruco 3	00.78 XXXXXXXX
3		01.39 XXXXXXXXXXXX XXXX
4		00.73 XXXXXXX
5–6		01.35 XXXXXXXXXXXX XXXX
7	Camoruco 2	00.70 XXXXXXX
8		00.75 XXXXXXXX
9	Camoruco 1	00.33 XXX
10		00.63 XXXXXXX
11		01.55 XXXXXXXXXXXX XXXXXX
12	Corozal 3	00.16 XX
13	Corozal 2	00.00 —
14		00.00 —
15	Corozal 1	00.00 —
16–16W		00.00 —
16E		00.00 —
17		00.00 —
18		00.00 —
19		(00.00)
20		(00.00)

TABLE 60 • CONT'D

LEVEL	PHASE	PERCENT OF TOTAL SHERDS IN LEVEL ($X = .1\%$)
16	West burial	(00.00)
16	Central burial	(00.00)
16	North burial	(00.00)
18	Child burial	(00.00)

STATISTICAL SIGNIFICANCE OF PERCENT DIFFERENCES BY LEVEL

Levels 4/7: 0.09	Levels 7/8: 0.13	Levels 7/9: 1.01
Levels 7/10: 0.24	Levels 9/10: 0.86	Levels 10/11: 2.13
Levels 10/12: 1.93	Levels 10/13: 2.70	Levels 11/12: 3.65
Levels 12/13: 1.35	Levels 12/14: 1.65	

Table 61. Frequency of mode #160, circle-stamp motif, Excavation 3

Level	Phase	Number of Examples (X = 1)	Total: 106
1	Recent	X	1
2	Camoruco 3	XXXXX	5
3		XXX	3
4		XXXXXXXXXX	10
5		XXXXXXXXXX X	11
6		XXXX	4
7		XX	2
8	Camoruco 2	XXXX	4
9		XX	2
10		XXXXXX	6
11–12A		XXXX	4
11–12B		XX	2
13	Camoruco 1	XXXXXXXXXX X	11
14		XXXXXXXXXX XXXXXXXXXX	20
15		XXXXXXXXXX	10
16	Corozal 3	XXXXX	5
17		XXX	3
21	Corozal 2	—	0
22		—	0
23		—	0
24	Corozal 1	—	0
25		—	0
26		—	0

TABLE 61 • CONT'D

LEVEL	PHASE	NUMBER OF EXAMPLES (X = 1)	TOTAL: 106
16–17	Skeleton 1	—	0
18	Skeleton 2	xxx	3
18–19	Skeleton 3	—	0
18–22	Skeleton 4	—	0
25	Feature	—	0
25	Skeleton 2	—	0
25	Skeleton 3	—	0

STATISTICAL SIGNIFICANCE OF FREQUENCY DISTRIBUTION BY PHASE

Excavation X^2 = 33.12
Camoruco 3/Camoruco 2 X^2 = 2.53
Camoruco 2/Camoruco 1 X^2 = 2.40
Camoruco 1/Corozal 3 X^2 = 0.24
Corozal 3/Corozal 2 X^2 = 14.23

Table 62. Percentages of mode #160, circle-stamp motif, Excavation 3

LEVEL	PHASE	PERCENT OF TOTAL SHERDS IN LEVEL (X = .1%)
—1—	—Recent—	(05.56)
2	Camoruco 3	01.10 XXXXXXXXXXX X
3		00.83 XXXXXXXX
4		01.27 XXXXXXXXXX XXX
5		01.47 XXXXXXXXXXXX XXXXXX
6		00.74 XXXXXXXX
—7—		00.34 XXX
8	Camoruco 2	00.80 XXXXXXXX
9		00.49 XXXXX
10		00.67 XXXXXXX
11–12A		00.94 XXXXXXXXXX
11–12B		00.56 XXXXXXX
13	Camoruco 1	00.88 XXXXXXXXX
14		01.39 XXXXXXXXXX XXXX
—15—		00.87 XXXXXXXXX
16	Corozal 3	02.72 XXXXXXXXXX XXXXXXXXXX XXXXXXX
17		00.54 XXXXXX
—21—		00.00 —
22	Corozal 2	00.00 —
—23—		00.00 —
24	Corozal 1	00.00 —
25		00.00 —
26		(00.00)

TABLE 62 • CONT'D

LEVEL	PHASE	PERCENT OF TOTAL SHERDS IN LEVEL (X = .1%)
16–17	Skeleton 1	(00.00)
18	Skeleton 2	(06.82)
18–19	Skeleton 3	(00.00)
18–22	Skeleton 4	(00.00)
25	Feature	(00.00)
25	Skeleton 2	(00.00)
25	Skeleton 3	(00.00)

STATISTICAL SIGNIFICANCE OF PERCENT DIFFERENCES BY LEVEL

Levels 13/14: 1.25   Levels 13/16: 2.22
Levels 13/17: 0.76   Levels 14/16: 1.37
Levels 14/17: 1.60   Levels 16/17: 2.48
Levels 16/22: 4.26   Levels 16/23: 5.32
Levels 17/22: 1.89   Levels 17/23: 2.37

Table 63. Frequency of mode #40, Arauquinoid large human-effigy jars, Excavation 2

Level	Phase	Number of Examples (X = 1)	Total: 79
──1──	── Recent ──	—	0
2	Camoruco 3	XX	2
3		X	1
4		XXX	3
──5–6──	────────	XXXXXXXXX	9
7	Camoruco 2	XXXXXXXXXX XXXXXXXXXX	20
──8──	────────	XXXXXXXXXX X	11
9	Camoruco 1	XXXXXXX	7
10		XXXXXXXXXX XX	12
──11──	────────	XXXXXXXXX	9
──12──	── Corozal 3 ──	XX	2
13	Corozal 2	XX	2
──14──	────────	X	1
15	Corozal 1	—	0
16–16W		—	0
16E		—	0
17		—	0
18		—	0
19		—	0
20		—	0
16	West burial	—	0
16	Central burial	—	0
16	North burial	—	0
18	Child burial	—	0

Statistical Significance of Frequency Distribution by Phase

Excavation X^2 = 49.65
Camoruco 3/Camoruco 2 X^2 = 13.98
Camoruco 2/Camoruco 1 X^2 = 0.05
Camoruco 1/Corozal 3 X^2 = 3.72
Corozal 3/Corozal 2 X^2 = 2.46

Table 64. Percentages of mode #40, Arauquinoid large human-effigy jars, Excavation 2

Level	Phase	Percent of Total Sherds in Level (X = .1%)	
1	Recent	(00.00)	
2	Camoruco 3	00.17	XX
3		00.11	X
4		00.37	XXXX
5–6		00.61	XXXXXXX
7	Camoruco 2	01.28	XXXXXXXXXXXX XXX
8		01.03	XXXXXXXXXX
9	Camoruco 1	01.15	XXXXXXXXXXXX XX
10		00.76	XXXXXXXX
11		01.27	XXXXXXXXXXXX XXX
12	Corozal 3	00.16	XX
13	Corozal 2	00.17	XX
14		00.06	X
15	Corozal 1	00.00	—
16–16W		00.00	—
16E		00.00	—
17		00.00	—
18		00.00	—
19		(00.00)	
20		(00.00)	

TABLE 64 • CONT'D

LEVEL	PHASE	PERCENT OF TOTAL SHERDS IN LEVEL ($X = .1\%$)
16	West burial	(00.00)
16	Central burial	(00.00)
16	North burial	(00.00)
18	Child burial	(00.00)

STATISTICAL SIGNIFICANCE OF PERCENT DIFFERENCES BY LEVEL

Levels 2/3: 0.40   Levels 3/4: 1.14   Levels 4/5–6: 0.77
Levels 5–6/7: 1.90   Levels 7/8: 0.58   Levels 7/9: 0.23
Levels 7/10: 1.45   Levels 8/9: 0.24   Levels 9/10: 0.89
Levels 10/12: 2.26   Levels 12/13: 0.09   Levels 13/14: 0.93
Levels 14/15: 0.67

Table 65. Frequency of mode #40, Arauquinoid large human-effigy jars, Excavation 3

Level	Phase	Number of Examples (X = 1)	Total: 91
1	Recent	—	0
2	Camoruco 3	—	0
3		—	0
4		X	1
5		X	1
6		X	1
7		XXX	3
8	Camoruco 2	XXX	3
9		XXX	3
10		XXXXXXXXXX XXXX	14
11–12A		XXXXXXXXX	9
11–12B		XXX	3
13	Camoruco 1	XXXXXXXXXX XXXXXXXXXX XX	22
14		XXXXXXXXXX XXXXXXX	17
15		XXX	3
16	Corozal 3	X	1
17		XX	2
21		—	0
22	Corozal 2	—	0
23		XXX	3
24	Corozal 1	X	1
25		XX	2
26		—	0

TABLE 65 • CONT'D

LEVEL	PHASE	NUMBER OF EXAMPLES (X = 1)	TOTAL: 91
16–17	Skeleton 1	—	0
18	Skeleton 2	—	0
18–19	Skeleton 3	XX	2
18–22	Skeleton 4	—	0
25	Feature	—	0
25	Skeleton 2	—	0
25	Skeleton 3	—	0

STATISTICAL SIGNIFICANCE OF FREQUENCY DISTRIBUTION BY PHASE

Excavation X^2 = 54.54
Camoruco 3/Camoruco 2 X^2 = 23.29
Camoruco 2/Camoruco 1 X^2 = 0.00
Camoruco 1/Corozal 3 X^2 = 9.14

Table 66. Percentages of mode #40, Arauquinoid large human-effigy jars, Excavation 3

Level	Phase	Percent of Total Sherds in Level (X = .1%)	
1	Recent	(00.00)	
2	Camoruco 3	00.00	—
3		00.00	—
4		00.13	X
5		00.13	X
6		00.19	XX
7		00.51	XXXXX
8	Camoruco 2	00.60	XXXXXX
9		00.73	XXXXXXX
10		01.56	XXXXXXXXXX XXXXXX
11–12A		02.12	XXXXXXXXXXX XXXXXXXXXX X
11–12B		00.84	XXXXXXXXX
13	Camoruco 1	01.75	XXXXXXXXXX XXXXXXXX
14		01.18	XXXXXXXXXX XX
15		00.26	XXX
16	Corozal 3	00.54	XXXXXX
17		00.36	XXXX
21		00.00	—
22	Corozal 2	00.00	—
23		00.29	XXX
24	Corozal 1	00.16	XX
25		00.48	XXXXX
26		(00.00)	

TABLE 66 • CONT'D

LEVEL	PHASE	PERCENT OF TOTAL SHERDS IN LEVEL (X = .1%)
16–17	Skeleton 1	(00.00)
18	Skeleton 2	(00.00)
18–19	Skeleton 3	(03.51)
18–22	Skeleton 4	(00.00)
25	Feature	(00.00)
25	Skeleton 2	(00.00)
25	Skeleton 3	(00.00)

STATISTICAL SIGNIFICANCE OF PERCENT DIFFERENCES BY LEVEL

Levels 3/5: 0.70
Levels 5/6: 0.23
Levels 6/9: 1.28
Levels 10/11–12A: 0.73
Levels 11–12B/13: 1.23
Levels 14/16: 0.78
Levels 17/22: 1.55

Levels 4/5: 0.04
Levels 6/8: 1.08
Levels 6/10: 2.48
Levels 10/11–12B: 0.99
Levels 13/14: 1.23
Levels 16/17: 0.34
Levels 17/23: 0.24

Table 67. Frequency of mode #32, Arauquinoid small human-effigy jars, Excavation 2

Level	Phase	Number of Examples (X = 1)	Total: 19
1	Recent	—	0
2	Camoruco 3	XXXX	4
3		XX	2
4		XXXXX	5
5–6		XXXXXX	6
7	Camoruco 2	—	0
8		—	0
9	Camoruco 1	X	1
10		—	0
11		X	1
12	Corozal 3	—	0
13	Corozal 2	—	0
14		—	0
15	Corozal 1	—	0
16–16W		—	0
16E		—	0
17		—	0
18		—	0
19		—	0
20		—	0
16	West burial	—	0
16	Central burial	—	0
16	North burial	—	0
18	Child burial	—	0

STATISTICAL SIGNIFICANCE OF FREQUENCY DISTRIBUTION BY PHASE

Camoruco 3/Camoruco 2 $X^2 = 4.97$

Table 68. Percentages of mode #32, Arauquinoid small human-effigy jars, Excavation 2

Level	Phase	Percent of Total Sherds in Level	(X = .1%)
— 1 —	Recent	(00.00)	
2	Camoruco 3	00.35	XXXX
3		00.21	XX
4		00.61	XXXXXX
— 5-6 —		00.41	XXXX
7	Camoruco 2	00.00	—
— 8 —		00.00	—
9	Camoruco 1	00.16	XX
10		00.00	—
— 11 —		00.14	X
— 12 —	Corozal 3	00.00	—
13	Corozal 2	00.00	—
— 14 —		00.00	—
15	Corozal 1	00.00	—
16–16W		00.00	—
16E		00.00	—
17		00.00	—
18		00.00	—
19		(00.00)	
20		(00.00)	

TABLE 68 • CONT'D

LEVEL	PHASE	PERCENT OF TOTAL SHERDS IN LEVEL ($X = .1\%$)
16	West burial	(00.00)
16	Central burial	(00.00)
16	North burial	(00.00)
18	Child burial	(00.00)

STATISTICAL SIGNIFICANCE OF PERCENT DIFFERENCES BY LEVEL

Levels 2/3: 0.57	Levels 2/4: 0.85	Levels 3/7: 1.83
Levels 3/4: 1.32	Levels 3/8: 1.51	Levels 4/7: 3.10
Levels 4/8: 2.56	Levels 8/9: 1.33	Levels 9/10: 1.61
Levels 9/12: 1.44		

Table 69. Frequency of mode #32, Arauquinoid small human-effigy jars, Excavation 3

Level	Phase	Number of Examples (X = 1)	Total: 35
1	Recent	—	0
2	Camoruco 3	XXXXX	5
3		XX	2
4		XXXXXXXX	8
5		XXXXXXXXXX XXX	13
6		XXX	3
7		X	1
8	Camoruco 2	—	0
9		—	0
10		XX	2
11–12A		—	0
11–12B		—	0
13	Camoruco 1	X	1
14		—	0
15		—	0
16	Corozal 3	—	0
17		—	0
21		—	0
22	Corozal 2	—	0
23		—	0
24	Corozal 1	—	0
25		—	0
26		—	0
16–17	Skeleton 1	—	0
18	Skeleton 2	—	0
18–19	Skeleton 3	—	0
18–22	Skeleton 4	—	0
25	Feature	—	0
25	Skeleton 2	—	0
25	Skeleton 3	—	0

Statistical significance of frequency distribution by phase

Excavation X^2 = 92.02
Camoruco 3/Camoruco 2 X^2 = 20.30

Table 70. Percentages of mode #32, Arauquinoid small human-effigy jars, Excavation 3

LEVEL	PHASE	PERCENT OF TOTAL SHERDS IN LEVEL (X = .1%)
1	— Recent —	(00.00)
2	Camoruco 3	01.10 XXXXXXXXXXX X
3		00.55 XXXXXX
4		01.02 XXXXXXXXXX
5		01.74 XXXXXXXXXX XXXXXXX
6		00.56 XXXXXXX
7		00.17 XX
8	Camoruco 2	00.00 —
9		00.00 —
10		00.22 XX
11–12A		00.00 —
11–12B		00.00 —
13	Camoruco 1	00.08 X
14		00.00 —
15		00.00 —
16	Corozal 3	00.00 —
17		00.00 —
21		00.00 —
22	Corozal 2	00.00 —
23		00.00 —
24	Corozal 1	00.00 —
25		00.00 —
26		(00.00)

TABLE 70 • CONT'D

LEVEL	PHASE	PERCENT OF TOTAL SHERDS IN LEVEL ($X = .1\%$)
16–17	Skeleton 1	(00.00)
18	Skeleton 2	(00.00)
18–19	Skeleton 3	(00.00)
18–22	Skeleton 4	(00.00)
25	Feature	(00.00)
25	Skeleton 2	(00.00)
25	Skeleton 3	(00.00)

STATISTICAL SIGNIFICANCE OF PERCENT DIFFERENCES BY LEVEL

Levels 2/3: 0.84	Levels 3/4: 0.78
Levels 3/9: 1.51	Levels 4/5: 1.22
Levels 4/9: 2.05	Levels 5/6: 1.89
Levels 6/7: 1.10	Levels 6/8: 1.67
Levels 6/9: 1.51	Levels 7/8: 0.92
Levels 7/9: 0.83	Levels 7/10: 0.23
Levels 8/10: 1.05	Levels 9/10: 0.96
Levels 10/11–12A: 0.97	Levels 10/13: 0.88
Levels 13/16: 0.38	

Table 71. Frequency of mode #136, Arauquinoid human bowl rim lugs, Excavation 2

LEVEL	PHASE	NUMBER OF EXAMPLES (X = 1)	TOTAL: 63
1	Recent	—	0
2	Camoruco 3	XXXXXXXXXX XXXXXXXXX	19
3		XXXXXXXXXX XXXXXXXXX	19
4		XX	2
5–6		XXXXXXXXXX XXXXX	15
7	Camoruco 2	XXXX	4
8		X	1
9	Camoruco 1	—	0
10		XX	2
11		—	0
12	Corozal 3	X	1
13	Corozal 2	—	0
14		—	0
15	Corozal 1	—	0
16–16W		—	0
16E		—	0
17		—	0
18		—	0
19		—	0
20		—	0
16	West burial	—	0
16	Central burial	—	0
16	North burial	—	0
18	Child burial	—	0

STATISTICAL SIGNIFICANCE OF FREQUENCY DISTRIBUTION BY PHASE

Excavation X^2 = 102.51
Camoruco 3/Camoruco 2 X^2 = 17.32
Camoruco 2/Camoruco 1 X^2 = 3.61

Table 72. Percentages of mode #136, Arauquinoid human bowl rim lugs, Excavation 2

Level	Phase	Percent of Total Sherds in Level (X = .1%)	
1	Recent	(00.00)	
2	Camoruco 3	01.66	XXXXXXXXXXXXXXXXX
3		02.03	XXXXXXXXXXXXXXXXXXXX
4		00.24	XX
5–6		01.02	XXXXXXXXXX
7	Camoruco 2	00.26	XXX
8		00.09	X
9	Camoruco 1	00.00	—
10		00.13	X
11		00.00	—
12	Corozal 3	00.08	X
13	Corozal 2	00.00	—
14		00.00	—
15	Corozal 1	00.00	—
16–16W		00.00	—
16E		00.00	—
17		00.00	—
18		00.00	—
19		(00.00)	
20		(00.00)	

TABLE 72 • CONT'D

LEVEL	PHASE	PERCENT OF TOTAL SHERDS IN LEVEL (X = .1%)
16	West burial	(00.00)
16	Central burial	(00.00)
16	North burial	(00.00)
18	Child burial	(00.00)

STATISTICAL SIGNIFICANCE OF PERCENT DIFFERENCES BY LEVEL

Levels 2/3: 0.63	Levels 2/7: 3.93	Levels 3/4: 3.43
Levels 3/8: 4.36	Levels 3/5–6: 2.06	Levels 4/5–6: 2.06
Levels 4/7: 0.05	Levels 4/8: 0.82	Levels 5–6/7: 2.66
Levels 5–6/8: 2.91	Levels 7/8: 0.94	Levels 7/9: 1.25
Levels 7/10: 0.83	Levels 9/10: 0.88	Levels 9/12: 0.70
Levels 12/13: 0.96	Levels 12/14: 1.17	

Table 73. Frequency of mode #136, Arauquinoid human bowl rim lugs, Excavation 3

Level	Phase	Number of Examples (X = 1)	Total: 70
1	Recent	X	1
2	Camoruco 3	XXXXXX	6
3		XXXXXXXXXX	10
4		XXXXXXXXXX XXXX	14
5		XXXXXXXX	8
6		XXXXXXXXXX	10
7		XXXXXXX	7
8	Camoruco 2	XXXXXXXX	8
9		—	0
10		—	0
11–12A		—	0
11–12B		—	0
13	Camoruco 1	XX	2
14		XX	2
15		X	1
16	Corozal 3	—	0
17		X	1
21		—	0
22	Corozal 2	—	0
23		—	0
24	Corozal 1	—	0
25		—	0
26		—	0
16–17	Skeleton 1	—	0
18	Skeleton 2	—	0
18–19	Skeleton 3	—	0
18–22	Skeleton 4	—	0
25	Feature	—	0
25	Skeleton 2	—	0
25	Skeleton 3	—	0

Statistical significance of frequency distribution by phase

Excavation X^2 = 113.89
Camoruco 3/Camoruco 2 X^2 = 20.09
Camoruco 2/Camoruco 1 X^2 = 3.06

Table 74. Percentages of mode #136, Arauquinoid human bowl rim lugs, Excavation 3

LEVEL	PHASE	PERCENT OF TOTAL SHERDS IN LEVEL (X = .1%)	
1	— Recent —	(05.56)	
2	Camoruco 3	01.32	XXXXXXXXXXX XXX
3		02.77	XXXXXXXXXX XXXXXXXXXXX XXXXXXXXX
4		01.78	XXXXXXXXXX XXXXXXXX
5		01.07	XXXXXXXXXX X
6		01.86	XXXXXXXXXX XXXXXXXXX
7		01.18	XXXXXXXXXX XX
8	Camoruco 2	01.61	XXXXXXXXXX XXXXXX
9		00.00	—
10		00.00	—
11–12A		00.00	—
11–12B		00.00	—
13	Camoruco 1	00.16	XX
14		00.14	X
15		00.09	X
16	Corozal 3	00.00	—
17		00.18	XX
21		00.00	—
22	Corozal 2	00.00	—
23		00.00	—
24	Corozal 1	00.00	—
25		00.00	
26		(00.00)	

TABLE 74 • CONT'D

LEVEL	PHASE	PERCENT OF TOTAL SHERDS IN LEVEL (X = .1%)
16–17	Skeleton 1	(00.00)
18	Skeleton 2	(00.00)
18–19	Skeleton 3	(00.00)
18–22	Skeleton 4	(00.00)
25	Feature	(00.00)
25	Skeleton 2	(00.00)
25	Skeleton 3	(00.00)

STATISTICAL SIGNIFICANCE OF PERCENT DIFFERENCES BY LEVEL

Levels 2/3: 1.49	Levels 3/4: 1.09	Levels 3/8: 1.17
Levels 4/5: 1.17	Levels 4/8: 0.22	Levels 5/6: 1.18
Levels 5/8: 0.83	Levels 6/7: 0.94	Levels 6/8: 0.30
Levels 6/9: 2.78	Levels 6/16: 1.86	Levels 6/17: 2.78
Levels 7/8: 0.61	Levels 7/9: 2.21	Levels 7/22: 2.80
Levels 8/9: 2.58	Levels 8/10: 3.81	Levels 8/11–12A: 2.62
Levels 8/13: 3.63	Levels 8/14: 3.94	Levels 10/13: 1.20
Levels 10/14: 1.12	Levels 13/14: 0.14	Levels 14/22: 0.96
Levels 16/17: 0.58		

Table 75. Frequency of mode #57, modeled limbs, Excavation 2

Level	Phase	Number of Examples (X = 1)	Total: 54
1	Recent	—	0
2	Camoruco 3	XXXXXXXXXX XXXXXXX	17
3		XXXXXXXXXX XXXXX	15
4		XXX	3
5–6		XXXXXXXXXX XX	12
7	Camoruco 2	XXX	3
8		X	1
9	Camoruco 1	—	0
10		XX	2
11		—	0
12	Corozal 3	X	1
13	Corozal 2	—	0
14		—	0
15	Corozal 1	—	0
16–16W		—	0
16E		—	0
17		—	0
18		—	0
19		—	0
20		—	0
16	West burial	—	0
16	Central burial	—	0
16	North burial	—	0
18	Child burial	—	0

STATISTICAL SIGNIFICANCE OF FREQUENCY DISTRIBUTION BY PHASE

Excavation X^2 = 86.60
Camoruco 3/Camoruco 2 X^2 = 14.99
Camoruco 2/Camoruco 1 X^2 = 2.41

Table 76. Percentages of mode #57, modeled limbs, Excavation 2

Level	Phase	Percent of Total Sherds in Level (X = .1%)	
1	— Recent —	(00.00)	
2	Camoruco 3	01.48	XXXXXXXXXXXX XXXXX
3		01.60	XXXXXXXXXX XXXXXX
4		00.37	XXXX
5-6		00.81	XXXXXXXX
7	Camoruco 2	00.19	XX
8		00.09	X
9	Camoruco 1	00.00	—
10		00.13	X
11		00.00	—
12	Corozal 3	00.08	X
13	Corozal 2	00.00	—
14		00.00	—
15	Corozal 1	00.00	—
16–16W		00.00	—
16E		00.00	—
17		00.00	—
18		00.00	—
19		(00.00)	—
20		(00.00)	—

TABLE 76 • CONT'D

LEVEL	PHASE	PERCENT OF TOTAL SHERDS IN LEVEL ($X = .1\%$)
16	West burial	(00.00)
16	Central burial	(00.00)
16	North burial	(00.00)
18	Child burial	(00.00)

STATISTICAL SIGNIFICANCE OF PERCENT DIFFERENCES BY LEVEL

Levels 2/3: 0.22	Levels 2/4: 2.43	Levels 3/4: 2.56
Levels 4/5–6: 1.27	Levels 4/7: 0.81	Levels 4/8: 1.28
Levels 7/8: 0.64	Levels 8/9: 0.75	Levels 8/10: 0.25
Levels 11/12: 0.75	Levels 12/13: 0.96	Levels 12/14: 1.17
Levels 12/15: 0.78		

Table 77. Frequency of mode #57, modeled limbs, Excavation 3

Level	Phase	Number of Examples (X = 1)	Total: 61
1	— Recent —	X	1
2	Camoruco 3	XXXX	4
3		XXXXXXXXX	10
4		XXXXXXXXXX XX	12
5		XXXXXXXX	8
6		XXXXXXX	7
7		XXXX	4
8	Camoruco 2	XXXXXXX	7
9		X	1
10		—	0
11–12A		—	0
11–12B		—	0
13	Camoruco 1	XXX	3
14		XX	2
15		X	1
16	Corozal 3	—	0
17		X	1
21		—	0
22	Corozal 2	—	0
23		—	0
24	Corozal 1	—	0
25		—	0
26		—	0
16–17	Skeleton 1	—	0
18	Skeleton 2	—	0
18–19	Skeleton 3	—	0
18–22	Skeleton 4	—	0
25	Feature	—	0
25	Skeleton 2	—	0
25	Skeleton 3	—	0

Statistical significance of frequency distribution by phase

Excavation X^2 = 87.08
Camoruco 3/Camoruco 2 X^2 = 15.19
Camoruco 2/Camoruco 1 X^2 = 1.55

Table 78. Percentages of mode #57, modeled limbs, Excavation 3

Level	Phase	Percent of Total Sherds in Level (X = .1%)	
1	Recent	(05.56)	
2	Camoruco 3	00.88	XXXXXXXXX
3		02.77	XXXXXXXXXX XXXXXXXXXX XXXXXXXX
4		01.52	XXXXXXXXXX XXXXX
5		01.07	XXXXXXXXXX X
6		01.30	XXXXXXXXXX XXX
7		00.67	XXXXXXXX
8	Camoruco 2	01.41	XXXXXXXXXX XXXX
9		00.24	XX
10		00.00	—
11–12A		00.00	—
11–12B		00.00	—
13	Camoruco 1	00.24	XX
14		00.14	X
15		00.09	X
16	Corozal 3	00.00	—
17		00.18	XX
21		00.00	—
22	Corozal 2	00.00	—
23		00.00	—
24	Corozal 1	00.00	—
25		00.00	—
26		(00.00)	

TABLE 78 • CONT'D

LEVEL	PHASE	PERCENT OF TOTAL SHERDS IN LEVEL ($X = .1\%$)
16–17	Skeleton 1	(00.00)
18	Skeleton 2	(00.00)
18–19	Skeleton 3	(00.00)
18–22	Skeleton 4	(00.00)
25	Feature	(00.00)
25	Skeleton 2	(00.00)
25	Skeleton 3	(00.00)

STATISTICAL SIGNIFICANCE OF PERCENT DIFFERENCES BY LEVEL

Levels 2/3: 2.07	Levels 3/4: 1.43	Levels 4/5: 0.78
Levels 5/6: 0.38	Levels 6/8: 0.15	Levels 8/9: 1.87
Levels 9/10: 1.48	Levels 11–12B/13: 0.92	Levels 13/14: 0.60
Levels 14/15: 0.39	Levels 14/17: 0.21	Levels 16/17: 0.58

Table 79. Frequency of mode #212, everted and/or beveled open bowl rims, Excavation 2

Level	Phase	Number of Examples (X = 1)	Total: 167
1	Recent	—	0
2	Camoruco 3	XXXXXXXXXX XXXXXXXXXX XXXXXXXXXX XXXXXXX	37
3		XXXXXXXXXX XXXXXXXXXX	20
4		XXXXXXXXXX XXXXX	15
5–6		XXXXXXXXXX XXXX	14
7	Camoruco 2	XXXXXXXXXX XXXXXXXXXX X	21
8		XXXXXXXXXX X	11
9	Camoruco 1	XXXXXXXXXX	10
10		XXXXXXXXXX XXXXXXXXXX XXX	23
11		XXX	3
12	Corozal 3	XX	2
13	Corozal 2	X	1
14		XXXXXXX	7
15	Corozal 1	XXX	3
16–16W		—	0
16E		—	0
17		—	0
18		—	0
19		—	0
20		—	0

TABLE 78 • CONT'D

LEVEL	PHASE	NUMBER OF EXAMPLES ($X = 1$)	TOTAL: 167
16	West burial	—	0
16	Central burial	—	0
16	North burial	—	0
18	Child burial	—	0

STATISTICAL SIGNIFICANCE OF FREQUENCY DISTRIBUTION BY PHASE

Excavation X^2 = 81.84
Camoruco 3/Camoruco 2 X^2 = 9.56
Camoruco 2/Camoruco 1 X^2 = 0.41
Camoruco 1/Corozal 3 X^2 = 14.10
Corozal 3/Corozal 2 X^2 = 0.09
Corozal 2/Corozal 1 X^2 = 0.06

Table 80. Percentages of mode #212, everted and/or beveled open bowl rims, Excavation 2

Level	Phase	Percent of Total Sherds in Level (X = .1%)	
1	Recent	(00.00)	
2	Camoruco 3	03.23	XXXXXXXXXXX XXXXXXXXXX XXXXXXXXXXX XX
3		02.14	XXXXXXXXXXX XXXXXXXXXX X
4		01.84	XXXXXXXXXXX XXXXXXXXX
5–6		00.95	XXXXXXXXXX
7	Camoruco 2	01.34	XXXXXXXXXXX XXX
8		01.03	XXXXXXXXXX
9	Camoruco 1	01.65	XXXXXXXXXXX XXXXXXX
10		01.45	XXXXXXXXXXX XXXXX
11		00.42	XXXX
12	Corozal 3	00.16	XX
13	Corozal 2	00.09	X
14		00.41	XXXX
15	Corozal 1	00.39	XXXX
16–16W		00.00	—
16E		00.00	—
17		00.00	—
18		00.00	—
19		(00.00)	
20		(00.00)	

TABLE 80 • CONT'D

Level	Phase	Percent of Total Sherds in Level ($X = .1\%$)
16	West burial	(00.00)
16	Central burial	(00.00)
16	North burial	(00.00)
18	Child burial	(00.00)

STATISTICAL SIGNIFICANCE OF PERCENT DIFFERENCES BY LEVEL

Levels 2/3: 1.52	Levels 3/4: 0.45	Levels 4/5–6: 1.82
Levels 5–6/7: 1.02	Levels 9/10: 0.33	Levels 9/11: 2.24
Levels 9/14: 3.06	Levels 10/11: 2.15	Levels 11/13: 1.52
Levels 11/14: 0.04	Levels 13/14: 1.60	Levels 14/15: 0.07
Levels 15/16E: 0.79		

Table 81. Frequency of mode #212, everted and/or beveled open bowl rims, Excavation 3

Level	Phase	Number of Examples (X = 1)	Total: 190
1	Recent	—	0
2	Camoruco 3	XXXXX	5
3		XXXXXXXXXXX XXXXXX	16
4		XXXXXXXXXX XXXX	14
5		XXXXXXXXXX XXXXXXXXXX XXXXXXXXXX X	31
6		XXXXXXXXXX XXX	13
7		XXXXXXXXXX XXXXX	15
8	Camoruco 2	XXXXXXXXXX	10
9		XXXXXXXXXX	10
10		XXXXXXXXXX XXXXXXXXXX XXXXXXX	27
11–12A		XXXX	4
11–12B		XXXX	4
13	Camoruco 1	XXXXXXXXXX XXXXXXX	17
14		XXXXXXXXX	9
15		XX	2
16	Corozal 3	—	0
17		—	0
23		—	0
22	Corozal 2	X	1
23		XXXXXXX	7
24	Corozal 1	XXX	3
25		XX	2
26		—	0

TABLE 81 • CONT'D

LEVEL	PHASE	NUMBER OF EXAMPLES (X = 1)	TOTAL: 190
16–17	Skeleton 1	—	0
18	Skeleton 2	—	0
18–19	Skeleton 3	—	0
18–22	Skeleton 4	—	0
25	Feature	—	0
25	Skeleton 2	—	0
25	Skeleton 3	—	0

STATISTICAL SIGNIFICANCE OF FREQUENCY DISTRIBUTION BY PHASE

$$\begin{aligned}
\text{Excavation } X^2 &= 101.88 \\
\text{Camoruco 3/Camoruco 2 } X^2 &= 1.27 \\
\text{Camoruco 2/Camoruco 1 } X^2 &= 19.24 \\
\text{Camoruco 1/Corozal 3 } X^2 &= 9.06 \\
\text{Corozal 3/Corozal 2 } X^2 &= 2.79 \\
\text{Corozal 2/Corozal 1 } X^2 &= 0.03
\end{aligned}$$

Table 82. Percentages of mode #212, everted and/or beveled open bowl rims, Excavation 3

Level	Phase	Percent of Total Sherds in Level (X = .1%)	
1	Recent	(00.00)	
2	Camoruco 3	01.10	XXXXXXXXXX X
3		04.43	XXXXXXXXXX XXXXXXXXXX XXXXXXXXXX XXXXXXXXXX+
4		01.78	XXXXXXXXXX XXXXXXXX
5		04.14	XXXXXXXXXX XXXXXXXXXX XXXXXXXXXX XXXXXXXXXX+
6		02.41	XXXXXXXXXX XXXXXXXXXX XXXX
7		02.53	XXXXXXXXXX XXXXXXXXXX XXXXX
8	Camoruco 2	02.01	XXXXXXXXXX XXXXXXXXXX
9		02.43	XXXXXXXXXX XXXXXXXXXX XXXX
10		03.01	XXXXXXXXXX XXXXXXXXXX XXXXXXXXXX
11–12A		00.94	XXXXXXXXX
11–12B		01.12	XXXXXXXXXX X
13	Camoruco 1	01.35	XXXXXXXXXX XXXX
14		00.63	XXXXXX
15		00.17	XX
16	Corozal 3	00.00	—
17		00.00	—
21		00.00	—
22	Corozal 2	00.15	XX
23		00.67	XXXXXXX
24	Corozal 1	00.47	XXXXX
25		00.48	XXXXX
26		(00.00)	

TABLE 82 • CONT'D

LEVEL	PHASE	PERCENT OF TOTAL SHERDS IN LEVEL ($X = .1\%$)
16–17	Skeleton 1	(00.00)
18	Skeleton 2	(00.00)
18–19	Skeleton 3	(00.00)
18–22	Skeleton 4	(00.00)
25	Feature	(00.00)
25	Skeleton 2	(00.00)
25	Skeleton 3	(00.00)

STATISTICAL SIGNIFICANCE OF PERCENT DIFFERENCES BY LEVEL

Levels 2/3: 2.99 Levels 2/4: 0.94
Levels 3/4: 2.62 Levels 6/7: 0.12
Levels 7/8: 0.56 Levels 9/10: 0.58
Levels 10/11–12A: 2.32 Levels 11–12A/11–12B: 0.25
Levels 11–12B/13: 0.34 Levels 13/14: 1.93
Levels 14/15: 1.76 Levels 15/16: 0.56

Table 83. Frequency of mode #213, flat, angled bowl bases, Excavation 2

Level	Phase	Number of Examples (X = 1)	Total: 53
1	Recent	—	0
2	Camoruco 3	—	0
3		—	0
4		X	1
5–6		X	1
7	Camoruco 2	XXXXXXXX	8
8		XXX	3
9	Camoruco 1	—	0
10		XXXXXX	6
11		XX	2
12	Corozal 3	XXXXXXXXXX XXXX	14
13	Corozal 2	XXXXX	5
14		XXXXXXXX	8
15	Corozal 1	XXX	3
16–16W		X	1
16E		—	0
17		—	0
18		X	1
19		—	0
20		—	0
16	West burial	—	0
16	Central burial	—	0
16	North burial	—	0
18	Child burial	—	0

Statistical significance of frequency distribution by phase

Excavation X^2 = 27.25
Camoruco 3/Camoruco 2 X^2 = 5.76
Camoruco 2/Camoruco 1 X^2 = 0.01
Camoruco 1/Corozal 3 X^2 = 6.87
Corozal 3/Corozal 2 X^2 = 3.03
Corozal 2/Corozal 1 X^2 = 0.18

Table 84. Percentages of mode #213, flat, angled bowl bases, Excavation 2

Level	Phase	Percent of Total Sherds in Level (X = .1%)	
1	Recent	(00.00)	
2	Camoruco 3	00.00	—
3		00.00	—
4		00.12	X
5-6		00.07	X
7	Camoruco 2	00.51	XXXXX
8		00.28	XXX
9	Camoruco 1	00.00	—
10		00.38	XXXX
11		00.28	XXX
12	Corozal 3	01.12	XXXXXXXXXXX X
13	Corozal 2	00.44	XXXX
14		00.47	XXXXX
15	Corozal 1	00.39	XXXX
16–16W		00.30	XXX
16E		00.00	—
17		00.00	—
18		00.78	XXXXXXXX
19		(00.00)	
20		(00.00)	

TABLE 84 • CONT'D

LEVEL	PHASE	PERCENT OF TOTAL SHERDS IN LEVEL ($X = .1\%$)
16	West burial	(00.00)
16	Central burial	(00.00)
16	North burial	(00.00)
18	Child burial	(00.00)

STATISTICAL SIGNIFICANCE OF PERCENT DIFFERENCES BY LEVEL

Levels 2/7: 2.42	Levels 2/8: 1.79	Levels 2/10: 2.09
Levels 4/7: 1.47	Levels 7/8: 0.90	Levels 8/9: 1.31
Levels 9/10: 1.52	Levels 10/12: 2.33	Levels 14/18: 0.49
Levels 16–16W/18: 0.70	Levels 17/18: 0.95	

Table 85. Frequency of mode #213, flat, angled bowl bases, Excavation 3

LEVEL	PHASE	NUMBER OF EXAMPLES (X = 1)	TOTAL: 43
1	Recent	—	0
2	Camoruco 3	—	0
3		—	0
4		—	0
5		—	0
6		—	0
7		—	0
8	Camoruco 2	—	0
9		x	1
10		XXXXXXX	7
11–12A		XX	2
11–12B		—	0
13	Camoruco 1	XXX	3
14		XX	2
15		XXX	3
16	Corozal 3	—	0
17		XXXXXXX	7
21		XXX	3
22	Corozal 2	XXXXX	5
23		XX	2
24	Corozal 1	X	1
25		XX	2
26		—	0

TABLE 85 • CONT'D

LEVEL	PHASE	NUMBER OF EXAMPLES ($X = 1$)	TOTAL: 43
16–17	Skeleton 1	—	0
18	Skeleton 2	XXXX	4
18–19	Skeleton 3	—	0
18–22	Skeleton 4	—	0
25	Feature	—	0
25	Skeleton 2	—	0
25	Skeleton 3	X	1

STATISTICAL SIGNIFICANCE OF FREQUENCY DISTRIBUTION BY PHASE

Excavation X^2 = 20.53
Camoruco 3/Camoruco 2 X^2 = 9.79
Camoruco 2/Camoruco 1 X^2 = 0.98
Camoruco 1/Corozal 3 X^2 = 5.37
Corozal 3/Corozal 2 X^2 = 0.53
Corozal 2/Corozal 1 X^2 = 0.13

Table 86. Percentages of mode #213, flat, angled bowl bases, Excavation 3

Level	Phase	Percent of Total Sherds in Level (X = .1%)	
1	Recent	(00.00)	
2	Camoruco 3	00.00	—
3		00.00	—
4		00.00	—
5		00.00	—
6		00.00	—
7		00.00	—
8	Camoruco 2	00.00	—
9		00.24	XX
10		00.78	XXXXXXXX
11–12A		00.47	XXXXX
11–12B		00.00	—
13	Camoruco 1	00.24	XX
14		00.14	X
15		00.26	XXX
16	Corozal 3	00.00	—
17		01.26	XXXXXXXXXXX XXX
21		00.88	XXXXXXXXX
22	Corozal 2	00.75	XXXXXXXX
23		00.19	XX
24	Corozal 1	00.16	XX
25		00.48	XXXXX
26		(00.00)	

TABLE 86 • CONT'D

LEVEL	PHASE	PERCENT OF TOTAL SHERDS IN LEVEL ($X = .1\%$)
16–17	Skeleton 1	(00.00)
18	Skeleton 2	(09.09)
18–19	Skeleton 3	(00.00)
18–22	Skeleton 4	(00.00)
25	Feature	(00.00)
25	Skeleton 2	(00.00)
25	Skeleton 3	(08.33)

STATISTICAL SIGNIFICANCE OF PERCENT DIFFERENCES BY LEVEL

Levels 3/9: 0.94 Levels 3/10: 1.68
Levels 5/9: 1.35 Levels 6/9: 1.15
Levels 8/9: 1.10 Levels 9/10: 1.16
Levels 14/15: 0.70 Levels 16/17: 1.53
Levels 21/22: 0.21 Levels 24/25: 0.95

Table 87. Frequency of mode #214, round bowl bases, Excavation 2

Level	Phase	Number of Examples (X = 1)	Total: 62
1		X	1
2	Camoruco 3	XXXXXXXX	8
3		XXXXXXXXX	9
4		XX	2
5–6		XXX	3
7	Camoruco 2	XXXX	4
8		XXX	3
9	Camoruco 1	X	1
10		XXXXX	5
11		—	0
12	Corozal 3	XX	2
13	Corozal 2	XXXXXXX	7
14		XXXXXXXXXX XXXX	14
15	Corozal 1	X	1
16–16W		XX	2
16E		—	0
17		—	0
18		—	0
19		—	0
20		—	0
16	West burial	—	0
16	Central burial	—	0
16	North burial	—	0
18	Child burial	—	0

Statistical significance of frequency distribution by phase

Excavation X^2 = 20.42
Camoruco 3/Camoruco 2 X^2 = 4.46
Camoruco 2/Camoruco 1 X^2 = 0.07
Corozal 3/Corozal 2 X^2 = 6.36
Corozal 2/Corozal 1 X^2 = 4.56

Table 88. Percentages of mode #214, round bowl bases, Excavation 2

Level	Phase	Percent of Total Sherds in Level (X = .1%)	
1	Recent	(01.23)	
2	Camoruco 3	00.70	XXXXXXX
3		00.96	XXXXXXXXXX
4		00.24	XX
5–6		00.20	XX
7	Camoruco 2	00.26	XXX
8		00.28	XXX
9	Camoruco 1	00.16	XX
10		00.32	XXX
11		00.00	—
12	Corozal 3	00.16	XX
13	Corozal 2	00.61	XXXXXX
14		00.82	XXXXXXXX
15	Corozal 1	00.13	X
16–16W		00.60	XXXXXX
16E		00.00	—
17		00.00	—
18		00.00	—
19		(00.00)	
20		(00.00)	

TABLE 88 • CONT'D

LEVEL	PHASE	PERCENT OF TOTAL SHERDS IN LEVEL ($X = .1\%$)
16	West burial	(00.00)
16	Central burial	(00.00)
16	North burial	(00.00)
18	Child burial	(00.00)

STATISTICAL SIGNIFICANCE OF PERCENT DIFFERENCES BY LEVEL

Levels 2/3: 0.67	Levels 2/7: 1.71	Levels 3/4: 1.90
Levels 7/8: 0.12	Levels 8/9: 0.47	Levels 10/12: 0.84
Levels 11/12: 1.06	Levels 12/13: 1.80	Levels 13/14: 0.65
Levels 13/15: 1.59	Levels 15/17: 0.39	Levels 16–16W/16E: 0.98

Table 89. Frequency of mode #214, round bowl bases, Excavation 3

LEVEL	PHASE	NUMBER OF EXAMPLES (X = 1)	TOTAL: 44
1	Recent	—	0
2	Camoruco 3	—	0
3		—	0
4		XXX	3
5		XXXXXX	6
6		—	0
7		XXX	3
8	Camoruco 2	X	1
9		—	0
10		XXXXX	5
11–12A		—	0
11–12B		XX	2
13	Camoruco 1	XXXXXX	6
14		XXX	3
15		—	0
16	Corozal 3	—	0
17		—	0
21		—	0
22	Corozal 2	XXXX	4
23		XXXXXXX	7
24	Corozal 1	XX	2
25		X	1
26		—	0

TABLE 89 • CONT'D

LEVEL	PHASE	NUMBER OF EXAMPLES (X = 1)	TOTAL: 44
16–17	Skeleton 1	—	0
18	Skeleton 2	—	0
18–19	Skeleton 3	—	0
18–22	Skeleton 4	—	0
25	Feature	—	0
25	Skeleton 2	—	0
25	Skeleton 3	X	1

STATISTICAL SIGNIFICANCE OF FREQUENCY DISTRIBUTION BY PHASE

$$\text{Excavation } X^2 = 9.49$$
$$\text{Camoruco 3/Camoruco 2 } X^2 = 0.01$$
$$\text{Camoruco 2/Camoruco 1 } X^2 = 0.04$$
$$\text{Camoruco 1/Corozal 3 } X^2 = 3.01$$
$$\text{Corozal 3/Corozal 2 } X^2 = 7.06$$
$$\text{Corozal 2/Corozal 1 } X^2 = 0.88$$

Table 90. Percentages of mode #214, round bowl bases, Excavation 3

LEVEL	PHASE	PERCENT OF TOTAL SHERDS IN LEVEL (X = .1%)	
1	Recent	(00.00)	
2	Camoruco 3	00.00	—
3		00.00	—
4		00.38	XXXX
5		00.80	XXXXXXXX
6		00.00	—
7		00.51	XXXXXX
8	Camoruco 2	00.20	XX
9		00.00	—
10		00.56	XXXXXXX
11–12A		00.00	—
11–12B		00.56	XXXXXXX
13	Camoruco 1	00.48	XXXXXX
14		00.21	XX
15		00.00	—
16	Corozal 3	00.00	—
17		00.00	—
21		00.00	—
22	Corozal 2	00.60	XXXXXX
23		00.67	XXXXXXX
24	Corozal 1	00.31	XXX
25		00.24	XX
26		(00.00)	

TABLE 90 • CONT'D

LEVEL	PHASE	PERCENT OF TOTAL SHERDS IN LEVEL (X = .1%)
16–17	Skeleton 1	(00.00)
18	Skeleton 2	(00.00)
18–19	Skeleton 3	(00.00)
18–22	Skeleton 4	(00.00)
25	Feature	(00.00)
25	Skeleton 2	(00.00)
25	Skeleton 3	(08.33)

STATISTICAL SIGNIFICANCE OF PERCENT DIFFERENCES BY LEVEL

Levels 3/4: 1.17   Levels 4/5: 1.08
Levels 5/6: 2.08   Levels 6/8: 1.04
Levels 8/9: 0.91   Levels 9/10: 1.52
Levels 10/11–12A: 1.54   Levels 10/13: 0.25
Levels 13/14: 1.21   Levels 14/16: 0.62
Levels 17/22: 1.83   Levels 22/23: 0.18
Levels 24/25: 0.23

References

ATHENS, J. S.
    1989   Pumpuentsa and the Pastaza Phase in Southeastern Ecuador. *Ñawpa Pacha* 24:1–19.

BARSE, W.
    1989   Preceramic Occupations in the Orinoco River Valley. *Science 250:*1388–90.

BENNETT, WENDELL C.
    1936   Excavations in Bolivia. *Anthropological Papers 35(4)*. American Museum of Natural History. New York.
    1937   Excavations at La Mata, Maracay, Venezuela. Anthropological Papers 36(2). American Museum of Natural History. New York.

BEZERRA DE MENESES, ULPIANO
    1972   *Arqueologia Amazônica (Santarem).* Museu de Arqueologia e Etnologia, Universidade de São Paulo. São Paulo.

BIRD, JUNIUS B.
    1943   Excavations in Northern Chile. *Anthropological Papers 38(4)*. American Museum of Natural History. New York.

BLACK, F. L., F. M. SALZANO, L. L. BERMAN, Y. GABBAY, T.A. WEIMER, M. H. L. P. FRANCO, AND J.P. PANDEY
    1983   Failure of Linguistic Relationships to Predict Genetic Distances between the Waiapi and Other Tribes of Lower Amazonia. *American Journal of Physical Anthropology 60:*327–335.

BOOMERT, ARIE
    1976   Precolumbian Raised Fields in Coastal Surinam. In *Proceedings of the Sixth International Congress for the Study of the Pre-Columbian Cultures of the Lesser Antilles. Guadeloupe,* pp. 134–144. University Presses of Florida. Gainsville.
    1980a   Hertenrits: An Arauquinoid Complex in North West Surinam. Part 1. *Journal of Archaeology and Anthropology 3(2):*68–104.
    1980b   The Sipaliwini Archaeological Complex of Surinam: A Summary. *Niew West-Indische Gids 54(2):*94–107.
    1983   The Saladoid Occupation of Wonotobo Falls, Western Surinam. In *Proceedings of the Ninth International Congress for the Study of the Pre-Columbian Cultures of the Lesser Antilles,* ed. by L. Allaire and F. Mayer, pp. 97–120. Centre de Recherches Caraïbes, Université of Montréal. Montreal.

BROCHADO, JOSE
1980 The Social Ecology of the Marajoara Culture. M.A. thesis, Department of Anthropology, University of Illinois, Urbana.

BROCHADO, JOSE, AND DONALD LATHRAP
MS Amazonia. University of Illinois. Urbana.

BURGER, R.
1984 *The Prehistoric Occupation of Chavin de Huantar, Peru.* University of California Publications in Anthropology, vol. 14. University of California Press. Berkeley.

BURGER, R., AND N. VAN DER MERWE
1990 Maize and the Origin of Highland Chavin Civilization: An Isotopic Perspective. *American Anthropologist 92(1):*85–95.

BUSH, M. B., D. R. PIPERNO, AND P. COLINVAUX
1989 A 6,000 Year History of Maize Cultivation. *Nature 340:* 303–5.

CARNEIRO, R.
1970 A Theory of the Origin of the State. *Science 169:*733–38.
1995 The History of Ecological Interpretation of Amazonia. Does Roosevelt Have It Right? In *Indigenous Peoples and The Future of Amazonia: An Ecological Anthropology of An Endangered World,* ed. by L. E. Sponsel, pp. 145–70. University of Arizona Press. Tucson.

CRUXENT, JOSE MARIA, AND IRVING ROUSE
1958–59 *An Archaeological Chronology of Venezuela.* Pan American Union, Social Science Monographs, no. 6. 2 vols. Washington.

DEBOER, W.
1975 The Archaeological Evidence for Manioc Cultivation: A Cautionary Note. *American Antiquity 40(4):*419–33.

DEBOER, W., AND D. LATHRAP
1979 The Making and Breaking of Shipibo Ceramics. In *Ethnoarchaeology: The Implications of Ethnology for Archaeology,* ed. by Carol Kramer, pp. 102–38. Columbia University Press. New York.

DEETZ, JAMES
1968 The Inference of Residence and Descent Rules from Archaeological Data. In *New Perspectives in Archaeology,* ed. by S. B. Binford and L. Binford, pp. 41–48. Aldine, Chicago.

DENEVAN, WILLIAM
1966 *An Aboriginal Cultural Geography of the Llanos de Mojos de Bolivia.* Ibero-Americana 48. University of California Press. Berkeley.

DENEVAN, WILLIAM, AND ALBERTA ZUCCHI
1978   Ridged Field Excavations in the Central Orinoco Llanos, Venezuela. In *Advances in Andean Archaeology,* ed. by David Browman, pp. 235–46. Mouton Publishers. The Hague.

DOOLITTLE, W. E., AND C. D. FREDERICK
1991   Phytoliths as Indicators of Prehistoric Maize (Zea mays sub-sp. mays, Poaceae) Cultivation. *Plant Systematics and Evolution 177:* 175–84.

DOUGHERTY, B., AND H. A. CALANDRA
1981–82   Excavaciones Arqueologicas en La Loma Alta de Casarabe, Llanos de Moxos, Departamento del Beni, Bolivia. *Relaciones de La Sociedad Argentina de Antropologia* [N.S.] *14(2):*9–48.

ERICKSON, C.
1980   Sistemas Agricolas Prehispanicos de los Llanos de Mojos. *American Indigena 40(4):*731–55.

ERICKSON, J. E., M. WEST, C. H. SULLIVAN, AND H. KRUEGER
1989   The Development of Maize Agriculture in the Viru Valley, Peru. In *The Chemistry of Prehistoric Human Bone,* ed. by T. D. Price, pp. 68–104. School of American Research. Cambridge.

EVANS, CLIFFORD, AND BETTY J. MEGGERS
1968   *Archaeological Investigations on the Rio Napo, Eastern Ecuador.* Smithsonian Contributions to Anthropology, no. 6. Washington, D.C.

1960   *Archaeological Investigations in British Guiana.* Bureau of American Ethnology, Bulletin 177.

EVANS, CLIFFORD, BETTY J. MEGGERS, AND JOSE MARIA CRUXENT
1959   Preliminary Results of Archaeological Invesetigations along the Orinoco and Ventuari Rivers, Venezuela. In *Actas, 33rd International Congress of Americanists,* vol. 2, pp. 359–69. Lehman. San Jose, Costa Rica.

FAGAN, B. M.
1987   *The Great Journey.* Thames and Hudson. London.

FALESI, C.
1974   Soils of the Brazilian Amazon. In *Man in the Amazon,* ed. by Charles Wagley, pp. 201–29. The University Presses of Florida. Gainesville.

FARABEE, WILLIAM
MS   Field Notebooks, Marajo. Archives, University of Pennsylvania Museum. Philadelphia.

FEIDEL, S.
1987 *Prehistory of the Americas.* Cambridge University Press. Cambridge.

FERNANDEZ DISTEL, A.
1978 *Las Cuevas de Huachichocana, Su Posición Dentro del Preceramico con Agricultura Incipiente del Noroeste Argentino.* Beiträge zur Allgemeinen und Vergleichenden Archäologie. Verlag Phillip Van Zabein. Mainz, Germany.

FERREIRA PENNA, D. S.
1885 Indios de Marajo. *Archivos do Museu Nacional 6:*108–15. Rio de Janeiro.

FOSTER, D. W., AND LATHRAP
1973 Further Evidence for Well-Developed Tropical Forest Culture on the North Coast of Colombia during the First and Second Millennia B.C. *Journal of the Steward Anthropological Society 4(2):*160–99.

GARSON, ADAM
1980 Prehistory, Settlement, and Food Production in the Savanna Region of La Calzada de Paez, Venezuela. Ph.D. dissertation, Yale University, New Haven.

GOWLETT, J. A. J., AND R. E. M. HEDGES, EDS.
1986 *Archaeological Results from Accelerator Dating.* Oxford University Committee for Archaeology, Monograph 11.

GUMILLA, JOSÉ
1955 *El Orinoco Ilustrado, Historia Natural, Civil y Geografica de Este Gran Rio.* Biblioteca de la Presidencia de Colombia, no. 8. Editorial ABC. Bogota.

HARRIS, EDWARD
1979 *Principles of Archaeological Stratigraphy.* Studies in Archaeological Science. Academic Press. London.

HARRIS, PETER O'B.
1973 Preliminary Report on Banwari Trace, a Preceramic Site in Trinidad. In *Proceedings of the Fourth International Congress for the Study of the Pre-Columbian Cultures of the Lesser Antilles. Guadeloupe,* pp. 115–26. University Presses of Florida. Gainesville.

HARTT, CHARLES, F.
1883 Contributions to the Ethnology of the Valley of the Amazons. Archives, Peabody Museum, Harvard University. Cambridge.

1885 Contribuicões para a Etnologia do Valle do Amazonas. *Archivos do Museu Nacional 6:*1–174.

HEDGES R. E. M., AND J. A. J. GOWLETT
1986 Radiocarbon Dating by Accelerator Mass Spectrometry. *Scientific American 254(1):*100–107.

HERRERA, L., W. BRAY, AND C. MCEWAN
1983 Datos Sobre La Arqueologia de Araracuara (Comisaria del Amazonas, Colombia). *Revista Colombiana de Anthropologia 23:*185–251.

HILBERT, PETER PAUL
1955 *A Ceramica da Região de Oriximiná.* Instituto de Arqueologia e Etnologia do Pará, Publicação 9. Belém.
1959a *Achados Arqueologicos num Sambaqui do Baixo Amazonas.* Instituto de Arqueologia e Etnologia do Pará, Publicação 10. Belém.
1959b Preliminary Results of Archaeological Investigations in the Vicinity of the Mouth of the Rio Negro, Amazonas. In *Actas del 33 Congreso International de Americanistas,* pp. 370–377. Lehman. San Jose.
1968 *Untersuchungen Archaeologische am Mittleren Amazonas.* Marburger Studien zur Volkerkunde, 1. Dietrich Reimer Verlag. Berlin.

HILBERT, PETER PAUL, AND K. HILBERT
1980 *Resultados Preliminares da Pesquisa Arqueologica nos Rios Nhamundá e Trombetas, Baixo Amazonas.* Boletim do Museu Paraense Emílio Goeldi, n.s., no. 75.

HOWARD, GEORGE
1943 *Excavations at Ronquin, Venezuela.* Yale University Publications in Anthropology, no. 28. New Haven.
1947 *Prehistoric Ceramic Styles of Lowland South America, Their Distribution and History.* Yale University Publications in Anthropology, no. 37. New Haven.

HUGH-JONES, CHRISTINE
1979 *From the Milk River: Spatial and Temporal Processes in Northwest Amazonia.* Cambridge University Press. Cambridge.

HUGH-JONES, STEPHAN
1979 *The Palm and the Pleiades: Initiation and Cosmology in Northwest Amazonia.* Cambridge University Press. Cambridge.

KEATINGE, R., EDITOR
    1988   *Peruvian Prehistory.* Cambridge University Press. Cambridge.

KIDDER, A.
    1944   *Archaeology of Northwestern Venezuela.* Papers of the Peabody Museum 26(1). Harvard University. Cambridge.

LABBÉ, A. L.
    1986   *Colombia before Columbus: The People, Culture, and Ceramic Art of Prehispanic Colombia.* Rizzoli. New York.

LANE, R., AND A. SUBLETT
    1972   Osteology of Social Organization. *American Antiquity 37:* 186–201.

LANGE, ALGOT
    1914   *The Lower Amazon.* G. P. Putnam's Sons. New York.

LANNING, EDWARD
    1967   *Peru before the Incas.* Prentice-Hall Publishers. Englewood Cliffs, N.J.

LATHRAP, DONALD
    1970   *The Upper Amazon.* Praeger Publishers. New York.
    1971   The Tropical Forest and the Cultural Context of Chavin. In *Dumbarton Oaks Conference on Chavin,* ed. by E. P. Benson, pp. 73–100. Trustees for Harvard University. Washington, D.C.
    1974   The Moist Tropics, the Arid Lands, and the Appearance of Great Art Styles in the New World. In *Art and Environment in Native America,* ed. by M. E. King and I. R. Traylor, Jr., pp. 115–58. Special Publications of the Museum, no. 7. Texas Tech University. Lubbock.
    1975   *Ancient Ecuador: Culture, Clay, and Creativity 3000–300 B.C.* Field Museum of Natural History. Chicago.

LATHRAP, DONALD, AND J. OLIVER
    1980   Una Evalucacion Critica de Las Culturas Formativas del Oriente de Venezuela. Por M. Sanoja (1979). *Interciencia 5:* 391–400.

LONG, A., B. F. BENZ, D. J. DONAHUE, AND J. A. HULL
    1989   First Direct AMS Dates on Early Maize from Tehuacan, Mexico. *Abstracts, Annual Meeting of the Society of American Anthropology,* no. 39.

LONGACRE, W.
    1968   Some Aspects of Prehistoric Society in East Central Arizona. In *New Perspectives in Archaeology,* ed. by S. Binford and L. Binford, pp. 89–102. Aldine. Chicago.

LOPES, DANIEL FROIS, M. IMAZIO DA SILVEIRA, AND M. P. MAGALHÃES
    1989   Current Research: Pará. *American Antiquity 54(1):* 186.

LYNCH, T. F.
    1983   The Paleoindians. In *Ancient South Americans,* ed. by J. D. Jennings, pp. 97–138. W. H. Freeman and Company. San Francisco.
    1990   Glacial-Age Man in South America? A Critical Review. *American Antiquity 55(1):*12–36.

MEGGERS, BETTY J.
    1954   Environmental Limitations on the Development of Culture. *American Anthropologist 56:*801–24.
    1971   *Amazonia: Man and Nature in a Counterfeit Paradise.* Aldine. Chicago.

MEGGERS, BETTY J., AND CLIFFORD EVANS
    1961   An Experimental Formulation of Horizon Styles in the Tropical Forest Area of South America. In *Essays in Precolumbian Art and Archaeology,* ed. by Samuel K. Lothrop et al. Harvard University. Cambridge.
    1957   *Archaeological Investigations at the Mouth of the Amazon.* Bureau of American Ethnology, Bulletin 167. Smithsonian Institution. Washington, D.C.
    1978   Lowland South America and the Antilles. In *Ancient Native Americans,* ed. by J. D. Jennings, pp. 542–91. W. H. Freeman Publishers. San Francisco.
    1983   Lowland South America and the Antilles. In *Ancient South Americans,* ed. by J. D. Jennings, pp. 287–335. W. H. Freeman Publishers. San Francisco.

MILLER, E.
    1987   Pesquisas Arqueologicas Paleoindigenas no Brasil Occidental. In *Investigaciones Paleoindias al Sur de La Linea Ecuatorial,* ed. by L. Nunez and B. J. Meggers, pp. 37–61. Estudos Atacameños, no. 8. San Pedro de Atacama.

MUNSELL SOIL COLOR CHARTS
    1975   Macbeth Division of Kollmorgen Corporation. Baltimore.

NETTO, LADISLAV
    1885   Investigacões sobre a Archaeologia Brasileira. *Archivos do Museu Nacional 6:*257–554. Rio de Janeiro.

NIMUENDAJU, CURT
    MS   A Survey of Amazon Archaeology. Manuscript translated by Stig Ryden. Göteborg Ethnographic Museum.

NORDENSKIOLD, ERLAND
    1930   *L'Archeologie du Bassin de L'Amazone.* Ars Americana 1. Les Editions G. van Oest. Paris.

NORR, L.
    1984   Prehistoric Subsistence and Health Status of Coastal Peoples from the Panamanian Isthmus of Lower Central America. In *Paleopathology at the Origins of Agriculture,* ed. by M. N. Cohen and G. J. Armelagos, pp. 430–90. Academic Press. Orlando.

OLIVER, J. R.
    1989   The Archaeological, Linguistic, and Ethnohistorical Evidence for the Expansion of Arawakan into Northwestern Venezuela and Northeastern Colombia. Ph.D. dissertation, Yale University, New Haven.

OSGOOD, CHARLES, AND GEORGE HOWARD
    1943   *An Archaeological Survey of Venezuela.* Yale University Publications in Anthropology, no. 27. New Haven.

PALMATARY, HELEN, C.
    1950   *The Pottery of Marajo Island, Brazil.* Transactions of the American Philosophical Society, New Series, vol. 39(3). Philadelphia.
    1960   *The Archaeology of the Lower Tapajos Valley, Brazil.* Transactions of the American Philosophical Society, New Series, vol. 50(3). Philadelphia.

PETRULLO, VINCENZO
    1939   *Archaeology of Arauquin.* Bureau of American Ethnology, Bulletin 123, Anthropological Papers, no. 12, pp. 291–98.

PHILLIPSON, D.
    1985   *African Archaeology.* Cambridge University Press. Cambridge.

PORRAS, P.
    1987   *Investigaciones Arqueologicas a Las Faldas de Sangay, Provincia Morona Santiago, Tradicion Upano.* Artes Graficas Señal, Impresenal Cia. Ltda. Quito.

PRANCE, GILLIAN T.
    1985   The Changing Forests. In *Key Environments: Amazonia,* ed. by G. Prance and T. Lovejoy, pp. 146–65. Pergamon Press. Oxford.

PRANCE, GILLIAN T., EDITOR
    1982   *Biological Diversification in the Tropics.* Proceedings of the Fifth International Symposium of the Association for Tropical Biology. Columbia University Press. New York.

PRICE, T. D., EDITOR
    1989   *The Chemistry of Prehistoric Human Bone.* School of American Research. Cambridge.

REICHEL-DOLMATOFF, GERARDO
    1965a   *Excavaciones Archaeologicas en Puerto Hormiga, Departamento de Bolivar.* Publicaciones de la Universidad de los Andes, Antropologica 2. Bogota.
    1965b   *Colombia.* Praeger. New York.
    1971   *Amazonian Cosmos.* University of Chicago Press. Chicago.
    1985   *Monsu: Un Sitio Arqueologico.* Biblioteca Banco Popular, Textos Universitarios. Bogota.
    1986   *Arqueologia de Colombia: Un texto introductorio.* Fundacion Segunda Expedicion Botanica/Litografia Arco. Bogota.

RICE, P.
    1987   *Pottery Analysis: A Sourcebook.* University of Chicago Press. Chicago.

ROOSEVELT, ANNA CURTENIUS
    1978   La Gruta: An Early Tropical Forest Community of the Middle Orinoco. In *Unidad y Variedad; Ensayos Antropologicos en Homenaje a José M. Cruxent,* ed. by Erika Wagner and Alberta Zucchi, pp. 173–201. Instituto Venezolano de Investigaciones Cientificas and Ediciones del Centro de Estudios Avancadas. Caracas.
    1980   *Parmana: Prehistoric Maize and Manioc Subsistence along the Amazon and Orinoco.* Academic Press. Studies in Archaeology. New York.
    1984a   Problems Interpreting the Diffusion of Cultivated Plants. In *Precolumbian Plant Migration,* ed. by D. Stone, pp. 1–18. Papers of the Peabody Museum of Archaeology and Ethnology 76. Harvard University. Cambridge.
    1984b   Population, Health, and the Evolution of Subsistence: Conclusions. In *Paleopathology at the Origins of Agriculture,* ed. by Mark Cohen, and George Armelagos, pp. 559–83. Studies in Archaeology. Academic Press. New York.

1986	The Developmental Sequence at Santarem on the Lower Amazon, Brazil. Proposal to the National Endowment for the Humanities.
1987a	Chiefdoms in the Amazon and Orinoco. In *Chiefdoms in the Americas,* ed. by Robert Drennan and Carlos Uribe, pp. 153–185. University Press of America. Lanham, Md.
1987b	Interpreting Certain Female Images in Prehistoric Art. In *Gender in Precolumbian Art and Architecture,* ed. by Virginia Miller, pp. 1–34. University Press of America. Lanham, Md.
1989	Resource Management in Amazonia before the Conquest: Beyond Ethnographic Projection. In *Natural Resource Management by Indigenous and Folk Societies in Amazonia,* ed. by Darrel Posey and William Balee, pp. 30–62. Advances in Economic Botany 9. Botanical Garden. New York.
1990a	The Historical Perspective on Resource Use in Tropical Latin America. In *Economic Catalysts to Ecological Change: 39th Annual Conference, Center for Latin American Studies,* University of Florida, ed. by S. E. Sanderson and K. H. Redford, pp. 29–64. Tropical Conservation and Development Program, Working Papers.
1991a	*Moundbuilders of the Amazon: Geophysical Archaeology on Marajo Island, Brazil.* Academic Press. Studies in Archaeology. San Diego.
1991b	Determinismo Ecologico na Interpretacão do Desenvolvimento Social Indigena da Amazônia. In *Origens, Adaptacões, e Diversidade Biologica do Homem Nativo da Amazônia,* ed. by W. A. Neves, pp. 103–42. Museu Paraense Emílio Goeldi. Belém.
1991c	Indigenous Peoples of the Brazilian Amazon before the European Conquest. In *The Construction of the South Atlantic: Brazilian and African Societies on the Eve of the Modern World,* ed. by J. Diaz, pp. 17–45. Comissão Nacional para as Comemoracões dos Desobrimentos Portugueses. Lisbon.
1992	Arqueologia Amazônica. In *History of Brazilian Indians,* ed. by M. Carneiro da Cunha, pp. 53–86. Editora Schwarcz. São Paulo.
1995	Early Pottery in the Amazon: Twenty Years of Scholarly Obscurity. In *The Emergence of Pottery,* ed. by W. Barnett and J. Hoopes, pp. 115–31. Smithsonian Press. Washington, D.C.
MSa	Prehistory of Amazonia.

MSb   Preliminary Report on the Survey and Excavations at Guajara, Marajo Island, Pará, Brazil.
MSc   The Developmental Sequence at Santarem on the Lower Amazon, Brazil.

ROOSEVELT, A. C., R. HOUSLEY, M. IMAZIO DA SILVEIRA, S. MARANCA, AND R. JOHNSON
1991   Eighth Millennium Pottery from a Prehistoric Shell Midden in the Brazilian Amazon. *Science 254:*1621–24.

ROOSEVELT, A. C., M. LIMA DA COSTA, C. LOPES MACHADO, M. MICHAB, N. MERCIER, H. VALLADAS, J. FEATHERS, W. BARNETT, M. IMAZIO DA SILVEIRA, A. HENDERSON, J. SLIVA, B. CHERNOFF, D. S. REESE, J. A. HOLMAN, N. TOTH, AND K. SCHICK
1996   Paleoindian Cave Dwellers in the Amazon: The Peopling of the Americas. *Science 272:*373–84.

ROOSEVELT, A. C., H. KRUEGER, AND C. H. SULLIVAN
MSa   Isotopic Evidence for the Role of Maize in Prehistoric Orinocan Subsistence.
MSb   Isotopic Evidence for the Role of Maize in Ancient Mayan Subsistence.

ROTH, W.
1915   An Inquiry into the Animism and Folklore of the Guiana Indians. *30th Annual Report of the Bureau of American Ethnology 1908–1909,* pp. 103–386.

ROUSE, IRVING
1953   The Circum-Caribbean Theory: An Archaeological Test. *American Anthropologist, n.s., 55(2):*188–200.
1960   The Classification of Artifacts in Archaeology. *American Antiquity 25(3):*313–23.
1978   The La Gruta Sequence and Its Implications. In *Unidad y Variedad: Ensayos Antropológicos en Homenaje a José M. Cruxent,* ed. by Erika Wagner and Alberta Zucchi, pp. 203–29. Instituto Venezolano de Investigaciones Cientificas and Ediciones del Centro de Estudios Avancados. Caracas.
1986   *Migrations in Prehistory: Inferring Population Movement from Cultural Remains.* Yale University Press. New Haven.
1990   Social, Linguistic, and Stylistic Plurality in the West Indies. In *Proceedings of the 11th International Congress on Caribbean Archaeology, San Juan, Puerto Rico.* Fundación Arqueológica e Antropológica e Histórica de Puerto Rico.

ROUSE, IRVING, AND LOUIS ALLAIRE
 1978 Caribbean. In *Chronologies in New World Archaeology,* ed. by R. E. Taylor and C. W. Meighan, pp. 431–81. Academic Press. New York.

ROUSE, IRVING, L. ALLAIRE, AND, A. BOOMERT
 MS Eastern Venezuela, the Guianas, and the West Indies. Department of Anthropology, Yale University. New Haven.

ROUSE, IRVING, AND JOSE MARIA CRUXENT
 1963 *Venezuelan Archaeology.* Yale University Press. New Haven.

ROUSE, IRVING, JOSE MARIA CRUXENT, FRED OLSEN, AND ANNA CURTENIUS ROOSEVELT
 1976 Ronquin Revisited. In *Proceedings of the Sixth International Congress for the Study of the Precolumbian Cultures of the Lesser Antilles, Guadeloupe, 1975,* pp. 117–22. The University Presses of Florida. Gainesville.

SANDERS, WILLIAM, AND BARBARA PRICE
 1968 *Mesoamerica: The Evolution of a Civilization.* Random House. New York.

SANOJA O., MARIO
 1979 *Las Culturas Formativas del Oriente de Venezuela: La Tradición Barrancas del Bajo Orinoco.* Biblioteca de La Academia Nacional de la Historia, no. 6. Caracas.

SANOJA O., MARIO, AND IRAIDA VARGAS ARENAS
 1978 The Formative Cultures of the Venezuelan Oriente. In *Advances in Andean Archaeology,* ed. by David Browman, pp. 259–76. Mouton Publishers. The Hague.

SCHMITZ, P. I.
 1987 Prehistoric Hunters and Gatherers of Brazil. *Journal of World Prehistory 1(1):*53–126.

SENDERS, VIRGINIA L.
 1958 *Measurement and Statistics: A Basic Text Emphasizing Behavioral Science Applications.* Oxford University Press. New York.

SIEGEL, P.
 1992 Ancestors, Power, and Complexity: The Evolution of Political Organization in the Caribbean. Ph.D. dissertation, Anthropology, State University of New York at Binghamton.

SIEGEL, PETER, AND PETER ROE
    1986   Shipibo Archaeo-Ethnography: Site Formation Processes and Archaeological Interpretation. *World Archaeology 18(1):* 96–115.

SIMÕES, MARIO
    1969   The Castanheira Site: New Evidence on the Antiquity and History of the Ananatuba Phase (Marajo Island, Brasil). *American Antiquity 34:*402–10.
    1976   Notas sobre duas pontas-de-projetil da Bacia do Tapajos (Pará). *Boletim do Museu Paraense Emílio Goeldi* [N.S.] *62:*1–14.
    1981   *Coletores-Pescadores Ceramistas do Litoral do Salgado (Pará). Nota Preliminar.* Boletim do Museu Paraense Emílio Goeldi, n.s., 78. Belém.

SMITH, C. E., AND A. C. ROOSEVELT
    MS   Prehistoric Plant Use in the Middle Orinoco Basin: Tree Products.

SMITH, NIGEL
    1980   Anthrosols and Human Carrying Capacity in Amazonia. *Annals of the Association of American Geographers 70(1):*553–66.

SMITHSONIAN ANTHROPOLOGY ARCHIVES
    1965–85   Radiocarbon records. No. 87–035, box 9–10. Smithsonian Institution. Washington, D.C.

SPENCER, C., AND, E. REDMAN
    1991   Investigating Prehistoric Chiefdoms in the Venezuelan Llanos. *World Archaeology 24(1):*134–57.

STEINHART, A.
    MS   Analysis of Human Skeletal Material. Unpublished manuscript on skeletons from Corozal, Guarico, Venezuela, Excavated by the Museum of the American Indian Parmana Project.

STERNBERG, HILGARD O'REILLY
    1960   Radiocarbon Dating as Applied to a Problem of Amazonian Morphology. *Comptes Rendus du XVIIIe Congrés International de Geographie,* vol. 2, pp. 399–424. Centro de Pesquisas de Geografia do Brasil. Rio de Janeiro.

STEWARD, J. H.
    1949   South American Indians. In *The Comparative Ethnology of South American Indians,* ed. by J. H. Steward, vol. 5, pp. 669–72. Smithsonian Institution. Washington, D.C.

STONE, DORIS, EDITOR
 1984 *Precolumbian Plant Migration.* Papers of the Peabody Museum, no. 76. Harvard University. Cambridge.

STRUEVER, STUART
 1968 Flotation Techniques for the Recovery of Small-Scale Archaeological Remains. *American Antiquity 33(3):* 353–62.

TANKERSLEY, K. B., C. A. MUNSON, AND D. SMITH
 1987 Recognition of Bituminous Coal Contaminants in Radiocarbon Samples. *American Antiquity 52(2):*318–29.

TAYLOR, R. E.
 1987 *Radiocarbon Dating: An Archaeological Perspective.* Academic Press. Orlando.

VAN DER MERWE, N., A. C. ROOSEVELT, AND J. C. VOGEL
 1981 Isotopic Evidence for Prehistoric Subsistence Change at Parmana, Venezuela. *Nature 292:*536–38.

VAN DER MERWE, N., J. LEE-THORP, AND J. SCOTT RAYMOND
 1993 Light Stable Isotopes and the Subsistence Base of Formative Cultures at Valdivia, Ecuador. In *Prehistoric Human Bone: Archaeology at the Molecular Level,* ed. by J. B. Lambert and G. Grupe, pp. 63–97. Springer-Verlag. New York.

VARGAS, IRAIDA
 1976 La Gruta, Un Nuevo Sitio Ronquinoide en Orinoco Medico. In *Proceedings of the Sixth International Congress for the Study of the Precolumbian Cultures of the Lesser Antilles, 1975,* pp. 123–24. The University Presses of Florida. Gainesville.

 1979 *Tradicion Saladoide del Oriente de Venezuela: La Fase Cuartel.* Biblioteca de la Academia Nacional de la Historia, no. 5. Caracas.

 1981 *Investigaciones Archaeologicas en Parmana: Los Sitios de La Gruta y Ronquin, Estado Guarico, Venezuela.* Biblioteca de la Academia Nacional de La Historia, Estudios, Monografias, y Ensayos. Caracas.

WILLEY, G. R.
 1971 *An Introduction to American Archaeology,* vol. 2. South America. Prentice-Hall. Englewood Cliffs, N.J.

WILLIAMS, D.
 1981 Excavations of the Balbina Shell Mound Northwest District. An Interim Report. *Journal of the Walter Roth Museum of Archaeology and Anthropology 4(1–2):*13–36.

1992 El Arcaico en El Noroeste de Guyana y Los Comienzos de la Horticultura. In *Prehistoria Sudamericana: Nuevas Perspectivas,* ed. by Betty J. Meggers, pp. 233–270. Taraxacum. Washington, D.C.

WING, ELIZABETH, AND ANTOINETTE BROWN
1979 *Paleonutrition: Method and Theory in Prehistoric Foodways.* Academic Press. New York.

WING, ELIZABETH, ADAM GARSON, AND ERICA SIMON
MS The Archaeological Faunal Remains from Parmana, Venezuela. Field Museum. Chicago.

ZUCCHI, ALBERTA
1972 New Data on the Antiquity of Polychrome Painting from Venezuela. *American Antiquity 37:*439–46.

1975 *Caño Caroni: Un Grupo Prehispanico de la Selva de los Llanos de Barinas.* Universidad Central de Venezuela. Coleccion Antropologia.

ZUCCHI, ALBERTA, KAY TARBLE, AND EDUARDO VAZ
1984 The Ceramic Sequence and New TL and C-14 Dates for the Aguerito Site of the Middle Orinoco, Venezuela. *Journal of Field Archaeology 11(2):*155–80.

Plates

Plate 1. False-color infrared image of the Middle Orinoco, 1986

Produced by the author and colleagues at the Boston University Center for Remote Sensing training session for archaeologists, August 1988. (Source of digital raw data: Landsat 5, BIL MSS Band 45678, Path 003, Row 55, aqu. 8/14/86, 022479, Scene ID 83035614032XO, SE 6 #1 of 1.)

Plate 2. The Corozal site

Top: view inland toward north. *Bottom:* view south toward the headlands of El Puyazo Island in the Orinoco channel.

Plate 3. Excavations 2 and 3 at Corozal after excavation

Left: Excavation 2 and 3 west sidewalls.
Right: Excavation 3 and 2 east sidewalls.

Plate 4. Artifact features during excavation

Top: artifacts exposed at top of the hearth feature in Stratum S, Excavation 3, Level 5. *Center:* sherd feature in Stratum M, Excavation 3, Level 10. *Bottom:* 2 views of large fragment of a human-effigy vessel (mode #40, provenience number 72–7; *see* Pl. 13, *top*).

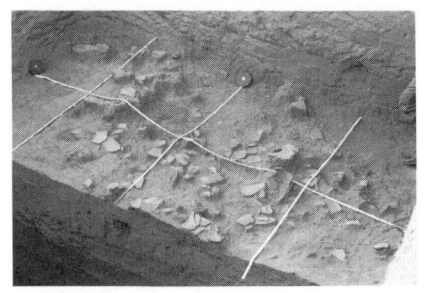

Plate 5. Human skeletons uncovered in Excavation 3

Left: Skeleton 2. *Right:* Disturbed Skeleton 4–5 lies around the feet and legs of Skeleton 2.

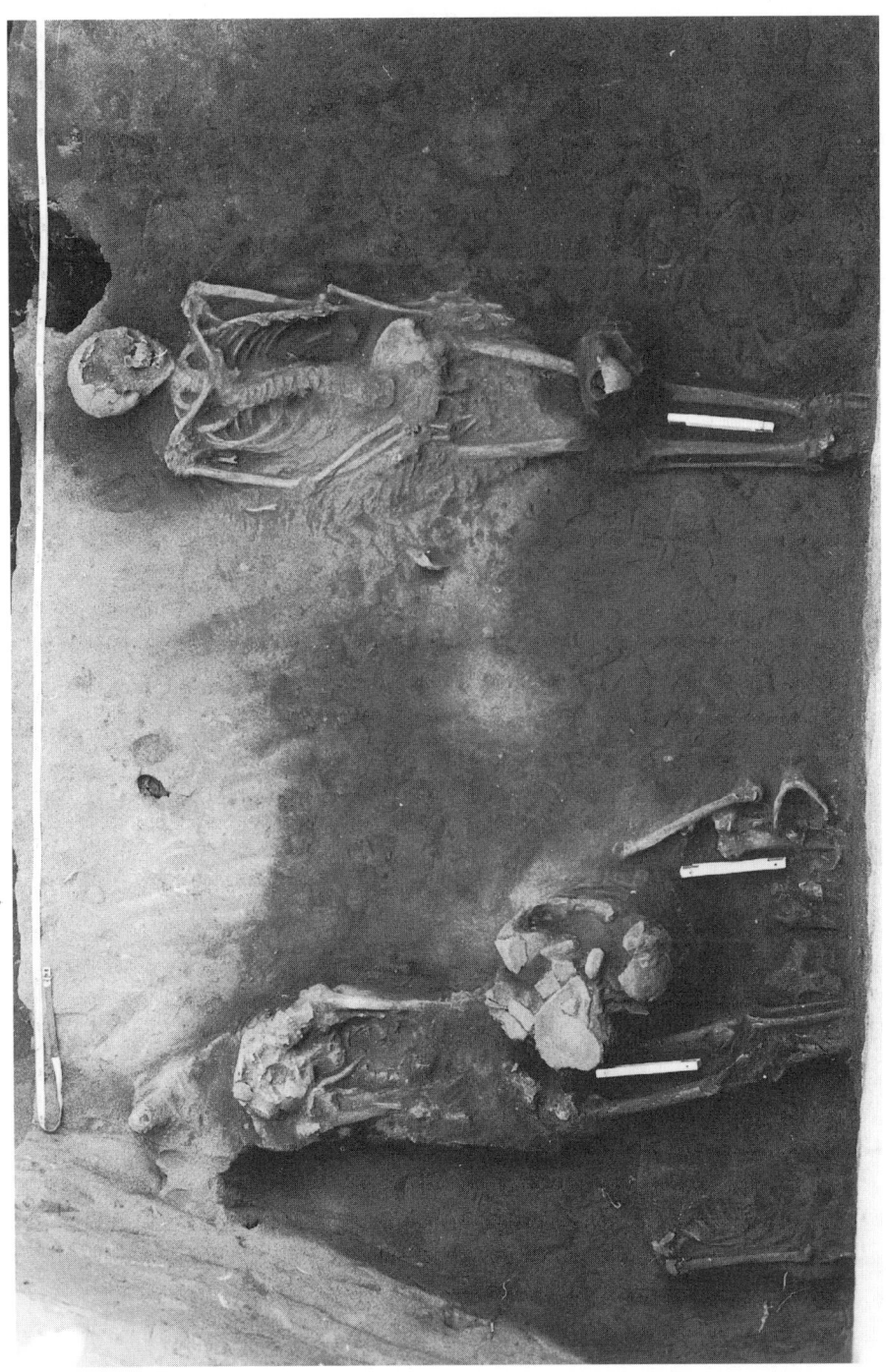

Plate 6. Human skeletons uncovered in Excavation 2

Top: skull of center skeleton. *Center* and *bottom:* child skeleton during excavation.

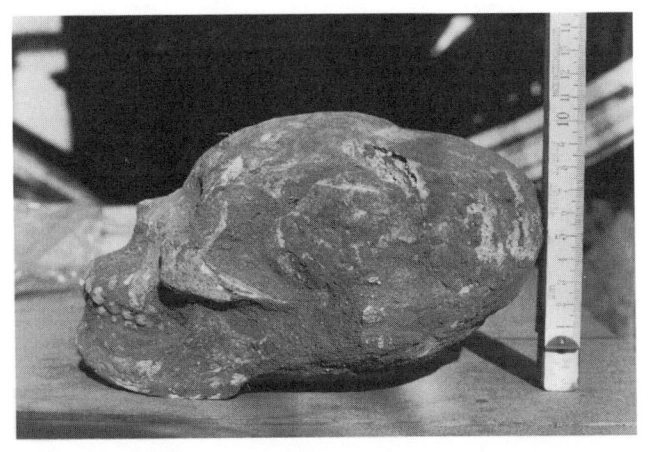

Plate 7. Corozal sherdware and gritware decorated sherds
Top: **sherdware sherds, mode #135;** *Bottom:* **gritware sherds, mode #140**

Provenience numbers: A: 8–27; B: 40–2; C: 7–11; D: 40–1; E: 22–16; F: 27–8; G: 27–6; H: 46–1; I: 42–3; J: 44–4; K: 42–4; L: 27–11; M: 47–15. A: 8–10; B: 7–1; C: 8–9; D: 8–28; E: 24–7; F: 8–40; G: 37–68; H: 2–92; I: 37–69; J: 42–3; K: 21–154; L: 37–70; M: 27–41; N: 2–472; O: 21–155.

Plate 8. Sherds of Corozal curvilinear incision, mode #133 *(top)*
and rectilinear incision, mode #132 *(bottom)*

Provenience numbers: A: 2–63; B: 8–2; C: 8–48; D: 21–3; E: 24–3; F: 152–1; G: 26–3; H: 3–4; I: 2–60; J: 3–78; K: 2–182; L: 21–66; M: 3–3; N: 31–122; O: 2–61; P: 7–8; Q: 10–5; R: 2–97; S: 2–69; T: 7–7; U: 21–10; V: 31–41; W: 31–45; X: 37–8; Y: 31–52; Z: 2–72; AA: 8–16; BB: 29–6; CC: 2–67 and 8–15; DD: 8–17 and 8–18.

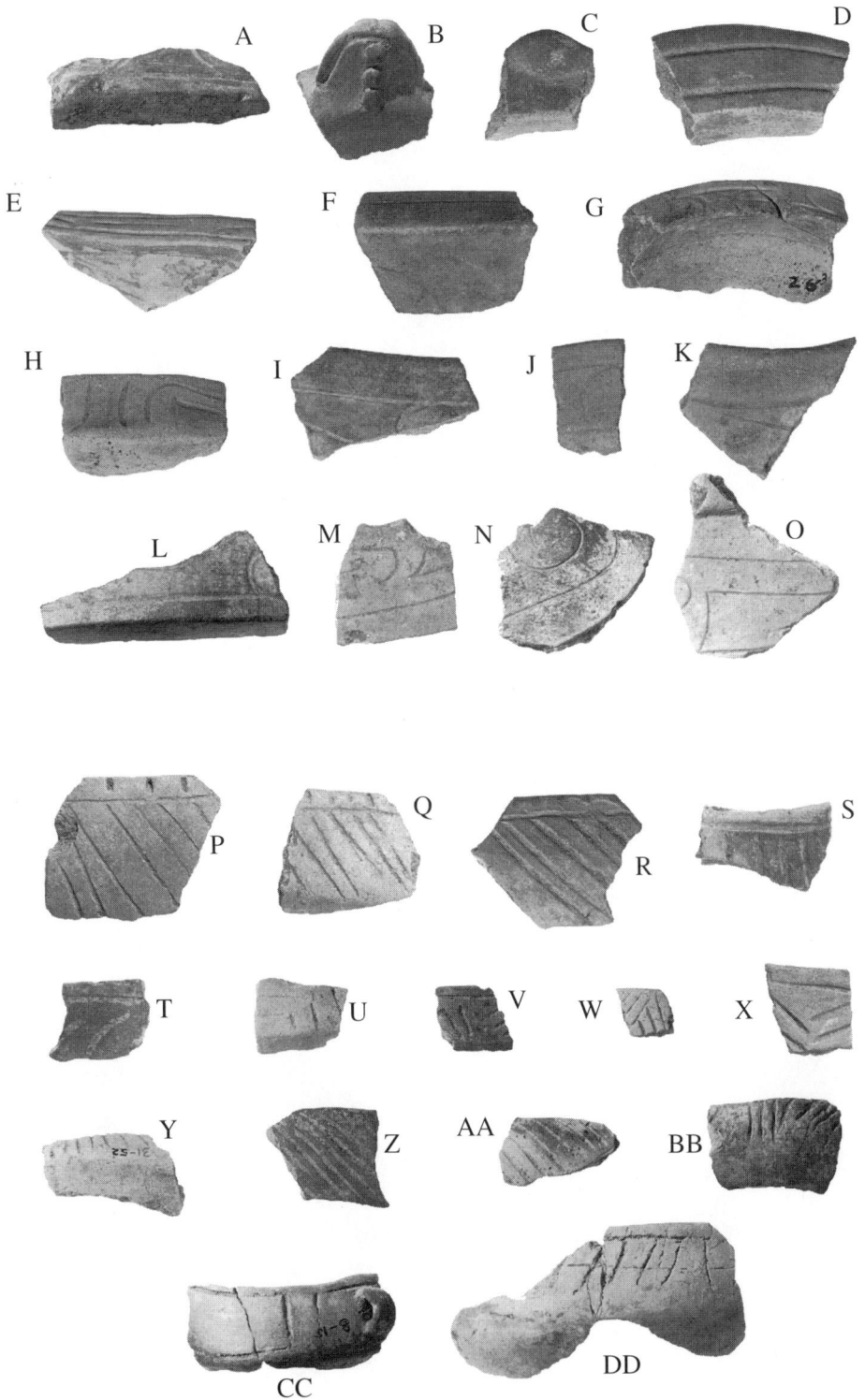

**Plate 9. Sherds of Corozal red-and-white paint, mode #8 (A–M),
Corozal polychrome, mode #20, (N–R), and
Corozal vertical rim strap handles; mode #126 (S–Z)**

Provenience numbers: A: 31–51; B: 2–75; C: 24–8; D: 31–53; E: 2–228; F: 8–21; G: 2–226; H: 7–22; I: 31–245; J: 2–197; K: 27–3; L: 2–162; M: 2–222; N: 29–1; O: 42–2; P: 2–76; Q: 2–164; R: 2–77; S: 2–157; T: 3–18; U: 41–31; V: 24–111; W: 2–82; X: 24–12; Y: 2–85; Z: 2–86.

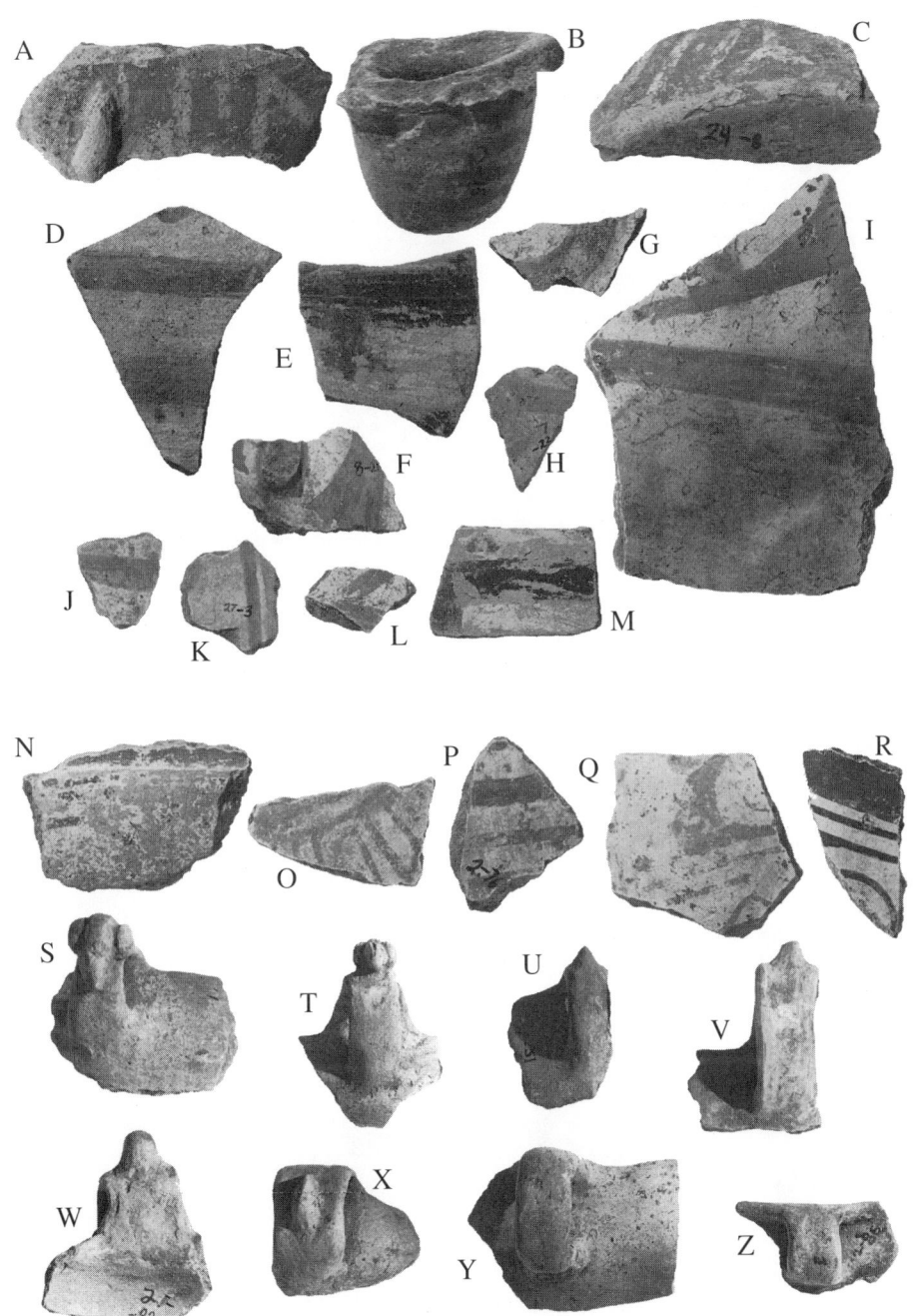

Plate 10. Sherds of animal-effigy bowls, mode #209 (*top*),
and Camoruco mauve paint, mode #152 (*bottom*)
Sherds from provenience #56 are from the offering with Skeleton 2, Level 18, Excavation 3

Provenience numbers: A: 12–87; B: 55–16; C: 55–126; D: 35–11; E: 35–12; F: 58–108; G: 34–164; H: 11–11; I: 12–146; J: 58–10; K: 23–4; L: 74–1 and 74–2; M: 10–2; N: 55–3; O: 23–3; P: 35–5; Q: 53–52; R: 4–10; S: 43–5; T: 48–342; U: 59–5; V: 12–5.

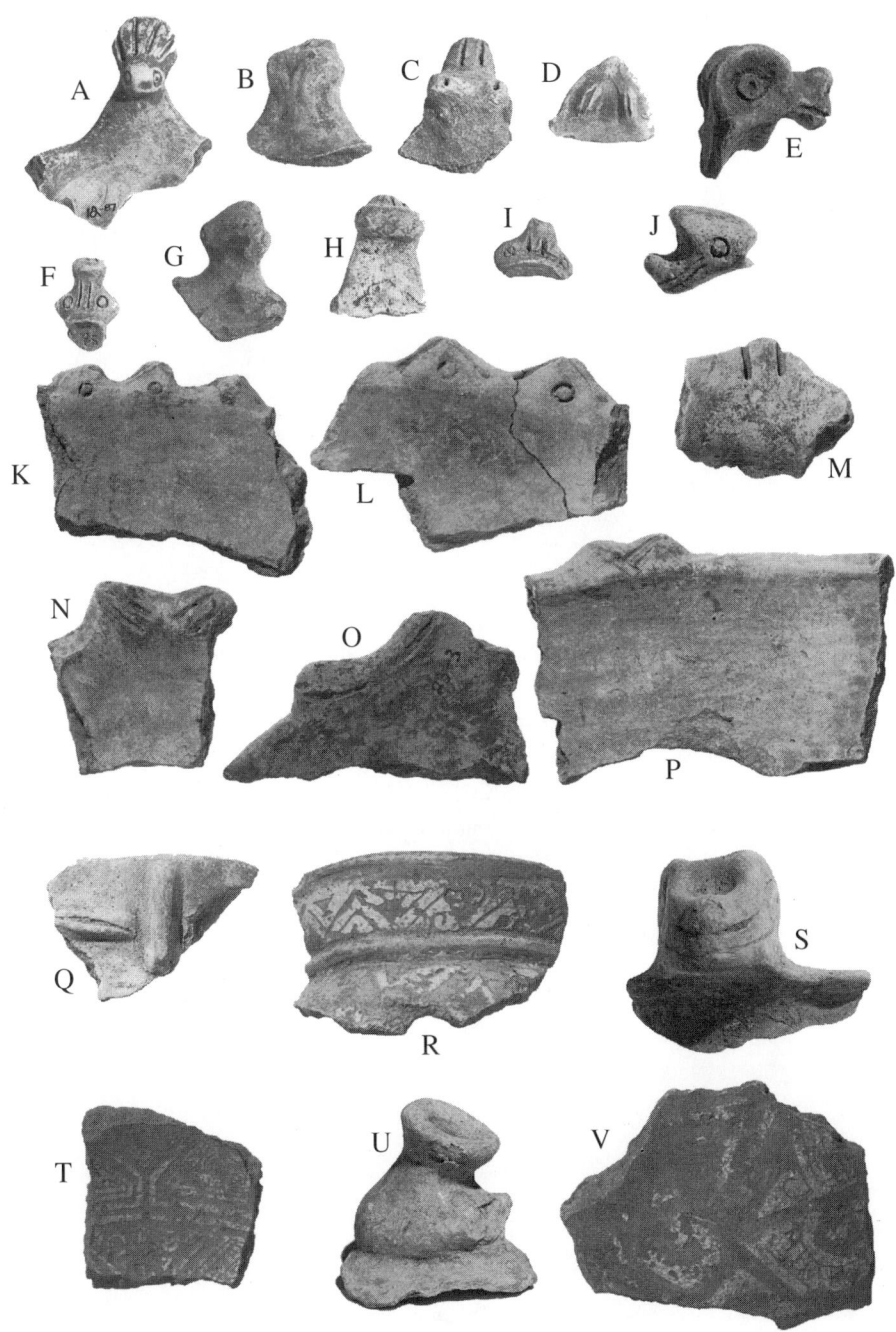

Plate 11. Sherds of Arauquinoid maroon paint, mode #14 (*top*), **and Arauquinoid rectilinear incision and punctation, mode #19**
(*center* and *bottom*)

Among the incised sherds, C–E, G, H, K, L, and Q, R also have maroon paint. Q and R also illustrate an example of the Arauquinoid human rim lugs of mode #136. Provenience numbers: A: 20–14; B: 1–22; C: 25–9; D: 34–4; E: 12–17; F: 25–10; G: 34–67; H: 20–11; I: 1–9; J: 20–10; K: 12–70; L: 34–11; M: 12–72; N: 12–73; O: 1–16; P: 12–71; Q: 32–110 (front); R: 32–110 (back).

Plate 12. Sherds of Arauquinoid human-effigy jars, modes #40 and #32, and Arauquinoid human bowl rim lugs, mode #136. The sherds in the third row of the plate and sherd U are mode #32, small Arauquinoid human-effigy jars. The remaining sherds in the top part of the plate are mode #40, large Arauquinoid human-effigy vessels. Sherds L, M, and O bear Arauquinoid maroon paint (mode #14), and sherds O and P bear Arauquinoid rectilinear incision as well (mode #19).

Provenience numbers: A: 76–2; B: 77–3; C: 48–14 and 48–115; D: 48–111; E: 72–2; F: 4–67; G: 23–165; H: 19–38; I: 48–341; J: 35–165; K: 32–98; L: 150–3; M: 25–3; N: 20–68; O: 63–19; P: 12–79; Q: 76–29; R: 48–97; S: 46–16; T: 12–74; U: 35–166; V: 34–60; W: 12–85; X: 20–3; Y: 32–108; Z: 21–84; AA: 25–7; BB: 48–107; CC: 12–83; DD: 30–2; EE: 12–86; FF: 150–1; GG: 150–60; HH: 1–3.

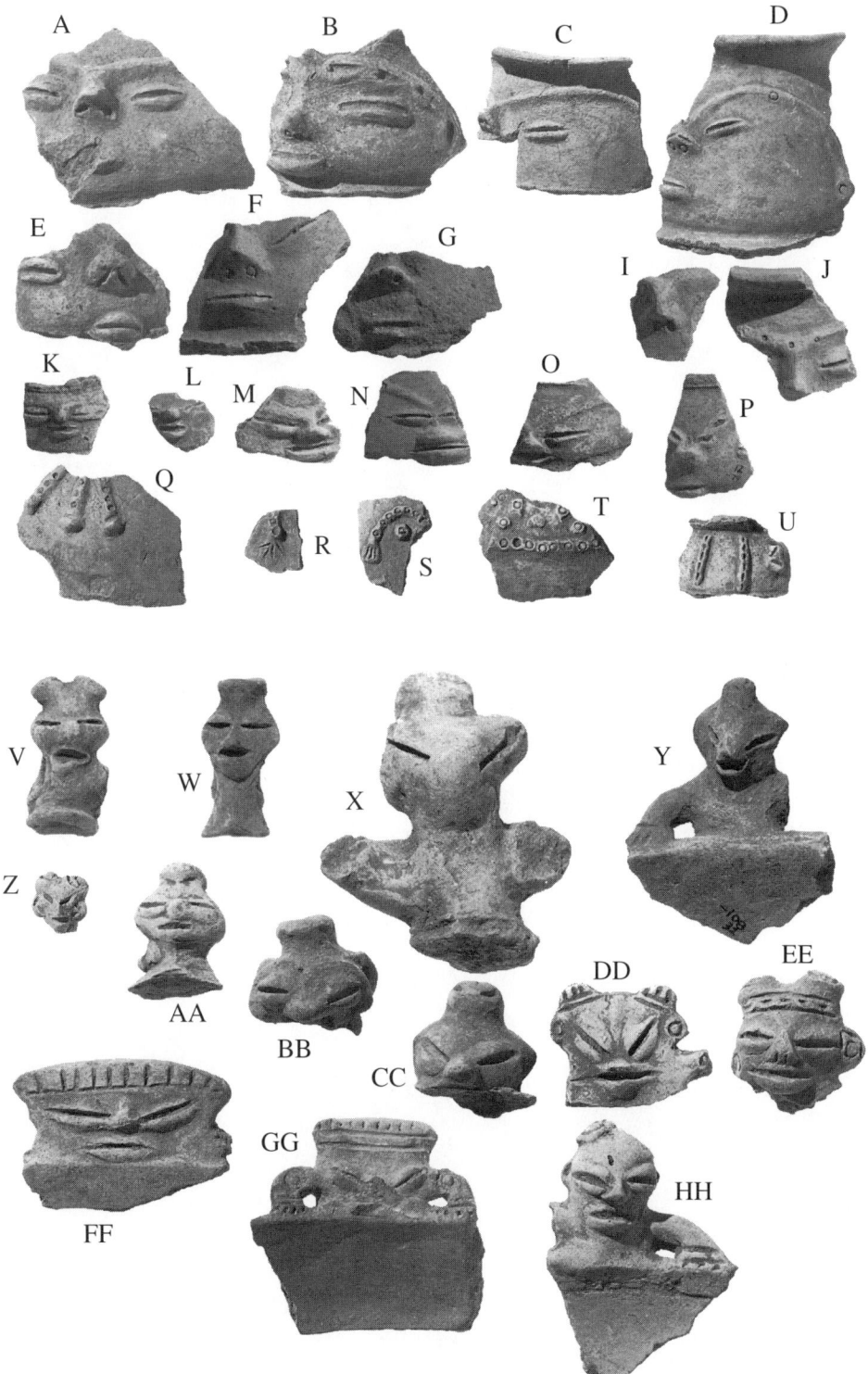

Plate 13. Fragments of human-effigy jars

Top: fragment of Arauquinoid large human-effigy jar, mode #40. *Bottom:* rare Corozal tradition human-effigy jar. Provenience numbers: 72–7 and 31–3.